HUBRIS

HUBRIS

The Inside Story of Spin, Scandal, and
the Selling of the Iraq War

MICHAEL ISIKOFF

AND

DAVID CORN

CROWN PUBLISHERS
NEW YORK

Library of Congress Cataloging-in-Publication Data
Isikoff, Michael
Hubris : the inside story of spin, scandal, and the selling of the
Iraq War / Michael Isikoff and David Corn.—1st ed.
p. cm.
Includes bibliographical references.
1. United States—Politics and government—2001– 2. United States—
Foreign relations—2001– 3. Iraq War, 2003—Causes. 4. Bush, George W.
(Geoge Walker), 1946– 5. Political corruption—United States.
6. Pride and vanity—Political aspects—United States. 7. Scandals—United States.
8. Spin doctors—United States. 9. Public relations and politics—United States.
10. Press and politics—United States. I. Corn, David. II. Title.
E902.184   2006
956.7044'31—dc22   2006025160

ISBN-10: 0-307-34681-1
ISBN-13: 978-0-307-34681-0

Printed in the United States of America

DESIGN BY BARBARA STURMAN

10 9 8 7 6 5 4 3 2 1

First Edition

For Trudy Isikoff and Willa

—M.I.

For Welmoed, Maaike, and Amarins

—D.C.

CONTENTS

CHARACTER LIST

Tyler Drumheller ...... European Division chief in the Directorate of Operations
Paul Pillar .... national intelligence officer for the Near East and South Asia
Robert Walpole .... national intelligence officer for strategic weapons
Alan Foley .... chief of the Center for Weapons Intelligence, Nonproliferation, and Arms Control (WINPAC)
Joe Turner .... WINPAC analyst
Bill Murray .... Paris station chief
Les .... biological weapons expert
Joseph Wilson IV .... former U.S. ambassador dispatched on mission to Niger

DEFENSE DEPARTMENT

Donald Rumsfeld .... defense secretary
Paul Wolfowitz .... deputy defense secretary
General Tommy Franks .... chief, Central Command
Vice Admiral Thomas Wilson ...... director of the Defense Intelligence Agency
Douglas Feith .... undersecretary of defense for policy
David Wurmser .... terrorism researcher for Feith
F. Michael Maloof .... terrorism researcher for Feith
Richard Perle .... chairman, Defense Policy Board
Lieutenant Colonel Kevin Benson .... U.S. Army war planner
Laurie Mylroie .... author and member of Pentagon advisory board on terrorism and technology
R. James Woolsey .... former CIA director sent by Wolfowitz on a special mission

STATE DEPARTMENT

Colin Powell .... secretary of state
Richard Armitage .... deputy secretary of state
Marc Grossman .... undersecretary of state
Lawrence Wilkerson .... chief of staff to Powell
Carl Ford, Jr. .... assistant secretary for the Bureau of Intelligence and Research (INR)
Simon Dodge .... nuclear weapons analyst at INR
Wayne White .... Middle East affairs analyst at INR
Douglas Rohn .... African affairs analyst at INR
William Howard Taft IV .... legal counselor
Kenneth Duberstein .... informal adviser to Colin Powell

JUSTICE DEPARTMENT

John Ashcroft .... attorney general
James Comey .... deputy attorney general
Mark Corallo .... public affairs chief

Patrick Fitzgerald ... U.S. attorney in Chicago and special counsel in CIA leak case
Jack Eckenrode .... senior FBI special agent on CIA leak case
Russell Fincher .... FBI counterterrorism agent

CONGRESS

Tom Daschle .... Democratic Senate leader
Bob Graham ..... Democratic senator and chairman of the intelligence committee
Joseph Biden .... Democratic senator and chairman of
the foreign relations committee
Carl Levin ..... Democratic senator and member of the armed services committee
Jay Rockefeller .... Democratic senator and member of the intelligence committee
Dick Durbin ..... Democratic senator and member of the intelligence committee
Chuck Schumer ..... Democratic senator and member of the judiciary committee
Trent Lott .... Republican Senate leader
Chuck Hagel .. Republican senator and member of the foreign relations committee
Dick Gephardt .... House Democratic leader
Dick Armey .... Republican House majority leader
Peter Zimmerman .... scientific adviser for the Senate foreign relations committee

WMD INVESTIGATORS

David Kay .... head of the Iraq Survey Group (until January 2004)
Charles Duelfer .... head of the Iraq Survey Group (after January 2004)
Jacques Baute ...... chief of the International Atomic Energy Agency's Iraq office

IRAQIS

Ahmad Chalabi .... head of the Iraqi National Congress (INC)
Aras Habib .... intelligence chief for the INC and suspected Iranian agent
Curveball .... a defector who claimed Iraq had mobile bioweapons labs
Adnan Ihsan Saeed al-Haideri .... INC-connected Iraqi defector who claimed
Saddam had an extensive WMD infrastructure
Sabah Khalifa Khodada al-Lami .... INC-connected defector who claimed
9/11 plotters were linked to Iraq
Naji Sabri .... Iraqi foreign minister in the Saddam Hussein
regime who almost became a CIA spy
Wissam al-Zahawie .... Iraqi ambassador to the Vatican who visited Niger in 1999
Mohammed Abdullah al-Shahwani .... general in charge of CIA-trained
Scorpions; Iraqi intelligence director

ITALIANS

Elisabetta Burba .... investigative reporter for the Italian magazine *Panorama*
Rocco Martino .... snitch who peddled phony documents

Laura Montini ("La Signora") . . . . a worker in the Niger Embassy in Rome
Antonio Nucera . . . . colonel in the Italian intelligence agency

NEWS MEDIA

Robert Novak . . . . syndicated columnist
Judith Miller . . . . *New York Times* reporter
Howell Raines . . . . *New York Times* executive editor (until June 2003)
Bill Keller . . . . *New York Times* executive editor (after July 2003)
Arthur Ochs Sulzberger, Jr. . . . . chairman of the board, New York Times Co.
Matthew Cooper . . . . *Time* White House correspondent
John Dickerson . . . . *Time* White House correspondent
Michael Duffy . . . . *Time* Washington bureau chief
Bob Woodward . . . . *Washington Post* reporter and author
Walter Pincus . . . . *Washington Post* national security reporter
Michael Allen . . . . *Washington Post* reporter
Tim Russert . . . . host of *Meet the Press*
Chris Matthews . . . . host of *Hardball*

LAWYERS

Robert Luskin . . . . attorney for Karl Rove
Floyd Abrams . . . . attorney for *The New York Times, Time,*
Judith Miller, and Matt Cooper
Robert Bennett . . . . attorney for Judith Miller
Richard Sauber . . . . attorney for Matt Cooper
James Hamilton . . . . attorney for Robert Novak
Joseph Tate . . . . attorney for Scooter Libby

TERRORISTS

Ibn al-Shaykh al-Libi . . . . captured al-Qaeda commander
Abu Musab al-Zarqawi . . . Jordanian terrorist cited by Colin Powell in UN speech
Mohamed Atta . . . . 9/11 ringleader
Ramzi Yousef . . . . planner of the 1993 World Trade Center bombings
Abdul Rahman Yasin . . . . plotter in the 1993 World Trade Center bombings

How is the world ruled and how do wars start? Diplomats tell lies to journalists and then believe what they read.

—Karl Kraus,
Austrian journalist and press critic
(1874–1936)

HUBRIS

I'm going to kick his sorry motherfucking ass all over the Mideast.
—President George W. Bush

Introduction

———

EARLY ON the afternoon of May 1, 2002, George W. Bush slipped out of the Oval Office, grabbed a tennis racquet, and headed to the South Lawn. He had a few spare moments for one of his recreational pleasures: whacking tennis balls to his dogs, Spot and Barney. It was a pleasant spring day in Washington and not an especially taxing one for the president. He had no pressing political worries. Having routed the Taliban regime in Afghanistan the previous fall, Bush was standing tall in the polls, with an approval rating hovering at 70 percent. That morning, there had been his usual terrorism briefings, then meetings with congressional leaders where Bush had talked about moving forward his domestic proposals, including a measure promoting faith-based social programs. Later in the day, the president was due to meet the vice president of China. Bush also had an unusual press interview on his schedule that afternoon. As he hit the balls and watched the dogs scamper, Bush prepared for that session with two press aides by reviewing questions he would likely be asked about one of his predecessors he admired most: Ronald Reagan.

Ever since September 11, 2001, Bush had increasingly identified with Reagan: his optimism, his firm convictions, his stark, uncompromising stand against Soviet communism. Bush had come to consider Reagan's battle against the Soviet Union a parallel of his own struggle against Islamic extremism. The Evil Empire was now the Axis of Evil—that trio of tyrannies, Iraq, Iran, and North Korea, that Bush had proclaimed the nation's foes months earlier during his first State of the Union speech.

Frank Sesno, the veteran newscaster, was due shortly at the White House to query Bush about Reagan and the parallels between his presidency and Bush's. The interview was for a History Channel special that would air upon the death of the former president, who was ninety-one years old and suffering from advanced Alzheimer's disease. On a two-page "pre-brief" memo prepared by his staff and containing questions that might be asked, Bush had written out by hand points he wanted to emphasize. The presidential scribbles, his aides thought, were revealing—perhaps a window onto Bush's view of himself. "Optimism and strength," Bush had scrawled on top of the memo. Also, "decisive" and "faith." Next to a question about Reagan's direct, blunt style, Bush had written, "moral clarity." He had drawn an arrow next to the word "forceful." Alongside a question about the 1983 suicide bombing attack on the U.S. Marines barracks in Lebanon (which killed 241 American troops) and how a president copes with such losses, Bush had written, "There will be casualties."

On the South Lawn, Press Secretary Ari Fleischer and another member of the communications staff, a burly, irrepressible former television producer named Adam Levine, reviewed these points with Bush. Then they all moved inside and headed upstairs to the Red Room so Bush could have makeup applied for the interview. Bush casually asked Fleischer how his day had been going and what the talk in the pressroom was. Fleischer mentioned Helen Thomas, the longtime correspondent then writing for Hearst News Service. She was a gadfly and constantly giving Fleischer a tough time about an issue much in the news: Iraq. Bush and other administration officials had been decrying Saddam Hussein, the dictator of Iraq, as a threat to the United States and the world. To many, it sounded like war talk. The media were filled with speculation that the White House was preparing for an invasion. But Bush had steadfastly refused to state his intentions. His aides repeatedly claimed that Bush had reached no decisions. Interviewed by a British broadcaster a few weeks earlier, Bush had resorted to a Clintonesque evasion: "I have no plans to attack on my desk."

At that day's daily press briefing, Thomas had peppered Fleischer with questions about Iraq. Referring to stories in the media about secret plans for military action, she asked, "What is the president's rationale for invading

Iraq?" What made Saddam different from other dictators and worth an invasion? Fleischer bantered with Thomas and pointed out that "regime change" in Iraq had been the official policy of the U.S. government since President Bill Clinton signed the Iraq Liberation Act in 1998. Thomas shot back: Did the law mandate that the United States overthrow the Iraqi government by force? Bush, Fleischer said, "believes that the people of Iraq, as well as the region, will be more peaceful, better off without Saddam Hussein." Thomas retorted, "That's not a reason" to go to war. "Well, Helen," Fleischer replied, "if you were the president, you could have vetoed the law." The reporters chuckled, and Fleischer called on another journalist.

As Fleischer recounted this exchange for the president, Bush's mood changed, according to Levine. He grew grim and determined—steely. Out of nowhere, he unleashed a string of expletives.

"Did you tell her I don't like motherfuckers who gas their own people?" the president snapped.

"Did you tell her I don't like assholes who lie to the world?"

"Did you tell her I'm going to kick his sorry motherfucking ass all over the Mideast?"

Fleischer paused. "I told her half of that," he replied. Bush laughed, as did his aides. Still, Bush's visceral reaction was telling. This wasn't bluster; this was real. The president had meant what he said—every word of it. This was the Bush that Levine admired. "You know where we're going here," Levine thought.

THE vice president's limousine sped through downtown Washington and headed over the Potomac River on its way to Langley, Virginia. It was days after Bush's outburst, and Dick Cheney was making another of his visits to CIA headquarters. These trips—unknown to the public at this point—had become the talk of the intelligence community. Cheney would arrive at agency headquarters and park himself in Director George Tenet's seventh-floor conference room. Then officers and analysts would be summoned to brief him—on Iraq and other matters—and often encounter a withering interrogation. How do we know this? What more do you have on that? What have you done to follow up? Cheney was proper and respectful. His questions were delivered in his soft, low, monotone voice, his arms folded. Still, they had an intimidating impact on his briefers. "I've seen him shake people," said John Maguire, an Iraq covert operations officer who often attended the Cheney briefings. "He would drill in on substantive details. If he asked you something that you didn't know, you better have an answer the next time you saw him. . . . He would say, 'I want answers on this. This is not acceptable.' " The worst thing to do with Cheney was to hedge or to waffle. "He'd say, 'Make a call,' " Maguire recalled. He didn't want to hear sentences that began, "We don't know."

During these sessions, Cheney demanded answers on Iraq. Cheney had long-standing and firm views on Saddam Hussein that went back to when he had served as secretary of defense during the first Persian Gulf War. Cheney had been convinced then that the CIA had blown it by badly underestimating how close Saddam had been to building a nuclear bomb before that war. And ever since the cataclysmic events of September 11, Cheney seemed obsessed with Iraq. He was sure that Saddam was a grave threat to the United States—and that the agency was missing the crucial intelligence that would prove it. In February 2002, Cheney had seized on a murky item presented to him during his daily morning briefing from the CIA: a report forwarded to the CIA by Italian military intelligence that Iraq had arranged to purchase 500 tons of yellowcake uranium from the impoverished African nation of Niger. If the report was accurate—if there had been such a transaction—this would be compelling evidence Iraq had revived a moribund nuclear weapons program that had been dismantled in the mid-1990s under the supervision of the International Atomic Energy Agency. But there was nothing to substantiate the report, and parts of it did not make sense. Still, Cheney had jumped on it. What more can you get on this? he had asked his CIA briefer. What more can you find out? As always, the answer from the CIA was, We'll get on this right away. And it did.

Another issue Cheney fixated on was Baghdad's ties to terrorists, especially the allegations of a connection between Saddam and al-Qaeda. The agency would write up answers to the vice president's repeated questions and send them to his office, often reporting that there was little to substantiate Cheney's darkest suspicions of an operational alliance between Saddam and Osama bin Laden. But Cheney and his hard-nosed chief of staff, I. Lewis Libby (who went by the nickname of Scooter), were never satisfied and continually asked for more. "It was like they were hoping we'd find something buried in the files or come back with a different answer,"

Michael Sulick, deputy chief of the CIA's Directorate of Operations, later said. There was no "obvious pressure" by Cheney and Libby to change the answers, Sulick recalled. But the barrage of questions and the frequent visits by the vice president had created an environment that was subtly, but unmistakably, influencing the agency's work. The CIA's analysts, Sulick believed, had become "overly eager to please."

Libby may have been harder to please than Cheney. He was one of the most powerful officials in the Bush White House. As Cheney's top national security adviser, he oversaw a "shadow" National Security Council, with tentacles reaching deep into the foreign policy and defense bureaucracy. One NSC staffer recalled being stunned to discover, years after he began working at the White House, that his internal memos to National Security Adviser Condoleezza Rice had routinely been routed to Libby without his knowledge. A CIA official was surprised to discover that Libby's staff was reading unedited transcripts of National Security Agency intercepts.

A cool, meticulous, and secretive Washington lawyer, Libby was an ideological and philosophical soul mate of his mentor, Paul Wolfowitz, the deputy secretary of defense and leading neoconservative hawk, who was even more preoccupied with Iraq than Cheney. Libby had been a student of Wolfowitz at Yale University in the 1970s; Wolfowitz had hired him as a speechwriter at the State Department in 1981 and again, as his principal deputy, nearly a decade later, when Wolfowitz was undersecretary of defense for policy and planning during the administration of George H. W. Bush. Libby and Wolfowitz shared with Cheney a congenital distrust of the CIA. They had a near-theological conviction that the agency's analysts were wedded to an inside-the-Beltway conventional wisdom that obscured the sinister plottings of America's enemies.

That was why Libby, on Cheney's behalf, relentlessly demanded that the agency supply the vice president's office with raw intelligence reports. Cheney's team believed that unanalyzed reports contained hidden nuggets that had been overlooked or ignored by the CIA because the data undercut the don't-rock-the-boat predilections of the agency's analysts. But the vice president's aides were confident that if *they* looked at the material, they could assess the *real* risks to America. In one nine-month period, starting in 2002, court records would later show, Libby sent requests to the CIA that generated between three hundred and five hundred documents, including e-mails, internal memos, and reports. The agency estimated that finding and retrieving from its files all the queries it had received from Libby—and all the responses it had sent back—would take nearly a year.

Libby was not popular at the CIA. "He had a reputation of being a prick," recalled one senior CIA official. In questioning analysts, "he was nasty and obnoxious about it." Libby was most aggressive on intelligence related to Saddam and al-Qaeda, according to this CIA veteran: "He wouldn't let go of the al-Qaeda–Saddam connection." A Bush NSC official recalled Libby as being aloof but skilled—and, if need be, devious—in the ways of bureaucratic infighting. "Whenever Scooter Libby walked into the elevator," this official said, "the temperature seemed to drop five degrees."

Libby was not with Cheney this particular May morning when the vice president arrived at the CIA. But as Cheney's top national security adviser, he would soon get a full report. Cheney had come to Langley to be updated on the latest intelligence on Iraq, including what was known about Saddam's unconventional weapons. But another subject was on the agenda, a matter of the utmost sensitivity. It was one of the most closely held secrets in the U.S. government: the Anabasis project.

DB/ANABASIS was the code name for an extensive covert operations plan that had been drawn up by the CIA to destabilize and ultimately topple the regime of Saddam Hussein. (DB was the agency cryptonym for Iraq.) At the direction of the White House, Tenet had commissioned the scheme, not too long after the U.S. military had defeated the Taliban. About this time, Bush asked Defense Secretary Donald Rumsfeld to order up a fresh war plan for Iraq. It was clear to top intelligence officials that Iraq was next on Bush's agenda, and the task of developing the CIA's secret plan was handed to two seasoned officers in the Iraq Operations Group within the agency's Directorate of Operations, or DO.

One of the officers was a stocky, balding Cuban American whose first name was Luis. He had previously been a special assistant to CIA Deputy Director John McLaughlin. Before that he had spent years as a case officer in CIA stations throughout the world. His father had participated in the CIA's Bay of Pigs debacle in 1961, when an agency-directed invasion of Cuba failed miserably. The other officer in charge of Anabasis was the forty-nine-year-old John Maguire, a strapping former Baltimore city cop who had specialized in busting down doors as a member of the city's SWAT team. Both were veterans of the CIA's covert wars of the 1980s, when CIA director William Casey, acting on orders from Ronald Reagan, was mounting secret paramilitary operations around the globe. Maguire had run guns to the Nicaraguan *contra* rebels fighting the Sandinista government, and he had participated in one of the more notorious episodes of that clandestine war: the mining of the ports of Nicaragua. In the middle of the night, he had directed local commandoes who would dump mines off the sides of speedboats. For cover, Maguire posed as an employee of the Johnson Outboard Motor Repair shop in La Union, El Salvador.

When the operation was exposed by the news media in April 1984, there was an uproar on Capitol Hill. "I am pissed off!" Senator Barry Goldwater, then the chairman of the Senate intelligence committee, wrote Casey. "[M]ine the harbors in Nicaragua? This is an act violating international law. It is an act of war." The mining program was shut down. Months later, Congress cut off money for the CIA's *contra* operations. Lieutenant Colonel Oliver North and the National Security Council covertly took over the program, and their clandestine scheming led to the Iran-*contra* scandal. Many CIA operatives whom Maguire had worked with became ensnared in the subsequent investigations. But Maguire escaped unscathed. He did learn a lesson about covert ops: they can get messy and not always go as planned.

Later, Maguire was dispatched to Afghanistan, where he provided explosives and weapons training for Ahmed Shah Massoud's Northern Alliance. Subsequently, he made his first foray into Iraq, where he helped plan a disastrous 1995 coup attempt—a debacle that he blamed in large part on the unreliability of Ahmad Chalabi, the self-promoting Iraqi exile the agency had been supporting. Maguire was bitter. Agents he had worked with and their family members had been murdered by Saddam. By the mid-1990s, he was also frustrated. The CIA, shuddering from the investigations and prosecutions triggered by Iran-*contra* and serving the more cautious Bill Clinton, had backed away from paramilitary operations and covert ops. Maguire left CIA headquarters to be an instructor at the Farm, the agency's training facility in rural Virginia.

On September 12, 2001, he returned to headquarters and, with Luis, jumped at the chance to put his experience in clandestine ops to new uses. Over an intense forty-five-day period beginning in late 2001, the two men cooked up an audacious plan, unlike anything Langley had seen in years.

James Pavitt, the DO chief, had given Luis and Maguire a blunt directive when he assigned this project: "Give me a plan that scares me." As Maguire later put it, "And so we did. We scared the crap out of him."

Anabasis was no-holds-barred covert action. It called for installing a small army of paramilitary CIA officers on the ground inside Iraq; for elaborate schemes to penetrate Saddam's regime, recruiting disgruntled military officers with buckets of cash; for feeding the regime disinformation about internal dissent in ways that would cause Saddam to lash out (most likely through mass executions); for disrupting the regime's finances and supply networks; for sabotage that included blowing up railroad lines and communications towers; and for targeting the lives of key regime officials. It also envisioned staging a phony incident that could be used to start a war. A small group of Iraqi exiles would be flown into Iraq by helicopter to seize an isolated military base near the Saudi border. They then would take to the airwaves and announce a coup was under way. If Saddam responded by flying troops south, his aircraft could be shot down by U.S. fighter planes patrolling the no-fly zones established by UN edict after the first Persian Gulf War. A clash of this sort could be used to initiate a full-scale war. "We were doing things in this program that we hadn't done since Casey," said Maguire.

For Maguire, it was also personal—a chance to settle an old score and avenge fallen comrades. "We wanted that fucker dead," he recalled. "We were willing to do anything to get Saddam."

The name Luis and Maguire had chosen for the program, Anabasis, had come from the title of a book by the ancient historian Xenophon that recounted the march of 10,000 Greek mercenaries to Babylon in the year 400 B.C. to capture the Persian throne for Cyrus the Younger from his brother. Wolfowitz, according to Maguire, was not keen on this particular name, though Maguire never understood why. But other CIA officials also thought the Anabasis program was inaptly titled—and wondered whether Luis and Maguire had misread history. The Greek army had been victorious at the critical battle of Cunaxa, but Cyrus had been killed, rendering the entire mission moot. The 10,000 Greeks then had to fight their way back to the Black Sea. Anabasis was the story of an unsuccessful operation that ended in retreat.

The estimated cost of Luis and Maguire's Anabasis was $400 million over two years. But it wasn't the price tag that frightened Pavitt and other senior agency officials. It was the lethality. In drawing up the plan, Luis and

Maguire had carefully avoided using the A-word: assassination. The agency had a long and troubled history of assassination plots. Most had failed and had cast a dark stain on the CIA's reputation. An executive order banning assassinations had been in place since 1976 (but occasionally circumvented during wartime). So Luis and Maguire referred instead to "direct action operations," a bland euphemism. But there was no doubt that, under Anabasis, people were going to die—and that innocent Iraqi civilians, not just government leaders and military officers, would likely be among the victims. When Pavitt and other senior officials in the DO reviewed the Anabasis plans, they were uncomfortable. Blowing up railroad lines? "You're going to kill people if you do this," Tyler Drumheller, chief of the DO's European Division, recalled saying when he first looked at Anabasis. He was stating the obvious.

But this was the post-9/11 era, when U.S. intelligence agencies, with the encouragement of the White House and fiercely conservative lawyers in the Justice Department, were pushing the envelope. The CIA was snatching terror suspects off the streets in Gambia, in Bosnia, in Sweden, and "rendering" them to friendly foreign intelligence services—where extreme interrogation practices would be used on them. The CIA set up its own network of secret prisons, where suspected al-Qaeda leaders were subjected to aggressive interrogation, including "water boarding," a technique in which the suspect was strapped to a board and dunked below water long enough to approximate (but not cause) drowning. In a rousing speech to CIA officers soon after the September 11 attacks, Cofer Black, then director of the CIA's Counterterrorism Center, had proclaimed, "The gloves are off." The line was widely quoted within the agency, and Black also used it during congressional testimony. But Black had said something to his CIA colleagues that did not attract public notice. There was some dispute as to his precise words. Drumheller recalled that Black had remarked that "someday we can all expect to be prosecuted for what we're going to do." Another counterterrorism official said that Black had simply commented that "someday we may all get called before a congressional committee for what we're going to do." Whatever the exact words, the message was clear: in the future, the missions the CIA was about to undertake might look different than they did right now.

On February 16, 2002, President Bush signed covert findings authorizing the various elements of Anabasis. The leaders of the congressional intelligence committees—including Representative Porter Goss, a Republican, and Senator Bob Graham, a Democrat—were briefed. Maguire and a team of his officers made their initial entry into Iraq in April 2002, crossing the Turkish border in Jeep Cherokees and driving into Kurdish areas in the north, a region outside the control of Saddam's regime. They met with the two rival Kurdish leaders, Massoud Barzani and Jalal Talabani, and briefed them on the details of the Anabasis plan. The Kurdish leaders were skeptical. They had heard talk from Americans like this in the past. Anabasis called for Kurdish irregulars to take risks—large risks—to recruit sources for the CIA and begin sabotage operations, even "direct action." People could die. "Is this real? Is the president serious?" Barzani and Talabani wanted to know. Maguire's response was one that he, and other CIA officials, would repeat: "We're really serious. This is not going to be some half-baked effort." Ultimately, the success of the plan rested on the credibility and the determination of George W. Bush—and about that, Maguire had no doubt. "This president is a man of his word," Maguire told the Kurds. "When we're finished, Saddam is not going to be there. When we're finished, we're going to be in Baghdad."

On this trip, Maguire himself headed south into Saddam-controlled territory, a white-mustachioed spy behind enemy lines. He drove in the backseat of a Toyota Super Salon dressed in the uniform of an Iraqi Army colonel with a red stripe on his shoulders. Maguire was waved through border crossings and checkpoints and drove right up to the perimeter of an Iraqi Army base. The unit was in disarray. There were soldiers milling about in flip-flops and shorts—with no guns or ammunition. "They looked like refugees," said Maguire. The Iraqi V Corps was supposedly the front line against an American invasion, but it seemed a shambles. On another occasion, a CIA officer working with Maguire inspected the line separating Kurdish-controlled territory from Saddam-controlled Iraq. On the other side were the deteriorating Iraqi military forces Maguire had seen. And one of those units, having spotted the CIA man, sent a runner across the line with a message: "Are you the Americans? We don't want to fight." When Maguire heard about this, he was pleased. It seemed that these Iraqi troops were eagerly awaiting an invasion—so they could surrender. He wrote it all up in a report that went directly to the president and the vice president. An invading American army, it appeared, could roll right through to Baghdad. Perhaps they would even be greeted as liberators.

BACK at headquarters, Luis and Maguire were eager to tell Cheney about Anabasis. The Kurdish leaders were fully on board; operations were beginning. The vice president, as always, asked tough questions: What kind of support are you receiving from the Kurds? Who are the people you're working with? Where are they placed? He was, Maguire recalled, "way in the weeds."

The answers Cheney received that day were reassuring. Luis and Maguire were can-do operatives firm in their conviction they were serving a righteous cause. After Cheney finished with them, he turned toward several analysts. He had a different set of questions for them: What was Saddam's force structure? How could the intelligence they have be used to support U.S. ground forces during an invasion? What Iraqi units were positioned where? Which ones might have chemical and biological weapons? Cheney was not posing the sort of questions a policy maker would need answered in order to determine whether Iraq posed a threat to the United States. He was not seeking information on *whether* Saddam was dangerous because he possessed weapons of mass destruction. He was not soliciting material that would help him decide if an invasion of Iraq was absolutely necessary. His queries were all pegged to the assumption that Iraq would be invaded. And he was not happy with what he was hearing, for the analysts were unable to provide concrete answers to his queries about the invasion to come.

Cheney's line of questioning was a logical follow-up to the briefing he had received on Anabasis, for from the start Luis and Maguire had made it clear that their top secret plan by itself should not be expected to eliminate Saddam. The various actions they had envisioned—the sabotage, the assassinations, the disinformation—could destabilize and weaken Saddam's tyrannical regime. They could create chaos and sow distrust. But truly ending the Iraqi dictator's grip on power would require the intervention of the U.S. military. Bush and Cheney, they believed, understood this. In response to a Bush directive, General Tommy Franks, commander of the U.S. Central Command, was already drawing up invasion plans. And Cheney was asking questions at the CIA that indicated he expected the United States to invade Iraq. Anabasis, from its inception, was a precursor and a complement to war—not a substitute.

There was even a timetable. When Maguire and Luis were instructed to devise a paramilitary plan, according to Maguire, the message they received from the agency leadership on the seventh floor was explicit: "Be ready to turn this thing on by January 2003. Be ready to go in a year. You got a year." That meant, as far as Maguire was concerned, there was going to be an invasion—and the clock was ticking.

WHILE Luis and Maguire were briefing Cheney on the top floor of CIA headquarters that day, another group of CIA operatives was toiling away on a related mission in the basement. In a space the size of a football field and divided into cubicles by partial walls, three hundred or so employees of the Counterproliferation Division (CPD) of the Directorate of Operations were mounting espionage operations aimed at obtaining intelligence on weapons of mass destruction programs around the globe. They also were plotting covert actions that might thwart these programs. A particularly busy unit in the CPD at this time was the Joint Task Force on Iraq, charged with digging up information on the top priority: Iraq's WMD programs. Its chief of operations was a career officer named Valerie Wilson.

Valerie Wilson, who had entered the CIA in 1985 as Valerie Plame, had been at the CPD for several years. Previously, she had served overseas in Europe, first as a case officer posing as a State Department employee and then as a supersecret NOC—an officer under "nonofficial cover." NOCs were the most clandestine of the agency's frontline officers. They did not pretend to work for the U.S. government—and did not have the protection of diplomatic immunity should anything go awry. They had to be independent, resourceful, confident—and careful. Valerie Wilson told people she worked for an energy firm. After returning from Europe and joining the CPD, she had maintained her NOC status. And now she was running ops aimed at uncovering intelligence on Iraq's unconventional weapons. Her job was to find the evidence of Saddam's clandestine efforts that Bush, Cheney, Libby, and other administration officials desired.

A year earlier—about the time Valerie Wilson joined it—the CPD's Iraq unit had been small, employing only a few operations officers. Not much was going on within it. In the years since 1998, when UN weapons inspectors had left Iraq, the CIA had not had a single source on Iraq's weapons programs. Prior to 1998, the CIA had used the UN inspection team to gather intelligence. With the inspectors gone, the CPD had utterly failed "to gain direct access to Iraq's WMD programs," as its deputy chief later told Senate investigators. Most of the Iraq action at the CIA—such as it was—had been occurring within the operations directorate's Near East Division, which had not done much better than the CPD. By 2001, the NE Division had developed only four sources in Iraq—and none was reporting on WMDs. But in the summer before 9/11, the word came down from the top brass: we're ramping up on Iraq. The CPD's Iraq unit was changed into the Joint Task Force on Iraq. And in the months after September 11, the JTFI grew to include about fifty employees; Valerie Wilson was placed in charge of its operations group.

By the spring of 2002, the JFTI, including Wilson, was under intense pressure to get more solid intelligence on Iraq's weapons programs. With Bush and his Cabinet members obviously focused on (or perhaps obsessed with) Saddam and Iraq, everyone in the intelligence community, from Tenet on down, realized it was crucial to do whatever they could—probe every corner, chase any lead—to penetrate Saddam's Iraq. The JTFI was frantic to do so.

Slowly, the JTFI began to develop sources within Iraq. Yet the group was coming up with nothing.

The JTFI's primary target was Iraqi scientists. The goal was to make indirect and surreptitious contact with these experts and find out what they knew about unconventional weapons in Iraq. JTFI operations officers tracked down relatives and associates of Iraqi scientists living in America. "It would be, 'Knock, knock, we're here from the U.S. government, we know you're a loyal citizen and we want to talk to you about your brother back in Iraq,'" a CIA officer recalled. "They would say, 'My brother is a good man.' We'd say, 'We know that.' They'd say, 'My brother knows nothing.' We'd say, 'I'm sure. But can we find a way to have *him* tell us that?'" JTFI officers occasionally persuaded an Iraqi émigré to pay a visit to a relative in Iraq and—when no one else was near—pose certain questions to the relative. Valerie Wilson and the operations officers of JTFI sought out Iraqi graduate students studying abroad who had previously studied under Iraqi scientists of interest to the CIA. What can you tell us about your mentor's work? Would you be willing to report secretly to us after returning to Iraq? What if we paid you? What if we could help you stay in this nice Western city? In some instances, JTFI attempted to persuade a defector to go back to Iraq.

"It was 'So glad you've risked your life getting out,'" one CIA official said. "'Now, will you go back for us?' Yeah, right, that was an easy sell."

By that spring, JTFI was sending out dozens of reports based on its new sources. But none of these sources had anything definitive to report about unconventional weapons activity within Iraq. At the same time, Valerie Wilson's operations unit was overwhelmed with walk-ins. As the anti-Saddam rhetoric coming from Bush administration officials had intensified, would-be informants were increasingly approaching U.S. embassies and offering—or peddling—information on Iraq's weapons programs. JTFI operations officers were traveling throughout the world to debrief these possible sources to determine if they were legitimate. Often it would take only minutes to conclude that someone was pulling a con. But the JTFI had to treat each case as potentially the breakthrough for which its officers yearned. "We knew nothing about what was going on in Iraq," a CIA official recalled. "We were way behind the eight ball. We had to look under every rock."

In one episode, an Iraqi showed up in Damascus claiming he had been taken blindfolded to a facility outside Baghdad where political prisoners or Iranian prisoners from the Iran-Iraq War (which ended in 1988) were being held. He was to repair equipment at this site. But, he claimed, he had witnessed the most gruesome experiment: Twenty or so subjects were strapped down and injected with a poison. Within hours, blood was pouring out of their noses and ears. And they died. JTFI officers flew to Syria to meet with this Iraqi. His story made them wonder if Iraq was testing a botulinum-based weapon. He told them how long he had sat blindfolded in the car that had ferried him to this site. He described the facility and the surrounding environs. Back in the CIA's basement, JTFI staffers pored over satellite photos and tried to determine where this facility was. They couldn't find anything. Then this fellow failed a lie detector test. Another nothing. Later, CIA officers would come to suspect that this informant, as well as other defectors bearing dramatic WMD allegations, had been sent their way by Chalabi's Iraqi National Congress, the exile group that had been lobbying Washington for years to overthrow Saddam.

A walk-in in India claimed he had been involved with a biological weapons program based at an Iraqi university. He had to be checked out. The Joint Task Force on Iraq dispatched one of the intelligence community's best BW experts to the subcontinent, a doctor named Les. (His last name remains a secret.) The shrewd doctor concluded the Indian was a fabricator.

"We were trying to find something," a CIA official recalled. "We were motivated. We knew this was important. But it was our job to be skeptical."

As the cases piled up, Valerie Wilson traveled overseas under assumed names to monitor walk-in operations and other activities. Members of the unit were putting in long hours. But the results were frustrating. None of the JTFI's operations was generating evidence that Saddam had biological or chemical weapons or a revived nuclear weapons program. Did the task force's lack of results mean it was not doing its job well enough—or rather, might Saddam not have the arsenal of unconventional weapons most CIA people (and White House officials) assumed he was hiding? Valerie Wilson and other JTFI officers were almost too overwhelmed to consider the possibility that the small number of operations they were conducting was, in a way, coming up with the right answer: that there was no intelligence to find on Saddam's current chemical and biological stockpiles and nuclear weapons programs because they did not exist. Instead, Valerie Wilson pushed on, doing all she could to uncover information—any information—on Saddam's weapons.

In over a year, she would become a household name—but not for anything she did to find Iraq's weapons of mass destruction.

THERE was a profound disconnect between Valerie Wilson's endeavors and those of her colleagues upstairs who were briefing Cheney on Anabasis. The operating premise of the officers of the Counterproliferation Division—and of the CIA as a whole—was that accurate intelligence mattered. It was the duty of the CIA and the other intelligence agencies to obtain truthful information, however they could, and to get it into the hands of policy makers. Spies, eavesdroppers, and analysts collected and processed intelligence so senior government officials, especially the commander in chief, could render the best decisions possible. But Bush, Cheney, and a handful of other senior officials already believed they had enough information to know what to do about Iraq. They still were seeking information about unconventional weapons in Iraq, but it was for reasons other than for evaluating whether Iraq was an immediate threat that would have to be neutralized by an invasion. They were drop-dead sure of their presumptions: Iraq was a danger, Saddam had to go, and war was the only option that would achieve this policy goal. They did not need intelligence to reach these conclusions—or to test them.

Intelligence on Iraq's weapons programs—and Saddam's ties to terrorists, including al-Qaeda—certainly had its uses for Bush and his aides. It could, as Cheney, a former secretary of defense, knew, help battlefield commanders prepare for the invasion. And just as important—if not more—it could help the Bush White House build a case for war and whip up congressional and public support for the course chosen. Bush and his aides were looking for intelligence not to guide their policy on Iraq but to market it. The intelligence would be the basis not for launching a war but for selling it.

So much of the coming debate over the intelligence on Iraq—did it indicate Iraq was a clear and present threat or not?—would be moot. The work of the thousands of intelligence professionals and the contentious tussles over the issue on Capitol Hill and within the media—all this was predicated on a false assumption: that the intelligence was a crucial element in whether war would happen. Much of what the CIA produced turned out to be embarrassingly flawed. But it was only window dressing for decision makers who did not need intelligence to know that they knew the truth.

The reasons why Bush invaded Iraq—and the precise moment he resolved to do so—will be debated by historians for years to come. Part of it, as Bush's outburst to Fleischer and Levine indicated, may well have been the president's gut instincts and a powerful—if not personal—antipathy toward Saddam Hussein, a dictator whom George Bush's father had defeated but left in place, a tyrant who had been accused of plotting to kill Bush's father, and a brute who, in the days after 9/11, provided an easy-to-hit target for a president who felt driven to take tough measures to safeguard America.

But for many others in his administration, the invasion of Iraq would be a faith-based war—predicated on certain ideological and geopolitical views. Cheney had his hardened Hobbesian views of power politics. Secretary of Defense Donald Rumsfeld was a haughty, self-styled transformer, convinced that he could see what needed to be done better than his generals could. Beside them was a fraternity of neoconservative academics, polemicists, and former government officials who had been advocating war with Iraq for years, long before September 11. Many of the most important of these neoconservatives had been influenced by an eccentric academic who claimed that Saddam was the hidden hand behind al-Qaeda. Now leading members of this group held senior positions in the Bush administration. Richard Perle was the chairman of the Defense Policy Board and an influential adviser to Rumsfeld. Wolfowitz was deputy secretary of defense. Libby was Cheney's chief of staff. Douglas Feith was undersecretary of defense for policy and running a secret unit that combed through raw intelligence reports seeking any information that linked Saddam to Osama bin Laden. In conferences at the American Enterprise Institute, in newspaper op-eds, and in articles in *The Weekly Standard* magazine, these hawks and their allies had been marshaling the case: Saddam was at the epicenter of world terrorism; he had assembled a massive arsenal of chemical and biological weapons; he was about to go nuclear; he was a threat to Israel, the Middle East, and the United States. Moreover, some of them argued, eliminating Saddam would serve larger policy goals: it would extend the United States' influence in the region and upend the toxic status quo in the Middle East. It would advance the cause of freedom, ushering in a new era of democracy. Imagine a pro-West, pro-Israel bastion of democracy in the middle of this uneasy part of the planet.

There was a case to be made. Saddam was a brutal ruler and a force for trouble, at least in the region. He had possessed chemical and biological weapons in the past and had sought nuclear weapons years earlier. He had gassed his enemies in the 1980s. He had not complied with UN Security Council resolutions demanding full disarmament. And after September 11, the United States had to be more vigilant about a prospective threat. He *might* still have biological and chemical weapons; he *might* be secretly developing nuclear weapons. He *might* one day hook up with anti-American terrorists. The continuing international sanctions imposed against his regime *might* be faltering and not thwart Saddam forever—especially if he used the billions of dollars he was skimming off the UN-supervised oil-for-food program to purchase WMD-related materials on the black market.

But the advocates for war went beyond depicting Saddam as a prospective threat. He was, they claimed, the number one danger to the United States and an American military defeat of this murderous thug would not only enhance the security of Americans but spark a historic and positive transformation in the Middle East. Many argued that a war against Iraq would not be difficult, the aftermath not a problem. The Iraqis would be grateful, and so would Arabs everywhere. Their case—before and after 9/11—was based on unproven, dubious assumptions and sketchy and, in many respects phony, intelligence. But it ultimately rested on a strong core belief: *we know what we're doing.*

There was no doubt. Information from intelligence analysts or other experts in or out of government that contradicted or undermined the operating assumptions of the get-Saddam crowd was ignored or belittled.

After the invasion, a bitter national debate would arise over how Bush had presented the case for war to the public. It was a damning question: had he—as well as Cheney, Rumsfeld, National Security Adviser Condoleezza Rice, Secretary of State Colin Powell, and other administration figures—hyped the threat to rally popular support for an elective war against a nation with no known connection to 9/11? Had Bush, Cheney, and their aides shared with the public what the U.S. government really did—and did not—know about Saddam, his weapons programs, and his alleged ties to al-Qaeda? Certainly, the intelligence services had failed miserably by issuing all-too-definitive statements about Saddam's WMDs. But had Bush compounded this failure by overselling the limited and flawed intelligence because war was his preferred option?

THE manner in which Bush would sell the war—promoting questionable intelligence—would hit Valerie Wilson directly. Months after the invasion, her maiden name (Valerie Plame) and her classified employment status at the CIA would be disclosed by conservative columnist Robert Novak, who had received information on her from two Bush administration officials. One of them, who much later insisted he had only confirmed what Novak already knew, was Karl Rove, the president's master strategist. Her career would be ruined, her operations and contacts possibly jeopardized. And all this would happen because her husband, former ambassador Joseph Wilson, had challenged Bush's use of a particularly lousy and misleading piece of intelligence to persuade (some might say, scare) Americans. Joseph Wilson was an imperfect critic. At points, he garbled some facts and overstated his case, even as he soundly raised questions about the administration's handling of the prewar intelligence.

The Plame affair would be full of ironies and twists. The investigation of the leak would entangle major media institutions, raise questions about the relationships between high-powered reporters and high-level sources, and land in jail one prominent journalist, whose prewar reporting on Iraq's WMDs would come to symbolize the media's complicity in the Bush White House's sales campaign. The episode would become another battlefront in the fierce partisan wars of Washington. The leak would be assailed as a vengeful act of treason engineered to discredit an administration critic, and it would be dismissed by administration allies as relatively routine political hardball. But while the White House—especially Cheney's office—would indeed train its sights on Wilson as a troublemaker, the original source of the leak was not a political hit man but a highly respected State Department official, who harbored deep doubts about Bush's march to war. He mentioned Valerie Wilson to Novak not as part of a White House smear campaign targeting Joseph Wilson. It was, according to the official's colleagues, a slip-up by an inveterate gossip—but one that occurred alongside a concerted White House effort to undermine a critic of the war.

Still, the Plame affair, fueled by White House deceptions, was a window into a much bigger scandal: the Bush administration's use of faulty intelligence and its fervent desire (after the invasion) to defend its prewar sales pitch. The Plame matter would lead to an investigation of the White House, the appointment of a special counsel, and the indictment of a senior White House official. But its real significance was larger than the sum of its parts. It would come to represent the disturbing and intrigue-ridden story of how the Bush administration—full of we-know-best, gung ho officials keen for a war that they assumed would go well—presented a case for war that turned out to be, in virtually every aspect, fraudulent.

It's a tragic tale partly because the inside account of the intelligence mess is replete with episodes in which intelligence analysts and government officials actually made the correct calls about Iraq's weapons, Baghdad's supposed ties to al-Qaeda, and the difficulties that a war would bring. But they either did not prevail in internal bureaucratic scuffles or were disregarded by a White House committed to (or hell-bent on) war against Saddam. What happened to Valerie Wilson was part of this larger story: how flawed intelligence was misused by the president and his top aides to take the nation to war.

WHEN Bush sat down for his History Channel interview on that spring day in 2002, ten months before he would send more than 150,000 American troops into Iraq, he did not seem to be thinking about nuances, conflicting intelligence reports, or the unknown consequences of bold action. The man in charge—the president who seemed to have resolved in his own mind that he would guide the nation to war—was thinking about moral clarity, about strong and decisive leadership, about standing tall against an evil tyrant. Reagan "didn't say, 'Well, Mr. Gorbachev, would you take the top three bricks off the wall?' " Bush told Frank Sesno. "He said, tear it all down. . . . And the truth of the matter is, I spoke about the Axis of Evil, and I did it for a reason. I wanted the world to know exactly where the United States stood." Reagan's hard line had been a success, Bush said to Sesno. Not only the top three bricks but the whole damn Berlin Wall had come tumbling down.

Now Bush had the chance to do something similar. He would get rid of Saddam Hussein. As he had told his press aides, he would "kick his sorry motherfucking ass all over the Mideast." But first he would have to convince Congress and the American public.

Mr. President, if you go in there, you're likely to be stuck in a quagmire.

—HOUSE MAJORITY LEADER DICK ARMEY

1

A Warning at the White House

THE PRESIDENT'S message was direct: There was no time to wait; the showdown with Saddam Hussein, the dictator of Iraq, had to start right away.

It was the morning of September 4, 2002, and George W. Bush had summoned eighteen senior members of the House and Senate to the Cabinet Room of the White House. Talk of war with Iraq had been under way for months. The prospect had been debated on cable news shows, dissected on op-ed pages, discussed at think tanks. And within the White House, the Pentagon, and the CIA, the planning had long since begun. Now Bush was making it quite real for his guests. In a few days, his administration would launch a major public relations campaign to persuade the American people—and the world—that Saddam was such a pressing threat that war might be the only option. But before doing so, the White House wanted to get Congress in line.

When the House and Senate members had taken their seats at the imposing oval mahogany table, they were given copies of a letter from the president. "America and the civilized world face a critical decision in the months ahead," it began. "The decision is how to disarm an outlaw regime that continues to possess and develop weapons of mass destruction." Since September 11, the letter said, "we have been tragically reminded that we are vulnerable to evil people. And this vulnerability increases dramatically when evil people have access to weapons of mass destruction." Bush told the assembled leaders that he would work with them on Iraq. But he needed a quick vote in Congress on a resolution that would grant him the authority to take on Saddam, perhaps with military action. He didn't have the proposed language yet. But he wanted this vote within six weeks—before Congress left town so members could campaign for reelection.

Listening to the president, Senate Majority Leader Tom Daschle felt trapped. Bush's promise to collaborate with Congress was a modest win for congressional leaders. Months earlier, White House Counsel Alberto Gonzales had insisted that Bush had the power to launch a war against Iraq without consulting Congress. But the White House had decided not to make a stand on this point.* Bush's concession, though, imposed a burden on him: he would have to present a case for war that could win over a majority of lawmakers. And that meant he would have to offer evidence—that is, the administration's secret intelligence on Iraq. But Daschle feared this apparent victory for Congress was part of a larger ploy.

House and Senate members were gearing up for the final stretch of the campaign, with control of the Senate up for grabs. Bush was informing them that the national debate would now focus on Iraq, not health care, not tax cuts, not the environment or anything the Democrats wanted to talk about. You want to be involved, he was saying, well, here are the terms.

The president's comments were a jolt to Daschle. His Democratic caucus was already deeply divided. Its liberal members were adamantly opposed to the idea of going to war in Iraq. Other Democrats—out of agreement with Bush or out of fear of opposing a popular president's confrontation with an anti-American tyrant—preferred to be on Bush's side. And the president's political strength was feared. Bush had smashed the Taliban and al-Qaeda in Afghanistan (even if Osama bin Laden remained at large).

---

*A secret Justice Department memo written after 9/11 concluded there were "no limits" on presidential power when it came to waging the war on terrorism. The memo, written by a young lawyer named John Yoo, stated that the president "may deploy force preemptively" against any terrorist group "or the states that harbor them," regardless of whether "they can be linked to the specific terrorist incidents of September 11." The president's decisions in a time of war, Yoo wrote, were "for him alone" and "unreviewable." Yoo's memo provided the legal underpinnings for a host of controversial actions that would include clandestine domestic eavesdropping conducted by the National Security Agency.

Memories of September 11 were fresh. In such a climate, could Senate Democrats running for reelection not support the president's assault on a brutal dictator wielding weapons of mass destruction?

In the Cabinet Room, Daschle pressed Bush on why there was a need to move quickly. Sure, Saddam was a problem that had to be addressed. But what was new? How immediate was the threat? Where was the tangible evidence?

And Daschle was thinking: Karl Rove. The previous January, Rove, Bush's political strategist, had telegraphed his intention to use terrorism and national security issues to hammer Democrats in the fall campaign. "We can go to the country on this issue," Rove had proclaimed at a Republican gathering, because the American people "trust the Republican Party to do a better job of strengthening America's military might and thereby protecting America." Then in June, a White House staffer had misplaced a computer disk containing a PowerPoint presentation that Rove and Kenneth Mehlman, his chief deputy, had prepared for GOP donors. In an odd twist, a Democratic Senate staffer found the disk across the street from the White House in Lafayette Park. "Focus on war and the economy," read the slide outlining the Republican strategy for the 2002 elections. *Focus on war.* Daschle and other Democrats saw this as the GOP plan for political domination.

Daschle wondered whether Bush was cynically pushing the Iraq threat as a campaign gambit. The day before the Cabinet Room meeting, Daschle had attended a breakfast with Bush in the president's private dining room with Cheney, Speaker of the House Dennis Hastert, Senate Minority Leader Trent Lott, and House Minority Leader Dick Gephardt. And he had put the same questions to the president. Wouldn't it be better, he asked, to postpone this until after the election and take politics out of the debate? Bush had looked at Cheney, who shot the president what Daschle would describe as a "half smile." Then Bush turned back to Daschle and said, "We just have to do it now." That was it, Daschle would later recall: "He didn't answer the question." But Bush's sidelong glance to Cheney was telling. It looked to Daschle as though the two of them had thought this through.

Now in the Cabinet Room, within a larger group of legislators, Daschle received no more satisfying a reply, as Bush insisted that the House and Senate proceed quickly. "The issue isn't going away," Bush told the congressional leaders. "You can't let it linger."

DASCHLE was not the only congressional leader in the White House that morning feeling uneasy. The most critical comments came from a Republican leader who infrequently weighed in on national security issues: House Majority Leader Dick Armey, the number two Republican in the House. A month earlier, Armey, a Texan, had bluntly voiced his own misgivings about a war against Iraq. While campaigning in Iowa for a GOP congressional candidate, Armey had told reporters that Saddam was "a blowhard." But as long as the Iraqi dictator didn't bother anybody outside his own borders, Armey had said, he couldn't see any basis for invading Iraq: "We Americans don't make unprovoked attacks."

Armey's Iowa comments had generated a brief flurry of media attention. They also upset the White House. Dan Bartlett, a deputy to White House communications director Karen Hughes, called Terry Holt, Armey's press secretary, and complained. "It isn't helpful for Armey to be out there speaking out against the president," Bartlett said, according to Holt. Armey dropped the issue. Armey was a plain-speaking former college professor with two great passions: free-market economics and country music. He didn't consider himself a foreign policy wizard—nor did anyone else in Washington. Still, the notion of going to war with Iraq made no sense to him. He assumed the administration's war talk was merely bluster on Bush's part, an effort to intimidate Saddam into accepting the return of UN weapons inspectors.

But in the Cabinet Room, watching Bush pressure his congressional colleagues, Armey realized that Bush was serious, that he seemed committed to launching a war and overthrowing Saddam. He thought of another president from Texas, Lyndon Johnson, and what a reckless war had done to his administration. Armey, who had not said anything else about Iraq after his Iowa outburst, decided this was the moment to speak his mind directly to Bush. "Mr. President," he said, "if you go in there, you're likely to be stuck in a quagmire that will endanger your domestic agenda for the rest of your presidency."

As he explained his thinking, Armey got worked up and ended his comments with a bowdlerized line from Shakespeare he had gleaned from a country music song: "Our fears make cowards of us all." What did he mean by this? Armey believed that Bush and other administration officials were overreacting to the country's post-9/11 fears. It was as if they were gripped by what he later called a "he-man macho psychosis where they felt the need to go out and shoot somebody to show they're the tough guy on the block." Armey could tell his comments were not going over well. "I was the skunk in the garden party," he said much later.

When Armey finished, Cheney spoke. It would be a good idea, the vice president said curtly, if Armey would not dissent from the president's position in public. Frankly, Armey replied, I didn't realize there was a specific White House position yet. Then Bush, according to Armey, "asked me if I would withhold any public comments until I had all the briefings. So I could understand how necessary this was." The president was saying, wait until you've seen the intelligence. That would prove why urgent action— maybe even a war—was required.

Had Armey spoken up after leaving the Cabinet Room, he might have sparked a ruckus that could have complicated the White House's upcoming efforts. But out of deference to Bush and Cheney, he agreed to hold his fire. "I won't speak publicly about this again," Armey promised the president, "until I'm fully briefed."

Upon exiting the meeting, the congressional leaders stood on the White House driveway and issued brief remarks for the assembled reporters. Senator John McCain said Bush had made a "convincing case" for action. Hastert commented that he expected Congress would vote on a resolution before the elections. Gephardt, who during the meeting had indicated he was willing to work with Bush to convince Americans that Saddam's WMDs were a real danger, said that Bush had to demonstrate to the public that "this is something that we need to do and to take seriously." Daschle, more guarded, repeated the concerns he had raised inside: "What new information exists? What has changed in recent months or years?" He added that he was "hoping for more information and greater clarity" in the weeks ahead. Armey walked by the TV cameras, saying nothing. But he still had the same questions: Why a war? Why now?

IN A way, the White House's answer was simple: Saddam was a ruthless dictator armed with dangerous weapons he could slip at any time to America-hating terrorists. But the idea of invading a country that had not attacked the United States—which would entail sending hundreds of thousands of

American troops into the heart of the Middle East—was seen by skeptics and critics as deeply unsettling and a distraction to the fight against al-Qaeda. After September 11, 2001, the nation's leaders did have to look ahead and consider proactive—possibly even preemptive—measures to prevent another (and conceivably worse) strike against America. But was Saddam truly a direct threat to the United States? Despite all the talk, both before and after the invasion of Iraq, of other reasons for the war (to transform the region, to liberate Iraqis, to spread democracy, to unseat a mass-murdering and repressive leader, to extend American influence in a vital area), the administration's public push for a confrontation with Iraq was fundamentally about one issue: the danger to the United States. Yet prior to the White House's public campaign for war, senior national security officials within the administration had conspicuously *not* been describing Saddam as a top-of-the-list threat.

In 2001 and in early 2002, various senior administration officials, including CIA chief George Tenet, Secretary of State Colin Powell, and Vice Admiral Thomas R. Wilson, the director of the Defense Intelligence Agency, had publicly said that Saddam's military ambitions had been effectively constrained by the problematic but still-in-place sanctions imposed after the first Gulf War and by the previous UN weapons inspections. Saddam "has not developed any significant capability with respect to weapons of mass destruction," Powell had said during a visit to Cairo in February 2001. Three months later, while testifying to the Senate, he expanded on this point: "The Iraqi regime militarily remains fairly weak. It doesn't have the capacity it had ten or twelve years ago. It has been contained. And even though we have no doubt in our mind that the Iraqi regime is pursuing programs to develop weapons of mass destruction—chemical, biological, and nuclear—I think the best intelligence estimates suggest that they have not been terribly successful."

As late as March 19, 2002—two months after Bush had pronounced Iraq part of an Axis of Evil along with Iran and North Korea—DIA chief Wilson, in little-noticed testimony before the Senate armed services committee, had not even listed Iraq as among the five most pressing "near-term concerns" to U.S. interests. Years of UN sanctions, combined with the American military presence in the region, had succeeded, Wilson said, in "restraining Saddam's ambitions," and his military had been "significantly degraded." Saddam's army was much "smaller and weaker" than during the

Persian Gulf War and was beset by manpower and equipment shortages and "fragile" morale.

Wilson also testified that Iraq possessed only "residual" amounts of weapons of mass destruction, not a growing arsenal. He made no reference to any nuclear program or to any ties Saddam Hussein might have to al-Qaeda. "I didn't really think they had a nuclear program," Wilson said years later. "I didn't think they were an immediate threat on WMD." And the State Department, in its annual report on global terrorism released in 2001, had offered scant signs of Iraqi support for terrorism beyond Baghdad's backing of the Mujahedin-e-Khalq, a militant group of Iranian exiles seeking to overthrow the Tehran regime. It too made no mention of any known connection between Saddam's government and Osama bin Laden.

These views were in sync with those of the spy service of the White House's closest ally, Britain. At the time of Admiral Wilson's testimony, British and American aides were intensely discussing what to do in Iraq. According to British documents that surfaced in 2005 (collectively known as the Downing Street memos), the British government assumed Bush was heading toward war in Iraq. Prime Minister Tony Blair and his aides were expressing support for military action in their conversations with their American counterparts, but they had reservations about portraying Iraq as a growing WMD threat. On March 22, 2002, Peter Ricketts, political director of the British Foreign Office, sent a memo to Foreign Secretary Jack Straw that laid out these concerns: "[E]ven the best survey of Iraq's WMD programmes will not show much advance in recent years on the nuclear, missile or CW/BW (Chemical Weapons/Biological Weapons) fronts: the programmes are extremely worrying but have not, as far as we know, been stepped up."

Ricketts also noted that "US scrambling to establish a link between Iraq and Al Qaida is so far frankly unconvincing." He concluded, "We are still left with a problem of bringing public opinion to accept the imminence of a threat from Iraq." Blair's aides were keen on orchestrating a scenario in which Saddam would refuse new WMD inspectors. That would, one memo said, be a "powerful argument" for a war.

Months later, elder statesmen quite familiar to Bush also questioned whether Saddam posed an urgent threat. During the summer of 2002, James Baker, secretary of state under Bush's father, publicly argued that the Bush administration ought to work through the United Nations and seek the return of inspectors, who could determine if Saddam truly did possess weapons of mass destruction and was building nuclear weapons. (Secretary of State Colin Powell had been advocating this approach within the administration.) Then Brent Scowcroft, who had been national security adviser for the first President Bush, weighed in with a *Wall Street Journal* op-ed that appeared under the headline "Don't Attack Saddam." He wrote, "An attack on Iraq at this time would seriously jeopardize, if not destroy, the global counter-terrorist campaign we have undertaken." It seemed as if the friends of the president's father were saying to the son, slow down. And in a speech in Florida, retired Marine General Anthony Zinni, the president's special envoy to the Mideast, signaled that the military was not in favor of a war in Iraq. "I can give you many more priorities," said Zinni, who as commander of CENTCOM, the U.S. military's central command, had overseen all U.S. troops in the Middle East between 1997 and 2000. He noted that a war would be expensive, stretch the military, and antagonize America's allies. It would interfere with efforts to defeat al-Qaeda and end up requiring the United States to keep troops in Iraq "forever." He added, "It's pretty interesting that all the generals see it the same way, and all the others who have never fired a shot and are hot to go see it another way."

In mid-August, Trent Lott had become concerned about the way the public debate was going. Bush had "made clear his intentions to wage war on Iraq in several of our private meetings," Lott later wrote in *Herding Cats: A Life in Politics*. But he feared popular opinion was not yet with the president. So he phoned the most ardent hawk of all—the vice president—and said that he didn't believe the "predicate" for war had been established. "Don't worry," Cheney replied. "We're about to fix all that. Just hold on."

Cheney started the "fix" on his own. On August 26, 2002, he delivered a speech at a national convention of Veterans of Foreign Wars in Nashville, Tennessee, that was laced with frightening rhetoric. "The Iraqi regime has in fact been very busy enhancing its capabilities in the field of chemical and biological agents," Cheney said. As for the nightmarish prospect of a nuclear-armed Saddam, the vice president declared, "We now know that Saddam has resumed his efforts to acquire nuclear weapons. . . . Many of us are convinced that Saddam will acquire nuclear weapons fairly soon." And, he added, "a return of inspectors would provide no assurance whatsoever of his compliance with UN resolutions. On the contrary, there is a great danger that it would provide false comfort that Saddam was somehow 'back in his box.'" Inspections, Cheney was arguing, would actually make the United States less secure.

Cheney didn't offer any evidence to back up his claims about Iraq's WMDs. But his assertions were bold and clear: "There is no doubt he is amassing [WMDs] to use against our friends, against our allies, and against us." If, as Cheney insisted, Saddam was building and stockpiling WMDs to deploy against the United States *and* weapons inspections could not address this grave threat, there was only one option: military action. Cheney did not say so explicitly. But there was no mistaking where he stood. The big question was whether he was speaking for himself or for the White House.

Another part of the "fix" Cheney promised Lott was the White House Iraq Group. Created that summer by White House Chief of Staff Andrew Card, the WHIG was a collection of senior staff members who met regularly in the highly secure Situation Room to discuss how best to promote the White House's message on Iraq. Among its members were National Security Adviser Condoleezza Rice, her chief deputy, Stephen Hadley, Scooter Libby, White House communications chief Karen Hughes, chief speechwriter Michael Gerson, and Karl Rove. "There was a recognition," one WHIG member subsequently said, that it would be "difficult to communicate" the Bush policy on Iraq.

On one occasion, Rove entered the Oval Office with polling data showing the public's doubts about an Iraq invasion. "The public isn't buying it," he told the president, according to a White House official who attended the meeting. Bush exploded: "Don't tell me about fucking polls. I don't care what the polls say." But Bush sought his political strategist's advice. "If there is a way to make the case more clearly, you tell me what it is," Bush said. The White House official thought this exchange was significant. Soon afterward, the WHIG campaign ramped up. "They started stretching it," the White House official said. "We were in a selling mode."

With the WHIG set up, the White House was working on the congressional leaders—as a prelude to a dramatic public relations offensive to sell the American public on the war. And the calculations did include a political element. It was clear from meetings in the Oval Office, this White House official said, that Bush wanted to use his political strength to prod Congress on Iraq—to give its members "backbone," as the president put it at one point—and that his clout would be at its zenith in the weeks before the November election.

Bush's aides knew that many Democrats (regardless of what the polls said about Iraq) would not want to defy a popular president—at the risk of being portrayed as soft on national security—prior to the elections. In that sense, "Daschle was right," this official said. The campaign calendar was driving the timing of the vote on Iraq. "The election was the anvil and the president was the hammer. That was when we had the most leverage."

THE day following Bush's meeting with the legislators in the Cabinet Room—a day on which a CNN/*USA Today*/Gallup poll noted that 58 percent of Americans believed that Bush had not "done enough to explain why" he might "take action in Iraq"—Cheney went to Capitol Hill to conduct his own briefing.

Cheney had arranged a special session with the Gang of Four, the four top leaders of Congress, Hastert, Gephardt, Lott, and Daschle. Normally allergic to sharing sensitive intelligence with Congress, the vice president now wanted to persuade the most senior congressional leaders that the White House had undeniable evidence that Saddam presented a direct and dire threat to the United States. The previous afternoon, Defense Secretary Donald Rumsfeld had held a closed-door briefing for the entire Senate—a session that had been deemed a failure by the White House. Rumsfeld had arrogantly hurled tautologies about the limitations of intelligence and had failed to provide any details to back up the administration's claim that Saddam was developing nuclear weapons. Lott left Rumsfeld's briefing midway through. Democrats marched out and complained to reporters that it had been a waste of time. But now Cheney had with him highly classified intelligence on Iraq's supposed weapons of mass destruction—information so sensitive it could be shared only with a very few.

Joining Cheney for this exclusive presentation was George Tenet, who had been staff director of the Senate intelligence committee before being tapped by Clinton to run the intelligence community. Tenet, a consummate bureaucratic player, had risen through the years by being an effective and efficient staffer who served his bosses well—by keeping them happy. And after Bush took office, Tenet, a cigar-smoking sports fanatic with a rough-and-ready manner, convinced Bush to retain him and then managed to avoid dismissal after the 9/11 intelligence failure. Tenet had bonded with Bush and became "extremely loyal" to him, according to A. B. "Buzzy" Krongard, the CIA's executive director. "It was beyond professional loyalty." (Bush had reciprocated by, among other things, ensuring that Tenet's wife was invited to functions of Cabinet member spouses—a small courtesy that Clinton had never extended the CIA chief.) But some CIA officers later griped that Tenet had gotten too close to the White House, that he had acted as if he were still a congressional staffer overly concerned with pleasing his employer—in this case, the president.

After the four lawmakers, Cheney, and Tenet gathered in the House intelligence committee briefing room inside the Capitol dome—a supersecret chamber routinely swept to guard against foreign eavesdropping—the vice president and the CIA chief began a highly classified show-and-tell. They displayed aerial photos of what appeared to be new construction at what Cheney said were Iraqi nuclear weapons sites. They showed drawings of what Tenet described as mobile biological weapons laboratories—tractor trailers that brewed deadly toxins and that could easily be hidden from international inspectors. They shared snapshots of unmanned aerial vehicles—sleek, pilotless drones said to be capable of carrying chemical and biological weapons great distances. The range of these UAVs, Cheney explained, had been enhanced; they could strike Israel. "That was the thing that spooked us all," Lott later recalled.

Lott was sold. Any doubts he had harbored were gone. He left the room thinking, *We have to take Saddam out.*

Daschle, once again, was torn. He wasn't sure what to make of the photographs. In and of themselves, they didn't mean anything. You couldn't see much: they were blurry pictures of buildings or warehouses that could be anything. He later admitted that he was "embarrassed" that he hadn't challenged Cheney. Daschle had once been a photo analyst intelligence officer in the Air Force. It had been his job to interpret photos. But here was Cheney telling the four leaders of Congress what they were looking at.

Daschle didn't trust Cheney. But the Senate majority leader wanted to grant Cheney and Tenet the benefit of the doubt on fundamental questions of national security. A part of him was also worried: *What if they're right about this?*

THAT same busy day, Tenet appeared in a secret session before the Senate intelligence committee. The CIA director highlighted the latest intelligence on Iraq—the agency's conclusion that Saddam was rebuilding his nuclear program, its estimate that there were 550 sites where WMDs were stored, its assessment that Iraq had developed UAVs that could deliver biological and chemical agents, perhaps to the U.S. mainland. After Tenet finished his briefing, Senator Dick Durbin, an Illinois Democrat, and Senator Bob Graham, a Florida Democrat and the panel's chairman, asked to see the National Intelligence Estimate on the Iraqi threat.

An NIE is the summation of the intelligence community's knowledge on any given issue, its most comprehensive assessment of an important subject. NIEs are supposed to be used by policy makers to render major strategic decisions. But the request from Durbin and Graham was met with "blank stares" from Tenet and his deputies, according to Graham. Tenet conceded that no NIE had been prepared. The Democrats were stunned. Bush was heading toward war, and the White House hadn't asked the CIA to produce an NIE on the most pressing national security question of the moment. For Graham and the Democrats, this was incomprehensible. The Democrats requested that Tenet assemble an NIE, but the CIA director said his people were too busy with other matters.

Though the intelligence committee briefing had done as much to rile as to reassure, Cheney's top secret presentation to the Gang of Four that day had paid off. When the congressional leaders departed that briefing, they looked grim. Hastert said the vice president had supplied important new information on Saddam's weapons. Lott and Gephardt said much the same. Daschle was tentative: he hadn't yet made up his mind; he still had questions needing answers. Nevertheless, he said, "It was a very helpful briefing."

On the cable news shows that night, Cheney's session with the four legislators was depicted as progress for the White House. Daschle, it seemed, might be coming around. One commentator was driven to sarcasm. "Will miracles never cease?" exclaimed columnist Robert Novak, a cohost of CNN's *Crossfire*. "Senator Tom Daschle, the Democratic majority leader, had a good word to say about Dick Cheney!"

The administration's warm-up was proceeding well. Next the White House would go public and selectively deploy intelligence—limited and flawed—to win popular support for the war to come.

We don't want the smoking gun to be a mushroom cloud.

—National Security Adviser Condoleezza Rice

2

The New Product

D AYS AFTER Cheney won over three of the Gang of Four, the public
became the Bush administration's target audience. The official rollout
was launched in a routine manner: on the Sunday morning chat shows. But
it relied upon a rather unusual device: a feedback loop exploited by the
White House. A leak of secret intelligence produced a dramatic front-page
headline that senior administration officials then used to corroborate their
most alarming claim. And Cheney, once more, was in the lead.

But before that happened, White House Chief of Staff Andrew Card
spelled out—perhaps too candidly—what was under way. On September 7,
a *New York Times* story quoted Card on the timing of the White House's
push on Iraq: "From a marketing point of view you don't introduce new
products in August." Apparently, the White House had decided the first
weekend after Labor Day—when the nation was about to mark the first anniversary of 9/11—was the optimal time to promote the "new product."*

---

*That same day, while at Camp David with Tony Blair, Bush declared that an International
Atomic Energy Agency report had concluded that in 1998—when UN weapons inspectors
left Iraq—Saddam's regime had been six months from producing a nuclear weapon. He also
said a *new* IAEA report showed that Iraq had recently been rebuilding its nuclear sites. An
IAEA spokesperson immediately said that no such 1998 report existed; to the contrary, the

Appearing on *Meet the Press* the next day, Cheney asserted that Saddam "has indeed stepped up his capacity to produce and deliver biological weapons, that he has reconstituted his nuclear program to develop a nuclear weapon, that there are efforts under way inside Iraq to significantly expand his capability." He maintained that there was "very clear evidence." When the host, Tim Russert, asked about the evidence related to the nuclear weapons program, Cheney replied that Saddam "now is trying . . . to acquire the equipment he needs to be able to enrich uranium to make the bombs. . . . Specifically, aluminum tubes." He then cited an authoritative source: "There's a story in *The New York Times* this morning . . ."

Cheney was referring to the paper's lead story. The front-page headline declared, "U.S. SAYS HUSSEIN INTENSIFIES QUEST FOR A-BOMB PARTS." The article was powerful—and very convenient—ammunition for the White House:

> More than a decade after Saddam Hussein agreed to give up weapons of mass destruction, Iraq has stepped up its quest for nuclear weapons and has embarked on a worldwide hunt for materials to make an atomic bomb, Bush administration officials said today. In the last 14 months, Iraq has sought to buy thousands of specially designed aluminum tubes, which American officials believe were intended as components of centrifuges to enrich uranium.

The story was full of other alarming details: Iraqi defectors had told U.S. officials that acquiring nuclear weapons was a top priority for Saddam; U.S. intelligence agencies were tracking construction at nuclear sites. The piece also extensively reported the assertions of a pseudonymous Iraqi defector who alleged that Iraq had been developing, producing, and storing chemical weapons at both mobile and fixed sites across the nation. This defector appeared to know a lot: Iraq had produced five tons of VX, a lethal nerve agent; there were secret labs in Mosul and Basra; Russian scientists were currently helping Iraq develop chemical, biological, and nuclear weapons; Iraq was storing 12,500 gallons of anthrax.

The article carried a shared byline: Michael Gordon and Judith Miller. Gordon was a respected and methodical defense correspondent for the

---

IAEA in 1998 reported it had demolished Iraq's nuclear weapons program. (The White House later suggested that 1991 press reports supported Bush's statements.) The IAEA also said it had issued no new report warning of any worrisome construction at nuclear weapons sites.

paper. He had been responsible for the portion of the piece involving the aluminum tubes. Miller, a storied and intensely controversial Pulitzer Prize–winning correspondent, had handled the second half of the article, devoted to the defector's frightening charges. The article conveyed an overwhelming impression: Iraq was a moveable feast of WMDs. And the story was loaded with quotes from unidentified senior Bush officials. One in particular stood out. Unnamed administration officials, according to the article, were worrying that "the first sign of a 'smoking gun' might be a mushroom cloud."

This hadn't been a spontaneous remark; it was the public debut of a carefully constructed piece of rhetoric. The smoking gun/mushroom cloud sound bite had been conceived by chief speechwriter Michael Gerson and discussed at a WHIG meeting just three days earlier. For the White House, Gerson's vivid metaphor, an administration official later said, perfectly captured the larger point about the need to deal with threats in the post–September 11 world. The original plan had been to place it in an upcoming presidential speech, but WHIG members fancied it so much that when the *Times* reporters contacted the White House to talk about their upcoming piece, one of them leaked Gerson's phrase—and the administration would soon make maximum use of it.

The Gordon-Miller scoop came at an opportune time for the Bush White House. A Saddam in possession of chemical and biological weapons—if he had them—was one kind of threat. A Saddam with a nuclear bomb was a much greater danger. It even looked as if the most important part of the story had been an orchestrated White House leak, for the lead sentence noted that Bush officials had told the *Times* about the aluminum tubes the previous day. But the article's appearance had been partly fortuitous.

Two weeks or so earlier, Howell Raines, the hard-driving executive editor of the *Times,* had ordered up an "all known thoughts" piece on what information U.S. intelligence agencies had on Iraq's WMDs. "All known thoughts" was Raines's phrase for Sunday megastories that would tell the *Times'* readers everything there was to know on an important subject in the news. It had been clear that the administration was preparing an argument for war based on the supposed WMD threat. Cheney's Nashville speech of mid-August suggested there was secret intelligence to back up the case. Raines wanted his readers to know what the White House knew.

Gordon had long been interested in nuclear weapons proliferation and had a history of writing articles that contested the assertions of Washington's hard-liners; Miller had contacts among Iraqi exiles and defectors and had written previously—though far too credulously—about allegations of biological and chemical weapons in Iraq. For this story, they each had worked their beats, asking sources repeatedly what was new about Iraq's WMDs. During one interview, a government source mentioned to Gordon that he had heard something about aluminum tubes intercepted in Jordan that might be for a nuclear weapons program in Iraq. Gordon found that other officials were not eager to discuss the tubes—a classified matter. But within days, he located sources who confirmed the story—or what appeared to be the story. He was told that the U.S. government had the tubes in its possession. Obviously, then, government experts could have determined the purpose of the tubes. And the experts, Gordon was informed, had concluded that the aluminum tubes were for use in a gas centrifuge that would enrich uranium for a nuclear weapon. The story seemed solid.

Miller's reporting for this article was based primarily on the word of an anonymous defector who had come to her via a group of former Iraqi military officials. But Gordon had discovered the big news: the first piece of physical evidence that Saddam was trying to go nuclear. That would be the lead. Gordon then contacted the National Security Council for a response—which gave members of the White House Iraq Group a heads-up and time to consider how best to use a leak the White House had not orchestrated. "They didn't want it out," recalled a *Times* source. "Then they totally used it."

So there was Cheney on television citing the *Times*. He said that he could not reveal intelligence sources, but with the *Times* story, "it's now public that, in fact, [Saddam] has been seeking to acquire" the tubes for his nuclear weapons enterprise. We know this, Cheney claimed, "with absolute certainty." Millions of *Meet the Press* viewers could be forgiven for not realizing that Cheney was citing an article based on information that had come from his own administration. And Cheney went further by remarking that he could not say whether or not Saddam already had a nuclear weapon, leaving that an open possibility. It was a disingenuous remark, for no U.S. intelligence analyst at the time believed that Saddam had his hands on a nuclear bomb.

But Gordon and Miller had missed an important detail: the significance of the tubes was based on a highly questionable judgment rendered by one single-minded CIA analyst. It was an assessment that this analyst had been pushing for a year and a half, but one sharply contested within the intelligence community by the government's most knowledgeable experts. The tubes were no smoking gun. They were just tubes.

A YEAR earlier, in the summer of 2001, David Albright, a soft-spoken physicist who ran a Washington think tank called the Institute for Science and International Security, received a phone call that rattled him. Albright, who had been a nuclear weapons inspector for the International Atomic Energy Agency in Iraq, was an influential figure in debates about nuclear weapons and had a history of being tough and critical of Saddam's regime. He, too, feared that Saddam might secretly be pursuing nuclear weapons—but he believed in the careful assessment of any evidence.

His caller, a scientist at the IAEA in Vienna, said, "The people across the river are trying to start a war." *Across the river*—that meant CIA headquarters in Langley, Virginia, across the Potomac River from Washington. "They are really beating the drum, they want to attack," Albright's friend said.

The phone call had been prompted by a visit to the IAEA by Joe Turner, a strong-willed CIA official who worked at the agency's Center for Weapons Intelligence, Nonproliferation, and Arms Control, a sprawling unit of seven hundred or so people in the Directorate of Intelligence. WINPAC, as the center was known, was charged with analyzing and tracking the proliferation of weapons of mass destruction, and Turner was among WINPAC's rising stars. His manner was mild. He spoke with a slight twang. "He was not a snappy dresser and had a doughy face," a colleague said. "He came across as an unassuming guy." But he was a tenacious and aggressive analyst with a background in nuclear research. He had once worked at the Energy Department's nuclear laboratory at Oak Ridge, Tennessee. During his visit to Vienna, he had startled the IAEA staff with his dogmatic presentation of an alarming conclusion: Saddam was attempting to enrich uranium for a nuclear weapon.

A few months earlier, Turner had seized on a single piece of intelligence: intercepted faxes indicating Iraq was seeking to purchase 60,000 aluminum tubes from Hong Kong. Why Iraq wanted the tubes was unclear. But Turner was struck by the fact that the tubes sought by Iraq were made from a high-strength alloy. Given their strength and size, he reasoned, Iraq could desire these tubes for only one reason: to use them as rotors that spin at extraordinarily high speeds in gas centrifuges that turn uranium into highly enriched uranium—the material needed for a nuclear bomb.

Turner's analysis quickly received high-level attention. This was the kind of hard-edged, out-of-the-box thinking that WINPAC wanted from its people. And it was the kind of analysis that policy makers in the Bush administration craved. Embracing Turner's analysis, the CIA officially concluded that the tubes were meant for a nuclear weapons program. That spring, the first report on Turner's assessment went straight to Bush in a superclassified President's Daily Brief (PDB). On April 10, 2001, a follow-up report based on Turner's analysis was included in another sensitive intelligence report circulated among top national security officials. The tubes, the brief said, "have little use other than for a uranium enrichment program." This could mean only that Iraq had embarked on a renewed and ambitious campaign to acquire a bomb.

The idea that Saddam wanted a bomb was plausible. He had sought to build one twenty years earlier and had been set back when the Israeli Air Force in 1981 bombed the country's Osirak nuclear reactor. Then after the 1991 Persian Gulf War, weapons inspectors had found signs that Iraq had once again sought nuclear weapons and had been further along than the CIA or other intelligence agencies had assessed. But the postwar international inspections and UN sanctions had essentially shut down Saddam's bomb program in the 1990s. The IAEA in 1998 reported that "there are no indications that there remains in Iraq any physical capability for the production of weapon-usable nuclear material of any practical significance." And the U.S. intelligence community, through 2001, had concluded that Iraq did not appear to have reconstituted its nuclear weapons program. The tubes—or rather Turner's analysis of the tubes—changed all that. "The tubes were everything for the administration's case," Albright later said. "They were something tangible that they could point to. Without it, they had nothing."

Yet Turner's analysis was based on a questionable assumption: that the tubes sought by the Iraqi were suitable *only* for centrifuges and could not be used for anything else. As soon as the CIA's reports started circulating within the U.S. intelligence community, Energy Department scientists— experts on nuclear weapons—began to challenge Turner's finding. A team of scientists headed by Jon Kreykes, chief of the Oak Ridge National Laboratory's Advanced Technology Division, had been assembled to review the CIA's evidence. Its first report, distributed on April 11, 2001, noted that the diameter of the tubes was half that of tubes used in a gas centrifuge tested by the Iraqis in 1990; that the tubes were only "marginally large enough for practical centrifuge applications"; and that the tubes had probably not been purchased for use in a centrifuge. A month later, the DOE reported that it had discovered another possible reason why the Iraqis had purchased the tubes: they were quite similar in size to aluminum tubes the Iraqis had previously used to build conventional rocket launchers.

There were other reasons why the DOE scientists were suspicious of Turner's conclusion: the Iraqis had been buying the tubes fairly openly, sending out multiple purchase orders and faxing them to international suppliers, and then haggling over the prices. The Iraqis had even advertised for the tubes on the Internet. None of that seemed consistent with a secret nuclear weapons program.

Then the CIA got hold of the actual tubes.

The agency had a whole platoon of operations officers and analysts tasked with tracking and penetrating Iraqi procurement efforts around the world. The electronic eavesdroppers of the U.S. intelligence committee were constantly on the watch for information—an e-mail, a conversation, a fax—pertaining to any equipment heading to Iraq that might be related to unconventional weapons. The CIA got advance notice of shipments of tubes from Asia heading for Iraq through Jordan. At the request of the CIA, Jordanian intelligence seized the shipment. In the summer of 2001, one CIA officer assigned to liaison work with the Jordanians regarding the tubes was Valerie Wilson. She traveled to Jordan. She saw the tubes, which were sitting at a storage yard, piled up and exposed to the elements. Samples had been sent to Langley.

Even with the tubes in hand, the battle lines did not change. DOE analysts found that the actual tubes indeed matched those Iraq had previously used for artillery rockets. And Turner was forced to concede that the samples did not fit the dimensions of most gas centrifuge designs. But he insisted they were a match for a centrifuge developed by a German scientist, Gernot Zippe, in the 1950s. Houston Wood, a University of Virginia nuclear scientist who served as a consultant to the Energy Department team, checked with the aging Zippe. Not so, Zippe told him, not even close. (As the Senate intelligence committee later found, although the inner diameter of the tubes was "close" to the dimensions of the Zippe design, the wall thickness of the Iraqi aluminum tubes was more than three times that of the

Zippe design. The tubes themselves were twice as long.) "Rocket production," not nuclear weapons, "is the more likely end-use for these tubes," read a classified August 17, 2001, Energy Department intelligence report.

Nor was the Department alone in its doubts. In late 2001, the State Department's Bureau of Intelligence and Research (INR) conducted an internal study of the Iraqi nuclear issue and the tubes. The INR canvassed the nuclear labs and interviewed several nuclear scientists. "We were talking to all these experts, and they were telling us, 'No, no, no, this is not the kind of [tubes] you use for centrifuges,'" Greg Thielmann, the director of proliferation for the INR, later said. In a lengthy memo to Powell late in 2001, and in a follow-up report in early 2002, the INR strongly disputed the CIA's tubes argument, as well as the rest of the case for a resurgent Iraqi nuclear program. "The consistent message from INR," Thielmann later noted, "was that there is no good evidence" at all that Iraq had restarted its nuclear program.

Turner refused to back down. In meetings and videoconferences with Energy Department scientists (and later with IAEA officials, who were also skeptical of his conclusions), he arrogantly dismissed the dissents and showed no willingness to engage in debate. "He was very condescending," recalled Robert Kelley, a weapons inspector with the IAEA, who sat in on meetings with Turner. "It was like he was on a kind of messianic mission. If you questioned him, he would just say, 'If you knew what I know.' Which is what intelligence people always say. It was like he didn't want to hear the right answer."

Some scientists were appalled at the idea that Turner (who held a bachelor's degree in mechanical engineering) had become the arbiter on such a highly technical—and critical—issue. "He was not an expert in the sense that he sold himself," said Houston Wood. "I think he was sort of in over his head." An intelligence analyst who worked at the DOE's Lawrence Livermore National Laboratory later noted that it was absurd that the DOE experts had been trumped by a CIA analyst. The Energy Department's nuclear scientists, this analyst said, "are the most boring people. Their whole lives revolve around nuclear technology. They can talk about gas centrifuges until you want to jump out of a window. And maybe once every ten years or longer there comes along an important question about gas centrifuges. That's when you really should listen to these guys. If they say an aluminum tube is not for a gas centrifuge, it's like a fish talking about water."

Between July 2001 and July 2002, Turner and the CIA pumped out report after slanted report on the tubes—at least nine. Each argued that the high-strength aluminum tubes were compelling proof that a reconstituted Iraqi nuclear program was proceeding. These reports went to high-level Bush administration officials and the Oval Office—without mention of the other opinions.

The Energy Department scientists and the State Department analysts—the dissenters—did not even see these reports. Wood was not aware that in the summer of 2002 the aluminum tubes issue was still in play. When the *New York Times* article on the aluminum tubes appeared, Wood, as he later put it, was "astounded." He had thought the tubes argument "had been put to bed." A CIA officer involved in the tubes episode called it a "perfect coming together of arrogance, incompetence, and basic human error. These screw-ups happen all the time, just not with consequences this enormous."

THE results of such screw-ups did not usually land on the front page of a national newspaper and become evidence cited by a vice president. But on *Meet the Press* Cheney was hailing the *Times'* tubes story as Exhibit No. 1 that Saddam was going nuclear.

The president's goal in Iraq was not merely disarmament, Cheney told Russert; it was regime change. But, he added, "No decision's been made yet to launch a military operation. Clearly, we are contemplating that possibility." Realizing that the public case for war rested on the perceived strength of the intelligence he claimed to have, Cheney talked up the U.S. intelligence services: "In terms of the quality of our intelligence operation, I think we're better than anybody else."

Other administration officials in media appearances that day reinforced Cheney's chilling message, especially regarding the aluminum tubes. On CNN's *Late Edition,* Rice declared Saddam a "danger to the United States" that "is gathering momentum." She said there was "increasing evidence that he continues his march toward weapons of mass destruction." She made the case sound beyond any doubt: "We know that he has stored . . . biological weapons." But like Cheney, the only concrete evidence she cited were the aluminum tubes, asserting they were "only really suited for nuclear weapons programs." Like Cheney, she didn't mention there had been dissension within the intelligence community on the tubes. And echoing the dramatic rhetoric attributed to unnamed officials in Gordon and Miller's article, Rice remarked, "We don't want the smoking gun to be a mushroom cloud."

Speaking to reporters that morning, Powell also beat the WMD drum: "I can assure you that as you see the information come out in the days and weeks ahead, there is a solid case that he has weapons of mass destruction."

It was all about the intelligence. We *know,* we *know*—Cheney and the others were saying. But Democrats on the intelligence committee wanted more than such assurances. The day after Cheney appeared on *Meet the Press,* Senator Dick Durbin sent a letter to Tenet, again asking for a National Intelligence Estimate on Iraq's WMDs. He also asked for an unclassified summary of this NIE so "the American public can better understand this important issue." Durbin was demanding that Bush and the CIA show the intelligence committee the full and best information justifying war. And several other Democrats on the committee—Bob Graham, Carl Levin, and Dianne Feinstein—joined Durbin in his request. After Tenet received Durbin's letter, the CIA began working on an estimate—on a rush basis.

THE White House's premiere of its anti-Iraq campaign had been well timed. In the days following the Sunday morning kickoff, the administration moved back and forth between 9/11-related concerns and its case against Iraq. On September 10, the White House announced that Cheney had spent the previous night at a secure, undisclosed location. Later that day, Attorney General John Ashcroft declared an orange terror alert—a scary reminder of the peril the country faced. Then, on the first anniversary of 9/11, Bush delivered an evening address from Ellis Island—chosen by White House image makers because it allowed Bush to use the Statue of Liberty as a dramatic backdrop. After honoring the fallen, he proclaimed, "We will not allow any terrorist or tyrant to threaten civilization with weapons of mass murder."

The next stop for the White House was the United Nations.

Ahmad would always say, "It's dangerous if you believe your own propaganda."

—AIDE TO IRAQI NATIONAL CONGRESS CHIEF AHMAD CHALABI

3

A Speech and a Spy at the United Nations

THE DAY after he commemorated an emotional 9/11 anniversary, Bush appeared before thousands of diplomats at the United Nations. It was time to take the confrontation with Baghdad to the world stage.

The General Assembly was holding its annual meeting, and it was customary for the American president to join the long line of national leaders delivering grandiose speeches to the body. Yet the diplomats before him, as well as the media, would be focusing on Bush's specific words on Iraq. How aggressive might he be? How clear a signal would he send? Bush arrived with two specific aims: to prod the United Nations into moving against Iraq and to present an argument why the United States, and its allies, would be within its rights to strike Saddam if the United Nations dragged its heels. For the members of the White House Iraq Group— Card, Rice, Rove, Libby, and the others—this was a strategic moment. But to bolster Bush's tough message, the White House, as before, was relying on some highly questionable evidence. In this case, it came from an especially dubious source: Ahmad Chalabi's Iraqi National Congress. And once again, *The New York Times* and Judy Miller would serve as the conduit. This episode was a prime example of how some journalists and Iraqi exiles, working in tandem, helped to create favorable conditions for the White House sales campaign.

SPEAKING beneath the olive branches and world map of the UN emblem, Bush claimed that Saddam—a brazen human rights abuser who had repeatedly not complied with UN resolutions related to disarmament—was a threat because he could supply anti-American terrorists "with the technologies to kill on a massive scale." Iraq, he maintained, was expanding its biological weapons facilities and maintaining stockpiles of chemical weapons. He referred to Iraq's attempts to buy high-strength aluminum tubes as proof Iraq had juiced up its nuclear weapons program. "Saddam Hussein's regime is a grave and gathering danger," Bush declared. He challenged the United Nations: "Are Security Council resolutions to be honored and enforced or cast aside without consequence? Will the United Nations serve the purpose of its founding, or will it be irrelevant?"

In the middle of all the tough talk, there was a momentary hitch. For much of the address, Bush's rhetoric could have been read as supporting immediate military action against Iraq. But Bush had come to the United Nations to announce that he would seek a new resolution that would give Iraq one more chance to comply with UN disarmament demands—or face the consequences. Bush's decision to try for a new and strong Security Council resolution was a victory for Powell over Cheney and Rumsfeld. For weeks, there had been a fierce internal debate within the administration. Powell had been pushing for a multilateral approach. Blair had bluntly told Bush that he required a new UN resolution to sell the war to a skeptical British public. Cheney and his senior staff had been contemptuous of the idea of relying on the United Nations for anything and of the need to appease Blair. Bush in the end sided with Powell and Blair, and the final draft of the UN speech contained a key sentence stating the United States would seek a new Security Council resolution.

To ensure against leaks, the sentence had been omitted from copies of the speech distributed to most staffers and agencies for review. And at the United Nations, a staffer had inserted the wrong draft into the TelePrompTer—the version without the key sentence. At the point in the speech when Bush was supposed to announce his support for a new UN resolution, he didn't say it—and moved on.

Back in Washington, senior aides watching the speech on TV were aghast. "What the hell happened?" one recalled thinking. Had Cheney and

Libby gotten to Bush at the last minute? Bush, though, caught the mishap and ad-libbed: "We will work with the UN Security Council for the necessary resolutions." That, too, was a gaffe: in the final approved text, Bush was supposed to call for only one singular resolution, not plural "resolutions." Still, the sentiment was the same: at the end of the day, with or without the United Nations, Bush vowed, the United States would act.

After the speech, Bush erupted at his staff for the TelePrompTer foul-up.

WHILE Bush was speaking at the United Nations, Bill Murray, the CIA station chief in Paris, thought there might be a way to avert war—and that he could be the man to do it. A few weeks earlier, Murray had met with a secret source on Iraq. The man was a Lebanese journalist and a longtime, reliable asset for French intelligence. For months, the journalist had been tantalizing Murray with information about an unnamed high-ranking Iraqi official who might be willing to work with the Americans. Murray had repeatedly pressed for details. Finally, in late August, the journalist had disclosed the Iraqi's identity: Naji Sabri, Saddam's foreign minister.

The journalist and Sabri were lifelong friends. Sabri hated Saddam, the journalist told Murray. The Iraqi dictator had killed his brother. The foreign minister wanted the regime gone. He might be willing to leave Iraq, to defect—if his family's safety could be guaranteed. Sabri also was interested in playing a role in Iraq's future, after Saddam was gone. That was important. After a war, the CIA might need a former regime official who was a Sunni. But Saddam's foreign minister also wanted money. The journalist asked for $1 million, most of which he promised to pass along to Sabri. But a chunk would be for himself—for expenses and, of course, for his fee as the middleman.

Murray was wary but intrigued. Sabri's defection would be a crippling psychological blow to Saddam's regime. Turning him into a CIA informant might be better. He could slip the agency reliable intelligence on what was going on inside Saddam's regime. Perhaps he could help the agency sort out whether Saddam possessed WMDs or was in league with al-Qaeda.

Murray, who had previously served as CIA station chief in Beirut, understood that extortionist money demands was how the game was played in the Middle East. It was all a question of bargaining, and $1 million was merely the first offer. More important, he already had some confidence in the journalist. In earlier meetings, the journalist had passed along good information he had received from Sabri, including a copy of Iraqi purchase orders for aluminum tubes being bought through front companies in Eastern Europe. The tubes had slightly different dimensions than the ones seized in Jordan the previous year. The journalist even got hold of two of the tubes—and handed them to Murray wrapped in burlap. The CIA officer sent the tubes to Langley, where they were passed to Joe Turner and other WINPAC analysts, who were excited to receive them. Whatever the significance of the new pair of tubes—the WINPAC guys naturally thought it strengthened their case—the transaction showed that the journalist could deliver.

In their meeting in late August, Murray had told the jounalist that *maybe* the agency would cough up the money. But he declared that the CIA wouldn't work through a cutout, that he had to meet with Sabri. In the meantime, Murray supplied the journalist with a series of questions to pose to Sabri. This would be a test of Sabri's willingness to help the Americans. Most of the questions concerned the issue of greatest urgency to Washington. Murray wanted an accurate update on the state of Saddam's WMD programs.

At a subsequent meeting, Murray—after getting approval from headquarters—advanced the journalist $200,000 cash. And Murray had a request. The journalist had mentioned that Sabri might go to New York for the UN General Assembly session. Murray told him to have a few high-quality, hand-tailored suits made for Sabri. If Sabri wore one of the suits in New York, it would be a signal that the journalist was on the level and that Sabri was willing to cooperate with the CIA.

After Bush finished his UN speech, Murray received a message: Sabri would be speaking at the General Assembly the following week. And he would be wearing one of the new suits. The Lebanese journalist was going to be in New York as well. Maybe a meeting between Murray and Sabri could be arranged. Murray immediately began making plans to fly to the United States—first to Langley to discuss the matter with the CIA brass and then to New York for a rendezvous where, he hoped, he could turn Iraq's foreign minister into an American spy.

WHAT the hell is this?

That's what John Maguire and Luis, the two covert action specialists who had drawn up the Anabasis plan for the CIA, were wondering after Bush finished his UN speech. For ten months, they had been led to believe that the White House was fully behind their covert project—and Anabasis meant war. Now they thought Bush might be shying away from that game plan and actually trying diplomacy at the United Nations. They were fretting over how this would play with the allies-in-sabotage they had developed in Iraq.

Maguire had promised the two prominent Kurdish leaders, Jalal Talabani and Massoud Barzani, that war was coming. Bases had been set up in Kurdish-controlled territory, and planning for antiregime operations already had begun. (The bases were used mainly for operations mounted by the Iraq Operations Group, but occasionally Valerie Wilson's operations officers at the Joint Task Force on Iraq would entice a source to a Kurdish base to discuss Saddam's WMDs—or lack of them—with a CIA officer.) Talabani and Barzani, though eager to get rid of Saddam, had been hesitant to saddle up with Washington. They had seen the United States encourage rebellion in Iraq in the past and then abandon the rebels—leaving them to be killed by Saddam. At the conclusion of the Persian Gulf War, the first President Bush had urged a Shia uprising and then done nothing when Saddam slaughtered the insurrectionists. And in the mid-1970s, Washington, after joining with the shah of Iran in supporting a Kurdish rebellion against Saddam, had precipitously cut off assistance to the Kurds when Saddam and the shah cut a deal. The Kurds had been crushed by Baghdad. (Explaining this betrayal in congressional testimony, Secretary of State Henry Kissinger said, "Covert action should not be confused with missionary work.") Forget the past, Maguire had assured Talabani and Barazani, it will be different this time.

But when Bush was done speaking, Maguire thought, "Goddamnit, here we go again." Soon the phone was ringing at the IOG office at the CIA. It was Talabani and Barzani in Kurdistan—and they were furious. Are you, they demanded to know, folding on us? Luis and Maguire tried to reassure the Kurds. Don't read anything into this, the CIA men said, we're not backing away; this is merely a necessary political maneuver. Maguire couldn't be certain. He had no direct pipeline to the Oval Office. But he hadn't lost faith in Bush's commitment to war.

———

BUSH'S decision to seek a new UN resolution was the big news of the day, but another significant development was the release of a major White House white paper on Iraq. The paper, entitled "A Decade of Deception and Defiance," had been commissioned by the White House Iraq Group to back up the rhetoric within Bush's UN speech. It had been drafted by Jim Wilkinson, a fast-talking former congressional staffer from Texas, who was deputy to White House communications chief Karen Hughes. The twenty-one-page document highlighted every aspect of Saddam's brutality. There were sections on Saddam's human rights abuses, political repression in Iraq, and violence against women. In preparing the document, Wilkinson had relied mainly on public sources—State Department and human rights group reports, as well as press reports from various publications, including two *New York Times* articles. Some White House officials, though, were troubled by the report. One staffer at the time saw it as a "spin job" that made no effort to assess the relative credibility of the barrage of allegations.

The document was the most extensive argument the administration had yet presented concerning the threat supposedly posed by Saddam. It maintained that Saddam was running a "highly secret terrorist training facility in Iraq known as Salman Pak, where both Iraqis and non-Iraqi Arabs receive training on hijacking planes and trains, planting explosives in cities, sabotage, and assassinations." And it portrayed Iraq as a storehouse of banned weapons.

Much of the weapons section focused on Iraq's past and well-known WMD record, such as its production of biological weapons agents in the early 1990s before its BW program was seemingly dismantled under UN supervision. For instance, the paper noted that gaps in Iraq's WMD accounting, previously identified by UN inspectors, "strongly suggest" that Iraq was stockpiling chemical weapons. This was a deductive case. But the white paper did zero in on three current signs that Iraq was dangerously active in the unconventional weapons business. It reported that Iraq was developing mobile biological weapons—an allegation the administration had not highlighted before—but no source was cited for this assertion. It cited the aluminum tubes as tangible evidence of an ongoing nuclear weapons program, using practically word for word the language of the September 8 *New York Times* piece by Gordon and Miller. And it referred to the chilling account of Adnan Ihsan Saeed al-Haideri, another Iraqi defector.

Al-Haideri claimed to be a civil engineer who had visited twenty secret facilities for chemical, biological, and nuclear weapons in Iraq. His account suggested that Saddam had an extensive WMD infrastructure. One of the secret sites, al-Haideri asserted, was located underneath Baghdad's main hospital. The white paper noted that al-Haideri had "supported his claims with stacks of Iraqi government contracts, complete with technical specifications." At the end of the White House paper's al-Haideri passage was a footnote that indicated all the information on this defector had come from a December 20, 2001, *New York Times* article written by Judy Miller.

The white paper did not disclose that the sensational al-Haideri allegation and the Salman Pak terrorist training camp charge had both been orchestrated by an especially problematic source: the Iraqi National Congress of Ahmad Chalabi.

AHMAD CHALABI—savior of Iraq or international scam artist? The U.S. government was bitterly divided. The reliability of Chalabi and his INC had been a contentious issue inside the U.S. intelligence community for years.

The scion of a wealthy Shiite banking family and a self-styled exile leader, Chalabi, as far as the CIA could tell, had no actual support inside Iraq. He hadn't lived there for decades, having emigrated with his family in the late 1950s, when he was thirteen years old. He was suave and charming. He boasted a Ph.D. in mathematics from the University of Chicago. But Chalabi also had a checkered background. He was a convicted embezzler, judged guilty in absentia in Jordan in 1992 for defrauding nearly $300 million from the Petra Bank, an institution he had owned and operated there. (Chalabi claimed he had been set up by Saddam.) Even some of his associates and allies acknowledged he had a manipulative air about him. "Ahmad would always say," recalled one of his former Washington deputies, " 'It's dangerous if you believe your own propaganda.' " Martin Indyk, who dealt with Chalabi when he served as an assistant secretary of state for the Middle East during the Clinton administration, said, "Of course, he was a con man. That was his charm." After spending a long evening with Chalabi, Wayne White, an Iraq expert at the State Department, concluded, as he later said, that Chalabi, "despite all his so-called winning charm," was no more than "a clever used-car salesman." This opinion was, more or less, the consensus view at Foggy Bottom.

Washington's decade-long relationship with Chalabi had been tumultuous. After the first Persian Gulf War, Chalabi had promoted himself as the next leader of Iraq, and the CIA, desperate for anti-Saddam assets, had bought the idea. The agency set up Chalabi in the Kurdish region of Iraq, an area not controlled by Saddam, as part of a quixotic plan to trigger an insurrection inside the country. The CIA supplied tens of millions of dollars in funds and equipment to Chalabi so he and his INC could foment dissent inside Saddam's regime. But the coup plotting turned into a disaster. Chalabi, working with Kurdish rebels and a few CIA officers on the ground, launched a revolt in 1995. But a hoped-for uprising of Saddam's army officers never materialized. "Chalabi didn't deliver a single lieutenant, let alone a colonel or a general," Robert Baer, the CIA officer who worked most closely with Chalabi, later said.

Shortly afterward, John Maguire, the CIA specialist in paramilitary operations, was dispatched to the Kurdish region to figure out what had gone wrong—and what Chalabi was doing with the agency's money. Chalabi, he discovered, was living out of a large house with a fleet of luxury cars in the driveway. (Chalabi at the time was also living well in London.) When Maguire went to the INC's CIA-funded newspaper office, he found two men working there but no newspaper. The same was true for the INC radio station. There was an office and a tower—but nothing was being broadcast. The entire Chalabi effort, Maguire concluded, was a sham. In January 1996, an indignant Maguire confronted Chalabi in a meeting in London and demanded an accounting of the agency's funds. "You've been lying to us," he told him. "You've been screwing us." Chalabi, caught off guard, accused the veteran CIA officer of being impossible to deal with and "thinking like an Arab." According to another CIA official, Maguire got so furious, he told Chalabi if he ever saw him walking down the street in London, he would swerve his car onto the sidewalk and mow him down. Years later, Maguire didn't deny the remark. "I was pissed off," he said. "It was an ugly meeting."

There was another problem that worried the CIA: Chalabi and the INC's connections to Iran. It was no secret that Chalabi, a Shia, frequently traveled to Iran (where he had a home) and maintained contact there. The INC even had a liaison office in the Iranian capital. The INC and Tehran shared a common aim of getting rid of Saddam. But there was more to the CIA's concern. The agency discovered, according to Maguire, that a senior Chalabi aide, Aras Habib, had been meeting in northern Iraq with officers of MOIS, the Iranian intelligence service. An analysis of intercepts bolstered the agency's suspicions. Habib, Maguire said, was receiving "tasking" instructions from MOIS officers—and passing back information to the Iranians about the identity of CIA officers and U.S. plans in the region. Bob Baer, who preceded Maguire as chief agency officer in the region, said that Habib was even using CIA safe houses in northern Iraq for his meetings with the Iranians. Zaab Sethna, who served for years as Chalabi's spokesman, would later insist that Habib had been fully open about his dealings with the Iranians—and that his contacts were no different than those of other Iraqi opposition groups. But by the mid-1990s, according to both Maguire and Baer, the CIA had concluded that Habib might well be an agent of Iranian intelligence.

In late 1996, the agency finally cut off Chalabi, and the Clinton White House distanced itself from him. But Chalabi found others to court in Washington. He aggressively worked Capitol Hill and developed relationships with conservative Republicans, such as House Speaker Newt Gingrich, who saw in Chalabi's cause an opportunity to bash Clinton for a feckless foreign policy. He forged alliances with an array of neoconservative intellectuals and policy wonks, including Paul Wolfowitz and Richard Perle, who as a hawkish assistant secretary of defense in the Reagan years earned the nickname "Prince of Darkness." The American Enterprise Institute, a think tank that was home to scholars favoring a confrontation with Iraq, was full of Chalabi advocates. (Cheney had been a senior fellow at AEI in the 1990s.)

In 1998, Congress passed, and Clinton signed, the Iraq Liberation Act, a law pushed by Chalabi, which formally committed the U.S. government to regime change. No one in the administration quite knew how that was supposed to be achieved, but Congress appropriated $97 million for the effort. The State Department subsequently handed out tens of millions of dollars to Iraqi opposition groups, with the INC receiving about $33 million from March 2000 to May 2003. Much of this money funded INC's "information collection program," essentially a U.S. government-sponsored propaganda operation under which Chalabi and his deputies were paid to troll Arab communities around the world in search of Iraqi defectors and exiles who could provide the U.S. intelligence community and the news media with information about Saddam's misdeeds.

With the election of George W. Bush, Chalabi's years of cultivating conservatives in Washington paid off. His most prominent champions were now in key positions throughout the government. Wolfowitz became deputy defense secretary; Perle, the new chairman of the Defense Policy Board. And Cheney's office was stocked with Chalabi fans, including Libby, John Hannah, and retired Navy Commander William Luti, a former foreign policy aide for Gingrich. Luti then moved to the office of defense undersecretary Douglas Feith to oversee a newly created unit to prepare for war, the Office of Special Plans. David Wurmser, an AEI scholar who had once called Chalabi a "mentor," would also go to work for Feith. These and other friends in the new administration looked to Chalabi to lead the way in any final confrontation with Iraq. Chalabi's past exploits and failures didn't matter. He had seduced the neoconservatives, and his previous trouble with the CIA was even a selling point among these national security intellectuals, who had long suspected the agency of being timid and too conventional.

Chalabi's friends, though, did try to turn around the skeptics at the CIA. A. B. "Buzzy" Krongard, the CIA's number three official, recalled being lobbied repeatedly by Perle and Wolfowitz before the September 11 attacks to drop the agency's opposition to the INC chief. Perle arranged a dinner at a downtown Washington restaurant, attended by Wolfowitz, so that Krongard could talk to Chalabi directly. Chalabi, Krongard recalled, was "as charming as he could be" and tried to convince Krongard that he was not the "scoundrel" that agency officials thought he was. (After the dinner, according to Krongard, Chalabi insisted—over the CIA man's objections—on picking up the hefty tab, a generous gesture that misfired when the waiter politely informed Chalabi that his credit card had been rejected.) Krongard and the CIA refused to reconsider. Not long afterward, Wolfowitz came to lunch at the CIA and pushed Krongard harder about Chalabi. In refusing to work with Chalabi, "you're undermining the president," Wolfowitz said gravely.

The battles over the INC and Chalabi grew more intense after September 11. The INC introduced a new wave of defectors to U.S. intelligence agencies. Most, the CIA concluded, were charlatans, asylum seekers, and hustlers simply saying what Chalabi and the INC wanted (or told) them to say in exchange for the group's assistance in getting them to Europe or America. Meanwhile, the INC's record keeping—which was supposed to track how U.S. funds were being used—was a shambles. In mid-2002, an internal CIA study, commissioned by the State Department's Bureau of Near Eastern Affairs, found that the information gathered under the "information collection" program was largely useless. Richard Armitage, the salty deputy secretary of state, was especially outraged. "We were doing everything we could to get rid of the program," one State Department official recalled. About that time, according to this official, Armitage convened a meeting to discuss the INC program. "The best thing that can happen is this thing gets shit-canned," Armitage proclaimed. "So shit-can it!" If that couldn't be done, Armitage had a fallback position: "Get this off our books and give it to somebody else." (The INC program was later transferred to the Defense Intelligence Agency.)

By this point, Chalabi didn't need the State Department or even the CIA. The INC was funneling its information to Chalabi's advocates in the Pentagon and Cheney's office. And the INC was also making its defectors available to friendly members of the press—and producing a stream of dramatic (but false) stories about Saddam's weapons and terrorism connections. A June 2002 list prepared by the INC boasted of 108 English-language media stories within the previous eight months that had included "product" from its "intelligence collection program." *The Sunday Times* of London, *Vanity Fair, Time, The Atlantic Monthly,* NPR, CNN, *The New Yorker, Newsweek,* Fox News, *60 Minutes, The National Review, The Weekly Standard,* the Associated Press, *The Washington Times, The Washington Post*—each had published or broadcast information from Chalabi's outfit, according to the INC.*

The INC official in charge of this program, which was designed to shape public opinion in the United States, was Aras Habib, the same Chalabi aide suspected by the CIA of being an Iranian agent. CIA officials aware of this, such as Maguire, wondered whether Iranian intelligence was working through the INC to influence American policy. But they sounded no alarms. "There was no fighting City Hall on Chalabi," Maguire recalled.

Despite the agency's suspicions, the INC continued its propaganda effort, and one major recipient of its intelligence was *The New York Times.*

---

*In 2004, Entifadh Qanbar, an INC spokesman, told the *Columbia Journalism Review,* "We did not provide information. We provided defectors. We take no position on them. It's up to you reporters to decide if they are credible or not."

Two INC-assisted *Times* stories—each based on false (or worse, fabricated) information from an INC-promoted defector—became the basis of the most alarming portions of the white paper drafted by White House aide Jim Wilkinson to support Bush's speech at the United Nations.

WILKINSON'S section on Saddam's "support for international terrorism" cited Salman Pak, a supposed training camp for terrorists—possibly anti-American terrorists. The white paper attributed this information only to unnamed "former Iraqi military officers." But the sources were INC-supplied defectors, primarily a former Iraqi captain named Sabah Khalifa Khodada al-Lami, who had emigrated to the United States in May 2001 and who claimed to have worked at this camp. After September 11, the INC brought Khodada to the attention of the United States with the help of an influential friend: R. James Woolsey, the former director of the CIA. Woolsey, an attorney, was representing, pro bono, INC exiles in deportation proceedings. His law firm, Shea & Gardner, lobbied for the Iraqi National Congress.

Shortly after 9/11, INC officials took Khodada to Woolsey's law office so the Iraqi could tell the former CIA director about the disturbing training that went on at the Salman Pak site. Woolsey then called friends in the Pentagon to arrange for Khodada to become a U.S. intelligence source. As for verifying the accuracy of Khodada's claims, the ex-CIA chief—who would later make a similar referral for another INC defector—subsequently remarked, "that's not my problem."

While Woolsey and the INC were injecting Khodada's serious charges into the U.S. intelligence stream, INC lobbyists Francis Brooke and Zaab Sethna were escorting Khodada to the offices of various news organizations. As Brooke acknowledged much later to *Vanity Fair*, the INC's overall plan at the time was straightforward: provide the Bush administration cause for invading Iraq and overthrowing Saddam. "I told [the INC], as their campaign manager," Brooke said, " 'Go get me a terrorist and some WMD, because that's what the Bush administration is interested in.' " And if this resulted in Chalabi becoming Iraq's next leader, no one in the INC would mind, least of all Chalabi.

Soon Khodada was cited in a series of press stories, starting with an op-ed column by *Washington Post* foreign affairs writer Jim Hoagland, who reported Khodada's claim that Salman Pak trained terrorists in airline hijacking and assassinations. Next, on October 27, 2001, a front-page story in *The New York Times* by Patrick Tyler and John Tagliabue noted that Khodada contended that non-Iraqi Arabs had been given training in terrorism at this camp. And PBS's *Frontline* reported that in an interview Khodada had said that "all this training" at Salman Pak was "directed towards attacking American targets" and that the 9/11 operation was "conducted by people who were trained by Saddam"—presumably at this camp.

But there was little, if any, corroboration for Khodada's tales, and U.S. intelligence agencies had discounted them from the start. There was indeed an Iraqi military facility at Salman Pak with a derelict Boeing 707 aircraft on site for training. The United States had satellite photos of the site. U.S. officials believed that years earlier Salman Pak had been used to train Palestinian terrorist groups. But U.S. intelligence agencies had a less disturbing explanation for what was currently happening there: Iraqi security forces were using the aircraft to train to respond to a terrorist hijacking, not to conduct one—the precise opposite of what Khodada was asserting. The INC, according to Zaab Sethna, soon cut off all contacts with Khodada after he started demanding money for his information. But by then, it didn't matter. Khodada had already been a key source for multiple news stories. And the White House was now using those problematic news accounts to spread his tales to the world.*

THE white paper's most serious WMD charge—Adnan Ihsan Saeed al-Haideri's account that he had personally visited clandestine facilities for the production of chemical, biological, and nuclear weapons in Iraq—was also the result of a successful INC operation that involved the nation's most prestigious newspaper.

After spiriting al-Haideri out of Damascus, where he had fled following his defection from Iraq in mid-2001, the INC flew him to Thailand and notified the Pentagon it had a potentially big catch. The DIA was more

---

*After the invasion, the CIA determined that one INC-linked Iraqi defector who described Salman Pak as a terrorist training camp to *Vanity Fair* had "embellished and exaggerated his access." Asked if any al-Qaeda operatives or other sources had confirmed that terrorist training occurred at Salman Pak, CIA and DIA analysts told the Senate intelligence committee that none had. A DIA analyst said that the INC "has been pushing information for a long time about Salman Pak and training of al-Qa'ida."

than interested. "This guy is the mother lode," the INC's Zaab Sethna recalled being told by an intelligence officer at the time, "and if even 5 percent of what he says turns out to be right, then we have hit the jackpot." But al-Haideri still had to be vetted. The DIA arranged for a CIA polygraph examiner to fly to Pattaya, Thailand, to administer a lie detector test to the forty-three-year-old Kurd. For days before the CIA polygraph expert arrived, Zaab Sethna prepped al-Haideri for the exam. But Sethna's coaching didn't work. The CIA official found the defector's responses about his background replete with deception. He concluded that al-Haideri had concocted his story.

Chalabi and Sethna weren't through, though. They contacted two journalists whom they hoped would carry al-Haideri's tales to the world. One was Paul Moran, an Australian freelancer (who previously had worked for the INC and the Rendon Group, a secretive Washington, D.C., consulting firm that years earlier had been contracted by the CIA to work with the INC). The other was Judy Miller. With Miller, the INC had the right vehicle to ensure that al-Haideri's story would receive wide circulation. And this was precisely the sort of story the *Times* and Miller wanted.

In the weeks after 9/11, *Times* executive editor Howell Raines had been, as one editor at the paper at the time later put it, "maniacal." He wanted his paper to be first and best in covering the horror that had occurred and anything related to it. But when *The Washington Post* kept scooping the *Times* on 9/11 stories—especially when the *Post*'s Bob Woodward disclosed the contents of a handwritten note that 9/11 ringleader Mohamed Atta had left behind in a piece of luggage—Raines went ballistic. At one point, he hauled Stephen Engelberg, the investigative editor, into a meeting and declared, "I don't want the first line on my obituary to be 'He was the editor of *The New York Times* when they blew the 9/11 story.'" Engelberg subsequently recalled that he left the meeting and told a deputy, "Have I lost my mind or what? Is this literally that personal, that Howell views this as, 'You're fucking up my place in history'?" Another *Times* reporter years later said that in the weeks after 9/11 there was a "lethal combination of ambition, anger and mania. A line that runs from Howell to Judy Miller."

Raines believed in the star system. He wanted star reporters chasing big stories. So he decided to send Judy Miller to Washington. "She has people in the White House who will talk to her and who will not talk to any other *Times* reporters," Raines told editors.

Miller was a controversial, irrepressible, and vivacious fifty-three-year-old reporter who had a history of breaking big stories. She had also alienated many colleagues and often operated with an unusual (and somewhat puzzling) amount of free rein within the heavily managed *Times* bureaucracy. For years, there had been widespread talk among her colleagues that she frequently became too close to sources. And there was never-ending catty gossip about her propensity to socialize with sources, including heads of state. In the 1970s and 1980s, she had dated U.S. officials—including Representative Les Aspin and Undersecretary of State Richard Burt—who worked in areas related to those she covered. Burt, who had previously been a correspondent at the *Times,* wondered about her reporting. When they were dating, he later recalled, she had shown him drafts of stories that he believed were overly dependent on a single source, and he would ask her, "Are you sure about this?" She was, he said, "an unguided missile."

She had been the paper's Cairo bureau chief from 1983 to 1986. In the late 1980s, she served as deputy editor of the Washington bureau in a stint widely perceived among *Times* people as a disaster due to her abrasive management skills and heavy-handed editing. Still, she had cowritten a best-selling book on Saddam in 1990 and then authored a much praised book on her reporting stint in the Middle East that explored the rise of Muslim fundamentalism.

In early 2001, Miller had cowritten a three-part series that alerted the public to the rising threat posed by al-Qaeda. The articles later won a Pulitzer Prize. But a reporter who shared a byline with Miller on the first article, Craig Pyes, pulled his name off the other pieces in the series because he was disgusted with what he viewed as Miller's fast-and-loose journalism. Before the series ran, Pyes sent his and Miller's editors e-mails noting his concern that Miller's reporting for the series was based too much on unconfirmed information from intelligence agencies. One of his e-mails read, "secret single source intel info that runs counter to the stated facts is nothing I hope we'd rely on." And in a note to Engelberg he lit into Miller: "I do not trust her work, her judgment, or her conduct. She is an advocate, and her actions threaten the integrity of the enterprise, and of everyone who works with her. . . . She has turned in a draft of a story . . . that is little more than dictation from government sources over several days, filled with unproven assertions and factual inaccuracies, which she then called the product of a year's investigation. Once she submitted the story . . . she then, as is her wont, tried to stampede it into the paper. This exact paradigm . . . has been her M.O. from day one." Pyes's note of alarm about Miller went unheeded within the *Times*. Pyes later remarked that it was "absolute hubris" for the *Times*' editors to believe that they could compensate for Miller's fault with effective editing: "Ultimately, the editor is a hostage of the judgments of the reporter."

Miller, though, was tireless and relentless; she was, as Raines knew, well connected in Washington. In early July 2001, she had learned from a high-level source about a U.S. government intercept that had picked up a conversation between two suspected al-Qaeda figures overseas, during which one said words to the effect of "Something big is coming. They're going to have to retaliate." Miller was excited. "This struck me as a major page one–potential story," she later said. She told Engelberg, her editor, about this. Who were these two men? he asked. Where were they? What sort of attack were they talking about? I don't know, replied Miller. "I can't put this story in the paper," he told her. After a breathless lead about a possible al-Qaeda attack, he added, "what would the third paragraph say?"

At the time of the September 11 attacks, Miller had been concentrating on germ warfare. (She had just finished a book with Engelberg and *Times* reporter William Broad on the subject.) After Raines unleashed her (and other reporters) to find the blockbuster stories of the post-9/11 era, she headed to Washington and made sure to look up one particular Bush official who had been a source for Engelberg on the germ warfare book: Scooter Libby.

Miller was the perfect outlet for the INC, especially since Chalabi had been a source of hers for years. When the INC contacted her in December 2001 and offered her a story about an Iraqi defector who possessed direct knowledge of Saddam's secret WMD sites, she hopped a plane to Thailand. Days later, al-Haideri's eye-popping tales were on the front page of *The New York Times* under Miller's byline.

Miller reported that al-Haideri had said he had personally helped renovate secret facilities in Iraq for biological, chemical, and nuclear weapons. His account, she wrote, "gives new clues about the types and possible locations of illegal laboratories, facilities and storage sites that American officials and international inspectors have long suspected Iraq of trying to hide." She did concede that "there was no means to independently verify" al-Haideri's allegations. But Miller signaled that this INC-backed defector deserved to be trusted because he "seemed familiar with key Iraqi officials in the military establishment, with many facilities previously thought to be associated with unconventional weapons, and with Iraq itself." She reported that an unnamed INC representative had said he trusted al-Haideri—as if that somehow enhanced the defector's credibility. Furthermore, she wrote, government experts—whom she didn't identify or characterize—"said his information seemed reliable and significant." (Engelberg would later say that the *Times* had no idea that al-Haideri had flunked his CIA lie detector test.)*

This was quite a chain of events: Raines's mania to Miller's sensationalist reporting to the INC's scheming to an official White House document. Wilkinson's white paper, commissioned by the White House Iraq Group, had supported a crucial WMD claim with a Miller article that had been orchestrated by the INC—and was based on nothing but the unconfirmed stories of a defector deemed a fabricator by the CIA. This was how the WHIG was prepping the public for an invasion of Iraq—by footnoting a fraud. Even though the CIA had been able to keep Chalabi's false intelligence out of official channels, the INC-to-Miller-to-WHIG nexus made the bogus information an important element of the president's case. And CIA officials did not see it as their job to vet a White House white paper or to reveal the findings of a lie detector test in order to show a front-page *New York Times* story was wrong.

IN WASHINGTON, there was one man who was trying to undo the damage done by a more recent Judy Miller article. After reading the September 8, 2002, *New York Times* story by Miller and Gordon on the aluminum tubes,

---

*Even if Miller hadn't known about the flunked polygraph, the *Times* story still hyped al-Haideri's account. The headline and the first sentence both stated that al-Haideri was asserting that his work had been "for" Iraqi WMD programs. But the story in the fourteenth paragraph pointed out that he acknowledged that he had not "personally visited" one of the purported biological weapons sites he had described to Miller. And it later more carefully stated that he only "believed" that the sites he worked on were for WMD programs. "It is important to note that [al-Haideri] always said he had no first-hand knowledge of any WMD," the INC's Sethna noted in an e-mail exchange with the authors in July 2006. "He said that he had been contracted to build laboratories and research facilities as well as some storage facilities that seemed suspicious." The *Times'* exaggerated account was further embellished in the White House white paper, which baldly stated that al-Haideri said he had visited "twenty secret facilities for chemical, biological and nuclear weapons."

David Albright, the former IAEA weapons inspector, was outraged. He knew that government scientists had debated the meaning of the tubes.

Miller had called Albright for the aluminum tubes story before it was published, but he had been out of town. He returned the call the day after the story hit, and he desperately wanted to set the record straight. He thought it was important that *The New York Times* inform its readers (including members of Congress, policy makers, and journalists) that most government scientists didn't accept the tubes argument. There's another side to this, an upset Albright told Miller. There's profound disagreement. Most people don't believe these tubes are for centrifuges. They think they're for artillery rockets. This is nothing to go to war over.

Don't yell at me, yell at Gordon, Miller told Albright. She explained that the article had been an accurate reflection of what the *Times'* sources knew of the intelligence on the tubes. But she listened to his complaints and passed them along to one of her editors, suggesting they do a follow-up. Albright assumed the *Times* would now run a story reflecting the deep skepticism within the government concerning the White House's prime piece of evidence in the nuclear case.

On September 13, the *Times* published a follow-up article. This time the double byline was reversed and Miller's name appeared before Gordon's. The short article was mostly about the WHIG-produced white paper released for Bush's UN speech. (Miller was echoing an echo: she was writing about a White House document that had been based in part on her own reporting.) On reading the *Times* article, Albright couldn't believe it. This article, he thought, was worse than the first.

In the middle of this piece, Miller and Gordon returned to the aluminum tubes issue and reported that there had been "debates among intelligence experts about Iraq's intentions in trying to buy such tubes." But the article went on: "it was the intelligence agencies' unanimous view that the type of tubes that Iraq has been seeking are used to make such centrifuges." The article acknowledged that "some experts" in the State Department and the Energy Department had raised questions as to whether the tubes were better suited for artillery rockets but added that "this was a minority view among intelligence experts and . . . the CIA had wide support, particularly among the government's top technical experts and nuclear scientists." It seemed the debate was over: "the best technical experts and nuclear scientists at laboratories like Oak Ridge supported the CIA assessment."

The new *Times* story, which ran on page A13, had been hurriedly put together, mainly by Miller, while Gordon had been stuck at home waiting for movers. Just as the first article had, this one relied on administration sources who depicted the CIA's case as solid. But the claim that the intelligence agencies were "unanimous" in the view that the tubes were for centrifuges was flatly wrong; both the State Department's INR and the Energy Department's intelligence division had strongly disputed the agency's position. As the Senate intelligence committee would put it in a later report, "the vast majority of scientists and nuclear experts at the DOE and the National Labs did not agree with the CIA's analysis."

Albright was furious. The reporters, relying on their administration sources, had gotten it completely wrong—again. Besides misleading the public about the tubes issue, this *Times* story had another serious consequence. The disclosure that there had been questions about the tubes prompted the Energy Department to issue an edict to its scientists: Don't talk to the news media about this. The order sent fear throughout the department's nuclear laboratories. It prevented scientists who could see that the White House was exploiting Joe Turner's incorrect assessment from countering the misguided intelligence.

Houston Wood, the University of Virginia scientist and DOE consultant who was sure Turner's conclusion was wrong, wrestled with what to do. He wanted to speak out, he later said. But like many other government scientists, he feared retaliation. He could lose his security clearance. So could his colleagues. "I think they were anguished about this," Wood recalled. "They were trying to dissent internally. They were expecting that somebody would listen to reason." At one point, Wood called one of the top scientists at Oak Ridge and discussed the issue of going public. "He was afraid he would give up his whole career if he went public," Wood said.

Albright was anxious to undo the damage of the second Miller-Gordon piece. He persuaded Wood to at least talk on background to *The Washington Post*. Albright had given *Post* reporter Joby Warrick a draft report on the tubes prepared by his think tank. The paper, which focused on technical issues (such as the type of aluminum involved and whether it was suitable for the welding that would be needed for a centrifuge program) concluded, "By themselves, these attempted procurements [of aluminum tubes] are not evidence that Iraq is in possession of, or close to possessing, nuclear weapons." Warrick wrote a story about the report. He noted that government scientists had disagreed about the tubes and that dissenters had been told to keep quiet. Within the *Post*'s newsroom, editors and reporters believed that Warrick had filed this story because he had been scooped by the *Times* on the importance of the tubes. The editors ran Warrick's story deep inside, on page A18.

The *Post* article wasn't much of a counter to the page-one blowout published by the *Times* on September 8. It caused few waves. Worse, it came out September 19, the day the White House sent Congress a draft resolution authorizing Bush to attack Iraq essentially whenever he saw fit. One reason for granting Bush this power, the resolution stated, was that Iraq was "actively seeking a nuclear weapons capability."

On September 18, in a hotel room in New York, Bill Murray, the CIA station chief in Paris, met with his secret source, the Lebanese journalist. Naji Sabri, the Iraqi foreign minister, was due to deliver his own speech to the United Nations the next day—Baghdad's response to Bush's UN address. But Sabri couldn't meet with Murray, the journalist told him. Swarms of FBI agents were tailing Sabri all over New York; he was nervous. But the journalist did have some good news: Sabri was interested in working with the Americans. He had answered all of Murray's questions about Saddam's weapons of mass destruction.

The WMD situation in Iraq, the journalist said, was complicated but quite different than what the White House was saying. Saddam's chemical weapons arsenal was all gone. What was left of the weapons had been disbursed to tribal and provincial leaders years ago. Saddam didn't want responsibility for them anymore. He didn't want such munitions to be found by UN inspectors. The supposed biological weapons program was amateurish. Perhaps there were a few vials of biological poisons left over from years earlier. But there was no program, no actively functioning laboratories. As for nuclear weapons, the journalist related Sabri's account of a meeting that Saddam had held with his nuclear scientists. The scientists had told Saddam that if they could obtain the right fissile materials, they could produce a nuclear bomb in eighteen to twenty-four months. But there was only one problem: the scientists didn't have any fissile material—and they had no prospect of obtaining any. Whatever Saddam's intentions, there was no revived nuclear program as the White House had claimed.

That night, Murray flew to Washington to share what he had been told with John McLaughlin, the CIA deputy director. The next day, Sabri appeared before the General Assembly to read a lengthy letter from Saddam. The Iraqi dictator assailed the "American propaganda machine" and its "lies, distortion, and falsehood" about Iraq. He declared that Iraq was "clear of all nuclear, chemical, and biological weapons." Watching the speech, Murray focused on something other than Saddam's rhetoric. He was studying Sabri's clothes. The Iraqi foreign minister was wearing one of the expensive suits the CIA had paid for. It was the signal that Sabri might be serious about becoming a CIA asset.

Sabri's inside intelligence suggested a WMD program far less menacing than what the White House had been claiming. "Bill, you may be a hero," Tyler Drumheller, the European Division chief in the CIA's operations directorate, told him. "You may be the guy who stopped a war."

But not everyone at CIA headquarters was impressed by Murray's burgeoning operation and its potential. Luis and Maguire, the chief and deputy chief of the Iraq Operations Group, had no use for it, which led to shouting matches between Murray and the two Anabasis men. Sabri's only value, Maguire later said, "was as a high-level defection. . . . We weren't interested in having Sabri stay in place and work for us because we knew we were going to war." Anything Sabri had to say about Iraq's WMDs while he remained part of Saddam's corrupt regime, Luis and Maguire argued, would be worthless, just disinformation. If the CIA took this sort of information to the White House, Maguire told Murray, the agency would be laughed out of the office

The face-off between Murray and the CIA paramilitary experts reflected the larger struggle within the national security circles of the Bush administration. It was a fight between those who wanted more information on Iraq's weapons programs so they could accurately assess the nature of the threat and those who were already sure they had a handle on what was at stake and were ready for war. Luis and Maguire's mission—arranging sabotage within Iraq and preparing for a U.S. invasion—signaled (at least to Luis and Maguire) that the Bush White House was well beyond caring what Sabri had to say. During one confrontation with Murray, Luis was blunt: "One of these days you're going to get it. This is not about intelligence. This is about regime change." (An intelligence community official later said that Luis denied making such a statement.)

Drumheller and Murray eventually heard that CIA Director George Tenet had told the White House about Sabri. The response came back: the White House would be interested if Sabri were to defect. What he had to say about WMDs was less important to the NSC. Probably all lies.

AFTER reading Bush's proposed Iraq resolution, Senator Chuck Hagel, a Nebraska Republican, thought, "My God, this crowd down at the White House is rolling right over the top of us—and we're letting them do it." The legislation that the White House sent to Capitol Hill was tremendously broad. It would permit Bush "to use all means that he determines to be appropriate, including force, in order to enforce the United Nations Security Council resolutions [demanding Iraq dismantle its WMD programs], defend the national security interests of the United States against the threat posed by Iraq, and restore international peace and security in the region." *Restore international peace and security in the region?* That was a tall and wide-open order; the measure itself a blank check. Congressional Democrats were stunned by the sweep of this resolution—as were some Republicans.

Hagel, who believed Saddam was bottled up and posed no pressing threat to the United States, quickly talked to Senator Joe Biden, the Democratic chairman of the foreign relations committee, and the two discussed whether the White House's war aims extended beyond Iraq. "I remember saying to Joe over the phone, the way this is written, the president could go to war anywhere in the Middle East," Hagel later said. "And I remember Joe and I talked about Iran and Syria. Maybe they're thinking, 'We just take them all down, just take two, three of them out, go after Syria and Iran too.' What's to stop them?"

The White House's draft resolution was full of "whereas" clauses that cited Iraq's persistent violations of UN Security Council resolutions and its previous use of unconventional weapons years ago. But several clauses went beyond the rhetoric of the previous weeks. They claimed that Iraq had demonstrated a "willingness to attack" the United States (with its futile efforts to shoot down U.S. fighter jets enforcing no-fly zones in Iraq) and that "members of al-Qaida . . . are known to be in Iraq." On the WMD front, the resolution stated there was a "high risk that the current Iraqi regime will either employ [WMDs] to launch a surprise attack against the United States or its armed forces or provide them to international terrorists who would do so." This was as serious an assertion as the Bush administration could toss at lawmakers and the American people. After the war, White House allies would insist that the president had never used the word "imminent" to describe the threat from Saddam. But the "high risk" of a "surprise attack" with weapons of mass destruction was just as stark and every bit as scary.

Bush and the White House were upping the rhetorical ante. And more charges were on the way.

Everything, everything, everything was connected to Saddam.

—Daniel Pipes, Middle East researcher

4

One Strange Theory

NOT LONG after the 9/11 attacks, Deputy Secretary of Defense Paul Wolfowitz dispatched former CIA Director James Woolsey on a secret trip to London.

Wolfowitz was not expecting Woolsey to come up with important new leads related to the events of September 11. Instead, Woolsey's unorthodox mission was primarily to press the Brits for any evidence they might have that would validate the theories of an eccentric academic named Laurie Mylroie. A onetime Harvard assistant professor, Mylroie was convinced she had unraveled mysteries no one in the CIA or the FBI had been able (or willing) to divine, mysteries she believed added up to a stunning and historic conclusion: Saddam was the mastermind behind much of the world's terrorism. In the aftermath of 9/11—with the U.S. government still trying to discern what precisely had happened and what should be done—Wolfowitz was focusing on far-fetched notions about Saddam promoted by this former college professor. But if Mylroie could be proven right—as both Wolfowitz and Woolsey ardently believed she was—her ideas could fundamentally shape the administration's response to those attacks. Her research, if validated, could provide the *casus belli* to wage war on Iraq.

Wolfowitz and Woolsey were just two members of a small crop of current and former U.S. officials who in recent years had become enamored of

Mylroie's anti-Saddam work. The elaborate conspiracy theories she had propounded—dismissed as bizarre and implausible by the U.S. law enforcement and intelligence communities—would have enormous influence within the administration. It ultimately wouldn't matter whether Wolfowitz and Woolsey could find information to confirm her ideas. They and others had already accepted them and would act accordingly.

THREE days after September 11, the conservative American Enterprise Institute held a press briefing. Former UN ambassador Jeane Kirkpatrick, past House Speaker Newt Gingrich, AEI scholar (and Chalabi champion) David Wurmser, and AEI fellow Michael Ledeen were corralled into a conference room in downtown Washington to offer instant analysis to members of the media, government officials, and fellow think-tankers. "The shock has been very great," Kirkpatrick said. To explain it all, she first called on Mylroie, another AEI fellow and panelist. Mylroie got right to the point:

> There has been no clear demonstration that Osama bin Laden was involved in Tuesday's assault on the United States, but there's been a lot of speculation to that effect, and it may turn out that he is. So assume that he is because I think the key question will be, how likely is it that Osama bin Laden's group or any other group carried out these attacks alone, unassisted by a state? I'd like to suggest that it is extremely unlikely—in fact, next to impossible.

Who, then, was *really* behind the attacks? Mylroie had the answer: Iraq. There was no way, she insisted, that al-Qaeda could have pulled off 9/11 without the support of Saddam Hussein.

The rumpled-looking Mylroie had been anticipating a moment like 9/11 for years. Finally, she thought, she might soon see the result of a decade of hard work: a war against Saddam. Her own personal odyssey—which had taken her from promoting Saddam's potential as a positive leader to decrying him as the leading source of evil in the world—was a key chapter in the war's back story, a tale that also featured a band of like-minded policy wonks who had been pushing for a full-scale invasion of Iraq practically since the end of the first Persian Gulf War. Mylroie and her neoconservative allies would demonstrate, perhaps beyond their most fanciful dreams, that a few committed souls could change the world—even if they didn't have their facts straight.

Mylroie made her reputation as a Middle East expert and a prodigious researcher in the 1980s, when she was a graduate student and then an assistant professor of political science at Harvard University. She was at that time a pragmatist regarding Saddam, arguably sympathetic to the tyrant. The Iraqi dictator, she pointed out then, was not an Islamic fanatic; he was not passionately anti-American. Saddam, she thought, could be turned into a U.S. ally in the Mideast. In a 1987 piece in *The New Republic*—headlined "Back Iraq: It's Time for a U.S. 'Tilt' "—Mylroie and Daniel Pipes, a pro-Israel hawk who worked with her at Harvard, called for the Reagan administration to swing behind Saddam's regime in its ongoing war with Iran. The two advocated sending weapons to Iraq and upgrading the intelligence Washington was already providing Saddam. The pair noted that Iraq had moderated its view of Israel and the United States (with which it had restored relations in 1984, thanks in part to the effort of Donald Rumsfeld, whom Reagan dispatched to Iraq as an envoy in 1983). A shift toward Iraq, Mylroie and Pipes wrote, "could lay the basis for a fruitful relationship" that would enhance both U.S. and Israeli security interests.

Beyond writing about the Middle East, Mylroie was looking to change the region through back-channel, private diplomacy—and she aspired to be a behind-the-scenes peacemaker who would broker a deal between Saddam and Israel. Amatzia Baram, an influential University of Haifa professor and an Israeli expert on Iraq, recalled that he had encouraged Mylroie in this endeavor. "Yeah, I was somewhat hopeful there could be a normalization of relations," he said. The pair hatched a plan: Mylroie would visit Iraq and approach high-level officials there to see if they might be interested in exploring talks with Israel. Baram took Mylroie to see Ezer Weizman, the legendary Israeli Air Service hero then serving in the Cabinet of the Likud-led Israeli government. "Ezer liked the idea," according to Baram, and gave this unofficial diplomacy a green light.

In 1987, according to Baram, Mylroie went to Baghdad and met with Tariq Aziz, the foreign minister, and Nizar Hamdoon, the Iraqi ambassador to the United States. She then visited Israel. Later, she organized an unofficial meeting at Harvard between Hamdoon and two Israeli Army generals. Hamdoon was coy and ultimately noncommittal. The Israeli Army generals, according to Baram, went back home with "mixed feelings," concluding that Hamdoon was really just playing along as a way of placating the United States—not because Saddam's regime had any real desire to make peace. Mylroie's efforts at playing Henry Kissinger had gone nowhere.

But Mylroie continued to advocate engaging Saddam, even after the Iraqi dictator slaughtered tens of thousands of Kurds in what became known as the Anfal campaign of 1987 and 1988. That horrific attack caused the Reagan administration to formally condemn Iraq for its use of chemical weapons in September 1988. In May 1989, Mylroie wrote in *The Jerusalem Post* that Israel and the United States should not "poke" Iraq "with a stick" and should refrain from tossing "idle threats and harsh words" at Baghdad. She suggested Iraq might become a benign, if not positive, presence in the region. She pointed out that Saddam had even announced a program of democracy—including allowing freedom of speech and permitting opposition parties to operate—that should not be dismissed out of hand. The following March, *The Jerusalem Post* quoted Mylroie as saying that Israel and Iraq ought to try to reach an informal understanding through a third party—perhaps an oblique reference to her own back-channel efforts.

Whatever hopes she harbored of being a Middle East peacemaker were dashed on August 2, 1990, when Iraqi troops poured across the border and occupied Kuwait. Saddam's invasion crushed Mylroie—and turned her view of the world upside down. "Laurie was utterly horrified and aghast," Pipes recalled. "She was in a state of shock." Almost overnight, she turned against the dictator she had once wanted Washington to help, with the passion of one who felt personally betrayed.

After the invasion, Mylroie was asked by a New York publisher to collaborate with Judy Miller on a book on Saddam and the current crisis. Written in just twenty-one days, the paperback positioned Mylroie and Miller as two prominent experts on the evil and brutal ways of Iraq's dictator. ("Saddam Hussein loves *The Godfather*," they wrote.) An editor who worked on the book recalled that Mylroie often became obsessed with individual facts and exaggerated their importance: "She was capable of great insight and of investing the smallest detail with the most disproportionate weight. She was not always capable of making a straightforward, linear argument. Left to her own devices, she would seize on reeds she would think were redwoods." Miller, though, found Mylroie a fine collaborator. "It was a great match," Miller said later. "I learned an enormous amount about Iraq from her."

Their book was no cry for military action. The conclusion took a cynical view of the first President Bush's deployment of 100,000 U.S. troops to the region: "American forces had been sent to Saudi Arabia to protect the nation's access to oil. . . . [T]he confrontation in the Gulf was prompted partly by greed—Saddam Hussein's and America's." Saddam's invasion, they wrote, was inexcusable, but Washington's failed policies were also responsible for this crisis. Mylroie and Miller cautioned against imperial overreach. The book became a number one bestseller.

But as the book was about to come out, Mylroie's past as secret freelance diplomat was exposed by an unlikely source: Egyptian President Hosni Mubarak. On October 4, 1990, Mubarak delivered a speech in which he claimed that Iraq and Israel had engaged in secret contacts in 1987 and 1989 through a Harvard University professor. Mubarak said this professor had carried a message from Saddam to Israel in 1987—that Iraq had no desire to go to war with Israel—and that in 1989 this professor had visited Israel to tell officials there that Saddam cared less about the Palestinian issue than his troubles with Iran and Syria. Mubarak was probably trying to embarrass Saddam. He did not name the professor, but Israeli newspapers did: Laurie Mylroie.

Mylroie refused to comment on Mubarak's speech. More recently, she said that she had "never conveyed any messages" between Saddam and Israel. But in interviews for this book, five of her former associates in Israel and the United States confirmed that she had been a secret go-between between Baghdad and Jerusalem. In 1990 Judy Miller cryptically said to *The Boston Globe* that Mubarak had been "right on the substance" but that her coauthor had never served as an intermediary between Iraq and Israel. Yet in 2006, Miller acknowledged that "Laurie told me about the alleged 'go-between' role after a report surfaced in the press. She said it was never a formal arrangement, just an informal kind of thing."

After the Saddam book was published, Mylroie was hired as a policy analyst at the Washington Institute for Near East Policy by Martin Indyk, a Mideast expert influential in Democratic circles. And when Indyk became an adviser to presidential candidate Bill Clinton, he asked Mylroie on one occasion to join a group of foreign policy specialists briefing Clinton on Middle East issues. Her fifteen minutes or so with the Democratic candidate, according to Indyk, were unremarkable, but long enough that Mylroie soon began advertising herself as an "adviser" to the Clinton campaign on Mideast policy.

After the 1993 World Trade Center bombing, which killed six people and injured more than 1,000, Mylroie's work took a more dramatic turn. She began poring over the evidence and theorized that the bombing had been an act of retaliation by Saddam for the Persian Gulf War. The notion was not utterly out of the question. There were a few intriguing threads. One of the minor figures in the plot, Abdul Rahman Yasin, had fled to Iraq after the attacks. And Yasin's precise status in Iraq was not clear. Born in Indiana of Iraqi parents, Yasin had grown up in Baghdad. After the bombing, Iraqi officials appeared to view Yasin as a potential bargaining chip, even offering at several points to hand him over to Washington in exchange for a shift in U.S. policy. Later on, evidence would emerge confirming what U.S. officials had suspected: that Yasin had been essentially placed under house arrest and was being watched closely by Iraqi security forces.* But in Mylroie's view, Yasin had been granted safe haven by the Iraqis, and that could only mean that Yasin had been an Iraqi agent.

Mylroie also zeroed in on phone records involving the bombing suspects. One of the men, Mohammed Salameh, was the nephew of a Palestinian terrorist, Abu Bakr, who was living in Baghdad. Salameh, Mylroie discovered, had called his uncle forty-six times in June and July 1992—before his phone was cut off for nonpayment. Mylroie had no idea what was being said in these calls, whether they had anything to do with the World Trade Center plot seven months later or involved any connection to the Iraqi government. But it didn't matter. "She would stare at you, and insist that unless you had studied all these phone records you couldn't understand what was going on," said Steven Emerson, a terrorism researcher who saw the World Trade Center bombing not as an Iraqi plot but as the act of Islamic extremists. "She would start rattling them off. At 4:07 A.M., this person called that person, then five minutes later they called someone else. How can you challenge something like that?"

Over time, Mylroie developed a Byzantine hypothesis about the 1993 bombing, one that seemed more the product of a Hollywood screenwriter

---

*Dobie McArthur, a Pentagon official dispatched by Wolfowitz after the war to examine voluminous Iraqi security records, reviewed the Iraqi security file on Yasin. He found no evidence that Yasin or anybody else associated with the 1993 World Trade Center attack had received any support from Baghdad for the 1993 bombing. McArthur did see records suggesting that Yasin, after fleeing to Baghdad, had been given a monthly stipend but was restricted in his movements and kept under constant surveillance.

than an Ivy League–trained scholar. She fixated on the mastermind of this first WTC attack, Ramzi Yousef. The FBI apprehended Yousef in Pakistan in 1995 and concluded that his name was but one of many aliases; that he was actually Abdul Basit Karim, a Pakistani national from the Baluch region who had been raised in Kuwait and who later studied engineering at the Swansea Institute in Wales. But Mylroie came to believe that there were, in a way, two Ramzi Yousefs. One was the real Basit, who under Mylroie's theory had been killed or had otherwise vanished along with the rest of his family during the Iraqi invasion of Kuwait. The other was Yousef, a cold-blooded Iraqi intelligence agent who had been trained by Saddam to kill Americans and who had absconded with Basit's identity.

To back up her theory, Mylroie pointed to missing pages from Yousef's passport and several small discrepancies. For example, witnesses recalled that the Basit they had known in Wales was a few inches shorter than the six-foot-tall man arrested by the FBI. She also maintained that the Iraqi intelligence services had forged the Iraqi passport that Yousef had used to enter the United States.

FBI investigators and federal prosecutors studied her ideas and rejected them. There were several fundamental problems that essentially stopped her conspiracy theory in its tracks. After Yousef was captured, bureau agents had located witnesses from the United Kingdom who testified at the terrorist's bail hearing that the man in custody was indeed the same person they had known in Wales as Abdul Basit. And there was testimony from eyewitnesses identifying Yousef as an Islamic radical who had spent time in Afghan training camps affiliated with al-Qaeda. (Yousef himself admitted to federal agents that he had been trained in explosives and bomb making in Afghanistan.) More important, the bureau checked Yousef's fingerprints with those for Basit in Kuwait and discovered they were one and the same. Thereafter, the FBI and federal prosecutors were pretty much convinced that Mylroie's double-man idea was dead wrong.

"I don't think there was any serious question of Yousef's identity," said Dieter Snell, a top investigator for the September 11 commission who, as a federal prosecutor, tried the terrorist in the summer of 1996 in a separate case that involved a plot to blow up eleven airliners heading toward the United States. (A law enforcement official recalled that Mylroie showed up at that trial and eyed the defendant up and down intensely when he walked into the courtroom, as though she were trying to measure him.)

Still, Mylroie relentlessly promoted her double-man thesis to past and present government officials, foreign policy experts, and journalists. The FBI's debunking of Mylroie's narrative was not a matter of public record, and several neoconservatives accepted Mylroie's work as compelling evidence of Saddam's sponsorship of anti-American terrorism.

Indyk, now overseeing Iraq policy for Clinton's National Security Council, had asked the FBI and CIA to review Mylroie's theory. He wanted to believe it, Indyk later said. The Clinton administration had entered office inclined to adopt an aggressive approach toward Iraq—and this would have helped. But the CIA and FBI reported back that they had conducted an extensive analysis, Indyk said, and that "there was nothing to it." As one CIA analyst later put it, "Not only was it not true, we proved the opposite"—that Saddam had had nothing to do with the 1993 WTC bombing.

Not long after that, Indyk received a visitor at his White House office. It was Paul Wolfowitz, who at the time was dean of the Johns Hopkins School of Advanced International Studies. Wolfowitz had one item on his agenda: Laurie Mylroie's theory about the World Trade Center. Wolfowitz asked why the Clinton administration was not paying adequate attention to her thesis. Indyk explained that, as far as he was concerned, it had been debunked by the CIA and FBI. Wolfowitz, according to Indyk, was "surprised" to hear this and not persuaded: "He was convinced that we were purposely refusing to see the link for policy reasons." Indyk considered it odd that Wolfowitz appeared so attached to Mylroie's ideas. He surmised that Wolfowitz felt personally guilty for the first Bush administration's failure to get rid of Saddam after the Persian Gulf War. Mylroie's theories could offer a justification for action that would rectify that past policy mistake. (Mylroie was also personally close to Wolfowitz's then-wife, Clare.) Whatever the reason, Wolfowitz was putting more faith in Mylroie than the CIA or the FBI.*

Over time, Mylroie became more persistent and more obsessive. She

---

*Wolfowitz and Mylroie had an old-school connection through the Telluride House—an elite, intellectually oriented residence at Cornell University, once known as a haven for followers of the prominent conservative philosopher Allan Bloom. As a Cornell student in the early 1970s, Mylroie lived in the Telluride House. Wolfowitz had resided there earlier and was a board member of the Telluride Association. As James Mann, author of *Rise of the Vulcans,* noted, Wolfowitz hired members of the Telluride community when he went into government. Mylroie was a part of this informal network, according to writer Francis Fukuyama, another Telluride alumnus.

was so convinced that the 1993 World Trade Center bombing had been an Iraqi operation that she offered herself as defense witness for Eyad Ismoil, one of the alleged terrorists in the 1995 trial of the blind sheik Omar Abdel-Rahman, who was accused of conspiring to encourage acts of terrorism in the United States, including the WTC bombings. Mylroie's position was that the defendants were patsies being held responsible for a monstrous crime committed by Saddam. Mylroie never took the stand. But she showed up at court hearings and at times appeared emotionally invested in the proceedings, according to Joan Ullman, a New York journalist who monitored the trial for Steven Emerson's terrorist-tracking outfit. At one court hearing for Ismoil, who was accused of having driven the bomb-laden truck to the World Trade Center, Mylroie was spotted "cradling Ismoil's father and at times, wiping tears from her own brimming heavily blue-eye-lined mascara," Ullman wrote in a memo at the time.

After the 1995 Oklahoma City bombing, Mylroie became convinced that that attack, too, was an Iraqi strike on America. She offered her services to the lawyers for Timothy McVeigh, the antigovernment zealot accused of setting off the bomb. Mylroie sent memos promoting the Iraq connection to the McVeigh defense team. Stephen Jones, McVeigh's chief lawyer, hired her as a consultant and even sent investigators to the Philippines. It was Mylroie's suspicion that McVeigh's coconspirator, Terry Nichols, might have met in the Philippines with Yousef, the theoretical Iraqi agent. But the trail went cold. "I couldn't make it go anywhere," recalled Jones. As he saw it, Mylroie was a piece of work: an impressive tireless researcher who worked at a "fanatic" pace, calling him at all hours with new ideas and potential Iraqi links to the plot. "She was sort of like *The Da Vinci Code* people," said Jones. "She had this one grand theory. I didn't see it."

In time, Mylroie saw the hidden hand of Saddam in almost every act of anti-American terrorism in the world, even the 1998 bombings of two U.S. embassies in Africa, Osama bin Laden's first major assault against the United States. As for the 2000 bombing of the USS *Cole* off the coast of Yemen, an al-Qaeda operation that killed seventeen Navy sailors—that, too, was, for Mylroie, the handiwork of the Iraqi dictator. "Everything, everything, everything was connected to Saddam," said her former collaborator Daniel Pipes. "She became monomaniacal on the subject." She also became hostile toward old friends and colleagues who didn't see the world her way. When Pipes publicly endorsed the predominant view that anti-U.S. terrorism was caused primarily by radical Islamic fundamentalists and questioned her Saddam-centric view of world terrorism, Mylroie accused Pipes of endangering the welfare of the republic. "My charge against you is that you are, at the periphery, responsible for the death of Americans," she e-mailed Pipes on March 7, 1999. "And furthermore, that more Americans will die, if people continue to listen to your version of events."

MYLROIE might have remained an oddball and offbeat academic insistently pushing a widely disregarded theory, but she had powerful friends, including Ahmad Chalabi and his compatriots within the Iraqi National Congress, who were certainly predisposed to depict Saddam as the world's greatest menace. In the late 1990s, Mylroie joined Chalabi's informal Washington kitchen cabinet. She advocated the INC's cause at conferences and in academic journals and the op-ed pages of *The Wall Street Journal* and other publications. She was frequently seen at the home of Francis Brooke, Chalabi's chief Washington lobbyist. Another new set of friends could be found at the offices of the American Enterprise Institute, where Mylroie landed a berth as an adjunct fellow. In the fall of 2000, the AEI published Mylroie's book about the 1993 World Trade Center bombing, called *Study of Revenge: Saddam Hussein's Unfinished War Against America.*

What was on the back of the book cover was as important as the text inside: a blurb from Paul Wolfowitz. It read:

> Laurie Mylroie's provocative and disturbing book argues powerfully that the shadowy mastermind of the 1993 bombing of New York's World Trade Center, Ramzi Yousef, was in fact an agent of Iraqi intelligence. If so, what would that tell us about the extent of Saddam Hussein's ambitions? How would it change our view of Iraq's continuing efforts to retain weapons of mass destruction and to acquire new ones? How would it affect our judgments . . . and the need for a fundamentally new policy? These are questions that urgently need to be answered.

Wolfowitz, who had helped Mylroie with the manuscript, was carefully attaching his seal of approval to her thesis.

Perle, too, provided an endorsement of the work. (Woolsey wrote a supportive foreword for a later version.) In the acknowledgments, Mylroie saluted Wolfowitz and noted that his wife, Clare, had "fundamentally shaped this book." She thanked John Hannah, who later would become a foreign policy aide to Vice President Cheney, for his guidance. She noted that the INC's Francis Brooke and his wife, Sharon, had offered her much support and "keen insights." She also expressed her gratitude to David Wurmser, Michael Ledeen, and John Bolton, a fierce hawk who would soon become the State Department's top arms control official. Scooter Libby, she noted, had supplied her with "timely and generous assistance."

When the Bush team took office soon after the book was published, Mylroie found herself with fans in high places. She was named to a Pentagon advisory board on terrorism and technology. And her most prominent champion, Wolfowitz, used his newfound power to seek confirmation of Mylroie's thesis. Sometime before September 11, according to DIA director Thomas Wilson, Wolfowitz pressed the DIA chief on whether he had read Mylroie's *Study of Revenge*. Wilson replied that he hadn't. Wolfowitz requested that Wilson have his analysts examine the book. Wilson dutifully passed along the request, and an answer came back: the DIA couldn't find anything to back up Mylroie.

In June 2001, Wolfowitz also tried to get the CIA to reinvestigate the Mylroie theory, according to the report of the 9/11 Commission. Nothing came of that, either. Wolfowitz had by then mastered the minutiae of Mylroie's research—and retained it. "Wolfowitz was an encyclopedia on this stuff," Undersecretary of Defense Doug Feith subsequently said. And years later, according to Dobie McArthur, a Wolfowitz aide, the deputy defense secretary became excited when fresh intelligence surfaced about the whereabouts of an obscure associate of Yasin, the indicted 1993 bomber. Wolfowitz got up from his chair, pulled out a copy of Mylroie's book, and opened it to the exact page where the associate was mentioned.

Within administration meetings in the early days of the Bush administration, Wolfowitz voiced a Mylroie-like view on terrorism. When the National Security Council of the new Bush administration held its first deputies meeting on terrorism in April 2001, Richard Clarke, then the White House counterterrorism adviser, talked about the urgent need to go after bin Laden and the al-Qaeda leadership in Afghanistan, according to Clarke's memoirs. Wolfowitz was dismissive. "Well, I just don't understand why we are beginning by talking about this one man, bin Laden," he replied. Wolfowitz tried to switch the subject to "Iraqi terrorism." An exasperated Clarke replied that the intelligence community had no evidence of any recent Iraqi terrorism against the United States—a position endorsed at the meeting by CIA Deputy Director John McLaughlin. Clarke started citing bin Laden's writings and his plans to overthrow Arab governments and set up a radical multination caliphate, adding "sometimes, as with Hitler in *Mein Kampf,* you have to believe that these people will actually do what they say they will do." Wolfowitz snapped back, saying that he resented any comparison between the Holocaust "and this little terrorist in Afghanistan."

FOR years, neoconservatives, not just Mylroie, had been fixating on Iraq and the need to topple its tyrannical dictator. Their approach was more geostrategic than Mylroie's, but they ended up in the same place. In 1996, Perle, Wurmser, and Feith were part of a study group that produced a paper for the Jerusalem-based Institute for Advanced Strategic and Political Studies, a conservative, pro-Israel think tank closely allied with the policies of Israel's hawkish Likud Party. They noted that "removing Saddam Hussein from power" was "an important Israeli strategic objective" and that toppling his regime would be "a means of foiling Syria's regional ambition."

The paper, entitled "A Clean Break: A New Strategy for Securing the Realm," was policy advice for the new hard-line Israeli prime minister, Benjamin Netanyahu. It had numerous other elements, the most important of which was a decisive rejection of the idea that Israel should swap "land for peace" to reach an accommodation with the Palestinians. But as part of a larger plan to secure Israel's security, the paper urged the removal of Saddam and the restoration of a Hashemite kingdom in Baghdad to box in the Syrian regime of Hafez Assad.

This report later led to another conspiracy theory: that eliminating Saddam was part of a neoconservative/Likud plot to benefit Israel. Yet the authors of "A Clean Break" had actually gone beyond the position of the Likud Party's own strategists. By the late 1990s, Israeli officials tended to consider Iran a much more significant worry than Iraq. Indyk, who was U.S. ambassador to Israel in the mid-1990s and then again in 2000 and 2001, recalled that Iraq was barely mentioned as an Israeli priority during his years in Tel Aviv. "It was Iran, Iran, Iran all the time," Indyk said. "The Israelis were not that bothered by Saddam." Though "A Clean Break" was not evidence that the neoconservative fixation on Saddam was made (or coordinated) in Israel, it did show that Perle and his allies saw Saddam as a chessboard piece that should be removed to further a larger strategic game plan. This scrappy band of policy fighters seemed to believe that toppling inconvenient regimes could be achieved with relatively small costs—and that such bold steps could reshape the geopolitical map of the Middle East for the better.

In late 1997, *The Weekly Standard,* a magazine financed by media baron Rupert Murdoch and edited by William Kristol, former chief of staff for Vice President Dan Quayle, ran an issue with a cover proclaiming, "Saddam Must Go." An editorial declared that the UN WMD inspections, under way since the end of the Persian Gulf War, had been ineffectual and that a containment policy would not work. In the same issue, Wolfowitz and Zalmay Khalilzad, then a strategist at the Rand Corporation, published an article that maintained that "only the substantial use of military force" with the goal of "the liberation of Iraq" would do the trick.

Kristol, Perle, and their allies were not plotting a conspiracy. They were advocating war in full public view. A month later, the Project for the New American Century, a foreign policy shop headed by Kristol, sent President Clinton a letter urging him to attack Iraq. If Saddam acquired WMDs, they wrote, "the safety of American troops in the region, of our friends and allies like Israel and the moderate Arab states, and a significant portion of the world's supply of oil will all be put at hazard." The letter said nothing about bringing democracy to Iraq or the regime or what would happen after an invasion. The eighteen signatories on the letter included several conservatives who would wind up with positions in the George W. Bush administration, including Rumsfeld, Wolfowitz, Perle, Bolton, Khalilzad, former Pentagon official Richard Armitage, and Iran-*contra* veteran Elliott Abrams.*

After Congress passed and Clinton signed into law in the fall of 1998 the Iraq Liberation Act, the advocates of regime change were hardly satisfied—especially when it became clear that neither the Clinton administration nor Congress had any real plan for achieving the goal set out in the law. Nor were they mollified when Clinton, in December 1998, launched bomb-

---

*By this point, the PNAC, which Kristol had created the previous June, had become the leading advocate for war in Iraq. In its founding statement, the group had called for expansion of the U.S. military so Washington could preserve and extend "an international order friendly to our security." That statement had been signed by twenty-five heavyweight political figures, including Cheney, Rumsfeld, Wolfowitz, and Libby.

ing strikes on military sites in Iraq, declaring that a Saddam regime in control of WMDs was a risk that could not be tolerated. (Explaining these air strikes, Clinton said, "Our mission is clear: to degrade Saddam's capacity to develop and deliver weapons of mass destruction.") Unless Clinton got fully behind the "Iraqi opposition" (meaning the Iraqi National Congress) and considered sending in U.S. troops, Robert Kagan of the Project for a New American Century wrote in *The Weekly Standard,* his policy would remain useless.

In September 2000, with a neck-and-neck presidential race under way, the PNAC produced a strategy paper that noted that the "United States has for decades sought to play a more permanent role in Gulf regional security. While the unresolved conflict with Iraq provides the immediate justification, the need for a substantial American force presence in the Gulf transcends the issue of the regime of Saddam Hussein." Taking out Saddam was about more than taking out Saddam. It was part of the larger strategic vision: expanding the United States' influence and showing its muscle in the Middle East. When the George W. Bush administration took office in January 2001, it was clear to Bush's Treasury secretary, Paul O'Neill (as he would recount later), that one top-of-the-agenda item was getting rid of Saddam: "It was all about finding *a way to do it.* That was the tone of it. The president saying, 'Fine. Go find me a way to do this.'"

IN THE shell-shocked days following 9/11, much of the world was looking for an explanation. At the AEI event, Mylroie had one ready. She claimed that al-Qaeda did not have the "sophistication" and "organization" to pull off 9/11 and that the group was nothing but a Keystones Kops–like band of terrorists. "There's evidence," she asserted, "to suggest that Iraq was involved with bin Laden in the 1998 bombing [of two U.S. embassies in Africa] because those bombings occurred in a certain context." For Mylroie, context *was* evidence. Mylroie concluded with the recommendation that all U.S. intelligence on terrorism be scrubbed and reexamined. Such a review, she maintained, would show that al-Qaeda was not a stand-alone outfit. Instead, Mylroie said, "a review will conclude that a good bit of the terrorism we have experienced since the Gulf War is merely another phase of the Gulf War— Saddam's part of the Gulf War." After she finished, Wurmser remarked, "I want to reemphasize everything Laurie just said. . . . We really do have to begin with Iraq." Ledeen then called on the administration to "unleash" Chalabi's INC. The debris from the World Trade Center had barely settled and cooled, and Mylroie and her allies were already pushing a war to overthrow Saddam.

THE Mylroie-bolstered belief that Saddam was America's number one enemy also gripped the most senior officials of the Bush administration. Within hours of the al-Qaeda strike, Rumsfeld was asking if Saddam could be targeted as well as Osama bin Laden. The next day, Bush, according to Richard Clarke, pulled him aside in the White House Situation Room and asked him to look for evidence that Saddam had staged 9/11. When Clarke replied, "Mr. President, al-Qaeda did this," Bush said, "I know, I know, but . . . see if Saddam was involved. Just look." Another counterterrorism official who witnessed the exchange said that Bush was "very forceful" in his direction to Clarke. After Bush left the room, this official stared straight ahead with mouth wide open and had one thought: "This is Wolfowitz." Days later, Clarke sent Rice a detailed memo that concluded there was no "compelling case" that Iraq had planned the 9/11 attacks. It also said there was no confirmed reporting that bin Laden and Saddam had cooperated on WMDs.

During the weeks following 9/11, Wolfowitz acted as if the terror attacks were proof of the theory he and Mylroie had advanced for years. After all, if Saddam had been behind the 1993 attack on the World Trade Center, it made perfect sense he would have tried again in 2001. At a Camp David meeting of the Cabinet on September 15, Wolfowitz argued that there was a 10 to 50 percent chance Saddam had been part of the 9/11 plot, and he suggested Bush consider attacking Iraq right away, noting a war in Iraq might be easier than one in Afghanistan. On September 17, he sent Rumsfeld a memo, entitled "Preventing More Events," that maintained that the odds were far better than one in ten that Saddam had been part of the 9/11 conspiracy; he cited the same thesis that Mylroie had developed that Iraq had been behind the 1993 WTC bombing. The next day, he fired off a similar memo to his boss. This one bore the ominous title "Were We Asleep?"—a suggestion that thousands of Americans were dead because the U.S. government had not perceived the real terrorist threat clearly. Then he dispatched Woolsey to London to find evidence that would back up Mylroie.

Officials at the Justice Department and CIA dismissed the trip as a wild-goose chase. "These guys don't give up," one senior Justice Department official said about Wolfowitz and his fellow Mylroie advocates. Justice reluctantly assigned a veteran prosecutor to accompany Woolsey on the mission. In London, Woolsey pushed British authorities to turn over more of Abdul Basit's records, which he believed would show that the former student from Pakistan was not Ramzi Yousef. The Brits patiently explained that they had cooperated with the FBI for years on this matter and that the fingerprint evidence was conclusive: Basit's fingerprints matched those of Yousef's. Woolsey remained unsatisfied. "He was being a real pain in the ass," recalled Tyler Drumheller, the CIA's European Division chief, who at the time received complaints from the CIA's London station about Woolsey's trip.

Another big booster of the Saddam-as-master-terrorist theory was Bush's new counterterrorism adviser, Wayne Downing, a retired general who once had designed an INC-backed plan for the overthrow of Saddam. In October 2001, Downing, Wolfowitz, and other proponents of a war with Iraq thought they had yet more ammunition for the case against Saddam. A series of deadly anthrax-laced letters had been sent to the Capitol Hill offices of Senator Daschle and Senator Patrick Leahy and to several newsrooms. Mylroie asserted that Saddam was behind the mailings. An early forensic test of the anthrax letters (which was later disputed) appeared to show that the anthrax spores were highly refined and "weaponized." To the Iraq hawks, the news was electric. "This is definitely Saddam!" Downing shouted to several White House aides. One of these aides later recalled overhearing Downing excitedly sharing the news over the phone with Wolfowitz and Feith. "I had the feeling they were high-five-ing each other," the White House official said.

The Iraq connection to the anthrax attacks never went anywhere. And Bush did not immediately embrace the advice of Mylroie, Wolfowitz, Perle, and their allies. His first concern was Afghanistan, and on October 7, 2001, he launched military operations against the Taliban regime. But as the Bush administration prosecuted its military campaign in Afghanistan, the prospect of striking Saddam remained a top-drawer item of consideration. On November 21—nine days after the fall of Kabul had sent thousands of Taliban and al-Qaeda fighters and supporters fleeing south—Bush took aside Rumsfeld, according to Bob Woodward's *Plan of Attack,* and asked him to draw up a fresh war plan for Iraq and to keep it a secret.

THE hawks who had accepted Mylroie's ideas about Saddam and terrorism were moving closer to their objective. In his first State of the Union speech, Bush decried the Axis of Evil, which in the speechwriting process had begun as a rhetorical attack only on Iraq. And over the next few months, there was a steady stream of preparation for war within the Bush administration but only the occasional leak indicating that a decision had been reached. On February 13, 2002, Knight Ridder reported that "President Bush has decided to oust Iraqi leader Saddam Hussein from power and ordered the CIA, the Pentagon and other agencies to devise a combination of military, diplomatic and covert steps to achieve that goal." (The news service had caught a hint of Anabasis.) At a press conference in March, Bush declared that Saddam was "a dangerous man who possesses the world's most dangerous weapons." All the while, Wolfowitz was championing Mylroie's thesis. At a March 17 lunch with England's ambassador to the United States, Christopher Meyer, Wolfowitz tried to convince the British that Iraq was tied to the first World Trade Center attack. And in a June 1 speech delivered at West Point, Bush laid out a grand national security vision and said that he would take "preemptive action" to defend the nation and to "confront the worst threats before they emerge." Strategies of containment or deterrence would no longer be considered sufficient. Iraq seemed to be the case he had in mind.

ON JULY 23, 2002, Tony Blair held a meeting with senior members of his government to discuss Iraq. Richard Dearlove, the head of British intelligence, briefed the group on his recent talks in Washington, where he had met with CIA Director George Tenet. The minutes of the meeting recorded his report:

> Military action was now seen as inevitable. Bush wanted to remove Saddam, through military action, justified by the conjunction of terrorism and WMD. But the intelligence and facts were being fixed around the policy. The NSC had no patience with the UN route, and no enthusiasm for publishing material on the Iraqi regime's record.

There was little discussion in Washington of the aftermath after military action.

The memo did not spell out what Dearlove meant when he said the intelligence was "being fixed." But at this meeting Foreign Secretary Jack Straw raised questions about the WMD rationale for war. According to the minutes, Straw noted:

It seemed clear that Bush had made up his mind to take military action, even if the timing was not yet decided. But the case was thin. Saddam was not threatening his neighbours, and his WMD capability was less than that of Libya, North Korea or Iran.

And at the meeting, Defense Secretary Geoff Hoon reported that the U.S. military had prepared several operations for the coming war.* The war, Hoon guessed, would start in January 2003.

BY NOW, Laurie Mylroie had become a talking head on Iraq, hitting the cable news shows, writing op-eds, talking up her book, and urging war against Saddam. Appearing on CNN on July 31, 2002, she told anchor Aaron Brown that Bush had already decided to get rid of Saddam. She asserted that Bush had ordered the CIA to "do it by covert means" but that "no one, including the CIA director," expected a secret attempt to overthrow Saddam to succeed. Thus, war was the only option. Fortunately, she noted, there already was a group ready and capable to lead Iraq to democracy following a military invasion: Ahmad Chalabi's Iraqi National Congress. Asked why Bush was committed to removing Saddam, Mylroie said it was "partly" due to Saddam's weapons and "partly it's [Saddam's] prior support for terrorism, including strong suspicions about Iraq's involvement in 9/11 in the part of the vice president's office and the office of the secretary of defense." But, Brown interjected, wasn't it the general view within the

---

*Two days earlier, a British Cabinet Office briefing paper had stated, "A post-war occupation of Iraq could lead to a protracted and costly nation-building exercise. As already made clear, the U.S. military plans are virtually silent on this point."

U.S. intelligence community that Saddam had not been mixed up in 9/11? The CIA's refusal to see the connection, Mylroie replied, was an "enormous scandal," bigger than Enron. The CIA, she added, was engaged in an "enormous cover-up exercise" by not, in essence, accepting her theory that Saddam was behind 9/11. "No reasonable person," she said, ". . . would conclude otherwise."

Honey, will you come into the office next week?

—VALERIE WILSON, CIA OFFICER

5

The Niger Caper

—

JOHN GIBSON, a young White House speechwriter, was at the Waldorf-Astoria hotel in New York on September 11, 2002, putting the final touches on the president's UN speech, when he received an urgent phone call on his cell phone. It was his boss, Michael Gerson, who had just been talking to White House communications aide Dan Bartlett. There was a new piece of intelligence that Gibson might be able to throw in the speech. They weren't sure yet. If they didn't use it in the speech, "it's something we might leak to *The New York Times*," Gerson said, according to Gibson. The speechwriter sensed that there was excitement at the White House about this latest nugget. What was it? he asked.

Gerson told Gibson to go to a secure line that had been set up at the Waldorf for White House staff and call a National Security Council aide, Robert Joseph. Gibson, who handled many of Bush's national security–related speeches, often worked with Joseph, and they were an odd couple. Gibson was a Democrat; he had been a national security speechwriter in the Clinton White House and stayed on to serve Bush. And he had doubts about a war in Iraq. "I'm not totally there yet," he had told Gerson weeks earlier, when his boss had assigned him the UN speech. Great, Gerson had told him, "then you're probably the perfect person to write the speech. If you can convince yourself, you can convince the country." Joseph, the NSC special assistant for proliferation issues, was the last person who needed convincing. A tough hard-line conservative academic known for his skeptical views about arms control and international diplomacy, Joseph had a reputation for pushing evidence related to Iraq as far as it could possibly go. Joseph, one colleague later recalled, "was quick to see darkness where others might see dusk."

When Gibson reached Joseph that day, the NSC aide had what seemed to be important new evidence of Iraqi darkness. Saddam, Joseph said, had been attempting to obtain a massive amount of yellowcake uranium in Africa. Gibson immediately realized what that meant. It was the worst-case scenario: Saddam was looking to enrich uranium for a nuclear bomb. For all his qualms about a war against Iraq, Gibson considered it his job to craft the most compelling case he could. And a charge like this would make the president's speech much more convincing.

As Gibson worked on the speech, Joseph and the NSC sent a message to the CIA, asking the agency to clear the use of three sentences:

> And we also know this: within the past few years, Iraq has resumed efforts to obtain large quantities of a type of uranium oxide known as yellowcake, which is an essential ingredient of this [uranium enrichment] process. The regime was caught trying to purchase 500 metric tons of this material. It takes about 10 tons to produce enough enriched uranium for a single nuclear weapon.

Go ahead, the CIA replied, suggesting that the words "up to" be placed before "500 metric tons." That day, Joseph and Gibson conferred several times about how to insert the yellowcake charge into the UN speech. Joseph even faxed to Gibson the language that had been cleared by the CIA. But, at the end of the day, the CIA wasn't comfortable with Bush issuing this allegation in public. The information had come from a single foreign source. It had not been confirmed. It was not solid enough for a presidential speech. The CIA wanted it out. Strike it, Joseph said, and Gibson did.

The president did not refer to Iraq's alleged uranium shopping in his UN speech. The White House had been warned not to use it—and had heeded the warning. It was the first of several such warnings. But Bush's eventual use of this allegation in the 2003 State of the Union address would epitomize his administration's determination to deploy any evidence it could to justify the invasion of Iraq, even disputed information produced by bizarre circumstances. The yellowcake episode would blow up into a scandal that would bedevil the White House and lead to a criminal investigation of the president's top aides. But nothing was stranger than how it began: with the intrigues of a shadowy, for-profit intelligence operator in Rome with a name straight out of a spy movie.

ROCCO MARTINO was the sort of character who resides at the fringes of the intelligence world. A onetime Italian military police officer, Martino was a dapper, well-dressed, silver-haired, mustachioed fellow who described himself as an international security consultant. In reality, he was a snitch. He collected and peddled documents to businesses and to journalists—and to intelligence agencies, for which he occasionally was an informer. That included SISMI, the Italian military intelligence agency. As Martino himself would tell Carlo Bonini, a journalist for *La Repubblica,* "That's my métier. I sell information." And not just for the Italians. "I worked for the French . . . but I worked for SISMI as well," he once told another Italian paper, *Il Giornale.* "I made a double, triple game." And this professional informant had a checkered past. In 1985, according to court records unearthed by *La Repubblica,* Martino was arrested in Italy for extortion. In 1993, he was arrested in Germany for possessing stolen checks.

Martino's chief contact at SISMI was Colonel Antonio Nucera, an old friend and deputy chief of the spy agency's counterproliferation division. As Martino would later recount to an Italian prosecutor, Nucera in 1999 put him in touch with a longtime SISMI source who worked as a clerk at the Niger Embassy, an elusive figure who would become known in the Italian press as "La Signora."* Nucera suggested that La Signora, an Italian woman in her sixties, could be helpful to Martino. "Maybe she could bring out of the embassy some interesting material for you," Nucera had said, according to Martino. Nucera's motivation in setting up Martino with La Signora was—like much of this tale—puzzling. Nucera later said he had merely been trying to help a SISMI asset—La Signora—make some extra money. But it is also possible the Italian spymaster was steering his friend, Martino, toward

---

*Eventually, her real name would be identified as Laura Montini, and she would, at one point, deny to reporters that she even knew Rocco Martino.

politically useful material that some SISMI officials wanted publicly disseminated—without being directly involved. The strange twists of the Martino saga prompted such conjecture. Was it mere coincidence that the SISMI officer in charge of WMDs would lead Martino to documents—which would turn out to be fraudulent—detailing a uranium deal involving Iraq?

Martino began meeting La Signora in early 2000 and plying her with gifts: a box of chocolate for her birthday, a fancy watch, some perfume. She later told Italian investigators that she first assumed that Martino was courting her. But news accounts noted that Martino had paid her a monthly fee. She in turn fed Martino documents from inside the Niger Embassy.

After the pair had been working together for months, something odd happened. Early on New Year's Day 2001, a break-in occurred at the offices of the Niger Embassy. Two days later, the embassy's second secretary reported the theft to the police: a few file cabinets had been broken into. A watch and two bottles of perfume were missing. Also, some Niger government letterhead, stationery, and official stamps were gone. The police report was circulated to foreign governments. Spy agencies keep an eye on embassy break-ins. An analyst at the CIA subsequently recalled seeing a brief item on the break-in at the time and thinking, "Hmmm, wonder what that's about?" The culprits were never apprehended.

Italian police later suspected that the break-in had been staged to create a (false) explanation for how Martino would soon come into possession of documents bearing the stationery and stamps of the Niger Embassy. Which would mean that someone was trying to provide cover for Martino or La Signora. But who? And for what purpose? The robbery was yet another mystery in a murky saga that encouraged fanciful speculation.

Niger, a landlocked, drought-ridden nation of 12 million in the sub-Sahara desert, is one of the poorest countries in the world. It has one principal economic product: a vast store of uranium deposits. Not surprisingly, most of the documents La Signora slipped to Martino concerned uranium deals, real and potential, including one in China. At one point, according to a statement La Signora later gave to an Italian magistrate, Martino told her that if she could produce documents showing Iraq had tried to obtain uranium from Niger, such papers could be sold for a lot of money.

Whether Martino knew it or not, Western intelligence services had a specific reason to watch for a possible Niger-Iraq connection. In February 1999, Wissam al-Zahawie, the Iraqi ambassador to the Vatican, had visited

Niger and three other African countries. The trip was officially an effort by the Iraqi diplomat to encourage African leaders to visit Baghdad and perhaps reestablish commercial relations—an obvious attempt to undermine the UN sanctions imposed on Iraq. Zahawie had an hour-long chat with Nigerien President Ibrahim Bare Mainassara. Years later, Zahawie claimed that all the two had talked about was the Iraqi's "invitation" to Bare and the sanctions on Iraq: "During my visit to all four African countries, not once did I hear the word 'uranium' mentioned." Bare "warmly welcomed the invitation and promised to visit Baghdad," Zahawie recalled. But the Nigerien president was assassinated a few months later. Zahawie's trip to Niger was duly noted by U.S. and European spy services.*

In the course of his dealings with La Signora, Martino obtained telexes, memos, and letters—some of which mentioned Zahawie—that purportedly showed that Iraq and Niger had signed a deal in July 2000 for Niger to sell Saddam's regime 500 tons of yellowcake uranium. There was also another document in the batch that chronicled a seemingly bizarre meeting of officials from Iran, Iraq, and other nations who had gathered to discuss creating a "Global Support" military alliance of rogue states. This weird memo would subsequently become a key clue for one sharp-eyed U.S. official trying to unravel the mystery of the Niger deal.

Years later, the FBI would conclude that La Signora, with the assistance of the Niger Embassy's first counselor, Zakaria Yaou Maiga, had forged the papers and then passed them along to Martino to sell to his intelligence agency contacts. "It was a financial scam," a senior FBI official familiar with the bureau's investigation said in 2006. "This was concocted by La Signora, the guy at the embassy, and Martino." But the bureau could not rule out any involvement by Nucera and SISMI, the Italian intelligence service, in the forgery scheme. The FBI's investigation was limited, a senior bureau official said. Its agents were unable to question Nucera, Martino, or Maiga. (The FBI had no means to compel foreigners to testify in this sort of inquiry.) There were no "definitive conclusions" on whether there had been any SISMI participation, another senior FBI official said. Some FBI offi-

---

*Coincidentally—or not—Zahawie himself was a figure of interest to the CIA and its Western partners, according to the CIA's Tyler Drumheller. The CIA suspected that Zahawie was disenchanted with Saddam's regime and thus might be open to recruitment by the agency or another Western intelligence service.

cials familiar with the case would still wonder whether elements of SISMI might have, for their own reasons, assisted in the caper.*

Whether SISMI had anything to do with the creation of the fraudulent documents, the Italian spy agency—directed by appointees of the conservative and pro-American prime minister, Silvio Berlusconi—ended up with copies of these papers in the weeks after 9/11. The Italian intelligence service then shared the information contained in these papers with its partners in American and British intelligence. As was customary among intelligence services, neither the CIA nor MI6 revealed to the other the source of the intelligence it had received on this troubling Iraq-Niger yellowcake deal. So neither service knew that each had gotten its intelligence on Iraq's worrisome procurement of uranium in Africa from the same poisoned tree—a questionable, hustling, down-on-his-luck, shadowy operator who had hooked up with a conniving Italian clerk turned forger. From this point, their con job would take on a life of its own.

The first sketchy report on the Iraq-Niger uranium sale was cabled by SISMI to the CIA's operations directorate on October 15, 2001. Initially, American intelligence analysts were not impressed by the report. CIA, Energy Department, and DIA analysts all considered the allegation "possible," though short on details. The State Department's INR thought such a deal was unlikely because a French consortium tightly controlled Niger's uranium industry. Still, the CIA put out a Senior Executive Intelligence Brief stating that according to an unidentified foreign intelligence service, Niger as of early that year "planned to send several tons of uranium to Iraq" under a deal signed the year before. But there was "no corroboration," the CIA cautioned. A month later, on November 20, 2001, the U.S. ambassador in

---

*Years later, Martino, when talking to *La Repubblica,* claimed that "SISMI wanted me to pass the documents of the Niger dossier on to the allied intelligence, but at the same time they didn't want anyone to know of their involvement in the operation." Considering Martino's track record and the fact that he had given varying accounts to different news organizations, his credibility was open to question. SISMI denied this charge. Another fact that fueled speculation about SISMI's role was a visit by Nicolò Pollari, the SISMI director, to Washington on September 9, 2002, during which he met with Deputy National Security Adviser Stephen Hadley. This was two days before the NSC asked the CIA to approve proposed speech language for Bush using the Niger charge. An NSC spokesperson said that this had been a courtesy meeting and the issue of Niger had not come up.

Niger, Barbro Owens-Kirkpatrick, sent a cable to Washington from her embassy in Niamey. The head of the French-led consortium in Niger had assured her there was "no possibility" that Niger had diverted any of the approximately 3,000 tons of yellowcake produced annually in its two uranium mines.

That could have been the end of it, but in early February 2002, the CIA got what seemed to be fresh information from SISMI—a "verbatim" text of the supposed Iraq-Niger yellowcake agreement, showing that the deal was not for "several tons" as originally reported but for a staggering 500 tons. This was more alarming, and the report's specificity seemed to impress some intelligence analysts. The CIA's operations directorate assured agency analysts that the information had come from "a very credible source." But a State Department analyst strongly doubted the transaction—even more so because of its size. (Five hundred tons was about one sixth the total annual output of Niger's uranium mines, hardly a small, on-the-side diversion.) In any case, no one within the intelligence community bothered to ask the Italians to see an actual copy of the Iraq-Niger contract. Nevertheless, the DIA distributed a report, on February 12, 2002, with an unambiguous title: "Niamey signed an agreement to sell 500 tons of uranium a year to Baghdad."

The report landed on Dick Cheney's desk. The vice president was ever on the watch for any scrap of intelligence that would confirm his worst suspicions about Iraq's WMDs—especially its nuclear weapons program. And a revived Iraqi nuclear program would be the most powerful argument to justify the overthrow of Saddam. As soon as he read the DIA report on Niger, Cheney asked his daily morning briefer from the CIA to follow up. He wanted to know what the agency could tell him about the Niger matter.

The CIA snapped to. On learning of the vice president's interest, WINPAC—the agency's analytical shop dealing with unconventional weapons—immediately circulated a memo cautioning that the report lacked "crucial details" and that the U.S. Embassy in Niger had obtained information undermining the allegation. At the same time, though, WINPAC sent word to the DO's Counterproliferation Division that the vice president had been intrigued by the Niger report. This was a big deal, recalled a CPD official: "A call from the vice president's office makes you feel important. The young staffer who took this call was practically shaking with excitement."

In response to the query from Cheney's office, the Counterproliferation Division began considering how it could unearth more details about the purported uranium deal that had caught Cheney's attention. Fortunately—or so it seemed at the time—the operations chief of the division's Joint Task Force on Iraq, Valerie Wilson, was married to a former U.S. ambassador who was something of an expert on African uranium. The CPD could turn to him for help.

Joseph Wilson IV was no quiet diplomat. He was brash and confident, smooth but blunt, with a flair for the dramatic and a fondness for cigars. He came from an old California family of well-established Republicans (one governor, one congressman); his parents were expatriate journalists and authors, who dragged Wilson and his brother across Europe in his teenage years. Wilson graduated from the University of California at Santa Barbara in 1971; he escaped the Vietnam draft when the Nixon administration temporarily suspended it. He became a carpenter—and a ski and surf bum. He married the first of what would be three wives (Valerie was the third), and in 1975 he passed the Foreign Service examination and was offered a job at the State Department. Citing his knowledge of French, he suggested a posting in France. Instead, his rookie assignment was to the former French colony of Niger.

Wilson first garnered headlines for defying Saddam Hussein during the run-up to the first Persian Gulf War. At the time, Wilson was deputy chief of mission in the Baghdad embassy (and acting ambassador), and he engaged in a months-long standoff with Saddam Hussein that produced one notable stunt. The Iraqis were demanding that the U.S. Embassy force American citizens who had taken refuge at the U.S. ambassador's residence to register at an Iraqi government office. Failure to comply was punishable by death. With 125 Americans already held hostage by the Iraqi government, Wilson refused to turn over the 40 Americans under his protection, and he appeared at an off-the-record press conference wearing a hangman's noose. If Saddam "wants to execute me for keeping Americans from being taken hostage, I will bring my own fucking rope," he told the journalists, one of whom reported the event. Wilson's tenure in Baghdad and his efforts to protect the hostages won him praise from President George H. W. Bush. He received kind words from conservative newspaper columnists Rowland Evans and Robert Novak. Wilson, they wrote in a 1990 column, "shows the stuff of heroism."

But it wasn't Wilson's past heroic deeds that interested the officers of the CIA's Counterproliferation Division in the winter of 2002. When Wilson was a junior diplomatic officer in Niger in the 1970s, the U.S. Embassy was tracking the growth of Niger's uranium industry. As ambassador to Gabon, another uranium-producing African nation, in the mid-1990s, he had again paid attention to the uranium business. And when Wilson was chief of the Africa desk at the National Security Council in 1997 and 1998, his portfolio included the continent's uranium trade, and he maintained frequent contact with Nigerien officials. Now retired from the government and pursuing a career in international finance, Wilson was probably as familiar with both the Niger government and the uranium business as anyone in Washington.

There later would be a heated dispute over how much of a role Valerie Wilson played in CPD's decision to dispatch her husband to Niger. A Senate intelligence committee report would note that Valerie Wilson "suggested his name for the trip" and pointed to a memo she had written stating that her husband had "good relations with both the PM [prime minister] and the former Minister of Mines." Wilson would insist his wife had merely been "the conduit" for a message from a colleague in her office asking if he would be willing to come by and talk about Niger's uranium industry. Valerie Wilson would tell friends that she had written an e-mail—not a memo—to the Counterproliferation Division's deputy chief explaining her husband's qualifications only after a CPD officer had approached her and asked if her husband might be willing to help out the agency. (The CIA had no officers in Niger.)

The CPD officer knew that Joe Wilson had done this sort of work before. In 1999, after Valerie Wilson mentioned to her supervisors that her husband was planning a business trip to Niger, the CPD asked if Wilson would be willing, while he was in Niger, to ask his contacts there about A. Q. Khan, the Pakistani nuclear scientist who was running a secret international proliferation network. The CIA had picked up intelligence indicating a possible Niger connection involving Khan. Wilson agreed to do so but returned with no fresh information on the subject. When Valerie Wilson's colleague inquired in 2002 if Wilson could help on the latest Niger matter, this mother of two-year-old twins was not especially eager to have her husband trek to Niger (for no pay). Just see if he'll come in to talk to us, her fellow CPD officer asked. Valerie Wilson would later tell a friend, "My supervisor said, 'Why don't we set up a meeting and have Joe come in?' My job was to go home and say, 'Honey, will you come into the office next week?' "

On February 19, 2002, Joseph Wilson made the ten-minute drive from the Wilsons' Washington town house across the Potomac to Langley to discuss Niger and uranium with assorted analysts. Valerie met him at the front entrance of CIA headquarters and escorted him to a basement meeting room. People were filing in when Wilson arrived, and, he later recalled, he asked his wife, "Why don't you stay?" According to Wilson, she said, "No, this is not my thing. I have my own work to do." Later—once this session had become a matter of controversy—Valerie Wilson told friends that she had merely introduced her husband to the assembled analysts and officers and then left.

But Douglas Rohn, an INR Africa analyst who attended the meeting, afterward wrote what would become a fateful memo that noted that the session was "apparently convened" by Valerie Wilson. His one-page report made it seem as if she indeed had been responsible for the meeting—and for the mission that would follow. But years later, Rohn said that he had arrived after it had started and "really didn't understand who had done the organization work for the meeting." He explained that he had used the word "apparently" in his memo because he hadn't been sure who had actually initiated the gathering. Valerie Wilson was not there when he entered. "I have never met her," he said. Rohn, who wrote the only known account of the meeting, acknowledged that his memo may have created a misimpression about Valerie Wilson's involvement.

In the meeting, Joe Wilson was told that a report of a uranium sale from Niger to Iraq had caught Cheney's eye. He shared with the CIA officers present what he knew of the uranium industry in Niger and the Nigerien officials who would have been in power at the time of the supposed Niger-Iraq agreement. He told them that the former minister of mines, who was overseeing the uranium business during the alleged sale, was a friend of his. Wilson was skeptical of the report, especially given its vague sourcing. Rohn, the INR analyst, was more dismissive.

Rohn was a career foreign service officer, who, like Wilson, had spent years serving in Africa, including one stint, in the 1990s, as deputy chief of mission in Niger. And, according to his memo, he pointed out that a 500-ton deal meant that "twice a year 25 semi tractor trailer loads of yellow cake would have to be driven down roads where one seldom sees even a bush taxi.

In other words, it would be very hard to hide such a shipment." And temperatures of up to 130 degrees Fahrenheit, drifting sands, and wear and tear on the vehicles would make such a trip "difficult in the extreme." Rohn added that "the French appear to have control of the entire mining, milling and transportation process and would seem to have little interest in selling uranium to the Iraqis." He "gently" noted that the U.S. Embassy in Niamey had good contacts with the government and that Ambassador Owens-Kirkpatrick was a "confidante" of the country's president. He also "a little less gently" made the point that the U.S. Embassy in Niger was a "reliable interlocutor and could be trusted to protect U.S. interests." Rohn was saying that there was no need for the CIA to send Wilson. The U.S. Embassy in Niamey and the State Department had the situation covered.

At the end of the meeting, Wilson was asked if he might be willing to travel to Niger and check out the yellowcake allegation. Given Rohn's objections and Wilson's own skepticism, why would the CPD even bother? The best explanation was Cheney—that is, the division was eager to do whatever it could in response to a request from the vice president. Wilson told the CIA officers he was game. But according to his own later account, he reminded them he was hardly a low-profile guy, especially in Africa.

Shortly after the meeting, the CPD officially requested that Wilson make the trip for the agency. Wilson agreed to go on a pro bono basis with the CIA covering his expenses. He was granted an "operational" security clearance, up to the "secret" level. He was not asked to sign a confidentiality agreement. He set off for Niamey in late February. One CIA official later recalled thinking how pathetic it was that the agency, which had shut down many of its African stations in the 1990s, had no sources of its own in Niger and that it had to turn to a retired diplomat—who would end up talking to the same sort of people the ambassador had already contacted. "What's this going to get us?" the agency official remembered thinking at the time.

It took Wilson five days to reach Niamey. (Two days before he arrived, the president of Niger had told Ambassador Owens-Kirkpatrick and the visiting General Carlton Fulford, the deputy commander of the U.S. European Command, that his goal was to keep Niger's uranium "in safe hands.") Once in Niger, Wilson met with Owens-Kirkpatrick, and she asked him to talk only to former Nigerien officials and private-sector officials, not any current government officials. The ambassador didn't want any CIA emissary mucking around on her turf.

Wilson went about talking to his contacts: former officials, Nigerien businesspeople, European expatriates, international aid workers. He confirmed what he already knew: the uranium consortium was strictly regulated and most of the uranium produced was for use in the nuclear energy plants of the countries represented by the French-led consortium. The yellowcake from Niger was not sold on the open market. It was mined in amounts determined by the needs of the consortium members. A significant boost in production to cover the 500 tons mentioned in the supposed Niger-Iraq deal would have been, Wilson subsequently noted, "absolutely impossible to hide."

And any such sale would have required multiple levels of approval from the Nigerien bureaucracy going all the way up to the prime minister. A secret sale, Wilson saw, would have been difficult, too, for it would have required the movement of thousands of barrels. Former Prime Minister Ibrahim Mayaki, who had led the nation from 1997 to 1999 (shortly before the deal was supposedly signed) told Wilson that he knew of no such accord between Niger and Iraq. Mayaki, however, did say that at an Organization of African Unity meeting in 1999 a Nigerien businessman had approached him and asked him to talk to an Iraqi delegation about expanding trade between the two nations. Mayaki interpreted this to mean the delegation might be interested in discussing uranium sales. Mayaki told Wilson that he had met briefly with a member of the Iraqi delegation. But, aware of the UN sanctions on Iraq, Mayaki insisted he had avoided any substantive conversation.* After eight days in Niger, Wilson concluded there was nothing to support the charge that Iraq had either sought or obtained the yellowcake.

While Wilson was in Niger, the State Department's INR produced a report, drafted by Rohn, entitled, "Niger: Sale of Uranium to Iraq Is Unlikely." It spelled out the multiple reasons to doubt the deal, including the fact that Niger was heavily dependent on foreign aid and would not risk jeopardizing its good relations with Washington by permitting such a transaction. "A payoff from Iraq of $50 million or even $100 million would not make up for what would be lost if the donor community turned off the taps

---

*In his book, *The Politics of Truth*, Wilson noted he had spoken to Mayaki again in early 2004, and the former prime minister told Wilson he now recalled the identity of the Iraqi with whom he had met at the OAU meeting: Mohammed Saeed al-Sahaf, also known as "Baghdad Bob," Saddam's reality-denying information minister at the time of the U.S. invasion. While watching television before the invasion, Mayaki had recognized al-Sahaf.

to Niger," Rohn wrote. The INR called the original intelligence a "report of questionable credibility." Its paper was sent to the White House Situation Room and to various embassies in Africa and around the world. A summation of this report was forwarded to Deputy Secretary of State Richard Armitage.

But Cheney hadn't forgotten about the first intriguing DIA report of a Niger-Iraq deal. In early March, he asked his morning CIA briefer a second time about the Niger uranium matter. In response, WINPAC sent an update to Cheney's briefer, noting that the Niger government had said it was doing everything possible to guarantee that its uranium wasn't heading toward any nuclear weapons programs. WINPAC's update reported that the Italian service "was unable to provide new information, but continues to assess that its source is reliable." WINPAC also told Cheney's briefer that the CIA would soon "be debriefing a source who may have information related to the alleged sale"—a reference to Joseph Wilson.

On March 5, two CIA officers debriefed Wilson at his home; Valerie Wilson didn't take part in the session. The former ambassador summarized his discussions with the ex–Nigerien leaders and explained his view that a uranium deal of this kind would be nearly impossible to pull off. One of the CIA officers wrote up a report and sent it to a colleague, who (as often happens in the intelligence community) rewrote the report. The rewritten report was then disseminated within the intelligence community. DO officials made sure to tell WINPAC analysts about the report because they knew, as a Senate intelligence report later noted, "the high priority of the issue." The report noted Wilson's judgment that it was unlikely such a uranium sale could have taken place. But it also included what Wilson had heard from Mayaki, the former prime minister, about the 1999 overture from an Iraqi delegation looking to talk about reestablishing commercial relations.

CIA analysts, according to a report of the Senate intelligence committee, considered Wilson's information nothing startling. They hadn't expected the Nigeriens to acknowledge such a deal had been signed. Moreover, the analysts focused on the part about an Iraqi representative having sounded out the Nigerien prime minister about expanded commercial relations in 1999. They thought this could be indirect confirmation of the Italian reporting—even though the Italian report had said the uranium transaction was a done deal. The CIA didn't brief Cheney on Wilson's trip.

Wilson assumed his report would be conveyed to Cheney. After all, it was Cheney who had asked the question that had led to Wilson's trip. But about this time, Cheney took off for an important trip to the Middle East to line up regional support for a confrontation with Saddam. Having heard nothing definitive from the agency, he seemingly lost interest in—or simply forgot about—the Niger deal. After the debriefing at his house, Wilson would have no more official contact with the CIA for a year and a half.

AT SOME point, Rocco Martino, who was trying to sell his hot (and bogus) documents on the Iraq-Niger uranium transaction, approached his contacts at the DGSE, the French intelligence service. Martino had previously attempted to peddle to the French information apparently obtained from SISMI on matters related to Bosnia and Kosovo. It was information the French service had already received directly from SISMI via official channels (for free). So when Martino came knocking with papers on a secret Niger-Iraq yellowcake agreement, French intelligence was skeptical—and a bit worried. Niger was a former French colony, and a French corporation led the international consortium that managed Niger's tightly controlled uranium industry. If the documents were authentic, French executives would be implicated in a massive illicit scheme. DGSE officials even wondered if someone was trying to set France up.

Martino wanted "a lot of money" for the material, recalled Alain Chouet, a deputy director of the French intelligence service. The going price for this sort of freelance intelligence was about $100,000. But the DGSE talked Martino down, paid him a small amount for a sample, and then quickly concluded the documents were phony. It was "no deal," Chouet said. "We dropped the whole thing."

Back at the CIA, the grounds for disbelieving the Italian report grew stronger—or should have—partly because of the DGSE. That summer, the French service received a request from the CIA for any information it could provide about a possible uranium deal between Iraq and Niger. The DGSE had already sent Martino packing, according to Chouet, but to reassure the Americans, the DGSE dispatched a team to Niger to determine if there had been any diversion to Iraq of uranium from the French-controlled mines. The team's report was conclusive: there was nothing to the allegation. "Our answer was that the information was not reliable at all and probably based on faked intelligence," Chouet subsequently said. DGSE officials considered the case closed. So, too, did Bill Murray, the CIA station chief in Paris. He had been sending report after report to Langley dismissing the whole idea. He finally wrote one frustrating cable that asked, "Do you want me to send a weekly report that the Eiffel Tower is still standing as well?"

BUT the White House kept pushing. Barely two weeks after the CIA had blocked the Niger claim from being inserted into Bush's UN speech, White House aides looking to fortify the Iraq nuclear case got a boost from the United Kingdom. On September 24, 2002, Tony Blair's government, in a major media event, released its own white paper on Iraq and WMDs. The document claimed that Blair's government possessed "significant" information on Iraq's WMDs obtained from "secret intelligence sources." This "secret intelligence" supposedly showed that Saddam was making progress in his WMD programs and that he was "ready to use" WMDs. Specifically, the paper said that Saddam was producing chemical and biological weapons; that he was developing mobile biological weapons labs; and that he possessed biological and chemical weapons that were "deployable within 45 minutes." The intelligence on the forty-five-minute claim was so iffy that the CIA had rejected it; Tenet privately referred to it as "shit." But it had the desired effect. "BRITs 45 Mins from Doom," screamed the headline in one London tabloid, which ran an article suggesting that British bases in Cyprus could be blown away by Saddam's WMDs at any time.

The white paper tracked with the White House's key allegations: Saddam had covertly sought equipment for a nuclear weapons program (a reference to the aluminum tubes);* he was developing long-range missiles that could carry WMDs; he had tried to turn a jet trainer into an unmanned aerial vehicle (UAV) that could carry chemical and biological weapons a long distance. But the British also declared that Saddam had "sought significant quantities of uranium from Africa."

The White House, which had just been warned off the same claim by the CIA, now jumped on this new uranium-shopping-in-Africa charge. At his daily White House press briefing, press secretary Ari Fleischer was asked

---

*The British report did note that there was no "definitive intelligence" indicating that the 60,000 aluminum tubes sought by Iraq were destined for a nuclear weapons program and that the British Joint Intelligence Committee "judged that while sanctions remain effective Iraq would not be able to produce a nuclear weapon."

if the British paper contained anything new and noteworthy. He pointed to two conclusions: that Saddam had unconventional weapons that could be launched within forty-five minutes and that he had been seeking to procure uranium in Africa. "That was new information," Fleischer said, adding, "We agree with their findings."

Following the release of the British white paper, Bush ratcheted up the rhetoric. "Each passing day could be the one on which the Iraqi regime gives anthrax or VX—nerve gas—or someday a nuclear weapon to a terrorist ally," he declared at a White House ceremony on September 26. Two days later, in his weekly radio address, Bush said that Saddam "could launch a biological or chemical attack in as little as forty-five minutes" (despite the CIA's rejection of this dramatic charge). He reported that he had spoken with both Democratic and Republican members of Congress and that "we are united in our determination to confront this urgent threat to America." He said that an agreement was near regarding the congressional resolution he was seeking from Congress. Indeed, the day the British white paper came out, Daschle had said, "Republicans and Democrats are prepared to give the benefit of the doubt under these circumstances to the administration."

The Niger charge was now fully in play—and would soon take on a significance that George W. Bush, Dick Cheney, Joe Wilson, and Rocco Martino could never have imagined.

Are you sure Elvis wasn't there also?

—9/11 COMMISSION INVESTIGATOR

6

The Secret Diggers

O N SEPTEMBER 16, 2002, a pair of dogged Pentagon researchers arrived at the White House to deliver an unusual briefing. The audience was high level: Scooter Libby, Cheney's chief of staff, and Stephen Hadley, the deputy national security adviser. The researchers were from a small unit, dubbed the "Iraqi intelligence cell," that had been created by Undersecretary of Defense Douglas Feith, Rumsfeld's loyal policy chief. They had spent months combing through raw intelligence reports and uncovering patterns that they believed had eluded the rest of the U.S. intelligence community. And they had turned all these data into a classified slide show designed to make one large point: Saddam Hussein's regime had a far more extensive relationship with Osama bin Laden and al-Qaeda than the CIA had acknowledged. There had been, one of their slides asserted, nearly two dozen "high level contacts" between Iraqi officials and al-Qaeda operatives dating back more than a decade. Another slide claimed that there had been "multiple areas of cooperation." And the Feith team reported that Saddam's intelligence service had played a "facilitation" role in the September 11 attacks. An Iraqi intelligence agent, the briefing said, had ordered that funds be disbursed to one of the hijackers. If that was not a reason for war, what would be?

The most important part of their case was a supposed meeting between

Mohamed Atta, the lead 9/11 hijacker, and an Iraqi intelligence agent in Prague in April 2001. This allegation was not new. It had been examined and dissected for nearly a year, both within the U.S. intelligence community and by the media. William Safire, the conservative *New York Times* columnist, had written about it frequently, calling the Prague meeting an "undisputed fact." Laurie Mylroie and James Woolsey had also cited it. Dick Cheney—when asked whether Saddam was connected to 9/11—had referred to the meeting repeatedly. "It's been pretty well confirmed that [Atta] did go to Prague and he did meet with a senior official of the Iraqi intelligence service," he insisted during a December 9, 2001, appearance on *Meet the Press*. And eight days before the Feith team's briefing for Libby and Hadley, Cheney had raised it again on *Meet the Press,* the same show on which he had touted the aluminum tubes.

"We have reporting that places him [Atta] in Prague with a senior Iraq intelligence official a few months before the attack on the World Trade Center," Cheney told Tim Russert.

"What does the CIA say about that?" Russert asked. "Is it credible?"

"It's credible," the vice president replied. "But you know, I think a way to put it would be it's unconfirmed at this point."

But Cheney had been disingenuous. The CIA and the FBI had already concluded that the meeting had probably never taken place. Yet that hadn't stopped Feith's briefers from presenting the Atta charge to Libby and Hadley as if it had been fully confirmed. One of their slides declared—as fact—that Atta had visited the Iraqi intelligence service office in Prague "at least twice" (in June 2000 and again in 2001, on April 8 and 9) and met with Ahmed Khalil Ibrahim Samir al-Ani, the Iraqi intelligence chief of station. Atta, according to the slide, had also "reportedly met" with the Iraqi chargé d'affaires in Prague, and al-Ani had ordered the Iraqi intelligence "finance officer" in Prague to issue funds to Atta. Finally, the slide stated, several workers at the Prague airport had identified Atta after September 11 and "remember him traveling with his brother Farhan Atta."

The Feith team could not say what Atta and Ani had discussed—had they met. There were no eyewitness accounts or tape recordings. There was no telling if the supposed meeting had been about 9/11. Still, the idea that Atta might have secretly rendezvoused with Iraqi intelligence was explosive—and much easier to comprehend than Laurie Mylroie's convoluted hypothesis about there being two Ramzi Yousefs.

Feith's slide show, especially the Atta portion, was a hit at the White House. The following day, a Feith aide reported to Wolfowitz that "the briefing went very well and generated further interest from Mr. Hadley and Mr. Libby." Hadley and Libby, the aide said, had requested more information, including a "chronology of Atta's travels."

But Feith's slide show left out plenty of information—such as all the material that had been dug up by the FBI and the CIA about the Atta-in-Prague allegation. After thorough investigations, agency and bureau officials doubted that Atta had even been in Prague at the time of the alleged meeting. There was not a scrap of reliable evidence that any Iraqi "finance officer" had passed money to Atta. And Atta, the son of an Egyptian attorney, could not have been spotted at the Prague airport with his brother. In fact, he had no brother.* As one 9/11 Commission investigator later commented about the Feith team's slide show, "Are you sure Elvis wasn't there also?"

FEITH's exploitation of the Atta-in-Prague allegation was a case of true believers twisting skimpy intelligence reports to create illusions of proof.

In the chaotic days after September 11, the CIA put out an urgent all-points bulletin to allied intelligence services, asking for whatever information they had that could shed any light (no matter how faint) on the hijackings. Czech intelligence, as it happened, received an intriguing report from an informant inside the Middle Eastern community. The informant said he had seen Atta's pictures in the paper and thought he had spotted the same man five months earlier with al-Ani outside the Iraqi Embassy. The Czech service passed along its informant's claim to the CIA. The Czechs also soon forwarded a surveillance photo taken outside the Iraqi Embassy that day that showed an unidentified Middle Eastern–looking man, who, they suggested, might have been the 9/11 hijacker.

"We knew right away that's not Atta," said one U.S. counterterrorism

---

*Two days after 9/11, FBI agents in Cairo sent in a report noting that Atta had two sisters and mentioning no male siblings. Later, Terry McDermott, a *Los Angeles Times* reporter, traveled to Cairo and met with Atta's father, mother, and sisters for research on his book, *Perfect Soldiers: The Hijackers, Who They Were, Why They Did It.* McDermott inspected all available public records, including birth certificates of members of Atta's family. "There are many things I'm not sure of, but one thing I am," McDermott told the authors in May 2006. "There's no brother."

official who examined the photo when it arrived at Langley. "The guy [in the photo] was bigger—a broad-shouldered guy in a leather jacket. He looked sort of like an Albanian thug. Atta was a little scrawny guy. There's no way it was Atta." The FBI and CIA technical labs analyzed the photo. They enlarged the image, scrutinized it, and compared it to all available shots of Atta. These labs tended not to issue definitive judgments. So they did not conclusively rule out the possibility that the unidentified fellow in the picture was Atta. Yet both the bureau and the agency's photo analysts reported that this person was *probably* not the 9/11 hijacker. Still, the slight wiggle room in their conclusion allowed Atta-in-Prague proponents—including those in the vice president's office and the Pentagon—to hang on to this uncorroborated single-source claim.

The FBI dug deeper. Agents reviewing Atta's travel records saw that he had left the United States twice in 2001: in January, to confer with Ramzi Binalshibh, his terrorist accomplice in Germany, and in July, to meet Binalshibh in Spain. On both occasions, Atta traveled under his own name with his own passport. The bureau couldn't find evidence that he had ever used an alias or that he had left the United States anytime in April, when the supposed Prague meeting occurred. On April 4, 2001, five days before his alleged rendezvous with al-Ani, Atta had been photographed by a surveillance camera cashing an $8,000 check at a bank in Virginia Beach, Virginia. On April 11, Atta and another of the September 11 hijackers, Marwan al-Shehhi, had leased an apartment in Coral Springs, Florida. In between—on April 6, 9, 10, and 11—Atta's cell phone was repeatedly used to make phone calls in Florida.

There was not one substantiated fact that indicated Atta had been in Prague on April 9—or anytime in 2001. "We looked at this real hard because, obviously, if it were true, it would be huge," one senior U.S. law enforcement official told *Newsweek* at the end of April 2002. "But nothing has matched up."

Wolfowitz, though, refused to let go of the Atta-in-Prague charge. In the summer of 2002, he summoned to his office Pasquale D'Amuro, the chief of FBI counterterrorism, and a senior agent to grill both about the Atta photograph and the Prague story. Questioning the pair intensely, he forced the FBI officials to admit that the FBI couldn't account for Atta's precise whereabouts every day of the week of the purported Prague meeting. So, Wolfowitz persisted, wasn't it theoretically possible that Atta had hastily flown out of the United States under an alias, had a short visit with al-Ani in Prague, and then quickly returned to America to continue his 9/11 plotting? Yes, it was "possible"—anything was "possible"—the FBI officials told the deputy defense secretary, according to a law enforcement colleague of theirs. That was all Wolfowitz and his allies inside Feith's shop needed. If it was possible, it was believable.

The White House would never officially embrace the Atta-in-Prague charge. Yet Cheney and others would continue to refer to the unconfirmed meeting as a reason to suspect that Saddam had been connected to 9/11. CIA officers and FBI agents, however, would roll their eyes whenever they heard an administration official cite the Atta–al-Ani meeting. None, though, would challenge the policy makers. "Who is going to question the vice president when he keeps espousing this shit?" asked the U.S. counterterrorism official who investigated the Atta issue. "Nobody at the FBI or CIA is going to speak up and say, stop the bullshit."*

THE Atta-in-Prague story lived on—at least in the minds of Cheney, Libby, and senior Pentagon officials.

Other parts of Feith's slide show were equally dubious. One slide referred to the fact that Abdul Rahman Yasin, a conspirator in the 1993 World Trade Center bombing, had fled to Iraq after that attack. It asserted (à la Laurie Mylroie) that this was evidence of Iraqi "facilitation" of that attack. Another slide displayed the story of Ahmad Hikmat Shakir, an Iraqi national who worked as an airport greeter in Kuala Lampur and had escorted two 9/11 hijackers in January 2000 when they arrived for a key al-Qaeda planning session in the Malaysian capital. Shakir had drawn the attention of U.S. intelligence officials. Wolfowitz was immersed in the details of the case. But CIA officials could find no connection between Shakir and the Iraqi regime.

---

*The 9/11 Commission later reported that Czech officials reviewed flight and border records and surveillance photos from the area near the Iraqi Embassy and found no evidence that Atta had been in Prague on April 9. The Czech government also reported that al-Ani had been away from Prague on the morning of April 9, when the meeting allegedly happened. The commission's report noted that Atta was an unlikely partner for Iraqi intelligence. It said that Binalshibh, who was captured in 2002, had told his interrogators that bin Laden was upset with Saddam for committing atrocities against Iraqi Muslims and would never have approved of a meeting between Atta and al-Ani. The commission concluded, "The available evidence does not support the original Czech report of an Atta–al-Ani meeting."

He was an Iraqi national, but al-Qaeda members and collaborators came from virtually every country in the Middle East. Fifteen of the nineteen September 11 hijackers were from Saudi Arabia. The citizenship of the hijackers and their accomplices was hardly evidence of government complicity in the attacks.

One key Baghdad–bin Laden "contact" in the Feith briefing involved an alleged July 1996 meeting between the director of Iraqi intelligence, Mani abd-al-Rashid al-Tikriti, and Osama bin Laden on the al-Qaeda leader's farm in Sudan. But there was a problem with this report: bin Laden had left Sudan for Afghanistan nearly two months earlier. His departure from the country had been no secret. By early July 1996, the British journalist Robert Fisk had reported interviewing bin Laden in a "remote and desolate mountainous area" of Afghanistan.*

Conventional evidentiary niceties didn't matter to Feith's crew. They eschewed a business-as-usual approach to intelligence analysis and pointed that out in the first of the slides they showed Libby and Hadley. That slide insisted that there were "fundamental problems" in the way the intelligence community had been assessing information about the shadowy world of international terrorism. The CIA, Feith's underlings claimed, was wedded to the thesis that secularist Baathists like Saddam wouldn't cooperate with fanatical Islamists like bin Laden. If you started with such a view, Feith's analysts argued, it was easy to dismiss or neglect evidence that was out of sync with that conformist perspective. But if you adopted an alternative view— that Iraq and al-Qaeda were actually cooperating—the available evidence looked different. Feith's team posited, as one slide noted, that al-Qaeda and Baghdad had developed a "mature" relationship and were able to conceal their alliance. There was no "juridical evidence" to verify the al-Qaeda–Iraq connection, the Feith team argued, because both parties to the devious pact had hidden the ties well. Wisps and crumbs were the best one could expect.

The Feith analysts were essentially claiming that because al-Qaeda and Iraq had joined together in a clandestine partnership to attack the United States, there would be little, if any, evidence to prove the conspiracy. "When

---

*Where did the Feith team get the idea that bin Laden was meeting on a farm in Sudan when he was actually thousands of miles away in Afghanistan? The information, the 9/11 Commission later found, had originated with a "third hand" report from a foreign intelligence service. This service had obtained the information through two unidentified intermediaries. Officers of this service had never spoken to or met with the original source.

operational security is very good," the opening slide in the Feith team's briefing read, "absence of evidence is not evidence of absence." That certainly was a contention that could not be disproved.

THE "absence of evidence" line—not coincidentally—was a mantra for Donald Rumsfeld. Imperious and cocksure, Rumsfeld had come into office with a deep-seated distrust of the U.S. intelligence community. Like Cheney, the secretary's old friend and former deputy, Rumsfeld, as well as Wolfowitz and Feith, were convinced the CIA was blind to the hidden threats the country was facing. This distrust dated to Cold War days, when Rumsfeld and other hard-liners (like Richard Perle and Wolfowitz) suspected the agency was underestimating the Soviet threat. The skepticism didn't dissipate with the fall of the Berlin Wall. In 1998, Rumsfeld chaired a national commission on missile defense and concluded that the CIA was insufficiently attuned to the possibilities that a rogue state might lob a missile at an American city. Rumsfeld's view was that the CIA was frequently too rigid or too timid—or maybe both.

In the summer of 2001, Rumsfeld called a group of influential Washington lobbyists and consultants, including Haley Barbour and Vin Weber, into his office. It was an odd meeting. What insights, wondered one participant, could lobbyists offer Rumsfeld about the national security issues on his plate? As it turned out, Rumsfeld used the occasion to rail at the CIA. "He kept talking about how what he was getting from the CIA was out of date and wasn't any good," recalled one attendee. On the wall of Rumsfeld's conference room was a huge map of the world, with the states possessing nuclear bombs and weapons of mass destruction highlighted. Rumsfeld had a solution for his dilemma. "I'm going to create my own intelligence agency," he told the group.*

---

*CIA officer John Maguire got a glimpse of Rumsfeld's view of the agency when he was briefing the secretary and others in Rumsfeld's office suite. In the middle of the briefing, Rumsfeld suddenly got up, went to his desk, and started working—without saying a word. Assuming the briefing was over, Maguire quietly left the office. But General Richard Myers, chairman of the Joint Chiefs of Staff, chased after him and tried to apologize. "Sometimes the secretary can be abrupt," Myers explained. Maguire replied, "You're the highest-ranking military officer in the country. You don't have to apologize to me." For Maguire, the incident reflected what Rumsfeld thought of the CIA: "He had no use for us."

Rumsfeld already had one, the Defense Intelligence Agency. But the DIA was part of the overall intelligence community headed by George Tenet, who was constantly jockeying with Rumsfeld for control of the intelligence budget. Perhaps worse for Rumsfeld, the DIA consisted mostly of career intelligence professionals committed to policy-neutral analysis. But Rumsfeld and his deputies in the Pentagon desired creative, out-of-the-box thinking that challenged the established orthodoxies. They wanted to begin with new paradigms (which just happened to reflect their policy preferences and inclinations) and then work backward to see if there might be evidence to support these theses. This was the opposite of how intelligence analysis traditionally operated: start with the available evidence (as fragmentary and contradictory as it might be) and build upward. While there was an undeniable logic to Rumsfeld's absence-of-evidence axiom, it could also lead policy makers astray—perhaps into believing what they wanted to believe, regardless of evidence or the absence of evidence. As Hans Blix, the chief UN weapons inspector, would later observe, the absence of evidence was not evidence of concealment either. It wasn't evidence of anything—other than, by definition, ignorance.

After the 9/11 attack, the Pentagon put Rumsfeld's mantra into practice. The CIA and FBI immediately suspected bin Laden, and within hours, they had gathered evidence directly linking al-Qaeda to the mass murder. Two of the hijackers, Khalid al-Midhar and Nawaf al-Hazmi, had been known to the U.S. intelligence community as bin Laden men.* But at the Pentagon, Rumsfeld, Wolfowitz, and Feith had different presumptions. The attack, they suspected, couldn't have been pulled off by a bunch of ragtag terrorists in Afghanistan plotting on their own. It had to have what terrorism experts called a "state sponsor"—and the most likely culprit was Iraq. Wolfowitz decried the CIA for lacking the imagination to explore the hidden truth of the attacks. But if the CIA was unable to see what needed to be seen, the Pentagon had options of its own.

---

*In early 2000, the CIA obtained intelligence indicating that these two suspected terrorists may have entered the United States. But it did not place them on the State Department's terrorist watch list and did not share this information with the FBI. The bureau did not learn about the two men's possible presence in the country until August 2001. The FBI then initiated a perfunctory search for the pair—a search that was still under way on September 11. Had the CIA passed along the information earlier, U.S. officials might have been able to locate these two would-be hijackers, who had been residing in San Diego under their real names. One had even been listed in the phone book.

Within weeks, the Pentagon leadership created a new, secret intelligence unit that would dig out the connections that the CIA had missed. The man in charge of this top-priority mission, Douglas Feith, was perhaps the most ideologically dogmatic and controversial of the neoconservatives in the new administration. A graduate of Harvard and Georgetown Law School, Feith had served on the National Security Council under Ronald Reagan and later moved to the Pentagon as an assistant to Perle. A fierce anti-Communist, Feith was also known for his unyielding stand on the Israeli-Palestinian dispute. His father, a Holocaust survivor and wealthy philanthropist, had been an activist in the Betar organization, the revisionist Zionist youth group founded by the Polish firebrand Ze'ev Jabotinsky, who preached that Jews were entitled to the entire territory of the original Palestinian Mandate, including both the West and East Banks of the Jordan River. The father had passed along many of his views to his son. During the Clinton years, Feith had denounced the Oslo Peace Accords or any swap of "land for peace" with the Palestinians. His law partner, L. Marc Zell, represented West Bank settlement groups. Feith for a time did legal work for the Israeli Embassy in Washington. He was also a consultant for the 1996 "Clean Break" paper calling for the overthrow of Saddam, prepared for Israeli Prime Minister Netanyahu.

Feith had a habit of irritating his Bush administration colleagues by injecting ideology—and his views of contemporary history—into policy discussions. "All he did was spout rhetoric," said one senior NSC official, who came to despise Feith. "He would launch into these diatribes about neofascism. . . . He had no interest in problem solving." Feith's other mission seemed to be waging intramural bureaucratic warfare. At deputies meetings, this senior official said, Feith was bent on protecting Rumsfeld and the Pentagon's turf, not fashioning governmentwide policies. "I've talked to Secretary Rrrrumsfeld about this," Feith would say, rolling his *R*s, according to the official. "Secretary Rrrrumsfeld has strong views about this." At times, tensions between Feith and Undersecretary of State Marc Grossman—over matters relating to Ahmad Chalabi's INC—grew heated, so much so that Deputy National Security Adviser Stephen Hadley at one session had to order the room cleared, the official said.

To run his new intelligence unit, Feith turned to two like-minded allies. One was David Wurmser, the young neoconservative analyst from the American Enterprise Institute, who had advocated war with Iraq, coauthored the

"Clean Break" report, and once called Chalabi a "mentor." Another member of Feith's new team was an impish veteran Pentagon policy warrior named Michael Maloof. Like Wurmser, Maloof was a longtime Perle ally. In the late 1990s, as chief of a small Pentagon office that oversaw export controls, Maloof had infuriated National Security Agency chief Michael Hayden by launching an investigation of Hughes Electronics, a major NSA contractor, for selling satellite equipment to China. Hayden then pushed for an FBI investigation of Maloof for allegedly leaking classified information about the Hughes case to the news media. Maloof, who in his spare time conducted paramilitary "combat tracking" courses, relished this sort of interagency combat.

In 2001, Wurmser and Maloof set up shop in a small windowless office on the third floor of the Pentagon, down the hall from the War Room. The project was eventually given the title of Policy Counterterrorism Evaluation Group. They created giant wall charts detailing the "linkages" and "associations" among terror groups that the CIA and DIA had ignored or dismissed. To establish the case that Iraq lurked behind terror organizations around the globe, they sought raw, highly classified intelligence reports. When the intelligence agencies balked at sharing such sensitive (and often unreliable) reports, Wolfowitz fired off messages to the CIA and DIA demanding that the unfiltered reports start flowing to Wurmser and Maloof. The friction between Feith's investigators and the intelligence agencies escalated. "The CIA was apoplectic about the work we were doing," Maloof later said. "They were so pissed off." The DIA, with CIA backing, "refused to give us the information, they were stonewalling us." One day, a top aide to Admiral Thomas Wilson, the DIA chief, confronted Maloof in the hallways of the Pentagon. "We don't like you guys looking over our shoulder," the aide told Maloof. Maloof couldn't have cared less. (Wilson later said that the two men didn't have the necessary clearances and his agency wasn't about to bend the rules.)

Soon enough, Maloof and Wurmser gained enough access to begin filling out their charts. The charts, Maloof recalled, looked "like a spiderweb" with crisscrossing lines stretching from Baghdad to the remote border jungles of Paraguay. "Iraq trains Palestinian terrorists associated with PFLP, PIJ, Hamas, ANO, PLF, Ansar al-Islam *which has direct ties to Al Qaeda*," Maloof wrote in a memo entitled "Iraqi Intelligence Shifts Terror Training Location" (adding his own italicized emphasis). In a secret 150-page report, the Maloof-Wurmser team depicted the 9/11 attacks as a complex operation carried out by al-Qaeda—but assisted by the Hizbollah Shiites, financed by Saudi royals, and sponsored (if not directed) by the secular Baathists of Baghdad. "Saddam used al-Qaeda as an indirect conduit because he needed plausible deniability," Maloof would later say, echoing the Mylroiean view of the world.

Maloof and Wurmser's spiderwebs attracted attention from senior Bush officials. A foreign policy aide to Cheney, Samantha Ravich, came to their office and studied the charts, taking notes so she could report back to Scooter Libby. So, too, did Wolfowitz, who one day spent forty-five minutes closely examining the charts. The deputy defense secretary was especially taken with the spaghetti lines that Maloof had drawn between the Abu Nidal terrorist organization in Iraq and training camps in Lebanon. From Lebanon, the lines then crisscrossed back to al-Qaeda in Afghanistan. The precise nature of these linkages was misty and, in the views of some intelligence analysts, nonsensical. The Abu Nidal organization, once a feared organization in the world of terror, was by this point essentially defunct. Still, Wolfowitz was impressed. Here were links that not even Mylroie had considered. "Great work," Wolfowitz told the team, according to Maloof.

In search of actual evidence, Maloof sought input from one decidedly nonobjective source: Ahmad Chalabi's INC. Perle helped set Maloof up with a liaison at the INC: Nibras Kazimi, a young college graduate who was a public affairs officer and intelligence analyst in the INC's Washington office. Over the next few months, Kazimi fed the Feith unit claims about Saddam's terrorism connections from INC-handled defectors—assertions that soon found their way onto the wall charts.

Maloof and Wurmser did not stay with the mission long. Maloof's usefulness diminished in January 2002, when he was stripped of his security clearances. The nominal reason was his unauthorized contact with a woman whom he had met in Georgia, the former Soviet Union territory. (He later married her.) Then Wurmser went to work for John Bolton, the hard-line undersecretary of state for arms control and international security. With Wurmser gone and Maloof hindered, Feith brought in Chris Carney, a Pennsylvania State University associate professor of political science and naval reservist, and Tina Shelton, a DIA analyst.

Carney and Shelton continued the work of Maloof and Wurmser, sharing their most promising data with Rumsfeld and Wolfowitz. The team's efforts soon put them in a headlong clash with the CIA. In June 2002, in response to repeated prodding from the White House and the vice president's office, the CIA finished and circulated a classified report, "Iraq and al-Qaida: Interpreting a Murky Relationship." The report was described in a cover note as "purposely aggressive in seeking to draw connections." But analysts in the Near East and South Asia division of the agency's intelligence directorate were offended by the whole process. They saw the document as an abandonment of the agency's "traditional analytic approach" in which intelligence had to be confirmed "with multiple sources" and based on "strongly supported reporting," according to a later study by the Senate intelligence committee. The NESA analysts believed the report had inflated "sporadic, wary contacts" between two independent actors into a "relationship," albeit murky, that didn't really exist. There was even a confidential complaint filed over the document with the CIA's ombudsman for politicization, an office set up to guard against undue political pressures. The ombudsman interviewed twenty-four analysts and later told Senate investigators that "about a half a dozen [analysts] mentioned 'pressure' from the administration; several others did not use that word, but spoke in a context that implied it." But the CIA ombudsman concluded that nothing untoward had happened.

Still, the CIA's "Murky Relationship" report—an effort by the agency to push the envelope on the critical topic of Saddam's alleged ties to al-Qaeda—wasn't good enough for the Feith cell. Shelton, the DIA analyst assigned to the unit, wrote a memo noting the report

> provides evidence from numerous intelligence sources over a decade on the interactions between Iraq and al-Qaida. In this regard, the report is excellent. Then in its interpretation of this information, CIA attempts to discredit, dismiss, or downgrade much of this reporting, resulting in inconsistent conclusions in many instances. Therefore, the CIA report should be read for content only—and CIA's interpretation ought to be ignored.

The battle continued through the summer of 2002, as the Bush White House was preparing to move on Iraq. On August 15, the Feith team presented its slide show to George Tenet and other senior CIA officials. Tenet listened politely for about ten minutes and then walked out.* Five days later,

---

*Later Feith would claim that Tenet had told him that the session had been "very helpful." Other CIA officials would say that much of the material in the briefing had already been

the Feith analysts returned to Langley to discuss the draft of an updated version of the agency's Saddam–al-Qaeda report, renamed "Iraqi Support for Terrorism." The report drew a distinction between the "patron-client pattern between Iraq and its Palestinian surrogates" and the arm's-length relationship between Iraq and al-Qaeda, which "appears to more closely resemble that of two independent actors trying to exploit each other." The report also found "no credible information that Baghdad had foreknowledge of the 11 September attacks or any other al-Qaida strike." Once again, the Feith team complained. "We raised numerous objections," they wrote in a memo after the meeting. Among them was that the draft made "no reference to the key issue of Atta."

If the CIA wouldn't listen, Feith and his team knew where they would get a more sympathetic reception: the White House.

DAYS after his staffers presented their slide show at the White House to Libby and Hadley, Feith made the pitch himself. On a Saturday morning in September, Hadley had convened a meeting in the White House Situation Room to ensure that all the administration's witnesses who were about to testify before Congress—Powell, Tenet, Rumsfeld—were on the same page regarding Iraq. Although Hadley had called the meeting, it was soon taken over by Feith. When a CIA officer pointed out that the available intelligence didn't support an assertion that the administration was planning to make about Iraq's link to al-Qaeda, Feith launched into a lengthy tutorial about the connections alleged in his secret unit's slide show: the meeting in Sudan, Atta's visits to Prague, and the rest. As he went on, Feith grew impassioned and accusatory, according to two officials present. He got up out of his chair and practically stepped on the toes of the officials standing behind him in the crowded room. "I know you guys don't believe this," he said to the CIA officials. But the agency, he claimed was "not putting it together . . . , not connecting the dots," one of the participants recalled.

When a CIA official mentioned that members of Congress might be skeptical about some of his claims, Feith brushed him aside. "Well, if some congressman is going to nitpick about this, he's going to look really dumb,"

---

discounted and that Tenet had never incorporated the Feith information into his briefings to Congress.

one person at the meeting remembered Feith saying. Larry Wilkerson, Powell's chief of staff, was astounded by what he viewed as Feith's arrogance. Feith's attitude toward the CIA officials present, according to Wilkerson, was, "You're all just dumb shits, I'm the smartest guy in this room." Wilkerson couldn't believe that Hadley was letting Feith dominate the discussion. "Finally," Wilkerson recalled, "Steve said something to the effect of 'Well, you know, that's not really what we came here to discuss. We should get back on the agenda. Why don't you sit down?' "

Paul Pillar, the national intelligence officer in charge of the Near East, was also stunned by Feith's presentation. As he saw it, Feith was a "zealot" and the work of his Iraq intelligence cell was a fraud: "It was a deliberate effort to try to stitch things together to try to make a case. It had nothing to do with intelligence analysis as I understood it—which is ultimately to try to get at the truth."

Feith later said he had no recollection of this White House meeting. He insisted that unlike Wolfowitz he had not been "immersed" in the details of the al-Qaeda–Iraq issue. But he had no apologies for his efforts to challenge the CIA's analysis on terrorism. The agency, he maintained, was doing its own spinning. "They would say an intelligence report was unconfirmed if they didn't believe it, but they wouldn't say it was unconfirmed if it fit their theories," he said. "We had our theories. Other people had their theories." He was adamant that he and his researchers never distorted the intelligence: "I think of myself as a very careful person and an honest one."

Many of the unconfirmed details peddled by the secret diggers of Feith's backdoor shop—with the notable exception of the Atta-in-Prague allegation—would not be shared with the public. His team was cooking up material on the Saddam–al-Qaeda connection for consumption within the national security community—to reinforce the case for war among the policy makers. But in the days to come, the White House would seize on yet another loose strand of intelligence in the agency's al-Qaeda files to promote a new claim about the supposed Baghdad–bin Laden connection—one even more frightening than those Feith had been advancing but just as dubious.

Trust me on this.

—Vice President Dick Cheney

7

A Tale of Two Sources

B Y LATE September, the White House was intensifying its campaign. Nearly every day, administration officials were trekking up to Capitol Hill to offer briefings, hoping to coax unsure lawmakers and bolster those already aboard. They were citing new claims—about Saddam's providing chemical weapons training for al-Qaeda and building a fleet of mobile biological weapons labs. At the same time, Bush seemed to be viewing the cause in stark and personal terms.

On the afternoon of September 26, 2002, Bush was at a Houston fundraiser for Republican senatorial candidate John Cornyn. Surrounded by old friends from Texas, he made his most bellicose public comments about Saddam yet. There would be "no discussion, no debate, no negotiation" with the Iraqi dictator. He repeated the standard litany: Saddam had tortured his own citizens, gassed the Kurds, invaded his neighbors: "There's no doubt his hatred is mainly directed at us. There's no doubt he can't stand us." But one line in this speech grabbed worldwide attention: "After all, this is a guy that tried to kill my dad at one time."

Bush was referring to a plot by a group of Iraqis and Kuwaitis who had been arrested walking in the Kuwaiti desert one night in April 1993. They were later charged by the Kuwaiti government with conspiring to assassinate George H. W. Bush with a car bomb during a ceremonial visit the former president and his family had made to Kuwait that month. George W. Bush had been invited on the trip but had begged off because he was busy as the managing partner of the Texas Rangers baseball team. But those family members who did go—and who might have also been killed in an assassination attempt—included his mother, two of his brothers, and his wife, Laura.

The Kuwaitis rested their case on the discovery of a car bomb and a confession made by the alleged ringleader, Wali al-Ghazali, after four days in Kuwaiti custody. Al-Ghazali later testified that he had been recruited barely a week before the Bush visit by an Iraqi intelligence agent who had pressured him to arrange the assassination plot and provided him with the car bomb. But much about the case was hazy. Amnesty International questioned whether al-Ghazali had been tortured, a practice not unheard of in Kuwaiti jails. A classified CIA report, leaked at the time to *The Boston Globe,* expressed skepticism about the Kuwaiti government's claims, noting that Kuwait might have "cooked the books." No testimony or documents ever tied Saddam to the plot. "I had no evidence of any direct order" by Saddam, the U.S. ambassador to Kuwait at the time, Edward "Skip" Gnehm, acknowledged in a 2006 interview (although Gnehm did endorse the Kuwaiti verdict). The FBI concluded that the car bomb uncovered by the Kuwaitis matched the known design of Iraqi-made bombs. The forensic evidence was deemed strong enough by President Clinton to order a Tomahawk missile attack on the headquarters of the Mukhabarat, the Iraqi intelligence service, in June 1993 in retaliation for the supposed assassination attempt.*

That Bush was citing the incident nine years later to explain his current policy made some members of Congress uncomfortable. House Majority Leader Dick Armey later said he had "just cringed" when he read about the president's comment. "Wow," he remarked to his wife, "I hope *that's* not what this is all about."

At one point, other members of Congress were able to witness Bush's

---

*The ultimate resolution of the assassination case raised further questions about the strength of the evidence. After the initial publicity surrounding the trial faded, the Kuwaiti State Security Court quietly commuted the sentences for four of the six plotters who had received the death sentence in the case. The emir of Kuwait then declined to sign the death warrants for the remaining two, including al-Ghazali. The Kuwaiti government gave no public explanation of these actions. After the Iraq invasion, the U.S. military seized millions of pages of Iraqi documents, including many from the files of the Mukhabarat. As of mid-2006, the U.S. government hadn't released any information pointing to Iraqi government complicity in the 1993 Kuwait incident.

intense feelings about Saddam up close. At a breakfast with a few congressional leaders in late September, Bush expressed exasperation when the issue of a diplomatic settlement arose. Saddam had shown his contempt for the United States, he told the legislators. There was no use talking to him. "Do you want to know what the foreign policy of Iraq is to the United States?" Bush asked angrily. The president then answered his own question by raising his middle finger and thrusting it inches in front of Senator Daschle's face, according to a witness. "Fuck the United States!" Bush continued. "That's what it is—and that's why we're going to get him!"*

BUT on Capitol Hill, the White House needed to make a case with evidence, not emotion. One critical hearing—a classified session—took place on September 24 for members of the Senate foreign relations committee. Tenet was the star witness, and Robert Walpole, the agency's national intelligence officer for nuclear weapons, had brought along a prop: one of the aluminum tubes. During the session, Tenet pushed the tubes case and presented other disturbing intelligence: Saddam had a fleet of mobile biological weapons labs and had been developing unmanned aerial vehicles (UAVs) that could be outfitted with chemical or biological agents. After listening to Tenet, Senator Joe Biden, the Democratic chairman of the committee, had the impression, as he later said, that these drones "could be put on oil tankers off the coast of the United States and fly into Philadelphia or Charleston [South Carolina] carrying chemical and biological weapons and hit with devastating effects." It was scary stuff—death labs on wheels, direct WMD attacks on America.

But when Biden and other committee members pressed Tenet on the sourcing for these claims, they got little in the way of answers. During the questioning, a committee staff member slipped Biden a note with a suggested query, and Biden put this question to Tenet: What "technically collected"

---

*Bush was also talking tough about Democrats. At a speech in New Jersey on September 23, 2002, Bush declared that Democrats in the Senate were "not interested in the security of the American people." He was referring not to Iraq but to the ongoing tussle over the legislation creating the Department of Homeland Security. Senate Democrats wanted to preserve traditional federal workplace rules at the new department; Bush wanted to remove these protections to ensure greater hiring-and-firing flexibility. Two days later, in a floor speech, Daschle, citing Bush's remark, yelled, "That is outrageous! Outrageous!"

evidence did the CIA have of Iraqi weapons of mass destruction? What the staffer had in mind was physical proof: radioactive emissions from nuclear sites, electronic intercepts, samples of biological agents. Anything that would be hard and irrefutable.

"None, Senator," Tenet replied.

There was a hush in the room. Oh my God, the staffer thought. " 'None, Senator'—that answer will ring in my ears as long as I live," the aide remarked later. Biden appeared bothered. He asked Tenet, "George, do you want me to clear the staff out of the room?" It was a way of asking if Tenet possessed superclassified information, some technical evidence that was so black, so secret, that it couldn't be shared with staffers.

"There's no reason to, Senator," Tenet replied, signaling that he wasn't holding anything back.

Tenet did insist that the CIA had solid human sources—strong reporting from defectors who had seen the mobile labs, reliable reporting on the UAVs. There was, Tenet said, nothing to be concerned about regarding the CIA's sourcing. Shortly after this exchange, Tenet left the hearing, explaining that he had to attend his son's basketball games. (Biden complimented him for having his priorities straight.) Some senators also began to slowly file out of the room.

But the hearing wasn't done. The committee had previously learned of the dispute within the government about the aluminum tubes, and Biden had invited witnesses to represent the skeptics. The State Department's chief intelligence officer, Carl Ford, Jr., was there to testify after Tenet, as was Rhys Williams, the chief of the Energy Department's Office of Intelligence. Both witnesses told the dwindling number of senators that their agencies didn't accept the tubes argument. But few senators were paying close attention to their testimony, and the hearing was petering out. "These dissents," another staffer present said, "were not front and center."

Peter Zimmerman, the committee's scientific adviser, left the closed-door meeting enraged. A former Pentagon contractor who specialized in nuclear technology, Zimmerman had drafted a report on nuclear centrifuges for the Defense Department in the late 1990s. As soon as he had heard about the aluminum tubes case, he had been doubtful. He had pored over the specifications of the tubes and had decided that they were too small to be used for centrifuges. After the hearing, he confronted Walpole. "Let's see your toy," he said, referring to the aluminum tube. Walpole took it out. The item looked like an aluminum sewer pipe. Zimmerman was not impressed; he grilled Walpole on assorted technical details. None of Walpole's answers was convincing. Walpole, Zimmerman thought, didn't understand the crucial technical issues. And Zimmerman was underwhelmed by almost everything else Tenet had said to the committee.

"I remember going home that night," he recalled, "and practically putting my fist through the wall half a dozen times. I was as frustrated as I've ever been. I remember saying to my wife, 'They're going to war and there's not a damn piece of evidence to substantiate it.'"

JUST about this time, administration officials began referring to intelligence reports that contained a dramatic new assertion: Saddam had already provided weapons training to al-Qaeda. On September 25, Condoleezza Rice appeared on PBS's *NewsHour* and said the Iraqi tyrant was supplying "training to al-Qaeda in chemical weapons development." The next day, Ari Fleischer pointed reporters to Rice's comments at the White House press briefing. On September 26, Rumsfeld said that there was "reliable reporting" of "possible chemical- and biological-agent training," and the following day he declared that the evidence of Saddam–al-Qaeda ties was "bullet-proof." This was not a Feith-like charge based on fuzzy past "associations" and "contacts." This seemed to be founded on fresh and solid intelligence: the Iraqi dictator was instructing the murderers of al-Qaeda in the use of weapons of mass death. Here was the connection—what Wolfowitz, Feith, Mylroie and others had obsessed over—in its most frightening manifestation.

The source of this allegation was the account of one man: a captured al-Qaeda commander named Ibn al-Shaykh al-Libi. His name was never mentioned publicly. Nor was an important part of the story: that some U.S. intelligence analysts doubted his claims and some FBI officials worried he might have provided an invented tale under torture.

After al-Libi was picked up by Pakistani security forces on December 19, 2001, the FBI quickly identified him as a major al-Qaeda figure—the highest-ranking operative yet apprehended. Al-Libi—whose real name was Ali Abdul Aziz al-Fakhiri—was from Libya but had spent considerable time in Syria, where he had studied engineering. He emigrated to Afghanistan and, according to U.S. officials, became a bomb maker. He was then the chief of bin Laden's Khalden training camp, in charge of preparing hundreds of fighters to wage jihad in the West.

Taken to Bagram Air Base in Afghanistan after his capture, al-Libi was handed over to two FBI agents from New York. The agents worked him hard. One of them, Russell Fincher, bonded with al-Libi, roping him in with a simple question: Do you pray? Of course, al-Libi replied. So did Fincher, a devout Christian. So they prayed together—and talked about faith and God, Jesus and Mohammed. Fincher and a colleague spent more than eighty hours with the al-Qaeda commander, talking religion, sipping coffee, playing to his ego, winning his trust. Fincher's basic view of interrogations was that no matter what horrible crimes your captives may have committed, they're still human beings. Treat them with respect, and you're likely to get a lot more out of them. The message was reinforced by his boss in New York, Jack Cloonan, a tough-talking, veteran FBI counterterrorism supervisor, who instructed Fincher to read al-Libi his rights and treat him exactly the way he would if he had picked him up on the streets of Brooklyn. That way, Cloonan explained, any confession al-Libi made, or any evidence he provided, could be used in an American court of law.

The tactics worked. Al-Libi began to open up. The agents started filing reports to the FBI in New York. Al-Libi identified two trainees at his camp who were of keen interest to the bureau: Zacarias Moussaoui, the would-be al-Qaeda pilot arrested in Minneapolis a few weeks before 9/11, and Richard Reid, the so-called shoe bomber recently arrested in Boston after he failed to ignite an explosive device on a transatlantic flight. The Justice Department was preparing cases against both men. Al-Libi, who seemed intent on cutting a deal, might be of use in those prosecutions. "He was giving us good information," recalled Cloonan, who reviewed Fincher's reports.

Fincher also questioned al-Libi closely about any al-Qaeda dealings with foreign governments. The al-Qaeda commander made no reference to any contacts with Saddam's regime. This was consistent with the message the FBI was getting from every other al-Qaeda captive it was questioning during this period. While al-Qaeda detainees did acknowledge ties to officials in some countries—such as Sudan and Pakistan—they denied having worked with Saddam. "It was always, 'No, no no,'" recalled Cloonan.

After a few days of interrogations, the FBI was convinced al-Libi could be a gold mine. But the CIA had a different view. Agency officials suspected al-Libi was holding out and might know of ongoing al-Qaeda operations that he wasn't revealing. CIA officials wanted control of al-Libi, and they were determined to get it.

In the intelligence community, few issues at the time were more contentious than the question of whether the CIA or the FBI should be in charge of interrogating al-Qaeda suspects arrested overseas or picked up in Afghanistan. Al-Libi became a test case. Tenet raised the issue at the White House—and won. At the time, the FBI was in no position to resist. The widespread perception (not entirely accurate) was that the bureau, not the CIA, had been primarily responsible for the intelligence failures leading to the September 11 attacks. And Tenet, with his cigars and tough talk, had bonded with Bush and displayed an aggressiveness that impressed the president. FBI Director Robert Mueller, who was much stiffer than Tenet, was new on the job. "We didn't have the political juice with the president," a senior FBI official subsequently said. "It was the agency that ruled the roost." The White House ordered that al-Libi be handed over to the CIA.

One day, before the FBI lost control of the suspect, a CIA officer at Bagram entered the cell where al-Libi was being held and interrupted one of Fincher's interrogations. He shouted at the prisoner, trying to intimidate him. He would be sent to Egypt, the CIA officer told him. Then he whispered in his ear: "When you're in Egypt, I'm going to find your mother and fuck her." Fincher heard the remark and later relayed it to Cloonan. Not long afterward, the CIA man returned with military personnel. In the presence of Fincher, they had the suspect removed. "They literally came into the room, strapped him to a stretcher, and wrapped his feet, his hands, and his mouth in duct tape," said a senior FBI official. A hood was placed over his head. The stretcher with al-Libi was then loaded into a pickup truck, which drove right onto a cargo plane that promptly took off. "The fucking guy just disappeared," said another top FBI agent. "We were pissed."

Al-Libi was flown to Egypt. He had fallen into the CIA's "extraordinary rendition" program. Started by the CIA's Counterterrorism Center in the 1990s to deal with recalcitrant terror suspects, this program had been expanded substantially after 9/11. Terror suspects were whisked away to allied countries—primarily Egypt, Jordan, and Morocco—where interrogation methods were known to be brutal and nasty. Once the program attracted publicity two years later, Bush and other senior administration officials would repeatedly say the United States did not engage in torture and did not send suspects to countries where they might be tortured. Yet the State Department's own human rights report for Egypt in 2001 reported there were "numerous credible reports" of torture by Egyptian security forces that year, especially regarding prisoners suspected of terrorism. Among the methods cited: "Being stripped and blindfolded; suspended from a ceiling or doorframe with feet just touching the floor; beaten with fists, whips, metal rods, or other objects; subjected to electrical shocks and doused with cold water." CIA officials would later say that they had been assured by the Egyptians that nothing improper was done to al-Libi while he was in their custody. Cloonan years later said his concerns were heightened when a U.S. military officer told him that al-Libi had been subjected to a particularly diabolical interrogation technique: a "mock burial" in which the prisoner is thrown into a hole that is gradually filled with dirt, causing him to believe that he is about to be buried alive.

Whatever happened to al-Libi while he was in Egyptian custody—and there has never been a public investigation—within a few weeks he changed his story about Saddam and al-Qaeda. He told his interrogators something he had not said to the FBI agents in Bagram. Bin Laden, he now claimed, had been frustrated by his inability to develop his own chemical and biological weapons capacity. So he had dispatched two operatives to Iraq for chemical and biological weapons training.

Intelligence reports about al-Libi's distressing claim—a chemical and biological weapons partnership between Saddam and bin Laden—were soon being sent to the White House. Though the CIA had resisted the Mylroie-Feith-Wolfowitz connect-the-dots theory of an alliance between Baghdad and bin Laden, in this case the agency had a direct report from a senior al-Qaeda operative in custody—even if the report was unconfirmed. It was at least *something* that CIA officials could circulate that appeared to substantiate the al-Qaeda–Iraq connection that was consuming influential administration officials.

Yet from the outset, there was also skepticism within the U.S. intelligence community. A February 2002 memo written by an analyst for the DIA noted that al-Libi "lacks specific details on the Iraqis involved, the CBRN [chemical, biological, radiological, or nuclear] materials associated with the assistance, and the location where training occurred." The analyst added that "it is possible he does not know any further details; it is more likely this individual is intentionally misleading the debriefers. Ibn al-Shaykh [al-Libi] has been undergoing debriefs for several weeks and may be describing scenarios to the debriefers that he knew will retain their interest."

The analyst was not only casting doubt on the al-Libi reporting; he was suggesting that the al-Qaeda captive may only have been telling his interrogators what he thought they wanted to hear, perhaps to get them to stop whatever aggressive interrogation techniques they were using. This was exactly why the FBI in the post-9/11 period had argued against the use of torture or other degrading interrogation techniques (particularly at the Guantánamo detention center, where FBI agents often clashed with military intelligence on this issue). Leave aside the human rights issues; you can never trust what you're getting, FBI officials asserted. The DIA analyst who authored the memo also cited an additional reason to question al-Libi's claims: "Saddam's regime is intensely secular and is wary of Islamic revolutionary movements. Moreover, Baghdad is unlikely to provide assistance to a group it cannot control."

The DIA analyst was adhering to the commonsense view held by most of the U.S. counterterrorism community. Why would Saddam pass along his chemical and biological know-how—presumably his most cherished possessions—to a terrorist group that owed its allegiance to someone else? For years, bin Laden had railed about "apostate" Arab states led by "infidel" leaders who failed to follow the words of the Prophet. Saddam was clearly one such leader. His secular Baathist regime would have to fall for bin Laden to achieve his goal of a new Islamic caliphate. "I never thought Saddam was crazy," said Michael Scheuer, a CIA analyst who once headed the bin Laden unit. "He was never going to give these guys weapons—because al-Qaeda would have been just as likely to use them against him as they would against the United States. They hated Saddam."

But the DIA's dissent never registered. At a critical moment in the Iraq debate—in late September—top administration officials such as Rice and Rumsfeld publicly exploited al-Libi's dubious tale to build support for the president's Iraq resolution. As it turned out, they were relying upon a source who would later recant his entire story. After the invasion of Iraq, al-Libi would again come into the custody of the FBI for a short period, and he would insist that he had told the truth to Russell Fincher the first time around. He would, according to two FBI officials, say of his WMD-training claims, "They were killing me. I had to tell them something."*

"TRUST me on this, Dick," Vice President Dick Cheney told House Majority Leader Dick Armey. "When I get done with this briefing, you're going to be with me."

It was an afternoon in late September, and Armey had been invited over to the vice president's small hideaway office in the U.S. Capitol. This was the briefing Bush had promised Armey three weeks earlier. Ever since then, Armey had acceded to the president's wishes and not said anything in public about his worries about Bush's stand. But the White House understood Armey's importance. He was the number two Republican in the House. If he broke ranks, that would be a problem. So Cheney was dispatched to do the job himself.

Armey thought Cheney's opening remark was odd: "He didn't say, 'You're going to be with us.' He didn't say, 'You're going to be with the president.' He said, 'You're going to be with *me.*'"

Over the next half hour, Cheney, surrounded by aides, pointed to pictures of the aluminum tubes, showed overhead images of nuclear sites supposedly under construction, and displayed drawings of mobile biological labs and photographs of UAVs that, he suggested, could hit Israel and spread mass death. He talked about the "associations" and "relationships" between Saddam and al-Qaeda. He noted that the Iraqis could slip miniaturized biological weapons (that fit into suitcases) to terrorists, who could bring them into the United States and kill thousands.

As Armey listened to Cheney and stared at the photos, it occurred to him—just as it had to Daschle—that he couldn't really see anything in the pictures. They were aerial shots of buildings and other sites. Who knew what was in those buildings? Armey realized he had to rely on what Cheney was telling him. "It wasn't very convincing," Armey later recalled. "If I'd gotten the same briefing from President Clinton or Al Gore, I probably would have said, 'Ah, bullshit.' But you don't do that with your own

---

*In early 2004, the CIA would formally recall all its reporting on al-Libi. "They needed some evidence, and he gave it to them," said one bitter veteran FBI counterterrorism agent years later. "In the court of public opinion, anything goes."

people." He assumed Cheney was leveling with him; it never occurred to Armey that the vice president was not telling him the whole story.

Armey asked few questions at the briefing; he didn't challenge Cheney on any point. As the briefing concluded, Armey thanked Cheney and promised to mull over the matter. He didn't commit to voting for the resolution. But he was coming around.

ON THE House side, with most Republicans supporting the president, Democrats were squabbling among themselves. The party's liberals were passionately opposed to giving Bush any resolution to wage war and scoffed at the administration's briefings. "There was one run by Rumsfeld and Powell," recalled Representative Bob Filner, a Democrat from San Diego. "They treated us like kids. They had all these military people standing around. It gave the thing an aura of authority. You'd feel stupid challenging them. They brought in one of those aluminum tubes. It was nothing. My attitude was 'You're taking us to war on that little tube?' I got up and walked out." Representative Jim McGovern of Massachusetts, another liberal Democrat, had the same complaint: "Here were Tenet, Rumsfeld, Powell, various undersecretaries. They would never get into the nitty-gritty of the reliability of their sources. It would be 'A source said this or that.' Well, who is this source? Why do we believe this source?"

But other Democrats were being tugged in a different direction. The party's leaders mounted their own briefings for House Democrats. These were conducted by the party's foreign policy wonks, the men and women who had shaped national security strategy for Bill Clinton. Most had grown increasingly frustrated with Iraqi recalcitrance in the 1990s and largely agreed that Saddam posed a danger. The briefings proved enormously important. Richard Holbrooke, Clinton's UN ambassador, talked about how Clinton had changed U.S. policy from containment to regime change and that, in his view, Saddam was the most dangerous man in the world. Kenneth Pollack, a former CIA analyst who had handled Iraq policy on Clinton's National Security Council, warned that Saddam might well be able to develop a nuclear bomb within a few years and that containment was no longer feasible. Dennis Ross, who had been Clinton's top Middle East negotiator, said that the Iraqi people would rejoice if Saddam were overthrown. Former Secretary of State Madeleine Albright reinforced the message that

Saddam must be dealt with: he was developing nuclear weapons, and deterrence was not a viable option. Most of these Clinton veterans would, after the war, point to caveats and qualifiers in their advice. They claimed they had never intended to back a war in which the president would invade without a broad international coalition, without enough troops, without engaging in sufficient postwar planning. But their bottom-line message—that military force was the only permanent solution—was what counted most in these crucial days.

For some of the Democrats, the most persuasive briefer was a plainspoken, nonpartisan weapons expert named David Kay. He boasted credentials that few other briefers could claim. As a UN weapons inspector in Iraq in the early 1990s, he had dealt with the Iraqis and knew how evasive they could be. Kay had repeatedly confronted Iraqi officials, challenging them when he suspected they weren't telling him the truth, and not notifying the Iraqis where he and his team were about to inspect. He hadn't minded bending—or breaking—the rules. In one dramatic incident that drew worldwide attention, Kay and his inspections team of several dozen had been forced out of an Iraqi government building after discovering documents indicating that Iraq, prior to the first Persian Gulf War, had been proceeding toward building a nuclear bomb (despite Baghdad's insistence it had not). The Iraqis ordered Kay to relinquish the records before departing the scene. Kay refused, and a standoff ensued in the parking lot that lasted four days. As armed Iraqi troops surrounded Kay and the inspectors, Kay and his colleagues used satellite phones to fax the crucial documents back to the United Nations, proving that the Iraqis had had a more extensive nuclear program than they acknowledged.

In his briefings to Democrats in the fall of 2002, Kay recounted this and other incidents to show that the U.S. government couldn't really trust the Iraqis to come clean. He also estimated that Saddam was in a position to spend up to $2 billion a year of his oil-for-food funds on illicit weapons programs. The only guaranteed way of disarming Saddam, and making sure he never got a nuclear bomb, was regime change, Kay said. Anything else, including relying on UN inspections, would entail risk and might not be sufficiently effective. "What mattered most to me was the fear of nuclear weapons," recalled Representative Henry Waxman, a liberal Democrat who would end up supporting Bush's resolution. "And these people were influential."

By the end of September, the president's war resolution was no sure thing. The White House had trimmed it back, dumping the language that authorized Bush to go to war to achieve stability in the region. Still, the White House faced a threat. Senator Joe Biden and two Republican senators on his foreign relations committee—Richard Lugar and Chuck Hagel—were pushing an alternative that would narrow the president's authority further. Under their proposal, Bush would be able to attack Iraq only for the purpose of destroying Iraq's WMDs and only after seeking UN approval. If the United Nations said no, Bush would have to come back to Congress and demonstrate that the Iraqi weapons threat was so "grave" that only military action could eliminate it. The Biden-Lugar measure was attracting support from both Democrats and Republicans. And, according to Biden, he and his allies were getting backdoor advice and encouragement from the administration's reluctant warriors: Powell and Armitage. The White House was worried about Biden's endeavor, and Bush was furious. "I don't want a resolution such as this that ties my hands," he told Senator Trent Lott. The president, according to Lott, gave him an emphatic order: "Derail the Biden legislation and make sure its language never sees the light of day."

But it was Dick Gephardt, the Democratic leader in the House and past and future presidential candidate, who derailed the bipartisan effort. He had already said he thought Iraq was a threat and that he was open to backing the president. He would later recall that he wasn't comfortable with the administration's resolution, but he felt at the time that he had few options. His party was in the minority in the House. At any moment, the House Republicans could put the president's bill to a vote on the floor, and it would pass—with a number of Democrats signing on. He had little room for maneuvering, and in negotiations with the White House he angled for small changes in the resolution. "At some point, the White House said, 'This is as good as it gets,' " Gephardt recalled, "and I became convinced we couldn't get more. You had to make a decision whether you were for giving the president the authority or not. Everything else was window dressing."

Gephardt's thinking had been shaped by the former Clinton national security aides, including Holbrooke, Pollack, and James Steinberg, who were arguing Saddam had to be confronted. But Biden and other Democrats wondered if another factor was influencing Gephardt: presidential politics. Gephardt, an earnest and dogged politician, was determined to run in 2004. And, like others in his party, including Massachusetts Senator John Kerry, he had a daunting post-9/11 political problem. Eleven years earlier, he had voted against the first Persian Gulf War. If he cast a similar vote now, he could expect to be tagged by Republicans as soft and too hesitant to use military force. Gephardt reached an agreement with the president's negotiators. At 1:15 in the afternoon on October 2, the White House held a Rose Garden ceremony with a crowd of senators and representatives from both parties to announce a resolution had been finalized. Standing right next to Bush, along with Hastert and Lott, was Gephardt.

Gephardt had been urged by his political advisers to be by Bush's side at the White House that day. But the move rankled plenty of congressional Democrats. On Capitol Hill, Gephardt held a meeting of House Democrats and gave an impassioned speech. Iraq posed a serious threat, he insisted. He went on to say (as he subsequently recalled), "I'm sorry he's the president. I didn't vote for him. But we're in a tough spot." He wasn't asking for a party-line vote. Rather, he told them, "Figure out what you believe and don't be political. I'll never mention this vote to you again." He knew that many in the room were livid with him.

"His message for us was implicit," Representative Jim McGovern said. "He did not want the Democrats to be blamed for the next attack." Representative Henry Waxman thought Gephardt was arguing that Democrats had no choice but to go along with Bush on Iraq: " 'Don't even try to fight the White House—keep it from becoming an issue in the election.' He was thinking about running for president, and he decided to be for it."

Gephardt's decision to back the president's resolution killed Biden's bipartisan alternative in the Senate and guaranteed a victory for the White House. When Biden consulted with Senate Republicans, they all said the same thing: How can we be to the left of Dick Gephardt? Biden's effort to impose conditions on Bush's march to war was finished. He didn't bother saying anything to Gephardt. "I was angry," Biden later remarked. "I was frustrated. But I never second-guess another man's political judgment."

By now Armey was being muscled by his own aides. His chief of staff laid it out for him: "This war is going to happen with you or without you." The train was leaving the station, no matter what he said or did. Armey concluded, he later said, that he could "participate in the process and give it guidance, or I could be a cranky voice on the outside and lose control." Armey decided to get on the train. He agreed to introduce the Iraq resolution on the floor of the House.

TYLER DRUMHELLER, the genial, heavyset CIA veteran who was chief of the Directorate of Operations' European Division, was sent on a sensitive mission in late September—to a Georgetown restaurant. Drumheller was due to have his monthly lunch with the Washington station chief for Germany's BND, or Federal Intelligence Service. But this time his boss, James Pavitt, the chief of the DO, wanted him to push the Germans about a particularly sensitive issue: a mysterious Iraqi defector under their control. His code name was Curveball.

The reports by this one defector had become the primary basis for one of the administration's most significant claims: that Iraq had built a fleet of mobile biological labs. The White House had publicly cited this charge, saying that Saddam was now capable of cooking up anthrax and other deadly agents on movable trailers that would never be found by weapons inspectors because they were constantly on the go. But Pavitt was concerned. The CIA had never talked to Curveball and had no idea how credible he was. It didn't even know his name.

Drumheller and the German station chief met at Georgetown's Sea Catch restaurant, and the CIA man delicately raised the subject: Could the agency, he asked, interview Curveball directly?

No, the German replied, there was no point to any American questioning Curveball.

Why not?

"You don't want to see him," the German told Drumheller. "The guy's crazy." Speaking to him would be a "waste of time." The German intelligence service was not even sure he was telling the truth. "We think he's had a nervous breakdown," the BND station chief said. "We think he's a fabricator." But, the German said to Drumheller, officially the BND still supported Curveball as a credible source. If the BND were asked about Curveball's problems or any concerns it had about him, the service would deny all of this. Drumheller was taken aback. He realized that Curveball could be a time bomb.

Only a few years earlier, the Iraqi defector had been a huge catch for the Germans. He was a dark-haired chemical engineer, with a young wife and child, who had arrived in Germany in 1999 seeking asylum. He told German authorities that he had embezzled money from the Iraqi government and would be imprisoned or killed if sent home. He was classified an exile and sent to a refugee center near Nuremberg. Then, as the *Los Angeles Times* would discover years later, the defector soon changed his story and told the Germans that he had once worked on mobile biological weapons labs in Iraq. He maintained that Saddam had several such trucks and that one had been concocting deadly germ weapons since 1997. The BND debriefed him and shared his reports with the Defense Intelligence Agency, which then spread them through the U.S. intelligence establishment.

From January 2000 to September 2001, the DIA disseminated almost a hundred reports based on Curveball's claims—reports that became part of intelligence briefings for senior Bush administration officials. And the reports became firmer as time went on. At first, the DIA reported that Curveball's claims "suggested" Iraq had a biological weapons program, and an early DIA report stated, "We cannot confirm whether Iraq has produced . . . biological agents." Yet as the White House's interest in Iraqi weapons programs grew, the reports became more definitive. By October 2001, relying principally on Curveball, the CIA's WINPAC—its analytical shop specializing in weapons proliferation—was reporting the existence of "mobile BW agent production plants" as fact, not supposition. And White House officials looking to catch Saddam red-handed embraced Curveball's reports of mobile bioweapons laboratories. An NSC staffer later recalled the excitement stirred within the White House by these intelligence reports: "We really thought the trailers were the smoking gun. When I saw that, I thought, 'We got him.' We were like, 'The bastard, we nailed his ass.' And finally, the agency was giving us something concrete."

But the Curveball operation was loaded with problems—not least of all Curveball himself. The reports based on his information came out of an awkward process—a linguistic version of the children's game of "telephone." Curveball usually spoke to the Germans in Arabic, and his information was translated into German. Then DIA officers translated the reports from German into English before sharing them with other U.S. intelligence services. Worse, the BND had not allowed U.S. intelligence direct access to Curveball, claiming he hated Americans. So the U.S. intelligence community was depending on double translations from a source they couldn't personally evaluate. And the DIA took no steps to ascertain Curveball's veracity. Years later, a DIA official told a White House commission on WMD intelligence that the DIA saw itself as merely a "conduit" for Curveball's Arabic-to-German-to-English reporting. "The whole handling of Curveball was a farce," said a CIA officer in the Counterproliferation Division who monitored the Curveball episode. "But it was a DIA operation. Our attitude was, it's their problem."

And there were red flags concerning the Iraqi from the outset. In May 2000, Les, the Defense Department physician detailed to the CPD and one of the intelligence community's leading experts on biological weapons, was able to meet Curveball—briefly. Curveball had told his German handlers that he had been an eyewitness to a 1998 biological weapons accident in which twelve technicians had died from exposure to biological agents. Les was dispatched to Germany to determine whether Curveball had been exposed to any biological agents or had been vaccinated. He was introduced to Curveball as a German for the sole purpose of obtaining a blood sample. He wasn't permitted to say anything to the defector, only to take his blood. The subsequent medical tests were inconclusive. But Les returned to Langley with a disturbing report. First, he had noticed, Curveball spoke English after all. The Germans had told the Americans he didn't and that was one reason why U.S. intelligence officials couldn't question him. Second, despite the fact that they met in the morning, Les had noticed that Curveball smelled of liquor. He seemed to be suffering from a hangover. Les wondered if Curveball might be a drunk.

In early 2001, there was another warning of sorts. The CIA station chief in Berlin sent a message to headquarters: a BND official had said that Curveball was "out of control" and couldn't be located. And in April 2002, England's MI6, which was also receiving the Curveball material, told the CIA that it had come across inconsistencies in Curveball's reporting. The British intelligence service reported it was "not convinced that Curveball is a wholly reliable source" and that "elements of [Curveball's] behavior strike us as typical of individuals we would normally assess as fabricators." But MI6, like the BND, officially continued to back Curveball. And neither the CIA nor the DIA dumped him. His reports on a fleet of mobile weapons labs kept circulating. "We were watching the whole Curveball thing in horror," recalled the Counterproliferation Division staffer. "We knew it was bad from the start. We felt powerless, but we also wondered if maybe we didn't know everything. In the aftermath of 9/11, could you afford to be negligent and dismiss a potential source as just another screwball? Most of our sources were strange in one way or another. Still, we couldn't believe this kept going on and on."

So by the time the CIA's Drumheller sat down with the BND station chief in Washington in late September 2002, there was more than sufficient reason for the CIA to worry. After the German intelligence chief told him that Curveball might be a fabricator, Drumheller reported this to Pavitt. "Stay on top of this," Pavitt told him. Drumheller sent a note to Alan Foley, the WINPAC chief, about what the German station chief had said about Curveball. He also asked his deputy to pull the files on the problematic source. "Find out what the hell is going on with this guy," Drumheller recalled telling her. She soon reported back, "This is a problem, boss." Curveball's information about bioweapons labs had just been accepted for inclusion in the National Intelligence Estimate then being drafted in response to a request from the Senate intelligence committee.

Oh boy, Drumheller thought, they have to have better stuff than this.

If I had to do it all over again, I would say,
"Hell no, I'm not going to do that!"

—CIA ANALYST PAUL PILLAR

8

Bent with the Wind

A S SOON as he could, Peter Zimmerman, the scientific adviser to the
Senate foreign relations committee, rushed to a secure room in the
U.S. Capitol to read the CIA's classified National Intelligence Estimate (NIE)
on Iraq's weapons of mass destruction. This was the report that had been
requested three weeks earlier by Democrats on the Senate intelligence committee. The ninety-page paper, delivered to Congress on the night of October 1, was supposed to be the most authoritative summary of the U.S.
government's intelligence on Iraq's deadly weapons and the threat they posed
to America. Zimmerman, who had been unimpressed by the closed-door
Tenet briefing a week earlier, was anxious to see what the CIA *really* had to
back up the WMD case for war.

He read the NIE twice. He was, he later said, astonished. The document offered bold and definitive conclusions in its "key judgments": Iraq,
it said, "has chemical and biological weapons" and "is reconstituting its
nuclear weapons program." But the actual evidence, he thought, was hardly
overpowering. Deeper in the NIE, there was information that undercut
those stark conclusions. On critical points—the tubes, the unmanned aerial
drones, the nuclear program—some government agencies had argued that
the NIE was wrong. "The dissents leaped out—they're in bold, almost like

flashing light," Zimmerman recalled. He had read NIEs before and never seen dissents as striking as these. "I remember thinking," he later said, " 'Boy, there's nothing there. If anybody takes the time to actually read this, they can't believe there actually are major WMD programs.' "

The NIE was something of a muddle. It eventually came to symbolize the entire WMD foul-up. The document did maintain that Iraq was full of deadly weapons. It was filled at some points with scary specifics. Iraq had amassed between 100 and 500 metric tons of chemical weapons (including mustard gas, sarin, and VX). Saddam possessed unmanned aerial vehicles (UAVs) that were "probably intended" to deliver biological agents. The drones could be "brought close to, or into . . . the U.S. Homeland." Iraq had "mobile facilities" for producing toxins and other biological agents that can "evade detection and are highly survivable." And the NIE stated that Iraq had begun "vigorously trying" to buy yellowcake and was "reportedly" working out a deal to acquire "up to 500 tons" from Niger. Its key judgment section suggested the WMD situation in Iraq might even be worse than what the NIE outlined: "We judge that we are seeing only a portion of Iraq's WMD efforts."

But, as Zimmerman noticed, there were plenty of doubts in the fine print. In an annex in the back of the document, the State Department's intelligence bureau, INR, stated that "claims of Iraqi pursuit of natural uranium in Africa are . . . highly dubious." (Notably, the yellowcake claims were also not included as a "key judgment" of the NIE.) Both the Energy Department's Office of Intelligence and INR had disagreed with the conclusions about the aluminum tubes—the only hard evidence to support the claim that Iraq had revived its nuclear weapons program. In a sidebar, INR also challenged the entire conclusion about Iraq's nuclear efforts. As for the UAVs, the Air Force's intelligence office (home to the government's main experts on such weapons) had concluded they were primarily intended for reconnaissance, not for spraying deadly biological agents on unsuspecting civilians.

And the details of the consensus portions of the NIE were not in all respects as bold as the overarching conclusions. None of the intelligence agencies claimed that Iraq was on the doorstep of the nuclear club. They concluded Iraq could produce a nuclear weapon "during this decade" (but not likely before 2007 to 2009) only if "left unchecked." But Iraq was still being checked by sanctions (as problematic as they were) and would soon face a new round of inspections. On chemical weapons, the NIE acknowledged, "we have little specific information on Iraq's CW stockpile." As for the mobile biological weapons labs, most of the NIE's section on this was based on a single source: Curveball.

The NIE said the intelligence community had "high confidence" in its conclusions that Iraq was expanding its chemical, biological, and nuclear weapons program, but it admitted it had little concrete evidence in hand: "we are not detecting portions of these weapons programs." In the eyes of other readers, the dissents and hedges might not have been as striking as Zimmerman considered them. But they were there, even if the public had no way of knowing they existed.

Only after the war began—when it was too late—would the NIE prompt hard questions about how the intelligence community had produced such a flawed document. It was a consensus paper thrashed out during hours of interagency meetings presided over by senior CIA officials. Had the process been politicized? Had analysts been pressured? Had Tenet and his deputy, John McLaughlin, been unwilling to impose tight standards to avoid displeasing the White House? An Energy Department official later said that the "DOE did not want to come out before the war and say [Iraq] wasn't reconstituting" its nuclear weapons program. One intelligence analyst subsequently told Senate investigators that when the NIE was being assembled, "the going-in assumption was we were going to war, so this NIE was to be written with that in mind. . . . This is about going to war and giving the combatant commander an estimate on which he can properly organize."

Two investigations—one by the Republican-controlled Senate intelligence committee, the other by a White House–appointed commission—would later conclude there had been no "political pressure" from the White House to alter the intelligence community's conclusions. But asking a blunt question—were analysts bullied into concocting conclusions that bolstered Bush administration policies?—overlooked how bureaucracies work. The dynamics that produced the NIE pervaded the U.S. intelligence community throughout the run-up to the Iraq War. "You were never told what to write," recalled Bruce Hardcastle, a veteran and widely respected DIA analyst for Near East affairs, who was deeply skeptical about some of the claims relating to Iraqi weapons programs. "But you knew what assessments administration officials would be receptive to—and what they would not be receptive to." In such an environment, Hardcastle added, what analyst was going to speak up and say "I don't think Saddam has any of these weapons"? Hardcastle was a walking example of the price that could be paid. After he clashed with a Feith deputy on Mideast issues, Hardcastle found himself shunted aside, bumped at the last minute from an overseas trip to the Middle East, and uninvited to key meetings.

The NIE was the product of a tainted intellectual environment—or so Paul Pillar, then the CIA's national intelligence officer for Near East and South Asia, argued more than three years later in a *Foreign Affairs* article. Pillar, a thoughtful, scholarly analyst with degrees from Oxford, Dartmouth, and Princeton, anguished over his own role in the CIA's handling of the prewar intelligence. "It was clear that the Bush administration would frown on or ignore analysis that called into question a decision to go to war and welcome analysis that supported such a decision," he wrote. "Intelligence analysts . . . felt a strong wind consistently blowing in one direction. The desire to bend with such a wind is natural and strong, even if unconscious."

The desire to "bend" with the wind, as Pillar put it, may be the only plausible explanation for one of the enduring puzzles of the NIE: Why did it have any reference at all to the mushy, unproven Niger charge? Barely two weeks earlier, the CIA had told the White House to strike a reference to the uranium deal from the president's UN speech, and it would do so again for another major speech in the days ahead. During interagency drafting meetings for the NIE, a State Department nuclear analyst, Simon Dodge, had tried to convince his colleagues to take it out of the NIE, arguing that the yellowcake claims were groundless and would draw a stiff dissent from his office. Still, agency officials were reluctant to remove an allegation that White House press secretary Ari Fleischer had already cited. They might also have wanted to make sure they didn't get criticized later for leaving it out—just in case it *might* turn out to be true. Robert Walpole, the national intelligence officer who oversaw this document, later told Senate investigators that he had decided to put the Niger charge into the NIE "for completeness" and so "nobody can say we didn't connect the dots." It was a decision that would soon cause great turmoil. "It's crystal clear we shouldn't have used the Niger allegation," deputy CIA director John McLaughlin subsequently said.*

In the end, the actual wording of the NIE probably didn't matter. By the time it was written, the Bush White House had already made extensive use of the faulty intelligence that had been packaged in the estimate. Bush, Cheney, Rumsfeld, Rice, Wolfowitz, and other administration officials had ignored the disputes (where they existed) and hardly questioned the limited (and flawed) intelligence that had been produced. Bush hadn't asked for the NIE, nor—as the White House would later acknowledge—did he even read it.†

Nor would most members of Congress. Senate aides would later calculate that no more than a half-dozen or so members actually went to the secure room where the highly classified NIE was kept under lock and key before the upcoming vote on Bush's Iraq resolution. Zimmerman, the Senate staffer, urged his colleagues with security clearances to go read the NIE, telling them the dissents were "pretty shocking." But it was too late. "There was not a goddamn thing I or any staffer could do to stop this. We had an election coming up. The Democrats were afraid of being seen as soft on

---

*To back its assertion that the Iraqis were "vigorously" procuring uranium, the NIE cited a "foreign government service" report of the Niger deal—a reference to the original SISMI cable—as well as "reports" that indicated that Iraq had also sought uranium from Somalia and "possibly" the Democratic Republic of the Congo. But, the NIE added, "we cannot confirm whether Iraq successfully succeeded in acquiring uranium . . . from these sources." In 2006, McLaughlin said, "There probably should have been more neon on the phrase 'that it hasn't been confirmed.'" (In fact, the CIA had not confirmed that Iraq had even tried to buy uranium from any of these countries.)

†As wrong and overstated as the NIE was, it was more sober than other intelligence that reached the White House. Years later, the White House commission on WMDs reported, "Even more misleading [than the NIE] was the river of intelligence that flowed from the CIA to top policymakers over long periods of time—in the President's Daily Brief (PDB) and in its more widely distributed companion, the Senior Executive Intelligence Brief (SEIB). These daily reports were, if anything, more alarmist and less nuanced than the NIE. . . . The PDBs and SEIBs, with their attention-grabbing headlines and drumbeat of repetition, left an impression of many corroborating reports where in fact there were very few sources. And in other instances, intelligence suggesting the existence of weapons programs was conveyed to senior policymakers, but later information casting doubt upon the validity of that intelligence was not. In ways both subtle and not so subtle, the daily reports seemed to be 'selling' intelligence—in order to keep its customers, or at least the First Customer, interested." This was a polite way of saying that Tenet and McLaughlin were serving up dishes they knew the boss wanted.

Saddam or on terrorism. The whole notion was, 'Let's get the war out of the way as fast as possible and turn back to the domestic agenda.'"

ONE of the few who did read the NIE was Senator Bob Graham, the Democratic chairman of the Senate intelligence committee. Graham, too, was struck by its "many nuances and outright dissents," he later said. But under committee rules, Graham and other skeptics were unable to say anything in public about them. At an October 2 closed-door hearing of the intelligence committee, Graham and Senator Carl Levin pressed Tenet and McLaughlin on the sourcing behind the NIE's assertions. Did the CIA have its own spies inside Iraq who could verify information about the country's supposed WMD stockpiles? Tenet acknowledged that there weren't any—and that the CIA hadn't had much in the way of assets in Iraq since UN inspectors had left in 1998. "I was stunned," Graham recalled. Graham and Levin requested a declassified version of the NIE, so that some of the equivocations and dissents could be shared with the public.

What came next was a crucial moment in the selling of the war. As it happened, in May, the White House had asked the CIA to prepare a white paper on Iraq's weapons. McLaughlin had passed the request to Pillar. A draft was completed within weeks. But it wasn't released. When the request came for a declassified NIE, Pillar was told to redo the old white paper and to keep it in sync with the NIE.

The CIA's new white paper, "Iraq's Weapons of Mass Destruction Programs," was publicly released on October 4, just as senators and representatives were beginning the floor debate on the resolution that would authorize Bush to launch a war against Iraq whenever he saw fit. The white paper was a slick document on glossy magazine-style paper with color maps, graphics, tables, and photos. One page displayed the location of Iraq's presumed nuclear facilities, complete with yellow-and-black radiation warning symbols. (They were, Graham would later note, "the modern equivalent of skull and crossbones.")

The white paper's conclusions were similar to those of the NIE, only more definitive. The CIA had removed the hedging language. It contained none of the dissents. The white paper falsely stated that "All intelligence experts agree that Iraq is seeking nuclear weapons," ignoring the State Department's pointed dissent. It said that "most intelligence specialists" thought the tubes were for a centrifuge program; it left out the fact that the Energy Department didn't agree. The white paper warned that "Baghdad's UAVs" could "threaten . . . the U.S. Homeland"; the Air Force's disagreement was not mentioned. And it dropped the NIE's telling concession that U.S. intelligence had "little specific information" on Iraq's chemical weapons stockpiles.

Afterward, Pillar was embarrassed by the white paper. "In retrospect, we shouldn't have done that white paper at all," he said. It wasn't really intelligence analysis, he believed. "The white paper was policy advocacy." He wished he had mustered the courage to tell the CIA leadership and the White House that he wouldn't put out such a document. "One of the biggest regrets of my career is, I didn't find a way to say no," he would later say. "If I had to do it all over again, I would say, 'Hell no, I'm not going to do that!'" Pillar, who had always prided himself on his independence and integrity, was ashamed of his role. He and his CIA colleagues, he thought, had been reduced to producing propaganda. He, too, had bent with the wind.

Pillar was operating under his own set of pressures. Shortly before the Bush administration began, he had published a book on terrorism that concluded that the major threat came from freelance groups operating independently of any governments, like al-Qaeda. This had been the CIA's long-standing position on the issue. But it was a direct challenge to the thinking of the neoconservatives and Laurie Mylroie, who believed that state-sponsored terrorism (meaning Saddam-sponsored terrorism) was the *real* problem. For administration hard-liners, Pillar was already suspect, a charter member of an imagined CIA cabal hostile to the president's agenda.

Pillar himself inadvertently sharpened the conflict a few weeks after the president's 2002 State of the Union speech highlighting the "Axis of Evil." He had been invited to speak to a class at the Johns Hopkins School of Advanced International Studies. He suggested the president, in his speech, should have been a "little clearer" about the distinction between terrorism and weapons of mass destruction. There was, he said, no evidence that the Iraqi government had shared such weapons with terrorists—and no evidence that Iraq had supported any terrorist acts since 1993. Pillar had thought he was speaking off the record. Yet within days, *Insight*—a conservative newsmagazine published by *The Washington Times*—carried a story reporting that Pillar had attacked Bush's speech and criticized Laurie Mylroie. Pillar suddenly found his job on the line and, he said, later heard that Wolfowitz wanted him fired.

The contentious dispute over the Iraq–al-Qaeda link, according to Pillar, was one explanation for the CIA's exaggerated conclusions on weapons of mass destruction in the NIE and the white paper. "What was going through the back of my mind," said Pillar, who worked on the NIE, "is that, unlike [the purported] terrorism [connection between Iraq and al-Qaeda], which was a manufactured issue . . . there was a consensus view on WMD." That was not entirely so. There was plenty of dispute within the intelligence community on crucial weapons-related issues. But the basic proposition— that Saddam had *some* chemical and biological weapons—had always been accepted by the CIA, just as it was by all allied intelligence services. The disagreement concerned whether Saddam possessed a vast and growing arsenal or merely "residual" stockpiles, as DIA chief Admiral Thomas Wilson had testified to Congress in March 2002.

Battered by administration officials on the al-Qaeda–Baghdad link, Pillar and other CIA officials were looking to be on the team in other ways. So the CIA, perhaps in an act of bureaucratic overcompensation, was willing to give the White House what it wanted on the WMD issue. Indirectly—but significantly—the obsession of Feith and Wolfowitz at the Pentagon and Scooter Libby and Cheney at the White House to find "the connection" between Saddam and Osama bin Laden was a factor that led to the CIA's overstating the WMD case.

The headlines generated by the white paper were good for the White House. "C.I.A. Says Iraq Revived Forbidden Weapons Program After the UN Inspectors Left," *The New York Times* declared. An Associated Press story reported, "Iraq is making new biological and chemical weapons and could have a nuclear weapon by 2010, a new report by U.S. intelligence agencies concludes."

WHEN Graham read the white paper, he went ballistic. He saw it had been shorn of the dissents and caveats of the classified NIE. "I had earlier concluded that a war with Iraq would be a distraction from the successful and expeditious completion of our aims in Afghanistan," Graham later wrote. "Now I had come to question whether the White House was telling the truth—or even had an interest in knowing the truth."

He called Tenet and lit into him, demanding to know how the CIA could have produced two such different documents: a secret NIE filled with dissents and a public "white paper" that conveyed unanimity and certainty. Tenet grew defensive, according to Graham, telling the senator he resented any questioning of the professionalism or the "patriotism" of his analysts. Graham shot back that he resented Tenet's suggestion that he lacked respect for the men and women of the CIA. He told Tenet he wanted more of the NIE made public. Tenet replied, testily, that he would look into it.

That night, Graham sent a letter seeking the public release of specific sections of the NIE showing there were doubts within the U.S. intelligence community about significant parts of the administration's case. He also wanted Tenet to permit the disclosure of a revealing exchange that had taken place at the October 2 closed-door hearing. In that back-and-forth, McLaughlin had been asked by Senator Carl Levin if it was "likely" that Saddam would launch an attack using chemical and biological weapons.

McLaughlin's response had been telling: "In the foreseeable future, given the conditions we understand now, the likelihood I think would be low." But if Saddam were to be attacked, McLaughlin added, the odds would be "pretty high" that he would retaliate with such weapons.

McLaughlin had also indicated that the CIA had concluded that Saddam had no intention of conducting terrorist attacks against the United States with conventional weapons or biological or chemical weapons. But the agency thought, he *might* assist anti-American terrorists to hit the United States with such weapons—if the United States attacked him.

This may have been no more than guesswork on the CIA's part. But Levin believed it offered quite a different picture from the one the White House was presenting to the public. In recent days, Bush had called Iraq "a threat of unique urgency." Echoing the British white paper, Bush had said that Iraq "could launch a biological or chemical attack in as little as forty-five minutes." He had warned that "each passing day could be the one on which the Iraqi regime gives anthrax or VX nerve gas or someday a nuclear weapon to a terrorist ally." Yet in this private hearing, the CIA's number two official had said that it was unlikely Saddam would do any of this unless the United States invaded Iraq.

"This was the most relevant possible testimony you could have," Levin later said. If this testimony could be declassified, Levin thought at the time, it could change the contours of the Iraq debate. Graham agreed it should be made public.

Three days later, with Congress still debating the Iraq resolution, the

CIA responded to Graham's request. In a letter for public release signed by McLaughlin on behalf of Tenet, the agency declassified some of its judgments about Saddam's WMD-related decision making. The letter noted that Baghdad "for now appears to be drawing a line short of conducting terrorist attacks with conventional or CBW against the United States." If Saddam thought a U.S.-led attack was coming, the letter said, "he probably would become much less constrained in adopting terrorist actions." Moreover, Saddam "might" take "the extreme step of assisting Islamist terrorists in conducting a WMD attack against the United States" as "a last chance to exact vengeance," if Iraq were under assault from the United States. The letter also declassified Levin's exchange with McLaughlin from the classified October 2 hearing.

But the CIA, in something of a preemptive strike, included in the letter other information that seemed to bolster the administration's case. "We have solid reporting of senior level contacts between Iraq and al-Qa'ida going back a decade," the letter said, during which the two parties "discussed safe haven and reciprocal non-aggression." It was the information from the Feith briefing—the same reporting that the CIA until recently had largely dismissed as unreliable. The CIA referred to "reporting" that Iraq had provided training to al-Qaeda concerning "poisons and gases and making conventional bombs." This was a reference to the al-Libi allegations—which the DIA had raised questions about months earlier and which may have been extracted under torture. The Tenet-McLaughlin letter made no mention of these doubts from intelligence community analysts. They were shoving into public view the same intelligence that had been the subject of intense debate and about which there was anything but a consensus.

Graham released the letter the next day. A *New York Times* front-page story called the letter a "new element" in the intensifying congressional debate over the Iraq resolution. But Tenet by this point was playing damage control—a highly unusual role for a CIA director. He had put out a statement claiming, "There is no inconsistency between our view of Saddam's growing threat and the view as expressed by the President." Tenet, who rarely talked to reporters directly, even called a *New York Times* reporter on deadline to ensure this point would make it into the paper—and it did.

Levin was enraged. "The head of the CIA was saying there was no difference between that CIA testimony and the administration," he later recalled. "That's a fabrication and bullshit. It was wrong and totally inappropriate for him to say that. That was important testimony, and they were lying about it. I believed it was likely that Saddam had chemical or biological weapons. But a lot of countries have WMDs. The question is, are they an imminent threat to you?" Levin saw the CIA's answer to that question as "no," and he was happy he had gotten this information into the public realm before the vote. But now Tenet was undermining his agency's own findings—and Levin's efforts. "I was bloody furious," Levin said. Tenet, he thought, was acting more like a White House spinner than the director of central intelligence.

THE day the CIA sent the letter to Senator Bob Graham, October 7, Bush was due to deliver a speech outlining the case against Iraq in Cincinnati. This would be Bush's effort to seal the deal as the congressional debate on the Iraq resolution headed toward a finale. The prospects for the White House looked excellent. The Biden-Lugar alternative had been shot down. The Republicans were fully behind the leader of their party; the Democrats were split. There were plenty of votes for Bush. But one last element of the White House's lobbying campaign remained: the big speech. The president would go on national television—in prime time—and share with the public compelling evidence the U.S. government possessed. This would be Bush's grand summation of the case for war. Neither before the invasion nor after would he again lay out the argument in such detail.

The White House wanted the speech loaded with as much ammunition as possible. So for days John Gibson, the White House speechwriter, had been doing what he had done prior to the UN speech: putting into the draft whatever alarming material the CIA would permit him to use. And even though Gibson had been told not to use the Niger charge for the UN speech, he now saw that it was part of the NIE. If it was in the NIE, he figured, it was good enough to use. He included it in a draft, and chief speechwriter Michael Gerson signed off. The pair, wanting to make the speech as powerful as possible, proposed a line saying that it would take only one canister of the chemical agents Saddam possessed to kill everyone in New York City—or wipe out some other major American city. The speechwriters pushed the CIA to give them a way to say this, so they could render the Iraq threat as frightening and close to home as possible. But the CIA wouldn't go along. There were too many variables, agency officials explained. Gibson and Gerson lost the line.

They also lost Niger. On October 4, the NSC had sent a draft of the Cincinnati speech to the agency for vetting. It contained a sentence that said that Iraq "has been caught attempting to purchase up to 500 metric tons of uranium oxide from Africa." It was an overstatement of the dubious language in the NIE. Iraq had certainly not been "caught" doing anything in Africa. And the CIA had even walked away from the Niger charge the day after the NIE was done. During his October 2 testimony to the Senate intelligence committee, McLaughlin had said of the recent British white paper, "I think they stretched a little bit beyond where we would stretch . . . on the points about Iraq seeking uranium from various African locations. We've looked at those reports, and we don't think they are very credible." (And during that testimony, Robert Walpole, the CIA official who had managed the production of the NIE, had been sitting right next to McLaughlin.)

On October 5, after the CIA had reviewed this draft, a senior CIA official, the associate deputy director for intelligence for strategic programs, faxed Deputy National Security Adviser Stephen Hadley and Gerson a memo telling them to strike the reference to the uranium shopping in Africa from the Cincinnati speech: "The amount is in dispute and it is debatable whether it can be acquired from the source. We told Congress that the Brits have exaggerated this issue. Finally, the Iraqis already have 550 metric tons of uranium oxide in their inventory." In other words, forget about it; the British were wrong to put the charge in their white paper. The president shouldn't use it.

But the next draft of the speech still contained the Niger charge. After the CIA received this version on October 6, the same CIA official quickly called Tenet. Then Tenet phoned Hadley and told him that his analysts thought the reporting on this allegation was weak and that Bush should not be a "fact witness" on this issue. The NSC dumped the reference. Still, the CIA sent a second fax that day to the NSC to reinforce the point: the evidence related to the Africa allegation was "weak," the "procurement is not particularly significant to Iraq's nuclear ambitions because the Iraqis already have a large stock of uranium oxide," and the CIA has already told Congress that "the Africa story is overblown." This was the fourth warning in less than a month that the CIA had sent the White House about this allegation. The Niger charge was gone—but only for the time being.

NIGER was not the only iffy intelligence the White House wanted to place in the Cincinnati speech. During the preparation for the Cincinnati speech, National Security Adviser Condoleezza Rice invited White House communications aide Adam Levine into the White House Situation Room to review hundreds of photographs strewn across the conference table. They were highly classified U.S. intelligence photos that supposedly illustrated Saddam's weapons of mass destruction. Rice wanted Levine's advice on what photos could be released with the Cincinnati speech to bolster the administration's case.

Levine, no expert on either intelligence or unconventional weapons, started to search through the pile and saw that all the shots had dates on the bottom. He wanted to see a recent one, figuring a current photo would have more impact. He spotted one that fit the bill: a highly detailed photo that appeared to show one of Saddam's UAVs that could be used to deliver chemical and biological agents. But Levine noticed something: the UAV had an insignia on it. He asked one of Rice's aides about it. It was a Czech flag, he was told. This UAV had been on display at a German air show. What, Levine asked, did this have to do with Iraq? The answer: This UAV is like the ones we believe Saddam has. *Like?* Not the real thing? Levine shook his head.

As Levine continued to pore over the photos, he realized the recent ones were all similar: shots that didn't prove anything. Aerial photographs in which the weapons or weapons site couldn't be seen. Before-and-after photographs of sites visited by United Nations inspectors—but from 1998. "I remember having this sinking feeling," Levine recalled. " 'Oh my God, I hope this isn't all we have. We've got to have better stuff than this.' "

Levine noticed something else that day. Inside the Situation Room, on the walls where a series of clocks showed the times at important capitals around the world—London, Tokyo, Moscow—there was one set to Baghdad time. Levine worried that word of this clock might leak—and that reporters might reasonably conclude that the decision to go to war against Iraq had already been made.

ON THE evening of October 7, Bush took the stage at the Cincinnati Museum Center. Before him was an audience of seven hundred or so invited guests, many from the local Republican organization. Outside, a few hundred yards away, were more than a thousand antiwar protesters, who were being kept from the museum by police on horses. (A Gallup poll released the previous day showed that popular support for an invasion of Iraq had dropped from 61 percent in June to 53 percent.)

In a stern, methodical manner, Bush depicted Iraq as a clear and present danger to the United States. Not surprisingly, he mentioned none of the doubts or dissents within the U.S. intelligence community. He called Iraq a "grave threat." He linked the peril posed by Saddam to September 11. In the wake of those attacks, he said, the United States must "confront every threat from any source . . . that could bring sudden terror and suffering to America." The Iraqi dictator, he proclaimed, "must not be permitted to threaten America and the world with horrible poisons and diseases and gases and atomic weapons." On the WMD front, he offered a whole range of evidence. He pointed out that previous UN inspections hadn't accounted for tens of thousands of liters of biological agents in Iraq and called this a "massive stockpile . . . capable of killing millions" (though UN inspectors had said that they didn't know whether this unaccounted-for material actually existed). "We know," Bush asserted, that Saddam has produced "thousands of tons of chemical agents." Iraq, Bush continued, was "exploring ways" of using unmanned drones bearing chemical and biological weapons "for missions targeting the United States."

Bush talked about the purported partnership between al-Qaeda and Baghdad, claiming that the pair had "high-level contacts that go back a decade." He then added, "We've learned that Iraq has trained al-Qaeda members in bomb making and poisons and deadly gases." (Bush was blending the Feith slide show and the information squeezed out of al-Libi.) Ignoring the CIA findings regarding Saddam's attitude toward sharing his unconventional weaons with terrorist groups, Bush said, "Iraq could decide on any given day to provide a biological or chemical weapon to a terrorist group or individual terrorists. Alliance with terrorists could allow the Iraqi regime to attack America without leaving any fingerprints."

Bush also raised the nuclear specter. He invoked the aluminum tubes and Saddam's "numerous meetings" with his "nuclear holy warriors." He said "we don't know exactly" how close Saddam was to getting a nuclear bomb. But were Iraq able to "produce, buy or steal" an amount of enriched uranium "a little larger than a single softball," it could have a bomb "in less than a year." Bush then deployed Gerson's rhetorical flourish, which Rice had road tested a month earlier: "Facing clear evidence of peril, we cannot wait for the final proof—the smoking gun—that could come in the form of a mushroom cloud."

Bush didn't advocate a military invasion—not yet. But he did dismiss other options. Inspections, sanctions, and strikes on suspected WMD sites, he asserted, hadn't stopped the Iraqi dictator from becoming a WMD power. He called on Congress "to authorize the use of America's military," noting that the House and Senate were "nearing a historic vote."

When Bush finished the speech, the crowd gave him a two-minute ovation.

IN ROME on the afternoon of October 7, the day of Bush's Cincinnati speech, Elisabetta Burba, an investigative reporter for *Panorama*, a Milan-based newsmagazine owned by conservative Italian Prime Minister Silvio Berlusconi, sat down for lunch at an upscale restaurant with an old source: Rocco Martino, the professional information peddler who had tried (unsuccessfully) to sell phony documents about a purported Niger-Iraq uranium deal to French intelligence. The two had done business in the past; Martino had once slipped Burba some papers about Islamic terrorists in the Balkans. A few days earlier, Martino had called Burba and told her he had something "very hot." Now Martino took out a thick envelope and showed the journalist what it was: documents that he said proved that Iraq had signed a deal to buy hundreds of tons of yellowcake from Niger. Martino (who was secretly tape-recording their meeting) made a reference to Bush's "big speech" that day. It was clear war was coming. But the two of them—Martino and Burba—could push it along, he suggested. "Let's make this war start," Martino told Burba. "This is a megagalactica situation."

Of course, Martino wanted money for this—20 million lire, or about $12,000. But Burba was not about to pay anything until she could verify the material. She said she would have to check out the documents. If they led to something, her magazine would pay. That was the practice in Italy. She flew back to Milan and started going over the documents with her husband, a historian.

They immediately spotted all sorts of problems with the papers. There were puzzling gaps in the documents and references that didn't seem to make sense. She started to wonder if the Niger documents were *una bufala*—a fraud. Still, she thought she should pursue the story. The next day, she told *Panorama* editor Carlo Rossella about this potential bombshell story. She proposed to fly off to Niger to check out the material. Before doing that, Rossella said, she should take the documents to the U.S. Embassy in Rome and show them to officials there. The Americans, no doubt, would know if there was anything to this deal. Rossella knew U.S. Ambassador Melvin Sembler, a shopping mall magnate who had been a fund-raiser for the Bush presidential campaign. He placed a phone call to the embassy and arranged a meeting.

Burba arrived at the U.S Embassy the following day, October 9, and was greeted by Ian Kelly, the press officer. He took her upstairs to his office to meet two embassy officials. They were cool—interested but careful. They wanted to know where she had gotten the material. A confidential source, she said. They said it wasn't the embassy's job to verify such material. But, they asked, could they have a copy? Sure, Burba said, and they photocopied the documents. But she left the embassy with no new information. Embassy officials immediately sent the copies to the State Department for review.

Eight months after Cheney had first asked about the Niger deal, the documents that had started the Niger episode—the documents that would become the most infamous intelligence forgery of recent years—were finally in the hands of the U.S. government. But the CIA still didn't have them.

Before the Burba meeting, a CIA officer who worked at the embassy had been informed of the session. But Jeff Castelli, the CIA station chief, had told his subordinate not to worry about it. We know all about this phony yellowcake report, Castelli had explained. "This is bullshit we don't have time to waste on," he had said, according to Drumheller, the CIA's European Division chief. Still, after the meeting, the station chief was given a set of the Niger documents—which he promptly forgot about. Castelli, Drumheller subsequently explained, was "not the most organized guy in the world. And his view was 'This is the least important thing that's coming across my desk now.' He just made a mistake." Langley wouldn't be able to vet the documents—because the Rome station chief had essentially lost the paperwork.

AFTER a week of debating, on October 10, the House was poised to vote on the legislation that would grant Bush the power to use military force "as he determines to be necessary and appropriate in order to defend the national security of the United States against the continuing threat posed by Iraq" and to "enforce all relevant" UN Security Council resolutions regarding Iraq.

Dick Armey, who had questioned the need for a war and Bush's motivations, gave the final emotional address before the members voted. Armey echoed the arguments that Cheney had made to him two weeks earlier. He talked about how Saddam, with his "ongoing working relationships with a myriad of evil terrorist organizations," could provide them with biological weapons that would be concealed in suitcases that could be left "in a train depot, a service station, an airport." He declared that Saddam could attack Israel at any time and "to me, an attack on Israel is an attack on America." Armey closed his remarks with an impassioned plea to the president to use his new power wisely. Choking up with tears, Armey referred to American troops and said, "Mr. President, we trust to you the best we have to give."

The measure passed easily in the House on a 296-to-133 vote, with all Republicans but six voting for the measure. The Democrats split, with 126 voting nay and 81 siding with Bush and Gephardt.

Armey had succumbed to Cheney's pressure. He had decided to be the good soldier, the loyal partisan. But this vote weighed on him. For weeks afterward, he would agonize about it and try to convince himself that he hadn't actually voted for a war. He wanted to believe that he had merely given Bush the option to use military force, to strengthen the president's hand in pursuing a diplomatic solution to the Saddam problem. "I'll tell my grandchildren that," he later said. "I'll split that hair until hell freezes over." But Armey suspected he was lying to himself. In December of that year, he would be driving along a stretch of Texas highway when a country song would come on about a fellow who looked in the mirror and saw a stranger. The line hit him hard. He had voted for the war against his better instincts, Armey now thought, and he had become that stranger. Disappointed with himself, Armey was thankful that a year previously, he had decided to leave the House at the end of this term.

Representative Walter Jones, a conservative Republican from a heavily military district in North Carolina, voted for the resolution. But after he left the House floor, as he later recounted, he was troubled. A member of the House armed services committee, Jones had never been quite convinced by the briefings he had received. There was something about the way the members of the Joint Chiefs of Staff and the rest of the Pentagon brass (including Rumsfeld) had answered the questions that told him they knew less than they were letting on. Jones was unsettled by the atmospherics that had surrounded the Iraq debate. It had been rushed, hectic, and at times too emotional. "There's something about this. I can't put my finger on it," he said to his chief of staff that night. "But I just don't feel good about this vote."

A DAY after the House voted, the resolution came up for a vote in the Senate. Every Republican but one was solidly behind the measure. On the floor of the Senate, Republican John McCain proclaimed that Saddam "has developed stocks of germs and toxins in sufficient quantities to kill the entire population of the Earth multiple times. He has placed weapons laden with these poisons on alert to fire at his neighbors within minutes." The vote on the resolution, he said, "will reveal whether we are brave and wise or reluctant, self-doubting." Senator Hillary Clinton echoed McCain and the president in outlining her support for the resolution: "Saddam Hussein has worked to rebuild his chemical and biological weapons stock, his missile delivery capability, and his nuclear program. He has also given aid, comfort, and sanctuary to terrorists, including al-Qaeda members."

Liberal Democrats passionately denounced the resolution. "What this resolution does," Senator Paul Wellstone declared, "is give the president the authority for a possible go-it-alone, unilateral military strike and ground war. . . . Our focus should be going to the United Nations Security Council."

Senator Joe Biden argued that Iraq's WMDs "do not pose an imminent threat to our national security." But he called the resolution a "march to peace and security" and said he would vote for it. If Bush were handed this authority, he reasoned, Colin Powell could cajole the Security Council to produce a tough new resolution that would compel Saddam to accept intrusive WMD inspections. And that, Biden argued, would decrease the prospects of war. "Thank God for Colin Powell," he proclaimed.

Senator Chuck Hagel, a Republican and Vietnam vet, voiced his mixed feelings. A war in Iraq would be no cakewalk, he warned: "We should not be seduced by the expectations of 'dancing in the streets' after Saddam's regime has fallen." He noted that Congress ought to be discussing the costs and commitments that would follow an invasion: "We have heard precious little from the president, his team, as well as from this Congress . . . about these most difficult and critical questions." He scoffed at war advocates who glibly spoke of Iraq as a "test case for democracy" in the Arab world. "How many of us," he asked, "really know and understand much about Iraq, the country, the people, [its] role in the Arab world?" He added, "Imposing democracy through force in Iraq is a roll of the dice." But Hagel still said he would vote for the measure.*

Senator Bob Graham, explaining his opposition to the resolution, quoted Winston Churchill: "Never, never, never believe any war will be smooth and easy, or that anyone who embarks on the strange voyage can measure the tides and hurricanes he will encounter. The statesman who yields to war fever must realize that once the signal is given, he is no longer the master of policy, but the slave of unforeseeable and uncontrollable events."

The Senate voted 77 to 23 for the resolution. Twenty-nine of the fifty Democrats said aye. That included John Kerry, who was preparing to run for president in 2004, and Tom Daschle, the Democratic leader. Daschle was still dubious of Bush's case for war, but that hadn't stopped him from acquiescing to Bush's demand. "We had just experienced 9/11," Daschle subsequently said. "Bush was telling me that Iraq had WMD and we had to move." Democrats who backed the resolution, he recalled, "were looking at where the country was. The country expected us to work together. We felt threatened."

It had taken the White House only one month to sell what Andy Card had described as its "new product": a confrontation with Iraq. Bush had won the power to strike at—and even invade—Iraq. Whether he would actually launch war was still—at least in public circles—open to speculation. Tough negotiations were under way at the United Nations, where Powell, with the support of the Blair government, was pressing France and other members of the Security Council to pass a resolution that would essentially force Saddam to accept vigorous weapons inspections or face attack. Was Bush serious about accepting a UN solution, or was he going through the

---

*Years later, Hagel said that the White House had used "the pressures of the election to get this thing done before the election. The intensity, the manipulation, the tone of the speeches, the urgency. They were maximizing the sense Americans had that we could be attacked tomorrow. There was no question that this was being manipulated."

motions for PR purposes to help Blair, who was encountering widespread public opposition in England to a war with Iraq? Some Washington players, such as Powell and Biden, clung to the hope that war wasn't yet a done deal. But Congress had just given Bush all the power he needed to make the decision on his own.

Two days after the Senate vote, a former U.S. ambassador published an op-ed piece in the San Jose *Mercury News,* a regional newspaper not closely followed in the nation's capital. Joe Wilson argued that Bush was being too confrontational, wrapping his obvious smash-Saddam desires within a thin argument on WMDs, and that the United Nations was not taking a hard enough line on a dictator who had flouted many of its resolutions. He suggested that a well-designed and well-orchestrated confrontation, in which Saddam's very existence wouldn't be threatened, could compel Baghdad to give up any WMDs it might have. "An aggressive UN-sanctioned campaign to disarm Iraq—bolstered by a militarily supported inspection process—would combine the best of the U.S. and UN approaches, a robust disarmament policy with the international legitimacy the United States seeks," he wrote.

Wilson sent copies of his article to Brent Scowcroft, James Baker, and George H. W. Bush, all of whom he knew due to his stint as the last acting ambassador in Iraq before the previous war. Scowcroft forwarded the piece to Rice at the White House. "I did think they ought to talk to somebody who had experience with Saddam," Scowcroft recalled later. "I made the point in a little note: 'Here's a person who has actually dealt with Saddam.'"

Wilson received a note from former president Bush, who said that he "agreed with almost everything" in the piece. Baker responded positively as well. And producers from cable television shows started calling and asking the former ambassador to come on air to discuss his perspective on Iraq. Wilson had reason to be pleased. His ideas had resonated among the Bush I crowd; perhaps they were also being considered within the current Bush administration.

But neither Scowcroft nor Wilson heard back from the White House.

The idea was to create an incident.

—JOHN MAGUIRE, DEPUTY CHIEF OF THE
CIA IRAQ OPERATIONS GROUP

9

A Secret in the Nevada Desert

WHO NEEDED evidence of weapons of mass destruction? John Maguire, the deputy chief of the CIA's Iraq Operations Group, and the agency officers working the Anabasis project had their own plan for starting the war, and it had nothing to do with the WMD debate. They also had a small and secret army of Iraqi commandoes—led by a former Iraqi war hero—willing to put the plan into action.

By the fall of 2002, the CIA's Anabasis team had set up a clandestine training site in the Nevada desert. The existence of the camp was one of the most tightly held secrets in the government. When Senator Bob Graham, the intelligence committee chairman, was first briefed on the training plan, he immediately thought of another era—when the CIA, in the early 1960s, had trained Cuban exiles in southern Florida for the disastrous invasion of Cuba that became known as the Bay of Pigs. The camp was located at the Energy Department's Nuclear Test Site, a vast isolated tract of land 65 miles northwest of Las Vegas and one of the most restricted stretches of territory in the country. Dozens of Iraqis had been brought to the site—some smuggled into the country—to train for a mission that Maguire and other CIA paramilitary officials hoped would trigger a war.

The plan was a core element of the original Anabasis program. These were the CIA-backed commandoes who would seize control of an isolated

Iraqi base at Nukhaib, near the Saudi border. Then they would go on the radio, announce a coup was under way, call on military units within Iraq to join them, and request that other nations support their bid to topple Saddam. Saddam, the thinking went, would be compelled to send troops to regain the base. But that would require him to violate the no-fly zone. The United States and Britain would then have a reason to attack Saddam's forces, and the war would be on. The Bush administration, Maguire later said, "was too wedded" to the WMD argument for war. "The idea was to create an incident in which Saddam lashes out." If all went as planned, "you'd have a premise for war: we've been invited in."

Maguire had been looking forward to such an operation since the day after 9/11. On September 12, 2001, he had called the man he wanted to lead this preinvasion invasion—Mohammed Abdullah al-Shahwani—and said, "It's showtime."

It was a bittersweet reunion. Years earlier, Maguire had met and worked with Shahwani, a former Iraqi general and special forces commander, and both men carried battle scars. Shahwani had been a hero of the Iran-Iraq War. He had led a daring raid in 1984 on a mountaintop in northeastern Iraq that had been taken by Iranian forces. In one of the biggest military assaults in Iraqi military history, Shahwani and his troops—using 150 helicopters—retook the strategically significant position. Three months later, Shahwani, who had on one occasion overseen the transportation of tons of mustard gas for battlefield use, was booted out of Saddam's army. The official reason: Iraq had too many high-ranking officers. But Shahwani assumed that Saddam considered a general capable of such derring-do a potential threat to his own rule.

Five years later, Shawani fled Iraq, fearing that Saddam was about to arrest him. He set up an import-export business in Amman and began establishing a secret network of former and current military officers inside Iraq who were willing to plot a coup. When the CIA learned of Shawani's network through Sarkis Soghanalian, a notorious arms dealer, it recruited him. Maguire became his control officer and reckoned the charismatic general a far more reliable partner than the conniving Chalabi.

Maguire and his colleagues in the CIA's operations directorate pressed the Clinton White House for permission to move ahead with Shahwani's coup, lest Saddam get tipped to what was in the works. But White House officials—spooked by Chalabi's botched 1995 insurrection and worried this network had been penetrated by Iraqi intelligence—withheld the go signal. By the spring of 1996, if not before, Saddam's security forces had uncovered Shahwani's operation, and the network was rolled up. About eighty of his operatives were executed, including three of Shahwani's sons. Others were tortured. Maguire was enraged, believing that a lack of resolve in Washington had directly led to the deaths of his friend's sons. Disgusted, Maguire considered resigning from the agency. A senior official talked him out of it, saying, "This will come around again."

And it did. In the Nevada desert six years later, Shahwani and Maguire were readying themselves for the next round—a chance, as Maguire would later say, "to make things right." After Maguire had set up Anabasis, Shahwani had contacted members of his old network—Iraqi exiles scattered across the globe—and had told them to gather in Kurdish-controlled Iraq. In the summer of 2002, the CIA began moving small bands of these Iraqis into the United States. After September 11, it wasn't easy for Arab men to enter the country. The CIA flew some of Shahwani's recruits across the borders in secret flights with no public records kept. (The agency used planes involved in its "extraordinary rendition" program, under which it flew captured terrorist suspects to secret interrogation prisons around the world.) In other instances, the CIA was able to provide the Iraqi fighters with passports, allowing them to enter the United States on commercial flights.

Come the fall, Shahwani and the agency had assembled about eighty members of this all-Iraqi squad of fighters at the secret camp in Nevada. They called themselves Scorpions 77 Alpha, named after a special forces unit Saddam had disbanded. (Another non-Iraqi Arab team of about fifteen saboteurs, mainly Egyptians and Lebanese, were also training at the site.) Most of the Iraqis had been professional soldiers, but they hadn't done such work in years. Maguire and his CIA teams provided refresher courses in shooting weapons, blowing up buildings and power lines, jumping out of helicopters, conducting raids. At one point, two of the men were badly injured and nearly killed when their vehicle rolled over. The assembled Scorpions were mean, angry, and eager to fight. Shahwani was the commander of the unit. And they had their own rallying cry: "Back to Baghdad."

Other Iraqi opposition groups had no idea of the existence of the Scorpions. The Iraqi National Congress attempted to recruit Shahwani to join its ranks; he ignored the invitation. (The Scorpions scoffed at Chalabi for having no support or operatives within Iraq.) "Nobody knew about us," one Scorpion later said. Inside the White House, officials responsible for Iraq planning were dimly aware of what was happening at the Nevada site. "We only knew that there were Iraqis who were being trained in small acts of sabotage and it was all being done by Tenet," recalled one senior National Security Council aide. The training, as this official understood it, was for "dirty tricks" that would create "chaos behind enemy lines." The Scorpions were indeed receiving training that could be put to such uses. But they were aiming to achieve more than dirty tricks; their goal was to trigger an invasion.*

WHILE building and training this covert force, the Anabasis men were achieving progress on another front: penetrating Saddam's regime. One of Maguire's deputies had established a relationship with the leader of Iraq's Sufi movement. The Sufis practiced a mystical brand of Islam, and their leader, a quirky holy man who believed in levitation, commanded a large and fiercely devoted following throughout Iraqi society. The leader, the CIA officers were told, could deliver sources at every level of the Iraqi leadership, including Iraqis who worked within Saddam's security forces. All he had to do was to ask his followers to cooperate with the CIA, and they would. But the Sufi leader was not about to take such a risk—unless he had a good reason to do so.

Back in September, when Congress was considering Bush's Iraq resolution, Luis and Maguire had the religious mystic flown to Washington. They met with him one night at Marrakesh restaurant on New York Avenue, a popular Moroccan establishment ten blocks from the White House where belly dancers entertained the patrons, who sat on cushions on the floor. Over dinner, the religious mystic asked the same question that the Kurdish leaders had repeatedly put to the CIA men: "You're not just going to come to Iraq, poke Saddam in the eye, and leave, are you?" No, Maguire assured

---

*The Nevada Test Site training of the Scorpions was separate from the Defense Department's effort to train a contingent of Iraqi exiles dubbed the Free Iraqi Forces at an air base in Hungary. These Iraqi exiles were supposed to serve as scouts who would accompany the U.S. military when it entered Iraq. The administration spent about $200 million on the program, which, as envisioned by the office of Undersecretary of Defense Doug Feith, would attract up to five thousand Iraqi exiles. "At the end of the day, about sixty guys showed up," recalled one White House official involved in this project.

him, this was for real. The United States was absolutely going to overthrow Saddam—and the CIA needed his help.

The Sufi leader explained that he could be persuaded—by the right amount of cash. He asked for $1 million a month. If that were forthcoming, the religious man would direct his followers—some from within Saddam's inner circle—to provide information to the Americans. The religious mystic didn't like Saddam, and he wanted a role in shaping a postinvasion Iraq. But first and foremost, Maguire thought, he wanted the money. "It was a rental agreement," the CIA man later said.

The CIA agreed to pay him, and eventually the amount did reach what the Sufi leader had requested. But Luis and Maguire considered it money well spent. Not long after the Marrakesh dinner, the religious mystic started to make Iraqi sources available to CIA officers based in Kurdish-controlled northern Iraq. The sources—who were almost too good to be believed—included Iraqi military officials who were more loyal to the mystic than to the dictator. These sources were given the code name ROCKSTARS. The information the Sufi followers supplied would be the best material the CIA would get on Iraq, including real-time information on Saddam's own movements.

THE results of the November 5 congressional elections further encouraged the Anabasis team—and anyone else hoping for war. The Republicans enlarged their margin in the House and regained control of the Senate. "It was pretty much everything George W. Bush wanted," CNN political correspondent Candy Crowley told viewers after the results were in. As it turned out, Iraq hadn't been as central an issue in the campaign as Karl Rove might once have desired. Many leading Democrats had voted for the president's war resolution. Still, Rove, who had directed much of the campaign from the White House (with the help of his chief political deputy, Ken Mehlman), had played the party's national security trump card as fiercely as he could. Bush and GOP candidates had hammered Democratic senators for failing to support the administration's version of a bill to create the Department of Homeland Security. In Georgia, a Republican challenger, Saxby Chambliss, had aired attack ads against incumbent Senator Max Cleland, that flashed pictures of Saddam Hussein and Osama bin Laden and accused the Democrat—a veteran who had lost three of his limbs while serving in

Vietnam—of voting "against the president's homeland security efforts." Cleland lost. The White House and the Republican Party were keeping the lines between fighting terrorism and the threat of Saddam Hussein as blurry as possible.

Three days after the elections, the White House triumphed again. The UN Security Council, at the urging of the Americans and the British, voted 15 to 0 to find Iraq in "material breach" of previous resolutions regarding its weapons of mass destruction. A new resolution, 1441, gave Baghdad "a final opportunity to comply with its disarmament obligations." Saddam was required to cooperate fully with "enhanced" inspections. If he did not, Iraq would face "serious consequences"—a term that the Security Council had purposefully left undefined but that hawks in the Bush administration chose to read as military action. At the State Department, there was hope that diplomacy and perhaps last-minute Iraqi compliance might avert an invasion. Right after the UN vote, Senator Joe Biden got a call from Secretary of State Powell. "We have a chance of avoiding war," Powell told him. "How bad can that be?"

Bush, though, did not greet the UN resolution with the words of a leader looking to avoid war. Moments after Resolution 1441 was passed, he declared that "any act of delay or defiance" on Saddam's part would justify military action. And even as the new UN inspection process began, the administration quietly moved ahead with its war plans. On November 26, the day before the new team of UN weapons inspectors led by Hans Blix entered Iraq, General Tommy Franks, the head of Central Command, sent Rumsfeld a request to begin deploying 300,000 troops to the Gulf. It was "the mother of all deployment orders," as Franks called it. Rumsfeld decided to stagger the order in two-week intervals, the better to avoid generating too much attention to a massive troop movement that might seem to be foreclosing the president's diplomatic options. By early December, U.S. aircraft carriers were streaming to the Gulf, and Franks moved into a newly created operational headquarters in Doha, Qatar, to manage the invasion that was on schedule to start in the next few months.

That fall, Cheney called together several of his favorite in-house intellectuals to discuss the upcoming conflict. Cheney occasionally held cozy get-togethers at the vice presidential residence on the grounds of the U.S. Naval

Observatory in northwest Washington. The guests were invariably conservative scholars and commentators who shared the vice president's distrust of diplomatic options. On this occasion, the guest list included Scooter Libby; Bernard Lewis, an Arabic scholar from Princeton; columnist George Will; and Victor Davis Hanson, a California raisin farmer and classical scholar, whose prolific writings about the virtues of American military power were read closely in the vice president's office. Cheney had even bought copies of one of Hanson's books for members of his staff, and he had assigned one of his aides to consult with Hanson regularly. Hanson was, as *New York Times* columnist Maureen Dowd acerbically dubbed him, Cheney's "war guru." Less than two weeks after 9/11, Hanson, writing in *The Wall Street Journal,* had argued that "battlefield stalwarts are rarely consensus builders" and that "great leaders are not only unpredictable, but often a little frightening." He had added, "We need generals who this time may well resign if told not to go to Baghdad."

On this evening, with the Iraq War on the horizon, Cheney wanted to discuss one of Hanson's books in particular: *The Soul of Battle.* The book profiled three fearsome military leaders: George Patton in World War II, William Tecumseh Sherman in the Civil War, and Epaminondas, a Theban general who had destroyed the Spartan army in ancient Greece. All three, in Hanson's study, were misunderstood figures. Each had been maligned during their day for employing ruthless tactics. But Hanson contended that their willingness to crush completely the armies of their enemies and (in Patton's and Sherman's cases) instill fear among the indigenous population had been effective. Cheney had read the book closely. "I think he was interested in the idea of people who are criticized as warmongers," Hanson later said. He wanted to explore the "reaction that society has toward people who want to create freedom and a better life . . . [but] have to do it in such a way that shocks people sometimes."

Cheney, it was clear to Hanson, viewed himself as one of those leaders. In the discussion that night, Cheney and Hanson talked about the historical parallels between the wars each of the three generals had fought and the modern-day struggle against Islamic fundamentalism and rogue dictators such as Saddam. Cheney was especially interested in the "bum rap" that Patton, Sherman, and Epaminondas had gotten in their respective day—and how each would later be vindicated by history, Hanson said. He warned the vice president and Libby that they, too, would face such scorn. "I just said,

'I hope you people know that once you go into Iraq, you're going to experience a level of invective that you won't believe . . . like nothing you've ever witnessed,'" Hanson subsequently remarked.

Cheney was not worried about that, according to Hanson. In fact, the vice president seemed impervious to such concerns. He was interested in the idea that defying this sort of criticism was "the responsibility of a statesman." Cheney, he added, was taking the "long view."

THE target was cars—those of Iraqi officials in Amman, Jordan. John Maguire wanted to destroy the fleet of vehicles used by Saddam's representatives in Jordan, as part of the secret Anabasis project.

As Maguire and Luis, the chief of the Iraq Operations Group, were speeding ahead with the various components of Anabasis—training operatives to conduct sabotage in Iraq, trying to penetrate Saddam's inner circle, preparing for "direct action"—they were doing whatever they could to mess with Saddam. And they were meeting resistance—from within the CIA. What to do about Saddam's cars in Jordan was one scuffle, but it was representative of the deeper conflict between the covert action squad and agency veterans, including station chiefs, who dismissed Anabasis as misguided adventurism.

Maguire, an expert in sabotage, saw the Iraqi auto fleet as an easy target. Amman had one of the largest concentrations of Iraqi government officials outside Iraq. There were two hundred or so vehicles used by Saddam's diplomats and security officers stationed there. Maguire considered three sabotage options: simple, subtle, and direct. Simple was slashing tires and drilling small holes in the windshields—small-time vandalism. Direct sabotage was more severe: blowing up or burning the cars. But that could track back to the CIA. He decided that in this case the subtle approach would be best. He devised a plan for the Amman CIA station to pour contaminants into the gas tanks of the Iraqis' cars. Within a week or so the motors would be corroded; all the vehicles would grind to a halt.

But the Amman station chief refused to move. In a cable to CIA headquarters, he huffed that he wouldn't engage in "juvenile college pranks." Maguire hit the roof. This is exactly what's wrong with the agency, he shouted. As he saw it, too many CIA stations were risk-averse timeservers who wouldn't get off their backsides and implement his plan. "We have a directive from the president of the United States to do this," Maguire shouted at the Amman station chief. "So shut the fuck up and do this! We're not interested in your grousing as to whether this is a wise move or not. The president has made a decision!" But the cars project never happened.

Luis and Maguire were increasingly infuriated by the lack of cooperation from CIA stations around the globe. Their plan called for aggressive action—*now.* They wanted to disrupt Saddam's finances and procurements, scare and intimidate his spy services, "ping" his regime with activities that might throw the dictator off his game. To block Saddam's access to money, the Iraq Operations Group had identified money managers who had access to Saddam's personal accounts. One idea was to target Saddam's top money-man in Geneva—set him up with prostitutes, get photographs, and blackmail him into shutting down the Iraqi dictator's accounts. It was a classic maneuver, called a "honey trap" in the spy trade. But this scheme and other ideas weren't happening—in large part, Luis and Maguire thought, because of lack of support from the field. These guys just don't get it, Luis and Maguire would gripe about the station chiefs. They don't understand we're serious—and that this is their job.

In several cases, the field did come through. The Athens station arranged to sting Greek-based Iraqi security officials in an arms deal. The CIA officers in Greece made it look as if the Iraqis had been buying guns for terrorists. And the terrorist gun sting hit the local press—with no mention of the CIA's role. For Luis and Maguire, it was a modest success.

But more often other parts of the Directorate of Operations were unresponsive. At one point, Luis and Maguire went to Pavitt, the chief of operations, and demanded he fire one of the station chiefs for insubordination. That would send the rest a message. Pavitt didn't do it, but he did convene a conference in London of CIA station chiefs from Europe and the Middle East. At that secret meeting, held at the U.S. Embassy, Pavitt and other agency officials laid down the word: the overthrow of Saddam was coming; everyone was expected to get with the program. It was a powerful reinforcement of the message Luis and Maguire had been hammering at hard for nearly a year: "There is no turning back."

———

THE Pentagon was preparing for an invasion. Anabasis paramilitary and intelligence operations were in motion. Yet critical elements of the WMD intelligence that propped up the administration's case for war were unraveling.

By mid-October, the Niger documents delivered by Elisabetta Burba to the U.S. Embassy in Rome had been forwarded to State Department headquarters in Washington and were in the hands of one analyst, who immediately suspected they were bogus. As he reviewed the papers purporting to document a uranium deal, Simon Dodge, the nuclear analyst at the INR, zeroed in on the bizarre companion document that had come attached to the Niger papers. It described a secret meeting at the home of the Iraqi ambassador in Rome on the afternoon of June 14, 2002. At this gathering, military officials of the world's leading outlaw states—Iraq, Iran, Sudan, Libya, and Pakistan—had come together, according to the document, to form a secret alliance to defend themselves against the West. This "plan of action" for "Global Support" would include "Islamic patriots accused of belonging to criminal organizations."

Iran and Iraq in a secret military pact? A worldwide alliance of rogue states and Islamic terrorists? This was something out of James Bond—or maybe Austin Powers. Dodge considered it "completely implausible," as he later told Senate investigators. The document bore what Dodge later described in an e-mail as a "funky Emb. Of Niger stamp (to make it look official, I guess)." The same stamp was on the uranium agreement papers. That was, for Dodge, a telltale sign. If the outlandish rogue state memo had come from the same source as the yellowcake documents, what did that say about the credibility of the Niger allegation? He concluded that the entire set of papers from Rome was probably fraudulent and e-mailed that conclusion to his colleagues.*

Dodge wasn't alone. When INR analyst Wayne White (who had once served in Niger) saw the papers, he, too, questioned their authenticity—within about fifteen minutes. The uranium deal, he thought, seemed completely impractical. And Larry Wilkerson, Powell's chief of staff, was visited

---

*The existence of the rogue state document also undermined the theory—later propounded by some journalists and bloggers—that the Niger papers were forged as part of a covert disinformation campaign designed to encourage Washington to invade Iraq. Proponents of this idea would have to account for why supposedly sophisticated operatives (presumably connected to intelligence agencies) would have concocted such a bizarre and unbelievable companion document.

at his office by an intelligence analyst who explained the implausibility of transporting massive quantities of uranium by trucks through the barely paved roads of Niger and across Africa to a port city—without any executives of the French consortium that controlled the uranium mines or any international inspectors noticing. By the time the two were done talking it through, Wilkerson later recalled, "we were laughing our asses off."

The documents—obviously forged—should have ended all talk within the U.S. government about this Niger deal. Here was concrete evidence that the Niger charge—which had been included in the National Intelligence Estimate (even though top CIA officials had doubts about it)—was phony. But the CIA didn't review the documents. The INR made a copy available to the CIA. Yet the agency did nothing with it. An officer at the agency's Counterproliferation Division merely filed the papers in a vault.

With the suspicious documents sitting unexamined in a safe, the administration could make good use of the Niger charge—perhaps more so than before. On December 7, Iraq filed a 12,000-page cut-and-paste declaration with the United Nations—required under Resolution 1441—asserting that it possessed no unconventional weapons stockpiles or any nuclear program. (Hans Blix, the chief UN inspector, called the Iraqi statement "not enough to create confidence.") The administration needed ammunition to show that the Iraqis were lying. On December 17, the CIA's WINPAC, which had aggressively pushed the nuclear claims, sent a paper to the National Security Council challenging Baghdad's assertion that it had no nuclear weapons program on two grounds: Saddam's regime had failed to explain its procurement of the aluminum tubes and it had not acknowledged its "efforts to procure uranium from Niger." (The next day, the State Department's Bureau of Public Affairs posted a fact sheet on the department's Web site pointing to these omissions. The fact sheet had been written in response to an order from Undersecretary of State John Bolton.) Tenet, McLaughlin, and other senior CIA officials had already dismissed the Niger allegation, yet WINPAC analysts—who were eager to show that Iraq was lying and determined to prove the nuclear case—couldn't let go and were treating the charge as established fact. It was one more sign of severe dysfunction at the CIA. What explained this? "There's no good answer," Dodge later said.

But Dodge was getting annoyed. In an e-mail to an Energy Department analyst, he complained that the authors of the WINPAC paper had failed to point out to the NSC that the State Department had dissented on both the aluminum tubes and the Niger claims. The Energy analyst wrote back: "It is most disturbing that WINPAC is essentially directing foreign policy in this matter. There are some very strong points to be made in respect to Iraq's arrogant non-compliance with UN sanctions. However when individuals attempt to convert those 'strong statements' into the 'knock-out' punch, the Administration will ultimately look foolish—i.e., the tubes and Niger!"

Dodge wouldn't give up. On January 12, 2003, he fired off his strongest e-mail yet to intelligence community analysts. He called the Iran-Iraq rogue alliance document ridiculous and noted again that it had the same stamp as the other material. In his e-mail, Dodge used words that should have sent a shock wave through the intelligence system. "The uranium purchase agreement," he wrote, "probably is a hoax," and the unbelievable rogue state alliance document that had come attached to the uranium deal records was "clearly a forgery."

Two Iraq analysts at WINPAC who finally looked at the Niger documents in mid-January 2003 noticed inconsistencies within the papers, but, as one later told congressional investigators, there was nothing "jumping out at us that the documents were forgeries."

WHILE Dodge (at State) was trying to counter the WINPAC analysts (at CIA), there was within the agency a brewing battle over Curveball, the elusive Iraqi exile who was the main source for the claim that Iraq had mobile weapons labs. In the weeks after Tyler Drumheller, a CIA division chief, had warned the brass that Curveball might be unreliable, the agency took no steps to investigate this all-important source. But in mid-December, the executive assistant to CIA Deputy Director John McLaughlin called a meeting to review Curveball's credibility. In preparation for the meeting, the Directorate of Operations' group chief in charge of German affairs sent out a cautionary e-mail to her colleagues. It raised the possibility that Curveball might have been "embellishing a bit" to get resettlement assistance from the German government. Now that he had received it, he appeared to be "less helpful"—and the Germans had their doubts about Curveball. "We have been unable to vet him operationally, and know very little about him," the e-mail warned. (One recipient of the e-mail was Stephen Kappes, the number two official in the operations directorate.)

At the meeting on December 19, this CIA official expanded upon her suspicions, suggesting that Curveball's stories about mobile labs may have been gleaned from public sources on the Internet. An analyst from WIN-PAC staunchly defended Curveball's reporting, insisting that his information had been corroborated (by one of the INC defectors). McLaughlin's executive assistant concluded that Curveball was "credible." McLaughlin would later insist he had never been told about any of the doubts.

Within days, the German group chief and Drumheller met with Pavitt, the head of the operations directorate, and Kappes and—once more—voiced their worries about Curveball. Pavitt, according to the German group chief, said this was a matter best left to the WINPAC analysts. The attempts to straighten out the Curveball operation had gone nowhere.

"We were reading the reports about him and scratching our heads and saying, 'What's going on?'" an officer at the CIA's Joint Task Force on Iraq later said. "We were following this with great interest. But thankfully, it was not our case. We knew he was a drunk. We knew this was beyond screwed up. But it had taken a life of its own, and it wouldn't go away. We watched it like a train wreck—with detached fascination."

THE case against Iraq was also crumbling on another front: the aluminum tubes. The agency had arranged for a private contractor to "spin" the tubes to determine if they could rotate fast enough for a nuclear centrifuge. (The tubes had to be able to spin at 90,000 revolutions per minute to work in a gas centrifuge.) The test results came back and appeared to show that the tubes were too weak for this purpose. But WINPAC refused to accept the results and ordered the data reexamined—and then it declared the new data proof the tubes were indeed usable in a centrifuge. Energy Department specialists, though, disagreed. Perhaps more important, IAEA inspectors, now back in Iraq, had rushed to the country's Nasser 81 mm rocket production facility and found 13,000 complete rockets—all made from the same aluminum tubes that the administration had been claiming were for nuclear centrifuges.

With the tubes case weakening, Joe Turner, the relentless WINPAC analyst, flew off to Vienna. In a conference room overlooking the Danube River, he again confidently argued his case to IAEA officials that the tubes *had* to be for a nuclear weapons program. But by now, he had completely lost his audience. The meeting was a disaster. "Everybody was embarrassed when he came and made this presentation," one participant later said. "Embarrassed and disgusted. We were going insane thinking, 'Where is he coming from?' "

On January 9, the IAEA released a report saying the tubes were "not directly suitable" for a nuclear centrifuge. *The New York Times'* article on the report—which noted that Bush's "key piece of evidence" had been challenged—was placed on page A10; the story was written by Michael Gordon, who had cowritten the original front-page *Times* story on the tubes.* Two and a half weeks later, on January 27, the IAEA reported to the UN Security Council that it had found no evidence of an active nuclear weapons program in Iraq. The aluminum tubes, the agency reported, appeared to be "consistent with the purpose stated by Iraq"—for artillery rockets.

The vivid imagery of a few months earlier—the "smoking gun in the form of a mushroom cloud"—was looking more like a mirage.

COME January, Shahwani and the Scorpions were all set. They had been trained. They knew the plan. The CIA moved them out of Nevada and flew them to Jordan. With comrades who hadn't made it to the training site, the unit now had more than a hundred members. Maguire and his CIA colleagues had also established a separate clandestine group that would conduct sabotage inside Iraq once the Scorpions moved on their target: the isolated Iraqi air base. The goal of the saboteurs would be to create havoc—blow things up, set cars on fire—to make it seem as if the Iraqi Army had mutinied and civil disorder was spreading. The only thing the Scorpions needed was a green light from the White House. They were waiting.

---

*Gordon's partner on the first tubes story, Judy Miller, had in recent weeks continued to report dramatic WMD allegations. In one piece, she noted that Iraq had purchased large quantities of a drug that could be used as an antidote for several chemical weapons. (Afterward, the AP noted that the United States and the United Nations had okayed Iraq's purchases of this drug, a medicine commonly used to revive heart attack victims.) In another story, Miller reported that an unidentified informant had told the CIA that Iraq had obtained an especially virulent form of smallpox in 1990 from a Russian scientist, who had died in 2000. In another piece, Miller said that "former Iraqi scientists, military officers and contractors have provided American intelligence agencies with a portrait of Saddam Hussein's secret programs to develop and conceal chemical, biological and nuclear weapons that is starkly at odds with the findings so far of the United Nations weapons inspectors."

FOR months, Valerie Wilson and the several operations officers she supervised in the basement of CIA headquarters had been frantically chasing after sources in Iraq who could tell them anything about Saddam's WMD programs. Wilson and her colleagues had developed only a small number of informants, mainly a few scientists working within Iraq. But all these sources had continued to say essentially the same thing: Iraq had no WMDs and no active WMD programs. The previous September, for example, the CIA had persuaded a Cleveland anesthesiologist to go to Baghdad and ask her brother, an electrical engineer whom the CIA believed was working on a covert nuclear weapons program, about Saddam's effort to develop nuclear weapons. The brother had told his sister that no nuclear weapons program existed.

The Joint Task Force on Iraq would write up reports detailing the denials they were getting from Iraqi scientists and shoot them into the CIA bureaucracy. But these reports were coming from only a few sources, perhaps not enough on which to base an unorthodox conclusion that would upset the White House. And CIA operations officers handling these Iraqi assets were never sure if they could believe their we-have-nothing pronouncements. "The working theory," said one CIA officer involved with the JTFI, "was that we were dealing with a similar mentality we had seen in Soviet scientists. These people were living in a society where lying was a way of life, a way to survive. We didn't just take their first answer when they said there was nothing or they themselves hadn't been involved in WMDs." Wilson and other JTFI officers couldn't tell whether they were actually getting the correct answer or whether they weren't doing their job well enough to find Saddam's WMDs.

"The fact that we were not getting affirmation of the WMDs did not mean they were not there," this CIA officer recalled. Besides, Valerie Wilson and the others were merely ops officers. It was their job to mount operations, ascertain whether sources were blowing smoke or telling the truth, and bring in whatever data they could. The analysts in the Directorate of Intelligence—such as the WINPAC analysts—were supposed to figure out what it all meant.

But on the Niger deal, Curveball, and the tubes, WINPAC analysts were making one profoundly wrong call after another—and consistently fending off challenges from other experts and even their own CIA colleagues. Their conclusions were exactly the material the White House wanted—and would soon use in the two final (and disastrous) acts of its sales campaign: the president's State of the Union speech and a historic presentation by the secretary of state at the United Nations.

I'm not reading this. This is crazy.

—SECRETARY OF STATE COLIN POWELL

10

The Final Pitch

IT WAS time to punch up another big speech on Iraq.

In mid-January 2003, two White House speechwriters, Michael Gerson and Matthew Scully, were huddled over their colleague John Gibson's shoulder staring at his computer in Room 191 of the Old Executive Office Building. The group had been working for weeks on the president's upcoming State of the Union speech, and they were focused once again on making the strongest indictment they could against Saddam Hussein. A familiar issue was back: the purported yellowcake deal in Niger. The charge had been stripped from the UN speech in September and cut from the Cincinnati speech in October. But the speechwriters had been handed a top secret binder of material that included the National Intelligence Estimate—and the Niger charge was still there. They talked about it briefly among themselves. If this was true, it was a big deal. The Niger allegation made the nuclear case much more powerful. The speechwriters agreed to put it into the speech. If there was a problem, they figured, Bob Joseph, the hawkish National Security Council staffer who handled nuclear matters, or somebody else in the intelligence community, would tell them to take it out.

In composing a litany of Saddam's offenses, the speechwriters had become enamored of a rhetorical device—which was to have Bush pronounce declarative, definitive statements. *We know* Saddam has chemical weapons agents. *We know* Saddam has biological agents. And they turned the Niger allegation into one such line: "We also know that [Saddam] has recently sought to buy uranium in Africa." Seeking CIA approval for this language, Joseph sent this part of the speech to his usual contact for such matters: the CIA's WINPAC, the analytical unit that had aggressively advocated the Niger claim and the aluminum tubes case.

When he got that portion, Alan Foley, the head of WINPAC, didn't express any concern about the credibility of the Africa line—still holding to an inexplicable position. The CIA had by this point warned the White House four times not to use the Niger allegation. Tenet had expressed skepticism about it to Hadley. And McLaughlin had told the Senate intelligence committee back in October that the CIA had looked at the yellowcake reports and "we don't think they are very credible." Yet WINPAC remained wedded to a flimsy claim that bolstered its nuclear case, and in Foley, Joseph had found a senior CIA official who wouldn't object. That was all Joseph needed to give the speechwriters the clearance they wanted.

Foley was a former Soviet analyst who, according to other intelligence officials, was not especially engaged in Iraq weapons issues. But he did raise a procedural matter. He was concerned that the line as written could be construed as revealing classified information that had come from a foreign intelligence service: the Italian SISMI. So Foley and Joseph worked out an agreement: the speech would refer to the British white paper, which had been publicly released in September and also included this charge. It was perhaps a distinction with little difference. But for Foley and Joseph, this formulation would protect the Italian secret, even if it was no longer much of one. And if anyone did have any concerns about the truth of the charge itself, attributing it to a British report would give them cover: We're not saying it's true; the British are.

Tenet and McLaughlin, according to a senior CIA official, weren't aware of Foley's discussion with Joseph.* What was on their minds was a small piece of the speech that had nothing to do with Iraq. The White House was planning to have Bush in this speech announce the creation of a Terrorist

---

*McLaughlin, according to an intelligence official, "saw one small piece of the [draft] speech which came over separately and was brought to his office by one of our staff officers. That section was focused on terrorism. John often had to fight to prevent White House speechwriters from overstating the Iraq–al-Qaeda connection."

Threat Integration Center that would compel the CIA, the FBI, the Pentagon, and the new Department of Homeland Security to share and analyze threat information in a single location. The proposal was creating the predictable bureaucratic tussles and headaches. For Tenet and McLaughlin, this was the critical part of the address, not the material that would be used to shore up the case for war.

Meanwhile, Karen Hughes, Bush's former communications director, who was now a White House consultant, was pressing Gerson and the other speechwriters to make the Iraq section of the speech as concrete as possible and to tie key charges to specific sources. Reading over a draft, she pointed out various charges and asked, "How do we know this?" She suggested the speechwriters erase the "we knows" and insert real sources: "the United Nations concluded"; "the International Atomic Energy Agency found"; "Iraqi defectors say." It would make the speech more persuasive, she suggested. So who had said that Saddam had been looking for uranium in Africa? The British had. The speechwriters could back up the charge by referencing the British white paper. Karen Hughes's attempt to firm up the speech led to the same formulation that Foley and Joseph had worked out independently.

Gibson was aware that the Niger charge had twice been knocked out of previous speeches, but he didn't dwell on that awkward detail. His assumption, he later recalled, was "maybe we had gotten better information on it." Perhaps something new had come in. Neither chief speechwriter Michael Gerson nor Deputy National Security Adviser Stephen Hadley—both of whom had been told by the CIA three months earlier to dump the Niger accusation—raised any objections to including the Niger claim in the State of the Union speech either.

On January 27, Tenet was at a National Security Council meeting and the White House handed him a copy of a near-final version of the speech, which was now loaded with references to assorted intelligence material and which included one sentence on the uranium-shopping-in-Africa claim. He put it into his briefcase and took it back to Langley. He handed it to an assistant and ordered that the draft be passed on to the director of the intelligence directorate. Tenet never read it.

The one line had become part of the speech due to a series of screw-ups and all-too-convenient memory lapses. But it was no simple accident. At the CIA, the NSC, and the White House speechwriting shop, officials were eager to go as far as they could to depict Saddam as a danger. Nobody insisted on rigorous fact checking, which might end up diluting the power of the president's message. Bush's State of the Union speech would contain other assertions about Iraq that would be wrong or overstated, yet it would be his sixteen words about uranium and Africa that would cause the greatest havoc for the administration and come to represent the White House's inflation of the WMD threat.

ON THE evening of January 28, 2003, George W. Bush strode into the U.S. Capitol. He walked past senators, representatives, Supreme Court justices, foreign ambassadors, and the Joint Chiefs of Staff and took his place in the well. Vice President Dick Cheney and House Speaker Denny Hastert sat behind him. Visitors to the Capitol this night had received instructions on how to escape a bioterrorism attack and had been informed that they could locate protective gear (called "escape hoods") in wooden cabinets in the hallways. One seat in Laura Bush's viewing box in the balcony was kept empty—a reminder of those killed in the September 11 attacks. There was much anticipation about what Bush would say about Iraq. Would he signal his intentions? In recent weeks, he had ratcheted up the rhetoric on Iraq in off-the-cuff remarks. But this was his chance to issue a full explanation of what he was thinking.

Bush devoted the first half of his speech to domestic matters. This was by design. The speechwriters wanted to build suspense. They knew what everybody wanted to hear most was what the president had to say about Iraq. But he first talked about tax cuts, Medicare, and hydrogen-powered cars. When Bush, about halfway through the speech, turned to foreign policy matters, he started with Afghanistan and AIDS in Africa. "We have the terrorists on the run," he declared. He didn't mention Osama bin Laden.

Then, after quickly referring to Iran and North Korea, Bush got to Iraq. The moment had come. The president claimed that Saddam was flouting the new UN inspections.* He once again depicted Saddam as a WMD menace, who was sitting on potentially huge stockpiles of chemical and biological weapons. He claimed Iraq had mobile biological weapons labs—

---

*A day earlier, Hans Blix, the chief UN inspector, had said that Iraq "has on the whole cooperated rather well so far" with the inspectors in Iraq but had failed to provide documentation sought by Blix.

information he said the United States knew "from three Iraqi defectors." He pointed to the aluminum tubes (even though they had recently been dismissed as evidence of a nuclear weapons program by the IAEA). And to bolster his claim that Saddam was trying to build nuclear weapons, Bush said, "The British government has learned that Saddam Hussein recently sought significant quantities of uranium from Africa."

Bush claimed that Saddam was aiding al-Qaeda and warned that the Iraqi tyrant could slip WMDs to his terrorist allies. He invoked the specter of September 11: "Imagine those nineteen hijackers with other weapons and other plans—this time armed by Saddam Hussein. It would take one vial, one canister, one crate slipped into this country to bring a day of horror like none we have ever known." The danger was growing, he insisted. The Iraqi people, he added, deserved liberation. "If Saddam Hussein does not fully disarm," Bush vowed, "for the safety of our people and for the peace of the world, we will lead a coalition to disarm him."

Bush's remarks pointed to war. But his speech contained no new evidence—other than his reference to uranium seeking in Africa, the first time the president himself had used the charge. Otherwise, the speech was a reformulation of what his administration had already declared and a rehash of critical intelligence findings that had been disputed—with no acknowledgment of the existence of the disputes. "Americans are still being asked to take it on faith that the government knows what it has yet to show—that Iraq is hiding weapons of mass destruction and has ties to al-Qaida," the Associated Press reported after the speech. "The allegations were thicker than the evidence in President Bush's State of the Union speech."*

In the speech, Bush had announced that he was asking the UN Security Council to hold a meeting in a week, at which Colin Powell would offer "information and intelligence" about Iraq's weapons and links to terrorist groups. Bush was leaving the heavy lifting to the member of his Cabinet

---

*Three years later, White House speechwriter Matthew Scully—the author of a book on the senseless slaughter of animals by big game hunters—would look back on his experiences writing Bush's Iraq speeches with no regrets. Neither he nor any of the other speechwriters, he said, had had any "independent knowledge" of the intelligence on Iraq. In any case, he noted, "I did not for one moment believe that I was involved in anything deliberately deceptive, and I don't believe that today. The basic argument was that ultimately it was for Saddam Hussein to prove he had no weapons of mass destruction, and without that proof, it was America's responsibility to act."

who was perhaps the most reluctant to guide the nation to war. It would be up to Powell to carry the argument for war over the finish line.

The next day, as Air Force One flew Bush and his entourage to Grand Rapids, Michigan, White House press secretary Ari Fleischer told reporters that Powell would go before the UN Security Council to "connect the dots." Would Powell, the reporters asked, be unveiling any fresh intelligence? "There's a review under way," Fleischer said. He added, "We are now entering the final phase."

JOE WILSON was puzzled. Watching the president give his speech, the retired ambassador had been struck by Bush's brief reference to Iraq's attempt to obtain uranium from Africa. The next day, he called a friend in the State Department. If Bush had been referring to Niger, Wilson told the State official, he may have misspoken. It wasn't only that Wilson (or so he believed) had shot down the Niger allegation. The U.S. ambassador there and a four-star Marine Corps general had also reported to Washington that such a deal was unlikely, he told his friend. Had other information come in since? If not, Wilson suggested, then the record ought to be corrected. Perhaps, the State Department official suggested, Bush had been talking about a different African country. "I had no reason to doubt my informant—his access and knowledge were more current than mine—so I didn't pursue the matter," Wilson later wrote. "It was my business only if the president was referring to Niger."

IN LATE January, days before the State of the Union speech, Bush had asked Powell to present the case against Iraq to the United Nations, and Powell had saluted and said yes. The idea—not a subtle one—was to attach Powell's credibility to the case for war. Powell's positive rating in opinion polls was over 70 percent, far higher than anybody else's in the administration. "You can afford to lose some poll points," Cheney told Powell, according to Powell's chief of staff, Lawrence Wilkerson. There was, Wilkerson thought, a real "coldness" between Powell and Cheney.*

---

*Wilkerson thought the chill went back to the first Bush administration. Powell had even alluded to this in his memoir, *My American Journey,* noting how at the end of the administration, Cheney had just disappeared from his secretary of defense office—with nary a good-bye

The presentation that Powell would deliver had been weeks in the making. After Iraq issued its WMD declaration in early December, the White House had asked the CIA to prepare a rebuttal. CIA analysts worked on this for several weeks. In late December, McLaughlin and Robert Walpole, the national intelligence officer who had overseen the National Intelligence Estimate, shared a draft with National Security Council staffers. The White House officials found it insufficient, complaining it lacked even the details of the NIE. Keep working on it, they told McLaughlin and Walpole. Weeks later, McLaughlin sent a revised version of the paper to the NSC and said, this is the best we can do.

It still wasn't good enough for the White House. Bush handed the assignment to Stephen Hadley and Scooter Libby. They were to take what the CIA had pulled together, whip it into shape, and produce a public case that would be irrefutable. The verdict—war—had essentially been reached; Bush was looking for the most compelling rationale to present to the public. The two lawyers went out to the CIA to search for whatever intelligence fragments they could find.

On January 25, in the White House Situation Room, Libby presented what he had assembled to Rice, Hadley, Wolfowitz, Rove, Armitage, Gerson, and Hughes. Libby claimed that intercepts and human intelligence reports indicated that Iraq had been concealing, moving, and burying items. What were they? Libby didn't know. But they had to be WMDs. He reported that Saddam's ties to al-Qaeda were extensive. He pointed to Mohamed Atta's alleged meeting in Prague with an Iraqi intelligence officer. All of this, Libby said, was a "Chinese menu" from which the various items could be selected. Armitage was stunned by Libby's blatant attempt to transform uncertain fragments into solid evidence. Wolfowitz, though, was impressed. Rove, too. Hughes cautioned Libby to stick to the facts. As for who should be the front man for the administration, the group agreed: Powell.

Powell was a good soldier who had earlier told Bush that he would stand by him in the coming war. He had tried hard to concoct a diplomatic resolution that Bush could accept. He and his top aides at State—Armitage and

---

to Powell, then the chairman of the Joint Chiefs of Staff. "Cheney left the Pentagon and never said a word to him," remembered Wilkerson, who was Powell's chief aide at the time. "No farewell, no bye-bye, no 'Job well done,' no 'Job poorly done.' One day he was there, the next day he wasn't."

Undersecretary Marc Grossman—had believed that they had a chance of pulling an end run on Cheney, Rumsfeld, Wolfowitz, and the go-for-war crowd. The Powell plan had been simple: keep the inspections process going for several more months, with increasingly intrusive inspections, and, at the same time, continue the military buildup and egg on the UN to threaten military action if Saddam did not capitulate. All of this might cause Saddam to step down, prompt an internal coup, or lead to other significant changes. But days earlier, on January 20, Powell and his allies at the State Department had practically given up. That day, French Foreign Minister Dominique de Villepin had said that France would not even consider war against Iraq—as long as the French believed peaceful alternatives (such as inspections) remained. The Chinese and German foreign ministers echoed his remarks.

The threat of a UN-sanctioned war was gone. De Villepin's statement enraged Powell and his team. It seemed a betrayal, for Powell was attempting to walk a tightrope, pushing the United Nations to pressure Iraq further and hoping muscular diplomacy would somehow prevent the war that Bush had already decided upon. Powell might have been hoping for more than he could reasonably expect. Still, he saw de Villepin's "no" as pulling the rug out from under him—whether or not there really had been a rug there. "All the hope of everybody went away," recalled a senior State Department official. "I was furious. . . . On that day, we were going to war."

THE day after Bush's State of the Union speech, Powell entered the office of Larry Wilkerson, his chief of staff, and handed him a draft script for the UN speech that was forty-eight pages long. Scooter Libby had given it to Powell at the White House. "We've done some work," Cheney had told Powell. "This is what you can work from." Powell instructed Wilkerson to start with the Libby draft and gave Wilkerson specific orders: he was to coordinate with the White House and the CIA to guarantee the speech would be as solid as possible. Wilkerson had been a senior aide to Powell for ten of the past fourteen years, and Powell trusted him completely. He told Wilkerson that he would be working with Will Tobey from the National Security Council, John Hannah from Cheney's office, Tenet, and McLaughlin. Powell wanted an airtight case, with multiple sources for every claim.

Wilkerson understood that the speech was a historic moment—both for his boss and for the country. Commentators were already comparing Powell's upcoming address to the dramatic moment during the Cuban Missile Crisis in 1962, when Adlai Stevenson, the U.S. ambassador to the United Nations, had displayed aerial photographs of Soviet missiles in Cuba at a special UN session and demanded an explanation from the Soviet ambassador. "I'm prepared to wait until hell freezes over," Stevenson had said. (Powell and Wilkerson would soon study tapes of Stevenson's talk.) Powell's speech at the United Nations would be his chance to galvanize world attention—just as Stevenson had.

The next morning, Wilkerson arrived at CIA headquarters to get to work. The team, including Tenet, McLaughlin, Tobey, Hannah, and Bob Joseph, assembled in Tenet's conference room and started reviewing the Libby draft. The process quickly proved tedious and exasperating. Wilkerson insisted on seeing the source for every assertion in the Libby script—not just the citation but the actual report or document. Wilkerson forced Hannah to page through his clipboard and pull out the supporting material.

For Wilkerson, this was the first peek under the hood of the administration's WMD case—and it was not pretty. "Hannah was constantly flipping through his clipboard, trying to source and verify all the statements," Wilkerson recalled. As the meeting wore on, Wilkerson became increasingly frustrated. "It was clear the thing was put together by cherry-picking everything from *The New York Times* to the DIA," he said. When Wilkerson and the team began to examine the underlying sources, they found that a Defense Intelligence Agency report was not being used properly, a CIA report was not being cited in a fair way, a referenced *New York Times* article was quoting a DIA report out of context. There were stories cited from *The Washington Times* by Bill Gertz, the conservative paper's defense writer, who specialized in receiving leaks from hard-liners inside the Pentagon. Much of the information in Libby's draft, Wilkerson concluded, had come from the Iraqi National Congress—laundered through Feith's operation at the Pentagon. It was maddening. Another State Department official present recalled that "we couldn't figure out where" the WMD allegations in the Libby draft were "coming from. . . . We took it apart piece by piece."

After six hours of work, only a few pages had been vetted. "Finally," Wilkerson recalled, "I threw the paper down on the table and said, 'This isn't going to cut it, ladies and gentlemen. We're never going to get there. We're going to have to have a different method.' And that's when George said, 'Let's use the NIE.' " Tenet turned to Hannah and rubbed it in: "I don't understand why we weren't doing that from the start. You've wasted a lot of our time." The Libby draft was tossed—and the team had a fresh script, the National Intelligence Estimate.

The new approach gave Wilkerson some comfort. In the days ahead, as Wilkerson and the others crafted the speech using assertions from the NIE, there was an illusion of professionalism. Tenet and McLaughlin would assure Wilkerson of the multiple sourcing for each claim—on mobile labs, aluminum tubes, UAVs. Wilkerson would press Tenet: You've got multiple sources for this and you're saying, George, they're independent of each other? "And then," Wilkerson recalled, "John [McLaughlin] would jump in and say, 'Yeah, this one was obtained this way, this one that way, they didn't collude, they're independent, and we've got satellite evidence to corroborate this man's remarks.' " On at least one occasion, there was a heated discussion over the aluminum tubes. "Without the tubes there was no nuclear case," a State Department official involved in this prep work recalled. Tenet and McLaughlin insisted on including the tubes; McLaughlin cited the spin tests that had been conducted, not disclosing that some experts had read the results as failures.

There was even talk of Powell holding up one of the tubes for dramatic effect. But a veteran communications strategist in the room balked. "If you do that, it will be on the front page of every paper the next day," noted Anna Perez, Condoleezza Rice's chief of communications. "Do you really want to do that?" Perez had a feel for these things; she had worked for Walt Disney, Chevron, and a top Hollywood talent agency. This would, she thought, be an awkward visual. Powell would be holding up the one piece of evidence that was most in dispute. Everybody would focus on that.

The idea was scrapped. Instead, the group came up with an alternative visual. When Powell was to start talking about biological weapons, he would raise a small medical vial. It was big enough to contain "less than a teaspoon" of dry anthrax—the same amount, he would note, that had shut down the U.S. Senate during the 2001 anthrax attack, killed two postal workers, and forced several hundred people to obtain emergency medical treatment.

As the back-and-forth continued, one of the State Department officials present started wondering, What about that Africa uranium charge? Bush had just highlighted it in the State of the Union. The State official kept waiting for Tenet or McLaughlin to mention it. "But nothing ever came up," the official recalled. It was curious.

On January 31, the State Department's INR, which had been vetting the work-in-progress draft, sent Powell a memo noting that thirty-eight allegations in the speech were "weak" or "unsubstantiated." The document noted that the draft's claim that Saddam had plans to hide WMDs (possibly in another country) had come mostly from "questionable sources." The draft asserted that the presence of decontamination vehicles at suspected sites was evidence that Iraq was stockpiling chemical weapons. But the INR analysis noted that these vehicles were "water trucks that can have legitimate uses." The draft also cited suspicious activity at a suspected chemical weapons site. INR wrote, "We caution, however, that Iraq has given [the UN inspectors] what may be a plausible account for this activity—that this was an exercise involving the movement of conventional explosives." The INR memo reported that the section on the aluminum tubes was "WEAK" and contained "egregious errors." INR analysts also objected to a section that stated that terrorists "could come through Baghdad and pick-up biological weapons."

Twenty-eight of the thirty-eight items identified by INR were excised from the draft. Two days later, the INR would object to seven items, three of which would be deleted. Since not all of INR's objections were heeded, Powell would be presenting evidence at the UN that even his own specialists did not believe.

On January 31, Bush met with Blair in the Oval Office for two hours. Blair had a request. He explained to Bush that he needed a second UN resolution that explicitly authorized military action against Iraq—despite France's opposition. He had promised his Labour Party he would seek one, and, with the British public decidedly opposed to an invasion of Iraq, a second UN resolution—at least an attempt to obtain one—was a political necessity. A memo written by a Blair aide recorded what the prime minister told Bush: "If anything went wrong with the military campaign, or if Saddam increased the stakes by burning the oil wells, killing children or fomenting internal divisions within Iraq, a second resolution would give us international cover, especially with the Arabs." Bush agreed to help his ally and to twist arms at the United Nations to win another vote there—even though Cheney never thought a second resolution was necessary and Powell now believed it wasn't achievable. But Bush told Blair that regardless of what happened at the United Nations or with the inspections in Iraq, there already was a tentative start date for the war: March 10.

Bush was clearly committed to an invasion. During the meeting, according to the memo, both Bush and Blair said they doubted that weapons of mass destruction would be discovered by the inspectors in Iraq in the near future. Given that, Bush raised the idea of provoking a confrontation with Saddam and floated several possibilities. "The U.S. was thinking," the document reported, "of flying U2 reconnaissance aircraft with fighter cover over Iraq, painted in UN colours. If Saddam fired on them, he would be in breach" of existing UN resolutions. And a retaliatory attack would be justified. Bush was considering creating an incident to start the war. Another option Bush cited, according to the memo, was producing "a defector who could give a public presentation about Saddam's WMD." Bush also mentioned assassinating Saddam. (If Bush wanted to stage a provocation, the CIA-trained Scorpions were ready to go in Jordan and the Anabasis men already had a plan to do it.)

Bush and Blair also talked about the aluminum tubes. The president assured the prime minister the IAEA was wrong to conclude that the tubes were for artillery rockets, not for a nuclear program. Bush insisted that the specifications of the tubes indicated they were indeed right for a nuclear centrifuge. And when the two talked briefly about postinvasion Iraq, Bush remarked that it was "unlikely there would be internecine warfare between the different religious and ethnic groups." Blair agreed.

THE drafting of Powell's presentation continued slowly, and tensions were growing. By Saturday morning, February 1, a proposed twenty-five-page script on Saddam's purported connections to terrorists had arrived—a compilation of the material that had been prepared by Feith's office. Cheney and Libby had been pushing to include a section on the supposed connections between Saddam and al-Qaeda. At this point, Powell himself was working on the speech in Tenet's conference room—joined at times by Rice, Hadley, Libby, and others. After Powell reviewed the new terrorism section, he pulled Wilkerson off to a side room and said, "I'm not reading this. This is crazy." The script, Wilkerson remembered, was a "genealogy" that strung together connections or associations and that were incomprehensible—and possibly meaningless: "It was like the Bible. It was the Old Testament. It was 'Joe met Bob met Frank met Bill met Ted met Jane in Khartoum and therefore we assume that Bob knew Ralph.' It was incredible."

The terror script was pared down to only the few assertions that the CIA would endorse, such as the claim that the Jordanian terrorist Abu Musab Zarqawi—who had been linked to a plot to assassinate a U.S. diplomat in Jordan—was being harbored in Iraq. (The evidence for the claims Powell accepted would prove sketchy as well.) Libby and Hadley, though, still wanted Powell to use a more dramatic allegation: the Atta-in-Prague story (Cheney had also asked Powell to use the charge). Powell had taken it out because Tenet had told him the agency was not sure the meeting ever occurred. But Hadley repeatedly tried to insert it in the speech. "What happened to Atta-in-Prague?" he asked during one discussion. Powell fixed him with a cold stare: "Steve, we took that out, don't you remember? And it's staying out." Hadley, according to Wilkerson, "kind of shrunk in his chair, looked at the secretary, and said, 'Oh yeah, I remember that.'"

Hunkered down at CIA headquarters, Powell kept poring over the intelligence, fighting off frustration. So much of the material was murky. On Sunday, February 2, he asked Armitage to join him at Langley. Armitage, too, was wary of the information piled before them. Powell's patience was wearing thin. "This is bullshit," he said at one point, throwing his papers down on the table.

Amid the fighting over what he should say in the speech, Powell received little support from another high-level official who had joined the group: Condoleezza Rice. Powell had been a mentor to Rice. They had worked together during the first Bush administration and were the two most visible African Americans in the government. But in the battles that weekend, Rice showed little deference to Powell, consistently siding with her deputy, Hadley, and the vice president's staff. She seemed almost dismissive of Powell's concerns and, as Wilkerson saw it, showed him little respect. "I was taken aback by the way Dr. Rice talked to him," Wilkerson said. "She would just say, 'Oh, come on, you know that ought to be in there.'"

AT THE start of the following week, the team assembled in New York and continued working on Powell's presentation. But unbeknownst to the secretary of state, the CIA was at war with itself over a critical piece of intelligence that he was about to share with the world.

One of the most alarming passages in the draft of Powell's speech was the claim that Iraq had mobile biological labs. Bush had cited these labs in his State of the Union speech, but the charge had not been played up and had received little media attention. The draft called for Powell to state that U.S. intelligence had "first hand descriptions" of these facilities and to show diagrams of the labs. With these illustrations, it would look as if the United States had caught Saddam red-handed. The plan was for Powell to back up this powerful allegation by citing four sources. The most important one would be an Iraqi chemical engineer: Curveball, the defector of questionable credibility. Another would be a former Iraqi major who had defected in 2001 and had supposedly confirmed the existence of the biolabs. This was Mohammad al-Harith, an INC-produced source who had been guided into the intelligence system by Jim Woolsey. Yet he had been judged a fabricator by the Defense Intelligence Agency a year earlier.*

But the mobile labs story was really all about Curveball. And within the CIA, some officers were still worrying about him. On January 24, the Germany group chief in the DO, who had previously raised concerns about Curveball, sent a cable to the Berlin station and asked if it could quickly obtain from the Germans the transcripts of Curveball's interviews with German intelligence. She had learned that there would be a Powell speech at the United Nations that would refer to the mobile biological weapons. As she later told investigators, she "couldn't believe" the presentation relied on Curveball reporting.

On January 27, the Berlin station replied that German intelligence "has not been able to verify [Curveball's] reporting." The station added a warning: "The source himself is problematical. . . . [T]o use information from another liaison service's source whose information cannot be verified on such an important, key topic should take the most serious consideration."

After this disturbing cable came in, Tyler Drumheller, the European Division chief, told John McLaughlin's executive assistant that the Germans

---

*A Pentagon intelligence officer who was aware of the fabrication notice sent out on al-Harith attended two preparation meetings for the Powell speech, but he raised no objections to using al-Harith as a source. He later told Senate investigators he was unaware that the source mentioned in the draft—who was not identified by name—was al-Harith.

were still blocking access to Curveball. And Drumheller followed up with an e-mail reporting that "we are not certain that we know where Curve Ball is" and that the Germans "cannot vouch for the validity of [Curveball's] information." Still, the Germans had told Drumheller that the Bush administration was free to use the Curveball information, as long as it did not attribute it to a German intelligence source; the Germans would not refute it.

This was not much of an endorsement. McLaughlin checked with a WINPAC analyst who assured him Curveball's reporting was solid.

Yet on February 3, with Powell's speech just two days away, McLaughlin's executive assistant sent a memo to Drumheller asking him to "touch base" with CIA stations in Berlin and elsewhere to get a fix on the "current status/whereabouts" of Curveball. The memo noted that "we want to take every precaution against unwelcome surprises that might emerge concerning the intel case; clearly, public statements by this émigré, press accounts of his reporting or credibility, or even direct press access to him would cause a number of potential concerns." McLaughlin wanted to be certain that after Powell displayed artist's renderings of the mobile BW labs to the whole world, Curveball wouldn't pop up in the media and say something to undermine the case. The CIA's number two man was worrying more about a post-speech problem than the legitimacy of the allegation.

But the only U.S. intelligence officer ever to have met Curveball was alarmed Powell would be depending on this iffy source. When Les, the Defense Department medical doctor and biological weapons specialist detailed to the CIA's Counterproliferation Division, read a draft of Powell's speech, he was upset. He had gone to Germany in 2000 to draw blood from Curveball and had returned troubled by the man he had met, suspecting he was a drunk and unreliable. Since then, Les had become frustrated as the Curveball operation continued. When he spotted Curveball information in Powell's draft, he later told Senate investigators, "I thought, my gosh, we have got—I have got to go on record and make my concerns known." On February 4, he sent an e-mail to the deputy chief of the CIA's Joint Task Force on Iraq: "I do have a concern with the validity of the information based on 'CURVE BALL.'" He noted there had been "major handling issues" with Curveball, including questions about whether "in fact, CURVE BALL was who he said he was." And he wrote, "These issues, in my opinion, warrant further inquiry before we use the information as the backbone of one of our major findings of the existence of a continuing Iraqi BW program!" The doctor's e-mail also reported that al-Harith—a supporting source for Curveball—had been branded a fabricator. "Need I say more?" he asked.

The deputy chief invited Les to see him and talk about this. But the deputy chief told Les not to expect that anything would change. His e-mail response reflected the attitude of the CIA leadership—and of much of the intelligence community—toward the administration's ongoing push for war: "As I said last night, let's keep in mind the fact that this war's going to happen regardless of what Curve Ball said or didn't say, and that the Powers that Be probably aren't terribly interested in whether Curve Ball knows what he's talking about. However, in the interest of Truth, we owe somebody a sentence of [sic] two of warning, if you honestly have reservations."

Les and the deputy chief met on the evening of February 4. Powell's speech was too far along, the deputy chief said to the doctor. What was done was done. The one U.S. intelligence employee who had ever had direct contact with Curveball could not prevent this disaster from happening.

Later that night, the Curveball issue came up yet again—this time with Tenet. The CIA director was already in New York City, helping with the final preparations for Powell's speech the next day. From his hotel suite at the Waldorf-Astoria, he called Tyler Drumheller at home and asked for the phone number of Richard Dearlove, the chief of the British intelligence service. He wanted Dearlove's approval to use British intelligence in the Powell speech. When Drumheller called Tenet back to give him the number, he mentioned Curveball. "Hey, boss, there's problems with that case," Drumheller later recalled telling Tenet. He quickly gave the CIA chief a boiled-down version of the Curveball issue. But Tenet, at this point, was in no mood to listen. He replied, according to Drumheller, with words to the effect, "Yeah, yeah, yeah, I'm exhausted," and said, "Don't worry about it." (Tenet would later claim he had no recollection of Drumheller's warning about Curveball and had never heard any complaints about the Iraqi source until after the war began.)

That wasn't the only last-minute distraction for Tenet. About 2:30 A.M., Phil Mudd, the CIA's top expert on terrorism, contacted him and passed along concerns from the White House. There were too many deletions to the passages on terrorism. Libby had called Powell's staff in New York and asked why certain material had been cut from that part of the speech. Tenet tried to reach Wilkerson through the State Department switchboard, but he couldn't get through.

SOMETIME in the days before the UN speech, Senator Joe Biden called Powell. He told the secretary of state that he thought it was encouraging that Bush was sending Powell to the United Nations and not blowing off diplomacy. Perhaps there still was a chance to get a second UN resolution authorizing military action—which might compel Saddam to capitulate or at least legitimize an invasion. Referring to Powell's UN presentation, Biden cautioned him, "Don't speak to anything you don't know about." That is, don't overstate the evidence. There was silence on the other end. Then Powell replied, "Someday when we're both out of office, we'll have a cup of coffee and I'll tell you why." Why what? Powell didn't explain, but Biden took the remark to mean that Powell was going to present a case about which he had his doubts.

THE day of the speech, Wilkerson got to the United Nations early. He wanted to be certain that everything would go as planned: the audiovisuals, the tapes of intercepted Iraqi communications that Powell would play. At one point, Wilkerson was told he had a call. It was the vice president's office. "Give that one to Barry," Wilkerson said, referring to Barry Lowenkron, a State Department official who had worked on the speech. But Lowenkron didn't take the call either. Wilkerson was later told the caller was Scooter Libby. The vice president's chief of staff had been making one last attempt to get the Atta-in-Prague allegation and other deleted sections of his terrorism draft back into Powell's speech.

Powell began at 10:30 that morning. Sitting right behind him at the United Nations was George Tenet. Powell had demanded that Tenet be there, a graphic demonstration that Powell was conveying evidence that had been vetted by the highest levels of U.S. intelligence. He told the members of the Security Council that he would "share with you what the United States knows about Iraq's weapons of mass destruction as well as Iraq's involvement in terrorism." *Knows,* he said. Not everything Washington knew could be disclosed, he said. Nevertheless, the evidence he had, Powell said, would demonstrate that "Saddam Hussein and his regime are concealing their efforts to produce more weapons of mass destruction."

Powell began with an intercepted conversation between two officers of Iraq's Republican Guard that had occurred on November 26, 2002. The pair apparently had been discussing hiding a prohibited (though unspecified) vehicle. Another intercept had supposedly caught another Republican Guard officer telling a subordinate to "clean out" an ammunition storage site before weapons inspectors were to visit it. Here was proof, Powell declared, that Iraq was moving and hiding items—presumably related to WMDs, but he didn't say what they were.*

"We know," Powell said, that Saddam's son Qusay had ordered the removal of prohibited weapons from various palaces, that government officials were hiding WMD stuff in their homes, that key intelligence files were being driven around the Iraqi countryside to avoid detection. "We know," he said, that warheads containing biological weapons had been disbursed to western Iraq.

The presentation went on for seventy-six minutes. He showed satellite photos that he said depicted WMD materials being moved from Iraqi facilities. He maintained that Iraq had not accounted for all the WMD-related material it had possessed in the mid-1990s. As for what Iraq had at this moment in time, Powell reported that "one of the most worrisome things that emerges from the thick intelligence file we have on Iraq's biological weapons is the existence of mobile production facilities used to make biological agents." These labs of death, he said, in a matter of months "can produce a quantity of biological poison equal to the entire amount that Iraq claimed to have produced in the years prior to the Gulf War." The source for this, he disclosed, was an eyewitness hiding in another country. He meant Curveball. Powell put up a slide showing a drawing of these mobile labs—as trucks and as railway cars. "We know how they work," he stated. ". . . We know that Iraq has at least seven of these mobile biological agent factories." These labs in just one month could produce enough biological agent "to kill thousands upon thousands of people." Iraq, he added, could use UAVs to launch a terrorist attack with biological weapons.

---

*The use of the NSA intercepts by Powell would seem to some observers one of the more persuasive elements in his presentation. But three months later, then NSA director Michael Hayden was a guest of *Newsweek* magazine at the White House correspondents dinner and was asked by a reporter to explain how the seemingly damning intercepts squared with the postwar failure to find any WMD. In a revealing moment, Hayden admitted the intercepts were arguably more ambiguous and open to interpretation than Powell had suggested. "If I were a defense lawyer," Hayden said, "I could make a case" that the intercepts didn't mean what Powell said they did.

Powell displayed a satellite photo of a facility where topsoil had been removed "in order to conceal chemical weapons evidence." As for nuclear weapons, he maintained that Saddam had never abandoned his nuclear weapons program. He didn't mention the Niger allegation, but he did cite the aluminum tubes. Powell, somewhat candidly, said there had been disagreement over the tubes but that "most U.S. experts" believed they were intended for centrifuges used to enrich uranium.

The danger was not merely Saddam's arsenal, Powell said, but the "sinister nexus between Iraq and the al-Qaeda terrorist network." To prove such a nexus existed, Powell claimed that Saddam was harboring Zarqawi's network and called Zarqawi a bin Laden "associate." Zarqawi, Powell reported, was running a camp specializing in poison and explosives training in northeastern Iraq. Had Zarqawi set up this base? What did it mean to be an al-Qaeda "associate"? It was all a bit fuzzy. And as if he were presenting a watered-down version of Feith's slide show, Powell reported that representatives of al-Qaeda and Saddam's regime had met "at least eight times" since the early 1990s.

THEN Powell offered his most powerful example of the "sinister nexus." It was the account of Ibn al-Shaykh al-Libi, the al-Qaeda commander who FBI agents feared had been tortured by the Egyptians. Powell, without using his name, stretched it out with dramatic effect:

> I can trace the story of a senior terrorist operative telling how Iraq provided training in these weapons [of mass destruction] to al-Qaeda. Fortunately, this operative is now detained, and he has told his story. I will relate it to you now as he himself described it.

This terrorist operative, according to Powell, had recounted how bin Laden had been unable to develop chemical or biological agents at al-Qaeda labs in Afghanistan and had turned elsewhere for help. "Where did they go? Where did they look? They went to Iraq." And Saddam's regime had provided "help in acquiring poisons and gases."

But the CIA now had its doubts about this entire story. CIA analyst Paul Pillar, who specialized in terrorism issues, had become, as he later recalled, deeply troubled when he had read the al-Libi interrogation reports, which had been passed to the CIA by Egyptian intelligence. They were sketchy and ambiguous—"almost James Joycean," Pillar subsequently said. It was hard to tell what al-Libi was really saying. One weekend, Pillar read them and reread them—and concluded that al-Libi was not actually claiming that the Iraqi training was real, only that it was something he had heard about from others. In January 2003, the CIA had produced a classified update on the relationship between Iraq and al-Qaeda that included a new caveat: al-Libi had not been in a position "to know if any training had taken place."

Powell was basing a key part of his argument for war on a source the CIA had, only days earlier, discounted.*

POWELL concluded with a few words about Saddam's atrocious human rights record. Iraq, he noted, was in material breach of UN Security Council resolutions, including the latest one. "We must not shrink from whatever is ahead of us," Powell said. It was almost as if he were trying to convince himself.

As Powell spoke, Wilkerson watched closely from a few rows back. Powell seemed in command of the material. But Wilkerson was not happy. He stared at the Iraqi delegation. He wanted to see if the Iraqis were rattled. But from what Wilkerson could tell, the Iraqis seemed unfazed. It looked as if they were rolling their eyes, as if to say, "Is this the best you have?" Wilkerson concluded that the speech was also not cutting it with the broader audience. He slumped in his chair. "I thought I had failed," he later said.

The reviews in the media were far kinder than Wilkerson had expected. That night, on MSNBC, David Kay, the former UN weapons inspector, said that Powell's presentation "was a well-integrated, very thorough case." The next day, *USA Today* reported that Powell had "forcefully laid out newly declassified evidence of Iraq's efforts to develop and conceal chemical, biological and nuclear weapons, as well as new signs that an al-Qaeda terrorist cell was set up in Baghdad last year." *The New York Times'* editorial page said

---

*Years later, Wilkerson noted that it was only *after* Powell's speech that he had heard about the earlier DIA dissent that had questioned al-Libi's charges and had learned that al-Libi, as Wilkerson put it, had been questioned "under conditions of torture or near torture." He noted, "This was disturbing because no such dissent was ever made known to me during the preparations [for Powell's speech] . . . Al-Libi's forced testimony was of course crucial to the secretary's assertions in the presentation that al-Qaeda had substantive links with Baghdad."

that Powell had delivered a "convincing" presentation. Mary McGrory, the veteran liberal *Washington Post* columnist, declared, "He persuaded me, and I was as tough as France to convince."*

Those aware of the disputes that had raged within the intelligence community were more in a position to be surprised by Powell's speech. "I was stunned and appalled by the nuclear portion of Powell's speech," Wayne White, an Iraq analyst at INR, later recalled. "After all the work [INR analyst] Simon [Dodge] had done in order to convince so many in the department that there was nothing to the aluminum tube story, I could hardly believe that the secretary would, in effect, make assertions contradicting the conclusions of his own in-house intelligence shop."

When Drumheller listened to the speech, he was astonished that the Curveball information had been included. So was an officer within Valerie Wilson's Joint Task Force on Iraq: "My mouth hung open when I saw Colin Powell use information from Curveball. It was like cognitive dissonance. Maybe, I thought, my government has something more. But it scared me deeply."

VIRTUALLY all of the allegations Powell presented would turn out to be wrong. But at the time, few in the media bothered poking at the details of Powell's address. The presentation was largely covered as a success, even if it did not win over reluctant allies. Powell's speech didn't have the power of Adlai Stevenson's showdown with the Soviets, but it achieved a boost in the poll numbers for the war-with-Iraq option. Powell had provided a measure of credibility to Bush's argument for war.

In later years, Powell would become increasingly embittered about the Security Council speech and the attention it continued to receive. "What I said was what they gave me to say," he said in the summer of 2006. "I'm not an intelligence officer. I was secretary of state. Whatever was in that speech was what they [the CIA] told me. I kept asking them, 'Are you sure of this? Are you confident of that?'" Powell said he had pressed hard on the mobile biolabs claim: "They said it was multi-sourced. I had no way of knowing it

---

*Weeks later, shortly before the invasion of Iraq, McGrory wrote a column clarifying her endorsement of Powell's presentation: "I did not make it clear enough that while I believed what Colin Powell told me about Saddam Hussein's poison collection, I was not convinced that war was the answer."

all went back to one guy." Powell blamed Tenet for the fiasco at the UN. And when, as Powell put it, "the sources started dropping like flies," he expressed his "disappointment" to the CIA director: "I had very little to do with the CIA after that."

It rankled Powell that his UN presentation had come to be considered a pivotal event on the path to war: "It's annoying to me. Everybody focuses on my presentation . . . Well the same goddamn case was presented to the U.S. Senate and the Congress and they voted for [Bush's Iraq] resolution. . . . Why aren't they outraged? They're the ones who are supposed to do oversight. The same case was presented to the president. Why isn't the president outraged? Its always, 'Gee, Powell, you made this speech to the UN.'"

But at the time, Powell was satisfied with his performance. When he returned to Washington, he told Wilkerson he was giving an award, a special plaque, to everyone who had worked on the speech. Wilkerson, though, was deflated and told his boss he didn't want it. (Another State Department official who received one of these plaques put it in his closet—and never took it out.) Wilkerson didn't think the speech was nearly as powerful as it should have been. Nor did Wilkerson have much confidence in the evidence Powell had vouched for. Later, he called the speech "the lowest point in my professional life" and "a hoax." He also said, "I never would have gone to war on that intelligence." But that was indeed what was happening—and his boss had cleared the way.

They had decided they were smarter than the rest of us.

—MILITARY ANALYST WHO DRAFTED A
STUDY PLANNING FOR POSTWAR IRAQ

11

Best-Laid Plans

A S THE war drew closer, President Bush sought to recast and broaden its purpose. An invasion of Iraq wasn't simply a preemptive strike against a menacing dictator; it would also be a transformative event for a troubled region. The president was now putting forth a grand and expansive vision, but one that obscured harsh realities that U.S. government experts were repeatedly warning about, both in public and behind the scenes.

The president outlined his larger war goals in a speech at an American Enterprise Institute fund-raiser on February 26, 2003. Standing before fourteen hundred AEI supporters and allies in a ballroom at the Washington Hilton that evening, he declared that "the world has a clear interest in the spread of democratic values" and that a "new regime in Iraq would serve as a dramatic and inspiring example of freedom for other nations in the region." After having spent months building a case for war primarily on the threat of weapons of mass destruction, Bush was fully embracing the idealistic, neo-Wilsonian rhetoric that Paul Wolfowitz and other neoconservative intellectuals had used to bolster their years-old case for war against Saddam. Their article of faith was that the overthrow of Saddam would be a catalyst for change in the Middle East—and Bush was accepting that far-reaching mission as his own. A liberal pro-Western democracy in Iraq, he said, would usher in a new era of political reform and "begin a new stage" for Middle

East peace. The president acknowledged that "bringing stability and unity to a free Iraq will not be easy." But he didn't dwell on the difficulties. His AEI speech was part of the White House's home-stretch effort to make the war sound easier and more noble—even as government experts and military officers were advising that the invasion and its aftermath would likely be costly and fraught with complexities.

WAYNE WHITE, the State Department Iraq analyst, was one of the government's most knowledgeable experts on Middle Eastern affairs. He had spent nearly a quarter century working in and studying the region. Having once served as a political officer in Baghdad, he was now the deputy director for Near East and South Asia Affairs in the State Department's Bureau of Intelligence and Research (INR). Just a few weeks before the president's AEI speech, White had begun work on a major paper on the very topic Bush would address: would a U.S. invasion of Iraq actually bring democracy to the region? No one had asked White to take this assignment on. But, he recalled later, "somebody needed to sit down and do some clearheaded thinking about an issue that was emerging."

White started by gathering polling data from Middle East countries. The numbers reinforced his worst expectations. It showed that the populations of these nations were far more anti-American and anti-Israel than were the governments in charge. The people were much more supportive of militant Islam and much less interested in such niceties as women's rights than their rulers were. Creating democracy in these countries would be tough— especially in Iraq, given the sectarian divisions that would probably arise there. The classified report he drafted concluded that political, economic, and social problems would likely undermine stability in the region for years and severely limit the prospects for democracy. An invasion of Iraq would not change these fundamentals. Even if democracy somehow did take root in Iraq or elsewhere, White wrote, it was likely that the governments elected would be more antipathetic toward the United States and Israel and closer to militant Islamism. "Liberal democracy would be difficult to achieve," the report read, and elections could actually bolster "anti-American elements."

White's findings weren't revolutionary. Other analysts outside the government had been raising similar points. But White realized this was a touchy matter. He sent a draft of his paper to other INR analysts. None had any objections. Nor did Tom Fingar, the deputy director at INR. Fingar had only one major suggestion. He wanted to change the title of the paper. White had called it "Iraq, the Middle East and Change." Fingar suggested adding the words "No Dominoes." The proposed title was a jab at Bush and the neoconservatives and their claim that an invasion of Iraq would create a chain reaction, spreading democracy through the region. (It was merely "serendipitous," White later said, that the report was ready for dissemination the day after Bush's AEI speech.) Would White mind the change in title? Fingar asked.

You're the boss, White told him.

Normally, INR would forward this kind of report—which was supposed to reflect the official view of the State Department—to recipients throughout the government: the National Security Council, the Pentagon leadership, the CIA, the congressional intelligence committees, various Cabinet members. But White asked Fingar to restrict the "No Dominoes" report to officials within the State Department. "It was too hot," White said. "This would leak." It was not his aim to pick a fight with the White House.

Fingar said he had never restricted an INR report in such a manner and didn't want to do so now. INR distributed the report throughout the intelligence community—and sent a copy to the White House.

"Usually," White recalled, "you'd get a response on a report like this from the seventh floor of State"—where the secretary of state had his office. "In the case of this report, I got nothing."*

THE same day "No Dominoes" went out, on February 27, Paul Wolfowitz appeared before the House budget committee, ostensibly to discuss the Pentagon's annual budget request (which notably didn't include any estimates to cover the costs of an invasion in Iraq). But Wolfowitz's main purpose that day was to douse a potential fire.

Two days earlier, while testifying before a Senate panel, General Eric Shinseki, the Army chief of staff, had said that "something on the order of several hundred thousand soldiers" would be necessary for a postwar occupying force.

---

*White was right. His study was leaked—but, he later said, not by him. On March 14, the *Los Angeles Times* published a front-page story disclosing the paper under the headline "Democracy Domino Theory 'Not Credible.'"

That certainly suggested a costly and significant occupation. After running through the latest Pentagon budget numbers, Wolfowitz took a sharp swipe at Shinseki. "The notion that it would take several hundred thousand U.S. troops to provide stability in post-Saddam Iraq," he said, is "wildly off the mark." He added, "[I]t is hard to conceive that it would take more forces to provide stability in post-Saddam Iraq than it would take to conduct the war itself."

This was quite a put-down: the civilian leaders of the Pentagon were saying they knew better than the head of the Army about how many troops it would take to manage postinvasion Iraq. The exchange was a continuation of Rumsfeld's internal fight with the uniformed services over the size of the force needed for an invasion of Iraq. The Army had recommended up to 400,000 troops, partly because it wanted a large force immediately available to handle the postinvasion tasks. Rumsfeld, who had championed a U.S. military that could fight leaner and quicker, initially thought 75,000 or so troops would be sufficient for the invasion. Fighting over the size of the postinvasion force was just another way of fighting over the preinvasion force—a tussle that had been resolved more in Rumsfeld's favor than the Army's. About 200,000 troops would be sent to the region for the war.

Wolfowitz's testimony that day offered a rare glimpse of his own rosy vision of the conflict to come. The Pentagon's postwar "requirements," he said, might be low because "there's been none of the record in Iraq of ethnic militias fighting one another." He disputed the idea that there would be "monstrous" costs.* Iraq's oil revenues, he asserted, could finance the postwar reconstruction. He maintained that the United States could expect other nations to share the financial burden of rebuilding a post-Saddam Iraq. And, he added, "based on what Iraqi-Americans told me in Detroit a week ago"—when he had attended a rally of proinvasion immigrants—

---

*The previous September, Lawrence Lindsey, Bush's senior economic adviser, had estimated that a war in Iraq could cost more than $200 billion—a rather steep bill. Later, the White House budget chief, Mitch Daniels, suggested that the war could be prosecuted for a much more reasonable $20 billion. (Lindsey was pushed out of the administration in December 2002.) As of January 2006, Congress had appropriated $251 billion for the Iraq War. A study by the Nobel prize–winning economist Joseph Stiglitz and Harvard University's Linda Bilmes estimated the long-term costs at $1.2 trillion, including money for the long-term health care of 16,000 wounded U.S. military personnel, 20 percent of whom had suffered major head or spinal injuries and another 6 percent of whom had lost limbs.

"I am reasonably certain that they will greet us as liberators and that will help us to keep requirements down."*

These were striking claims expressed with certitude and conviction. But in support of them Wolfowitz didn't cite any studies or intelligence assessments. He seemed to be basing the Defense Department's operating assumptions on what he had heard from several hundred Iraqi Americans yearning for an invasion. He was trusting his own instincts more than the views and work of generals and experts under his own command. Within the military and the intelligence community, there were officers and officials (not just Shinseki) who were attempting to sort out the postinvasion needs and challenges. Few of them shared Wolfowitz's fanciful optimism.

THE president had made a few cursory inquiries about the plans for a postwar Iraq. But the subject wasn't a focus of sustained, high-level attention. At a National Security Council meeting back in January in the White House Situation Room, Bush had asked General Tommy Franks, the CENTCOM commander in charge of the invasion, about security in Iraq after Saddam's regime was toppled. Who, he inquired, would maintain law and order? Who would keep the peace?

Franks had reassured the president. Don't worry, he said, according to a senior NSC official present for the exchange. We've got that covered. The U.S. military would keep the peace. Each major Iraqi town and village, Franks explained, would have a "lord mayor"—an appointed U.S. military officer—who would be in charge of maintaining civic order and administering basic services. Lord mayor? The NSC official had no idea what Franks was talking about.

Nearly two months later, at a final prewar planning meeting on March 10, 2003, the subject was raised again—by either Bush or Rice, according to the NSC official. This time, Franks bristled. He had already explained this, Franks said. There would be a lord mayor. Neither the president nor any other senior officials pressed Franks to explain what he meant by his use of this quaint British title.

---

*Wolfowitz was in sync with Rumsfeld, who was publicly downplaying the challenge in Iraq. Weeks earlier, the secretary of defense had said of the war, "It could last, you know, six days, six weeks. I doubt six months."

Pentagon officials actually never planned anything of the kind. Army Colonel Kevin Benson, the Third Army officer assigned by CENTCOM to draft the plans for a Phase IV (postinvasion) Iraq, later said his own documents had never incorporated anything like a lord mayor concept. "I never heard anyone talk of lord mayor," Benson remarked. "I never heard that term used."*

WHEN Colonel Benson saw that Wolfowitz had rudely dismissed Shinseki's estimate, he thought to himself, *What does the deputy secretary know that I don't?* Working out of Camp Doha in Kuwait, Benson had been toiling away on his Phase IV plan with his own staff and planners in Central Command, the Joint Chiefs of Staff, and other services.

After the war began, the conventional view would be that such plans barely existed. That was wrong, Benson said, recalling that "there was an enormous amount of planning done." The question was, what happened to the plans? He and his team, for example, drew up a plan for Phase IV that envisioned that violence would continue after the initial defeat of Saddam's standing army. It anticipated there would be substantial security concerns in post-Saddam Iraq. "We took all of this seriously," Benson said—especially the issue of how many troops would be needed after the invasion. Benson and his team started with this premise: Iraq was about the size of California. "We asked how many troops Gray Davis [then the California governor] had." They added up all the police officers, sheriff's deputies, peace officers, corrections officers, and the like in the Golden State and discovered the number was greater than the number of American troops being sent into Iraq—and California was a stable and secure entity. So when Benson saw that Shinseki had testified that a couple hundred thousand troops would be needed after the invasion, he had thought to himself, "That Shinseki is one helluva smart guy."

But after Rumsfeld and Wolfowitz disputed Shinseki, Benson realized there was a serious gap between his work and the view at the top. He could not see what real-life information Wolfowitz was relying on. "I was assum-

---

*The NSC official who twice heard Franks mention the lord mayor plan to the president years later asked a senior U.S. officer in charge of U.S. troops in Iraq about this idea. "What are you talking about?" the officer replied. "We were never told to do that."

ing that the guys in Washington must know something that I don't know," Benson recalled. "I never saw any intelligence that led me to the conclusion that the people in D.C. were making. I never saw intelligence that we would be met with cheering crowds and bands and people throwing flowers at us. I never saw any intelligence that would allow me to conclude it would be a cakewalk."*

Benson and his team weren't the only planners within the Defense Department worrying about Phase IV. In October 2002, Lieutenant General Richard Cody, the Army deputy chief of staff for operations and plans, asked the War College's Strategic Studies Institute to do a study—fast. By the end of January 2003, the Strategic Studies Institute produced a report that noted that "ethnic, tribal and religious schisms could produce civil war or fracture the state after Saddam is deposed," that Iraq reconstruction would require "a considerable commitment of American resources," and that the "longer U.S. presence is maintained, the more likely violent resistance will develop." An occupation, the report said, would last for "an extended period of time," and the Iraqi population would be more suspicious of than grateful toward the United States.

The study noted that the most likely development would be for political parties to emerge based on ethnic, tribal, and religious identities and free elections among ethnically based political parties could actually "increase divisions rather than mitigate them." And—worse—armed militias would likely be a problem. Terrorists could be expected to engage in horrific acts, even suicide bombings, to alienate Iraqis from the Americans. An occupier would find it "exceptionally challenging" to supply the population with the basics: electricity, water, food, security. The oil infrastructure of Iraq would not generate the revenues necessary to pay for reconstruction. Sabotage would be a "serious threat."

The paper listed 135 postinvasion tasks that would have to be accomplished to reestablish an Iraqi state. They included securing the borders, establishing local governments, protecting religious, historical, and cultural sites, establishing a police system, restoring and maintaining power systems,

---

*Given that the war on Iraq was an elective one, Benson later noted, "we could've had the best war plan ever, but it wasn't." The U.S. government's failure to develop and implement an effective postinvasion plan haunted Benson. "I took Pepcid AC for a year after I got back," he said.

operating hospitals, reorganizing the Iraqi military and security forces, and disarming militias. The paper advised against abolishing the Iraqi Army after the war. "Massive resources need to be focused on this [postoccupation] effort well before the first shot is fired," the report declared. But the authors knew that the Pentagon hadn't yet worked out much of this. The Defense Department had only recently established an office to handle the postwar period— the Office of Reconstruction and Humanitarian Assistance (ORHA), which was headed by retired General Jay Garner. The paper's overall conclusion was troubling: "The possibility of the United States winning the war and losing the peace in Iraq is real and serious."

The War College's Strategic Studies Institute sent a draft of the paper to the Army command staff and various field commanders in late January. It also mailed out about a thousand copies, including to members of Congress. "We heard that Central Command really liked it," recalled a military analyst who helped draft the report. But the authors received no feedback from the civilian leadership of the Pentagon. "At that point, the Bush administration was moving rapidly to war," the military analyst said. "Nothing would derail them, and their assumption was that it would be a lot easier than we had put it. They felt arguments that it would be hard were actually designed to cause people to rethink whether the war was worth doing in the first place. This was appalling. They were trying to rig the cost-benefit analysis. So they ended up not properly planning for the aftermath of the invasion because that might interfere with getting the war they wanted. Paul Wolfowitz's whole reason for living was to start that war. They didn't have to listen to us. Somewhere along the line they had decided they were smarter than the rest of us."

It was easy for the White House and the civilian leaders of the Pentagon to ignore a report from a small Army think tank. And it wasn't too difficult to swat aside a single remark from a general. They also disregarded the work of the CIA and the State Department. In January 2003, Paul Pillar, the national intelligence officer in charge of the Middle East, produced a high-level report examining the challenges the Bush administration would face in a post-Saddam Iraq.

The paper made the obvious point: turning Iraq into a state even remotely resembling a liberal democracy would be difficult. Iraq's political culture, Pillar recalled the report as saying, was not "fertile," and the mission would be "long, difficult and turbulent." It noted that Iraq didn't have a tradition of loyal opposition or the transfer of power and that a post-Saddam period would likely be marked by ethnic and religious conflict that could turn violent. The situation might explode—if the United States didn't maintain a large enough military presence in Iraq to smother the smoldering tensions. Moreover, a debt-ridden Iraq wouldn't be able to finance reconstruction with oil revenues.

Like the Third Army's planners and the Army War College analysts, Pillar and the CIA experts foresaw a costly occupation that would be riddled with problems and that could go bad rather easily. It was the exact opposite of the picture the administration wanted to share with the public. Pillar sent the report to Tenet's office. It was "bleak," a senior CIA official later said. Still, the report was forwarded to the White House and the Pentagon. Did the report register? Years later, Pillar recalled that he did receive a response from an administration official he wouldn't identify: "You guys just don't see the possibilities. You're too negative."

The White House and the Pentagon shoved aside the work of the State Department's Future of Iraq project, as well. In the spring of 2002, Thomas Warrick, a longtime State Department official, had set up seventeen working groups, full of Iraqi exiles (lawyers, engineers, academics, and businesspeople), to consider how to remake a post-Saddam Iraq: how to reorganize the military and police, how to create a new legal system, how to restructure the economy. The $5 million project predicted postinvasion "plunder and looting" and said that it would be necessary to "organize military patrols . . . in all major cities to prevent lawlessness." It warned that Iraq's electrical and water systems would be in need of extensive repairs and reconstruction. It produced thirteen volumes that included wide-ranging recommendations.

The Pentagon wasn't interested. One reason was Ahmad Chalabi. His champions at the Defense Department had contemplated forming a government in exile led by Chalabi, which could be put into place quickly following the invasion. The State Department, still suspicious of Chalabi, wasn't in favor of that. Warrick refused to let the Future of Iraq project become a game plan for a Chalabi coronation, and he made his views known. Years after the invasion, David Phillips, a conflict prevention expert at the Council on Foreign Relations who worked on the Future of Iraq project, would describe how bitter squabbling between the Pentagon and Warrick had sabotaged the planning effort. After Warrick had the temerity to criticize the Pentagon's prewar planning, officials in charge of ORHA were ordered to stop working with him, according to Phillips. Rumsfeld rejected a request by General Garner, the ORHA chief, to hire thirty-two State Department experts who had been involved in the project. Some of the experts were "blacklisted" because they didn't support Chalabi, Phillips wrote in his book *Losing Iraq.* "They were victims of the ideological rivalry that caused a virtual collapse of interagency process," Phillips noted. "By February 2003, State and Defense officials were barely on speaking terms."

Postwar Iraq planning paralleled what happened with prewar Iraq intelligence. The work of government experts and analysts was discarded by senior Bush administration policy makers when it conflicted with or undermined their own hardened ideas about what to expect in Iraq. They were confident—or wanted to believe—that the war would go smoothly. They didn't need other views, notions, or plans—not from the State Department, the CIA, or the military. It was their war, and they would run it as they saw fit.

IN LATE February, Bill Murray, the CIA station chief in Paris, hadn't yet abandoned hope of reeling in Naji Sabri, the Iraqi foreign minister. The information that Sabri had passed to the CIA through the Lebanese journalist months earlier—that Saddam had no active WMD programs—had run counter to everything the White House was saying. It was at odds with what the CIA was reporting. Possibly it was just lies from the chief diplomat of a murderous regime. Still, Murray wanted to talk to Sabri face-to-face. But five months had gone by, and nothing had happened—and the war was approaching.

The Lebanese journalist had told him that Sabri was still interested in cooperating with the CIA. But the logistics were difficult. Sabri couldn't find an excuse to visit a country where a meeting could be set up. At this point Murray was furious with colleagues back at headquarters for doing little to help him. James Pavitt, the director of operations, had instructed officers from the Iraq Operations Group to work with Murray on this sensitive project. And there had been one idea: to arrange for the Jordanians to invite Sabri to Amman for a summit. Then Murray could hold a secret rendezvous with him there. But John Maguire and other officers in the Iraq

Operations Group thought it was all a waste of time. They had no use for Murray's source—not unless the Iraqi minister was willing to defect.

Now Murray had another chance. Sabri would be flying to Kuala Lumpur for an Islamic conference. He would, the Lebanese journalist told Murray, talk to him there. The CIA man hopped a plane to Malaysia. When he landed, he learned that Sabri had already departed Kuala Lumpur for an Arab League meeting in Sharm el-Sheikh in the Sinai desert. Murray immediately flew to Cairo. He then looked for a connecting flight to the Sinai.

Meanwhile, at the Arab League conference, on March 1, Sabri was mobbed—by journalists and by diplomats. War seemed imminent. And he was busy echoing Saddam's line: "[W]e know that this American administration, with encouragement from Israel and the Israeli lobby in the U.S., is gearing up for war against Iraq." But what did he want to tell the CIA? Baghdad's official position was that it had no WMDs and no nuclear weapons programs. Was there anything Sabri could say to Murray that would indicate the Iraqis were telling the truth?

Murray would never find out. Sabri once again eluded him. The big catch—recruiting the Iraqi foreign minister as a CIA source—didn't happen. Murray was at the Cairo airport desperately trying to get a connecting flight to Sharm el-Sheikh when he learned Sabri had already flown back to Iraq.

ON THE eve of war, the Niger charge disintegrated—completely.

The day that Colin Powell delivered his presentation to the United Nations, Jacques Baute, the International Atomic Energy Agency's chief for Iraqi nuclear matters, had picked up a sealed envelope at the U.S. Mission to the United Nations. Six weeks earlier, the State Department had publicly accused the Iraqis of lying in their WMD declaration because they hadn't acknowledged their efforts to obtain uranium from Niger. The Vienna-based IAEA, which was responsible for nuclear weapons inspections in Iraq, wanted to resolve the dispute. It asked Washington to share with it information that would back up Foggy Bottom's assertion. It took a while to get a response. But then Baute was handed the envelope. Inside were the Niger documents. The material was considered sensitive; only Baute and IAEA Director General Mohamed ElBaradei could look at it.

At first glance, as he later recalled, Baute thought the documents were legitimate. (The package didn't include the unbelievable memo chronicling a far-fetched scheme of Iraqis, Iranians, Sudanese, Libyans, and others to create an anti-Western rogue-state alliance.) But Baute was too busy to conduct a thorough review. Over the next ten days, he and ElBaradei hopped from one country to the next, including a stop in Baghdad. Meeting with Iraqi officials, Baute and ElBaradei asked whether Baghdad had sought yellowcake in Niger (without revealing they possessed secret records about the uranium deal). The Iraqis denied the accusation and, Baute later said, were "quite cooperative" in answering questions about the purported accord.

Baute and his IAEA colleagues asked to speak to Wissam al-Zahawie, who had been Iraq's ambassador to the Vatican. His name was on the sales agreement as an Iraqi official who had apparently brokered the deal. Zahawie had retired from the Iraq foreign service and was living in Amman, Jordan. The Iraqis were eager to have Zahawie talk to the IAEA officials and debunk this allegation. An official in the Iraqi Embassy in Amman called Zahawie and told him the Foreign Ministry wanted him in Baghdad immediately. He was back in the Iraqi capital the next day. The day after that, February 12, he was interviewed by Baute and other IAEA officials.

Zahawie, as he later recounted, assumed that the subject at hand was his trip to Niger, for he had noticed Bush's reference in the State of the Union speech to Iraq's attempts to obtain uranium in Africa. First, the IAEA officials asked Zahawie about the details and purpose of his 1999 visit to Niger. Then they asked if he had signed a letter about a uranium purchase in 2000. Absolutely not, Zahawie told them.

Baute, ElBaradei, and the IAEA officials were not satisfied that Zahawie was telling the truth. After all, they had what they assumed to be concrete evidence. Another interview was held the next day. Zahawie once again denied any involvement in a uranium deal and indignantly demanded the IAEA produce any documents it possessed suggesting otherwise. They must be forgeries, he insisted. Zahawie later recalled that he told the IAEA officials that he could sue them for libel "as I was being accused of something of which I was totally ignorant."

Baute didn't show Zahawie the Niger papers. He was not ready to reveal all he knew—or thought he knew. He considered the documents his ace in the hole, and he wanted to research the matter before confronting the Iraqis with this powerful evidence. Despite the Iraqis' denials, he was still hoping he could use the documents to push them to admitting that something had indeed happened in Niger. Until he took a closer look.

On February 17, he was back in Vienna, and he finally had a moment to scrutinize the details of the deal outlined in the papers. He started plugging key words and phrases into Google. Within minutes, his basic research disclosed there was something wrong. The papers included a letter noting that the Nigerien president had approved the transaction under the authority of the 1965 Constitution of Niger. Yet Baute found a newspaper article that mentioned that the Constitution had been revived in 1999. Wouldn't the Nigerien government have gotten the date of its own constitution right?

Baute kept researching. He called the Niger Mission in Vienna to obtain information. And he changed his aim. He was no longer seeking to use the documents to corner Zahawie and the Iraqis; he was now trying to determine whether they were authentic. Within a couple of hours, he discovered about fifteen significant anomalies in the papers. The letterhead, the signatures, the dates, the format of the document—none of them matched up. One letter, dated October 10, 2000, was signed by Niger's minister of foreign affairs, Allele Habibou—a man who hadn't served in that office for more than ten years. It bore the heading "Conseil Militaire Suprême"—an organization that had gone out of existence in 1989. Another document dated July 30, 1999, referred in the past tense to deals that the other documents indicated had been arranged in June 2000.

Baute worked into the evening and concluded that the papers were completely bogus. "I stared at my computer screen," he recalled. "I was shocked." Late in the night, he phoned ElBaradei at home and said there was a problem with the Niger charge. ElBaradei had an easy solution, according to Baute. The IAEA chief said, "We'll report what we found. Goodnight." He hung up the phone.

Baute shared his finding with his IAEA colleagues. They all agreed: the papers were fakes. Baute, using Google and public domain records, had been able to do quickly what the CIA had failed to do for a year: ascertain that the Niger papers were a hoax. Baute asked the Bush administration for any other information it might have on the alleged Niger deal. Nothing came. On March 3, the IAEA officially notified the U.S. Mission in Vienna that it had determined the papers were fraudulent. Four days later, in a public report to the Security Council, IAEA Director General Mohamed ElBaradei stated that the documents were "not authentic."*

The forged documents made headlines. *The Washington Post* put the story on its front page: "A key piece of evidence linking Iraq to a nuclear weapons program appears to have been fabricated, the United Nations' chief nuclear inspector said yesterday in a report that called into question U.S. and British claims about Iraq's secret nuclear ambitions." Senator Jay Rockefeller called for an FBI investigation, to determine whether somebody had deliberately fed disinformation to the U.S. intelligence community. But as embarrassing as this was for the White House and the CIA, a full controversy didn't erupt. The White House ably fended off questions about how Bush had come to make a claim in his State of the Union address that was apparently based on a crude fraud. "It was the information that we had," Powell said. "We provided it [to the IAEA]. If that information is inaccurate, fine." And Rice dismissed the importance of the discovery: "We have never rested our case on nuclear weapons programs in Iraq on this issue about some uranium from Niger."

U.S. intelligence agencies tried lamely to defend themselves. The DIA, which had produced the original yellowcake report that had caught Cheney's eye, sent a new memo to Rumsfeld asserting that it had other information to support the Africa uranium charge. This included a U.S. Navy intelligence report that a West African businessman had arranged to store a large quantity of Niger uranium destined for Iraq in a warehouse in Benin. The memo failed to mention a pertinent detail: a U.S. Defense Department official had checked out the warehouse in question just a few weeks earlier and discovered that it was filled with bales of cotton. And the CIA's WINPAC maintained it had other reports indicating that Baghdad had tried to obtain uranium but admitted this information was "fragmentary and unconfirmed."†

---

*ElBaradei also reported that the IAEA's analysis had definitively concluded the aluminum tubes hadn't been destined for uranium enrichment. "We have to date found no evidence or plausible indication of the revival of a nuclear weapon program in Iraq," ElBaradei said. At the same time, Hans Blix reported that Iraq was providing "active"—but not "immediate"—cooperation with the UN weapons inspectors and noted that more time would be needed to oversee Iraq's final disarmament tasks, including destroying a set of prohibited missiles.

†A month later—after the invasion of Iraq—the CIA would acknowledge that there was nothing to the Niger charge, that there was no evidence to back up the allegation that Iraq had purchased uranium from Niger or that it even had mounted a serious effort to obtain yellowcake. In a Sense of the Community Memorandum, the National Intelligence Council said, "We

The day after the IAEA declared the papers bogus, Joe Wilson appeared on CNN and blasted the Bush administration for mishandling the Niger papers. "We know a lot about the uranium business in Niger," he said, "and for something like this to go unchallenged by the U.S. government is just simply stupid. . . . [I]t taints the whole rest of the case that the government is trying to build against Iraq. . . . The U.S. government should have or did know that this report was a fake." *The U.S. government did know?* What was Wilson suggesting?

Wilson had become a familiar figure on the cable news shows in recent months, a member of the foreign policy establishment who vocally opposed the war and the administration. He assumed that Iraq did possess some WMDs, but he argued that intrusive inspections were disrupting Saddam's weapons. "This war is not about weapons of mass destruction," Wilson had written in *The Nation* magazine. ". . . The underlying objective of this war is the imposition of a Pax Americana on the region and installation of vassal regimes that will control restive populations."

As Wilson pointed to the phony Niger documents as proof the Bush administration was hyping the case for war, he didn't mention his own involvement in the story. A State Department spokesman had said of the documents, "We fell for it." But in his remarks on CNN, Wilson hinted there was more to the tale.

THE intelligence supporting the premise that Iraq was a threat had become weaker, not stronger, in the months since Bush had started pushing for war against Saddam. The two key elements in the nuclear weapons case—the Niger deal and the aluminum tubes—had not held up. The White House's gripping metaphor, the smoking gun in the form of a mushroom cloud, now looked empty. Questions about Curveball had not been answered. The CIA also had recently discovered that another Iraqi defector, a former chemist, whom it had relied upon for critical intelligence reporting on Iraq's supposed

---

judge it highly unlikely that Niamey has sold uranium, yellowcake to Baghdad in recent years. The [intelligence community] agrees with the IAEA assessment that key documents purported showing a recent Iraq-Niger sales accord are a fabrication. We judge that other reports from 2002—one alleging warehousing of yellowcake for shipment to Iraq, a second alleging a 1999 visit by an Iraqi delegation to Niamey—do not constitute credible evidence of a recent or impending sale."

chemical weapons was a faker.* In early March, the agency revised its view on another big issue: Iraq's drones or unmanned aerial vehicles. The assertion that these vehicles could be used to attack the U.S. mainland with chemical or biological weapons had been based on intelligence reports that an Iraqi procurement agent had sought to buy U.S. mapping software for the weapons in the spring of 2001. But by early 2003, a CIA analyst had interviewed the procurement agent and concluded his purchase order for the mapping software had most likely been inadvertent; the Iraqi agent was really seeking other pieces of equipment from a manufacturer's Web site. In a memo to the House intelligence committee, the CIA reported it now had "no definite indications that Baghdad [was] planning to use WMD-armed UAVs against the U.S. mainland."

None of this had an impact (on the Bush administration) as the war approached. The administration's rhetoric stayed the same—or became more dramatic. Bush claimed an Iraqi UAV containing biological weapons "launched from a vessel off the American coast could reach hundreds of miles inland." Rumsfeld declared, "We know that [Saddam] continues to hide biological or chemical weapons, moving them to different locations as often as every twelve to twenty-four hours." Powell pointed to a new bin Laden audiotape as evidence al-Qaeda was "in partnership with Iraq." (In fact, bin Laden had only called upon Muslims to fight against an American invasion of Iraq.) At a public congressional hearing, Tenet claimed that Iraq had provided "training in poisons and gases" to al-Qaeda, once again invoking the questionable claims of Ibn al-Shaykh al-Libi. At his last press conference before the war began, Bush charged that Saddam had "financed" al-Qaeda.

On March 7, Britain introduced a U.S.-backed resolution in the Security Council that would essentially authorize war if Iraq failed to demonstrate

---

*This source—whose information had been included in the National Intelligence Estimate—had claimed that Iraq had produced a combined nuclear-chemical-biological weapon. Intelligence analysts had rightfully recognized this charge as absurd. Still, they had accepted his other tales about Iraq's CW efforts. In February 2003, he was given a polygraph test, and he failed. It turned out he was an information peddler whose allegations against Iraq, according to a report the CIA had received from a foreign intelligence service, had possibly been "directed" by a hostile intelligence service.

its unconditional commitment to disarmament by March 17. France and Russia signaled they would veto the measure. Nevertheless, a date had been set.

In the days before the invasion, the echo chamber of the war's most vocal advocates resounded strongly. "We'll be vindicated when we discover the weapons of mass destruction," Bill Kristol said on *Nightline*. He noted elsewhere that "very few wars in American history were prepared better or more thoroughly than this one by this president." Asked by Chris Matthews if post-Saddam Iraq would be dominated by fundamentalist Shia, Richard Perle pointed to Chalabi's Iraqi National Congress as a force for pluralistic democracy in the new Iraq. He claimed there was little chance of civil war arising in Iraq, that the war would be "quick," and that it would "not take anything like" Shinseki's estimate of several hundred thousand troops "to maintain peace and order." Appearing on a talk show on March 9, he said, "Forgive me. No one is talking about occupying Iraq for five to ten years." *New York Times* columnist Bill Safire urged Bush to get on with the war: "Smoking guns and hiding terrorists will be found."*

It wasn't just the partisans, either. On March 6, *The Washington Post*'s Bob Woodward went on CNN's *Larry King Live* and asserted that "the intelligence shows . . . there are massive amounts of weapons of mass destruction hidden, buried, unaccounted for" in Iraq.

On the eve of war in Washington, journalists and others gathered at a cocktail party at the home of Philip Taubman, the Washington bureau chief of *The New York Times,* to celebrate his new book on high-tech espionage during the Eisenhower years. Judy Miller was one of several *Times* reporters there, and she seemed excited. Another journalist present asked if she was planning to head over to Iraq to cover the invasion. Miller, according to the other guest, could barely contain herself. "Are you kidding?" she replied. "I've been waiting for this war for ten years. I wouldn't miss it for the world!"

---

*Months earlier, the conservative columnist Charles Krauthammer had said, "There is one thing that I think everybody has overlooked—we are going to have retroactive evidence." That is, the invasion of Iraq would produce the proof—WMDs—to justify the invasion. He also said, "Iraq will be the first act in the play of an America coming ashore in Arabia. . . . It's not just about weapons of mass destruction or American credibility. It's about reforming the Arab world."

THE marketing campaign that had begun the previous September with a Cheney appearance on *Meet the Press* ended with a Cheney appearance on *Meet the Press*. On March 16, while Bush was in the Azores to meet with the British and Spanish prime ministers, his future allies in the Iraq War, the vice president told Tim Russert that Saddam was hoarding unconventional weapons and had "a long-standing relationship" with al-Qaeda. Cheney dismissed the IAEA's finding that Saddam had not revived its nuclear weapons program. "We believe," Cheney said, "he has, in fact, reconstituted nuclear weapons." (This was a misstatement, he later acknowledged. He meant to say that Iraq had reconstituted its nuclear weapons program.) He pooh-poohed Shinseki's estimate that several hundred thousand troops would be needed for an occupation. "We will be greeted as liberators," the vice president said.

The next evening, Bush delivered a nationally televised address. He hailed his administration's "good-faith" efforts to disarm Iraq peacefully and declared that Saddam had thwarted the inspection process. "Intelligence gathered by this and other governments leaves no doubt that the Iraq regime continues to possess and conceal some of the most lethal weapons ever devised," Bush said. *No doubt.* Bush issued an ultimatum: Saddam and his two sons would have to leave Iraq within forty-eight hours, or there would be war.

About this time, John Gibson, the speechwriter who had done his best to craft a compelling case against Saddam, ran into Sean McCormack, the press spokesman for the National Security Council. McCormack, according to Gibson, asked, "What if we invade Iraq and we don't find any weapons?" "We both kind of laughed," Gibson recalled. But he didn't think it was that funny. He had written the words Bush had used to lead the country to war, even when he hadn't been sure of the wisdom of this endeavor. No weapons? That would be a problem, he thought.

And on the night of March 18, White House press aide Adam Levine fielded a call from Tim Russert. "All I can tell you, man," NBC's Washington bureau chief said to him, "is you guys better find the WMD." Levine replied, "You're telling me." Then the Bush aide said, "Either that, or we'll find the CIA version of Mark Fuhrman." It was Levine's attempt at humor:

he was referring to the notorious LA cop accused of planting evidence in the O. J. Simpson murder case.

The following evening, after the first bombing raid had occurred, Bush spoke to the nation from the Oval Office for a few minutes and announced that the war had started. "We will," he declared, "accept no outcome but victory."

WITHIN the CIA's Joint Task Force on Iraq—where Valerie Wilson and her colleagues were still running operations out of the basement at CIA headquarters in search of evidence of Saddam's WMDs—the start of the war brought a sense of frustration. "I felt like we ran out of time," one CIA officer recalled. "The war came so suddenly. We didn't have enough information to challenge the assumption that there were WMDs. It was very disappointing. How do you know it's a dry well? That Saddam was constrained? Given more time, we could have worked through the issue. We were trying to think creatively. But the war came too fast, and we did not have the time to look everywhere we could. From 9/11 to the war—eighteen months—that was not enough time to get a good answer to this important question. It was just not enough time."

FOR those who wanted to overthrow Saddam, everything had worked out. The American intervention, for which planning had begun sixteen months earlier, was about to unfold. But the public case had been built on a flimsy foundation: a faulty and misleading National Intelligence Estimate; the phony Niger charge; the false claims of fabricating defectors such as Curveball; the White House Iraq Group's spin campaign; the misleading media reports seeded by the manipulative Iraqi National Congress; the disputed aluminum tubes; the CIA white paper that concealed intelligence agency dissents; Rice's "mushroom cloud"; the imaginary Atta-in-Prague story that obsessed Cheney, Wolfowitz, Libby, and Feith; the flawed Powell presentation; and Bush's overstated (if not overheated) rhetoric that exceeded the actual and exaggerated intelligence. This was all part of the "product"—as chief of staff Andrew Card had called it—that the White House had rolled out the previous September.

The war would not turn out as Bush administration officials had promised. Because of that, the debate over the Iraq War—had it really been necessary, had Bush hyped the threat, had the administration prepared adequately, had the American public been misled?—would continue long after the invasion. That bitter and fierce brawl would yield controversy and scandal that would burden and shape the rest of the Bush presidency.

Holy shit, we're in trouble.

—CARL FORD, JR.,
STATE DEPARTMENT INTELLIGENCE CHIEF

12

The Missing Weapons

THE WAR went well—at first.

On the night of March 19, Bush ordered an air strike on a compound outside Baghdad in the hope of killing Saddam—and perhaps ending the war before it even started. Three ROCKSTARS sources—members of Saddam's security detail recruited for the CIA by the well-compensated Sufi mystic—had placed the Iraqi dictator at the site. But either their intelligence reporting had been wrong and Saddam was not there or Saddam survived the attack, because several hours later the Iraqi tyrant was on television decrying the raid. On March 21, U.S.-led coalition forces mounted nine hours of "shock and awe" bombing and missile strikes. Then ground forces entered Iraq.

The CIA Scorpions—the unit of former Iraqi special forces headed by retired General Shahwani and trained at the secret camp in the Nevada desert—had not been given the green light to seize the Iraqi air base and start the war. General Tommy Franks, according to John Maguire, had nixed the operation; he didn't want a sideshow interfering with his carefully designed invasion plans. The Scorpions would join the assault in a more traditional manner, helping to cut roads in the south and assisting U.S. commanders as they took cities and tried to establish ties with local mullahs.*

---

*Prior to the invasion, the CIA's Anabasis project ended up mounting only a limited number of sabotage operations. CIA-trained paramilitary teams entered western Iraq to blow up power

In the next weeks, U.S. troops marched toward Baghdad. Embedded reporters enthusiastically chronicled the actions—even the mundane ones—of American military units. The coalition forces consistently defeated Saddam's troops. But sandstorms did slow down the invasion, and the irregulars of the Fedayeen Saddam forces were more of a problem than military planners had expected. For a few days, critics expressed concern that the war plan wasn't sufficient. But the complaining didn't last long.

In some portions of Iraq, liberated Iraqis did celebrate. Iraq didn't counterattack against Israel. No refugee crisis developed. Oil fields were protected. Coalition casualties were moderate. No WMDs were fired at coalition forces. And when the U.S.-led troops reached Baghdad, there was no final, bloody battle. The troops rolled in, and on April 9 a giant statue of Saddam was pulled down by a small but excited crowd. The next day, Ken Adelman, a neoconservative defense intellectual close to Cheney, Rumsfeld, and Wolfowitz, wrote an op-ed article in *The Washington Post* crowing that he had been right fourteen months earlier when he had predicted Iraq would be a "cakewalk."

A few days later, Cheney held a small celebratory dinner party at the vice president's residence with Adelman, Wolfowitz, and Libby. They congratulated themselves, cheered Bush, and derided Powell for never having been a true believer. Asked for his thoughts, Libby said, "Wonderful." But, Adelman asked, what about the weapons of mass destruction? Where are they? "We'll find them," Wolfowitz said. Cheney repeated the words. This confidence on the part of the war's architects would soon be challenged by reality. The search for the weapons wouldn't meet the expectations they had set. And that would lead to yet more spinning and more distortion, including a new CIA white paper that would roil the intelligence community and become another black eye for the agency. At the same time, securing Iraq would turn out to be anything but a cakewalk.

---

pylons. The operation was compromised, and only one of four towers was destroyed. More successful were the "direct action" ops. Kurdish paramilitary teams, working closely with the CIA, conducted a deadly series of drive-by shootings and ambushes of Iraqi military and Baath Party security officials. These were in effect targeted assassinations against identified regime figures.

AFTER the statue came down, trouble began. With the collapse of Saddam's regime, Baghdad became a city of chaos. The decrepit water and electricity systems collapsed. Extensive looting occurred at government ministries, palaces, private homes, stores, hospitals, and the Iraqi National Museum. Media reports noted that the museum, a repository of treasures dating back to the cradle of civilization, had been ransacked and that up to 170,000 of its artifacts had been pilfered. It was a powerful symbol: coalition forces were guarding oil facilities but not the sites critical to the welfare and identity of the Iraqi people.* (American soldiers had been sent to destroy a disrespectful tile mosaic of the first President Bush on the floor of the al-Rashid Hotel; they weren't dispatched to safeguard hospitals or cultural institutions.) "The widespread anarchy that followed the first moments of liberty here this week," *The New York Times* reported, "has become a central problem for American soldiers and marines, who constitute the only visible presence of any form of order. The mayhem gave rise today to signs of widespread Iraqi anger over the direction of the American enterprise here." Suicide bombers began targeting American troops. Outside Baghdad, nuclear facilities and ammunition storehouses were looted. It was looking as if the Bush administration hadn't adequately prepared for what would come after the defeat of Saddam's army.

The administration responses to the rapid deterioration of civil order weren't reassuring. On April 11, Rumsfeld dismissed the reports of bedlam: "Stuff happens. . . . It is a fundamental misunderstanding to see those images over and over and over again of some boy walking out with a vase and say, 'Oh, my goodness, you didn't have a plan.' That's nonsense. [The occupation forces] know what they're doing. And they're doing a terrific job. And it's untidy. And freedom's untidy." Retired General Jay Garner, who as head of the Pentagon-created Office of Reconstruction and Humanitarian Assistance was in charge of managing the postinvasion rebuilding in Iraq, criticized the media's focus on the looting as "unfair." There were, he said,

---

*As it turned out months later, the looting at the museum was not as terrible as initially reported. Prior to the war, museum officials had hidden more than 8,000 of the museum's more important pieces. Still, 10,000 artifacts, mostly items of use for study and research purposes, had been stolen, and about 30 pieces of significant value were missing. By the time the real damage to the collection had been assessed, though, the looting of the museum had become a symbol of an inept occupation.

"not near the problems we thought there would be." Garner and his operation were based in Kuwait, waiting for a safe time to enter Iraq.

Others were not as sanguine. On April 12, Colonel Kevin Benson, who had been overseeing postwar planning for Central Command, briefed Major General William G. Webster, Jr., deputy commander of U.S. ground forces in Iraq. Benson had prepared a "sequel" to his original postinvasion plan. The situation on the ground now appeared far more complicated and ominous. Benson's new plan, called "Eclipse II," outlined a "most likely scenario" for postwar Iraq that included "continued resistance" from Republican Guard units and other Baathist elements and a wave of sectarian violence (including "score settling" and "ethnic cleansing" among Shiites, Sunnis, and Kurds). It also predicted that Islamic jihadists would stream into the country. Webster asked Benson how long he expected "the whole thing" to last. "Boss, I think it's going to last three to five years," Benson said.

There was another conspicuous problem: not only had no WMDs been deployed against U.S. troops, but no weapons were found—at all. In the initial days after the invasion, administration officials had exuded complete confidence that locating Saddam's weapons cache would not be an issue. "We know where they are," Rumsfeld had said on March 30 about Saddam's chemical and biological stockpiles. "They're in the area around Tikrit and Baghdad and east, west, south, and north somewhat." On April 10, White House press secretary Ari Fleischer asserted, "We have high confidence that they have weapons of mass destruction. This is what this war was about and is about. And we have high confidence it will be found."

But by the second week in April, within the White House and throughout the administration, there was nervousness. It was, press aide Adam Levine subsequently recalled, a "roller coaster." White House officials anxious for news related to unconventional weapons would become excited with each fresh report that something related to WMDs had been located in Iraq—only to learn the next day that it was nothing after all. One day, there was a report about the discovery of containers of ricin; the next day, they turned out to be barrels of curdled milk. "It seemed like every two or three days there would be some report that would turn out not to be true," recalled Victoria Clarke, the assistant secretary of defense for public affairs. Rove, in particular, was sensitive to the potential political danger; the failure to unearth WMDs, he feared, could undermine the president's credibility and Bush's 2004 reelection campaign was just beginning. Rove wasn't alone. Michael Gerson, the chief speechwriter, returned from one senior staff meeting and told a colleague that some White House officials were insisting it didn't matter whether any weapons were actually found—so long as the war was viewed as a success. They were wrong, Gerson said. It mattered for the president's legacy.

Some intelligence officials also saw that the WMD issue could blow up. "As each day passed, it became more and more difficult to hold to the line that we're going to find them," recalled Carl Ford, Jr., the assistant secretary in charge of the State Department's Bureau of Intelligence and Research (INR).

Ford had inside information. He was reading classified U.S. intelligence community reports based on the interrogations of captured senior Iraqi officials and scientists, including some who were on the so-called deck of cards of Iraqis most wanted by the U.S. military. All of those interrogated denied knowing about any weapons stockpiles. But as he read the reports, it didn't seem to Ford that the Iraqis were parroting a cover story. "Each person had a slightly different take on it," he recalled. "They were not saying the same thing." Yet they all conveyed the same bottom line: they had no idea where any weapons were to be found. Then the U.S. military began polygraphing the Iraqis—and they all passed. The response among high-level administration officials, Ford said, was, "These guys really are good." That is, good liars—who could beat the lie detector. Senior administration officials, according to Ford, were in "denial." But Ford and some of his colleagues at State were starting to come around to a different view. "Our common reaction was," Ford said, " 'Holy shit, we're in trouble.' "

JUDY MILLER was hoping to prove otherwise. And she believed she had the scoop of the war—the key to resolving the mystery of the missing weapons.

The New York Times' star was on the ground in Iraq, traveling as an embedded reporter with Mobile Exploitation Team (MET) Alpha, one of only two units looking for the weapons of mass destruction that Bush and his aides had claimed would be found in Iraq. Miller was the only journalist to get this coveted assignment, and that was no accident. Victoria Clarke, Rumsfeld's chief spokesperson, had personally approved it. "She was fairly knowledgeable on the subject [of WMDs] and had written responsibly on it," Clarke later said. "It wasn't a hard call."

In mid-April, Miller, wearing her military khakis, and the MET Alpha team were at a suspected weapons site in the desert. Off in the distance, an Iraqi man wearing a baseball cap was pointing out various spots in the sand to members of the unit. Miller couldn't hear what the fellow was saying. She wasn't permitted to speak to him. But she was confident she had something big.

At this time, Miller and the MET Alpha team were based in an abandoned chemical facility outside Karbala. The conditions were harsh. There was no electricity; the unit's generator had broken. From inside this facility, she worked on the article with her editors in New York over a satellite phone. Outside it was cold and windy. And she had a tough decision to make: whether to sleep outside in the elements or on the floor of a laboratory, where she would be surrounded by various chemical substances. She chose the floor.

Her piece, which landed on the front page of The New York Times on April 21, reported that the Iraqi with the baseball cap had the answer to the most pressing mystery of the war: Where were the weapons of mass destruction? The Iraqi, she wrote, was a scientist who had worked on Iraq's chemical weapons program for more than a decade. He had told his military interrogators that days before U.S. troops stormed into Iraq, Saddam had destroyed his stocks of chemical weapons and his biological warfare equipment. The scientist, according to Miller, also had disclosed to the WMD hunters that Iraq had been secretly sending WMD materials and equipment to Syria for years, that Baghdad had recently been cooperating with al-Qaeda on weapons-related matters, and that he himself had buried material from Iraq's illicit arms program. Miller reported that this Iraqi had led MET Alpha to banned precursors for chemical weapons.

This one man's story appeared to be confirmation of virtually everything the Bush administration had asserted before the war to justify an invasion of Iraq. Miller quoted Major General David Petraeus, commander of the 101st Airborne Division, saying that this "may be the major discovery" of the war.

But Miller's article contained obvious weaknesses. She noted that she had been permitted to watch the baseball-capped scientist leading MET Alpha members to various sites. But she hadn't been allowed to talk to or even identify him, under the terms of her embedding agreement with the 75th Exploitation Task Force (XTF), which was in charge of the MET units, and she had also been forced to hold the story for three days so material in it could be deleted by military censors. The *Times* reporter had gotten close to a most important source—yet had ended up with a censored, secondhand account of his assertions.

When Steven Erlanger, a veteran foreign correspondent for the *Times* and now its culture editor, read the article on the morning of April 21, it struck him as weird. Erlanger had long thought that Miller, particularly after writing the Saddam book with Laurie Mylroie, was "too engaged" to be covering this issue. And in the months before the war, he had sent memos to other editors noting that the paper should be careful in its coverage of the WMD question. Erlanger had worried that *Times* editors were not being sufficiently skeptical in reviewing the paper's reporting on unconventional weapons in Iraq. And now he wondered if this particular Miller story was solid.

At a planning meeting for the next day's paper, he waited for Executive Editor Howell Raines or Managing Editor Gerald Boyd to say something about the Miller article. But neither did. So Erlanger spoke up. "I said, 'Excuse me, are we going to follow up the Judy Miller story?' " he later recalled remarking. What do you mean? Boyd asked. Erlanger said words to the effect of, "We're way out there on this. We have a story on the front page that justifies the administration's entire case for war, and it is based on information from someone we didn't identify and we didn't talk to." There was silence in the room. Years afterward, Erlanger said, "It was like I crapped on the table."

Immediately after the meeting, according to Erlanger, Boyd came into Erlanger's office and angrily said, Don't ever do that to me again. He insisted that Erlanger was not aware of all the work that had gone into that story. Erlanger rejoined, "That's right, I read the article as any average reader would." Boyd said if Erlanger had any concern, he could send him a memo. Then he left.

Within the *Times,* word spread of Boyd's irate reaction to Erlanger. Miller was already considered a loose cannon by many of her peers at the *Times,* and some suspected her of embellishing stories (even while acknowledging she sometimes did get the goods). Her prewar reporting on Iraq's WMDs had worried colleagues. "There was a general unease," recalled one

Times correspondent. "This was not because anyone knew her stories were wrong but because they were enthusiastic and boosterish. . . . She was reporting about the [WMD] intelligence with breathlessness and naiveté." Still, Miller seemed to enjoy a special status at the paper. Why? She had won a Pulitzer Prize, but so had other reporters. She had once been a close pal of the publisher, Arthur Ochs Sulzberger, Jr., when they had both worked at the paper's Washington bureau in the late 1970s. *Times* people wondered if that afforded her protection. They also saw that Raines was now keen on Miller's stories "for the buzz" they created, as one *Times* reporter put it. In any event, reporters at the paper assumed—rightly or wrongly—that criticism of Miller or her work would not be appreciated by the higher-ups. By asking questions about her guy-in-a-baseball-cap story, Erlanger had trod upon sensitive territory. His confrontation with Boyd was regarded by other reporters, according to one *Times* correspondent, as a message from Raines and Boyd: We are riding Judy Miller and her reporting all the way. There was no backing down.

In a way, the *Times* editors were behaving like White House officials: both institutions were standing by their prewar assertions. The *Times* hadn't been the only major news outlet before the invasion to publish or broadcast stories that made it seem that Saddam had hoarded nightmarish amounts of WMDs. And Miller hadn't been the only *Times* correspondent who had engaged in such reporting. But she had written more of such stories than most, and, due to her prominence, they had been the most consequential. They had been quoted by Cheney and been cited in the White House paper "A Decade of Deception and Defiance" drafted by WHIG member Jim Wilkinson to bolster Bush's UN speech in September. And now Miller was still working that beat, determined to prove she had been right all along.

THE day after her Iraqi-in-the baseball-cap story ran, Miller was interviewed from Iraq about her scoop on PBS's *NewsHour*. "I think they found something more than a smoking gun," she said about the discovery of the alleged scientist. "What they've found is what is being called here by members of MET Alpha . . . a silver bullet." Miller asserted that Saddam had engaged in "mass destruction" of WMD stockpiles right before the invasion. "What's become clear," she stated, "is the extent to which Iraq and this regime was able to pull the wool over the eyes of the international inspectors."

Miller was vindicating the faith that top Pentagon officials had placed in her when they approved her unique MET Alpha embed. Judy Miller "is probably the best ally we have out there in the media," Colonel Richard McPhee, the commander of the 75th Exploitation Task Force told one of the unit's public affairs officers, Sergeant Eugene Pomeroy, according to an e-mail Pomeroy sent to a colleague.

The next day, Miller had a follow-up article in the *Times*. It reported the supposed Iraqi scientist had caused MET Alpha to change its strategy.* The unit was now trying to find Iraqis who had worked on unconventional weapons programs. Toward that end, she noted, the MET Alpha team would be turning for help to an important new source of information: Ahmad Chalabi. The INC chief had returned to Iraq with Pentagon backing and had set up a compound in a former sporting club in Baghdad. MET Alpha, in its search for postwar leads, would soon be relying on the same questionable source who had provided so much faulty prewar intelligence to the U.S. government and to Miller and the *Times*.

Miller hadn't lost any of her faith in Chalabi. She quickly started serving as the broker between MET Alpha and the INC chief. In a brazen move for a journalist, she also started influencing the WMD unit's activities. At one point, she led MET Alpha officers to Chalabi's headquarters and arranged for the transfer of Saddam's son-in-law, Jamal Sultan al-Tikriti, from the INC to the U.S. military. A Chalabi spokesman later told *The Washington Post* that the INC had gotten into contact with Miller to hand over Sultan because "we thought it was a good story" and "we needed some way to get the guy to the Americans."

When Colonel McPhee, commander of the 75th XTF, ordered MET Alpha to leave Baghdad for Talil, a town in the south, Miller was infuriated.

---

*After his brief prominence, the baseball-capped scientist vanished from the pages of the *Times,* as well as the rest of the media. *Washington Post* reporter Barton Gellman, who was also in Iraq covering WMD issues at the time, tried to follow up on Miller's scoop and was told that U.S. military officials had been unable to authenticate the Iraqi's claims or even verify that he was a scientist. Gellman said he was subsequently told that the man was in fact a minor intelligence functionary. Asked about the baseball-cap story several years later, Miller told the authors of this book, "I won't talk about the baseball-cap guy."

She thought MET Alpha should remain in Baghdad and continue working with Chalabi and the INC. She confronted Eugene Pomeroy, the unit's public affairs officer, and protested the order. He told her to put it in writing, and Miller quickly dashed off a snippy handwritten note:

> The hunt for WMD is *here*, not in Talil. I'm assigned to cover that hunt. I want to remain here in Baghdad *without disembedding* until MET Alpha *returns to* Baghdad with the 75th XTF, when I shall rejoin them. I see no reason for me to waste time (or Met Alpha, for that matter) in Talil. . . . Request permission to stay on here with Ahmad Cha

Miller then crossed out the reference to Chalabi and continued writing:

> colleagues at the Palestine Hotel til Met Alpha returns or order to return [to Talil] is rescinded. I intend to write about this decision in the NYTimes to send a successful team back . . . just as progress on WMD is being made.

Pomeroy couldn't believe Miller's note. "It was a threat, of course," he later said. She was trying to blackmail the military: reverse this order, or I'll blast you in *The New York Times.* "I thought to myself, this is something that is going to bite her in the ass," Pomeroy recalled. "The journalist is here as an observer. If you want to run around with Ahmad Chalabi, looking for baseball-hatted scientists, that's your own business. But to interfere with the operations of a military unit, it was unconscionable." But Miller got her way. She complained directly to General Petraeus, who then suggested to Colonel McPhee he cancel the order to return to Talil. The colonel did so.

Miller's note indicated that she considered Chalabi the key to finding WMD-related evidence—just as she had before the war. Days later, after she was chastised by John Burns, the chief of the paper's Baghdad bureau, for writing about Chalabi without coordinating with his bureau, Miller sent Burns an e-mail noting that she had been "covering Chalabi for about 10 years" and that he had "provided most of the front page exclusives on WMD to our paper." She was acknowledging that the *Times'* coverage of perhaps the most important national security issue of recent years had been shaped by a controversial Iraqi exile whose reliability and honesty had repeatedly been challenged by the CIA and the State Department.

Years later, Raines would tell *The New Yorker* that "I did not know Judy's sources." But Miller's reliance on Chalabi was no secret—to Raines or to top editors at the *Times*. In a May 5, 2003, e-mail to Raines and Boyd in New York, Miller even sought to lay exclusive claim to the INC leader. Miller protested in the note that Patrick Tyler, another *Times* reporter who had just been made the paper's Baghdad bureau chief, had organized a lunch for Chalabi without inviting her. She complained that Tyler intended to write about Chalabi's relationship with Jordanian King Abdullah and his problems at the Petra Bank (the institution Chalabi had been convicted in absentia of defrauding). Miller told the two editors that she had planned to do that same story—and that Chalabi had promised *her* files on this matter. "As you know," Miller wrote, "I'm at Chalabi's every day because MET Alpha has a very sensitive relationship with his intell people—a sharing of people and documents on WMD."

In the e-mail, Miller boasted of her "extremely close contacts with Chalabi" and the INC and noted that ever since she had arrived in Iraq, she had been "systematically cultivating their trust and renewing our relationship." She added, "Ultimately, Chalabi may provide not only the most important WMD info, but other info on terrorists, which, quite frankly, he has promised to give to me. That relationship is not transferable."

But Chalabi was unable to help Miller or the MET Alpha unit find any weapons. And the mood within the unit was getting antsy. The other two MET teams, assigned to investigating Saddam's war crimes, were scoring successes. They were discovering mass graves that were visceral and undeniable evidence of Saddam's brutality. But within MET Alpha and its companion unit, MET Bravo, the questions were growing. "It was extremely frustrating," Tewfik Boulenouar, MET Alpha's translator, later said. The team was being sent to locations that had been on a prewar list of possible WMD sites. But, Boulenouar said, "it was obvious to us that the Iraqis wouldn't leave the WMDs in the same place. We knew before we got to these places we wouldn't find anything." Every day, Pomeroy recalled, the members of those units would be asked the same thing: "So did you guys find anything?" The answer was always no. "I remember this feeling, so why did we do this?" Pomeroy said. "Everything we'd been told up to that point is, we had WMD there. We were scouring the landscape, and we hadn't found squat."

———

ON MAY 1, in a carefully choreographed event, the White House arranged for Bush to land on a jet aboard the aircraft carrier USS *Abraham Lincoln*. Speaking under a huge banner that declared "Mission Accomplished," Bush proclaimed that "major combat operations" in Iraq were over and that the United States had "prevailed." He was equally bullish on the hunt for weapons, saying the U.S. military had "begun" the search and we "already know of hundreds of sites that will be investigated."

But two days later, during a brief meeting with reporters at his ranch in Crawford, Bush offered a new take, one of many such shifts he would be forced to make on the weapons issue. First, Bush offered what had become the official line: "We'll find them. And it's just going to be a matter of time." But then he remarked, "But what we're going—the world will find is, the man had a program to develop weapons of mass destruction." The president was not talking about actual stockpiles of chemical and biological weapons, the prewar claim. He was now talking about a *program* to *develop* weapons.

THAT same weekend, Joe Wilson was hobnobbing with dozens of Democratic senators at a hotel on the Chesapeake Bay in eastern Maryland. The lawmakers had gathered to discuss various policy matters and to listen to experts. Wilson was there to serve on a panel examining what might lay ahead in Iraq. Other speakers participating in this session included University of Maryland professor Shibley Telhami and *New York Times* columnist Nicholas Kristof. The mood of the Democrats was quite dark. "At the conference, in private, they were far more critical of the decision to go to war and of Bush's handling of the war than they were in public," recalled one participant.

Throughout the weekend retreat, conversations continued between the panels. And Wilson freely participated in them, as he made the rounds with his wife. "I've known Joe for years," Telhami later said, "and this may have been the first time I met Valerie. I thought she was something like an energy executive." At some point—either during the panel or an informal discussion—Wilson referred to his trip to Niger. This caught Kristof's attention. He asked Wilson if he could write about it. Wilson said yes, as long as Kristof didn't name him. And days later, on May 6, the first public reference to Wilson's trip appeared—on the op-ed page of *The New York Times*. In his column, Kristof, addressing the absent WMDs, wrote, "There are indications that the U.S. government souped up intelligence, leaned on spooks to change their conclusions and concealed contrary information to deceive people at home and around the world." He referred to the Niger charge:

> Consider the now-disproved claims by President Bush and Colin Powell that Iraq tried to buy uranium from Niger so it could build nuclear weapons. . . .
>
> I'm told by a person involved in the Niger caper that more than a year ago the vice president's office asked for an investigation of the uranium deal, so a former U.S. ambassador to Africa was dispatched to Niger. In February 2002, according to someone present at the meetings, that envoy reported to the C.I.A. and State Department that the information was unequivocally wrong and that the documents had been forged.
>
> The envoy reported, for example, that a Niger minister whose signature was on one of the documents had in fact been out of office for more than a decade. In addition, the Niger mining program was structured so that the uranium diversion had been impossible. The envoy's debunking of the forgery was passed around the administration and seemed to be accepted—except that President Bush and the State Department kept citing it anyway.

Kristof got the story more right than not—though there were some mistakes. The CIA's report on Wilson's mission hadn't had the impact within the administration that Kristof's column suggested. And Wilson had not debunked the Niger documents by reporting that a particular minister had been out of office at the time of the deal (as the IAEA had later found). In fact, Wilson had never seen the Niger papers. His trip had occurred eight months before the State Department and CIA had received the actual forged documents from Italian journalist Elisabetta Burba in October 2002.*

---

*Wilson later wrote that he had been told by the CIA at his pretrip meeting that the Niger charge was based on an actual sales agreement. (The INR memo written by analyst Doug Rohn about this meeting refers to a discussion of an "alleged contract.") But Wilson had not been told which Nigerien officials had signed the purported contract. So he had been in a position to suggest that this sales agreement was false but not to challenge specific details within the documents. Over a year after Kristof's column appeared, Wilson's critics would point to the Kristof column and accuse Wilson of having overstated the results of his trip by claiming he had personally refuted the Niger papers.

Still, Wilson had returned from Niamey with a report that he thought seriously discredited the Niger allegation—and his information was ignored. It was a tangible, discrete example of how prewar intelligence had been mishandled; and what's more, there appeared to be a real-life source out there willing to talk about it. Few in the Washington media and political world knew who Kristof's unnamed ambassador was. But it wouldn't take long for a *Washington Post* reporter to figure it out.

On May 12, 2003, L. Paul Bremer III, the administrator appointed by Bush to head the newly created Coalition Provisional Authority, arrived in Baghdad. Bremer, a cool, self-confident State Department veteran, had been dispatched to replace the seemingly befuddled Jay Garner as the number one U.S. official on the scene. Four days later, Bremer issued Order Number One: a sweeping directive for the de-Baathification of Iraqi society. The idea of uprooting all remnants of Saddam's hated regime had been approved by the White House—and championed by Chalabi and the INC. It was part of the fundamental vision of the war's advocates: to create a new liberal democracy in the Middle East built in America's image. The order had been drafted by Doug Feith's office in the Pentagon. "We've got to show all the Iraqis that we're serious about building a new Iraq," Feith had told Bremer before he left. "And that means that Saddam's instruments of repression have no role in that new nation."

But how exactly was the decree to be implemented? There were more than 2 million members of the Baath Party. Under Saddam, party membership had been a requirement for almost all government jobs—in the police, in the universities, in sanitation. How many government workers were to be fired? Bremer, under instructions from Bush, took an expansive view of the order. The top three layers of management in every government institution—even the hospitals—were to be reviewed for possible Baath Party connections, he decreed. When he first briefed the staff he inherited from Jay Garner's ORHA about de-Baathification, Bremer wrote in an e-mail to his wife, there had been "a sea of bitching and moaning with lots of them saying how hard it was going to be. But I reminded them that the president's guidance is clear: de-Baathification will be carried out even if at a cost to administrative efficiency."

Iraq's new de-Baathification commission was cochaired by Chalabi.

Working closely with his nephew and political adviser, Salem Chalabi, the INC chief obtained Baath Party membership and payment records and implemented a sweeping purge. "He was using it to settle scores," said one senior NSC official. The White House, according to this official, was soon getting alarming reports of basic civic services breaking down, because thousands of trash collectors, police, and teachers were being ousted in Chalabi's purge.

On May 23, Bremer issued CPA Order Number Two, "Dissolution of Entities," abolishing the Iraqi Army. Overnight, 400,000 Iraqi soldiers were out of work, without pay, and with nowhere to go. Angry former soldiers were soon gathering outside the gates of the CPA; the disbanding of their army was a "humiliation to the dignity of the nation," read one banner. Like de-Baathification, the order had been drafted by Feith's office and approved by the White House, ignoring the advice of the State Department's Future of Iraq Group. By dissolving the Army, the Bush administration, State Department adviser David Phillips subsequently wrote, had "committed one of the greatest errors in the history of U.S. warfare: It unnecessarily increased the ranks of its enemies."

The CIA's John Maguire, who had just arrived in Iraq to help set up the CIA's Baghdad station, started getting complaints about both actions from his Iraqi contacts. The dissolution of the Army, Maguire later said, "disenfranchised people with guns, and it got rid of the technocrats—the people who ran the society—because it was a militarized society. It was a cataclysmic mistake." De-Baathification might have been worse. The Arabic word used in official documents to describe the de-Baathification decree was *ijtithaath*. It meant to uproot by root and branch, like a weed. But the connotation for many Iraqis was annihilation or eradication. To many Iraqis, Maguire later explained, it sounded like the Final Solution. Maguire was appalled. "We told Bremer that's a heinous word," he recalled. "He blew it off." This was a disaster in the making, Maguire feared.

Maguire, who had helped write the Anabasis plan and fervently believed in the war, was already worried that U.S. policies in Iraq were heading the wrong way. There seemed to be no real plan for what to do now. Iraqis, he noted, saw the lack of electricity and the U.S. failure to stop the looting as punishments being inflicted on them by Washington: "The goodwill was dissipating." From the outset, the CIA station, according to Maguire, was warning about the problems—and was cut out of critical planning sessions by the Pentagon and Bremer.

BY THE end of May, the news out of Iraq was getting worse. On the ground, looting was continuing, crime was rising, and there were increasing signs of an insurgency taking root. Military commanders were grousing that Rumsfeld had not supplied enough troops to manage the postinvasion challenges. Lieutenant General David McKiernan, commander of U.S. ground forces in Iraq, was telling reporters that the "war has not ended" and that the violent actions of the resistance were "not criminal activities, they are combat activities." And Bush's management of the war was coming under fire. "When is the president going to tell the American people that we're likely to be in the country of Iraq for three, four, five, six, eight, ten years, with thousands of forces and spending billions of dollars? Because it's not been told to them yet," Democratic Senator Joe Biden demanded of Paul Wolfowitz at a foreign relations committee hearing. Republican Senator Chuck Hagel complained, "We may have underestimated or mischaracterized the challenges of establishing security and rebuilding Iraq."

And still there were no weapons. Democrats on Capitol Hill were calling for investigations into prewar intelligence. How, they asked, could the White House have been so wrong about everything it had told the American public?

THEN the CIA came through—or seemed to. On May 28, the CIA released a new and extraordinary six-page report declaring that a critical part of the prewar WMD case had been proven right. Earlier in the month, the Pentagon had announced the discovery of a tractor trailer outfitted with industrial equipment and maintained it was one of the mobile biological weapons labs that had been graphically described by Powell in his UN presentation. Judy Miller, just before leaving Iraq, had hailed this news in an article that quoted an unidentified Pentagon WMD expert saying that the trailer was "a smoking gun."* But for weeks there had been no official confirmation.

---

*David Kay, the former weapons inspector who was now working for NBC News, filed a report showing the inside of the supposed bioweapons lab. Pointing to equipment within the trailer, Kay said, "This is where the biological process took place." Was the production of bioweapons, an NBC News anchor asked, the only conceivable purpose of this trailer? Kay replied, "Literally, there's nothing else for which it could be used."

Now the CIA had it figured out. The agency's public affairs office arranged a rare conference call for Washington reporters so officials could brief them about this important finding. This trailer and another one, the agency declared that day, were indeed the mobile bioweapons labs cited by Powell. The agency's report, which also carried the imprimatur of the Defense Intelligence Agency, noted that the trailers contained a fermenter capable of producing biological agents as well as support equipment such as water supply tanks, an air compressor, a water chiller, and a system for collecting gases. It all amounted to an "interconnected" and "ingeniously simple, self-contained bioprocessing system" for "biological warfare." The paper also dismissed one explanation for the trailers that had been offered by senior Iraqi officials—that they were to produce hydrogen for artillery weather balloons. This was a "cover story," the white paper said, that was typical of the Iraqis' "sophisticated denial and deception methods."

The CIA report was a godsend for the White House. "We have found the weapons of mass destruction," Bush proclaimed the next day in an interview with a Polish television journalist. When the reporter asked what argument Bush could "use now to justify this war," Bush pointed to the mobile BW labs: "You remember when Colin Powell stood up in front of the world, and he said, Iraq has got laboratories, mobile labs to build biological weapons . . . and we've so far discovered two. And we'll find more weapons as time goes on. But for those who say we haven't found the banned manufacturing devices or banned weapons, they're wrong, we found them."

Inside the intelligence community, however, the paper generated fierce controversy. Many intelligence professionals found it full of holes, a shoddy piece of work that had been prepared more for public relations purposes than legitimate analysis. The document itself conceded that not a trace of biological agents had been found in the trailers. Why not? How was that possible? The CIA claimed the absence suggested that the Iraqis had "thoroughly decontaminated" the trailers—a claim some weapons experts thought implausible because it would have been virtually impossible to scrub trace residues from the trailers. There was also another problem spotted by government weapons analysts: the tanks in the supposed trailer labs didn't have a drain. That was, one senior DIA analyst later noted, a "killer" issue. "You can't foment biological weapons agents in a tank without a drain. You'd never be able to get rid of [the toxins]. You'd end up killing yourself."

Objections to the CIA analysis had emerged even before the white paper was released. In mid-May, a team of DIA contractors in Iraq examining the trailers had concluded that the trailers were not biological weapons labs. These results had been e-mailed back to Washington by the contractors—and ignored. But the CIA, particularly the analysts at WINPAC, had kept pushing the case and wouldn't back down. The agency had tried to get DIA analysts to sign on to its assessment, but almost all of the defense agency's experts on the subject refused to do so. It was almost as though the DIA's analysts, feeling guilty for their prewar acquiescence, were now drawing a line in the sand. Then one night CIA officials contacted the one DIA analyst sympathetic to their position and obtained this analyst's approval to place the DIA's logo on the paper. "We were tricked," the senior DIA analyst later exclaimed. "It still boggles my mind. That report was bogus. That was not one of the finest moments in intelligence analysis."

Officials at the State Department's intelligence arm, INR, were also outraged. The CIA had refused to let INR participate in the review of the trailers. But when INR analysts read the CIA-DIA report, they "went ballistic," according to Carl Ford, the State Department's intelligence chief. Ford sent Powell a note: Be careful on this one. Don't get out in front on it. It's got problems. (The day the CIA released its report, Richard Boucher, the State Department spokesman, pointed to the paper to show that Powell had been on the money during his Security Council speech in February.) Then Ford received a phone call from Tenet's office. The director of central intelligence wanted to see him.

The next day, Ford entered the director's conference room; Tenet and McLaughlin were waiting for him. And Tenet tore into him—for sending Powell that cautionary note questioning the CIA's report. It was the first time he had ever seen the agency's director so visibly upset. "Tenet was saying, how dare I write something like that!" Ford recalled. "'You're misinformed!'" Ford held his ground. Tenet told him, "You don't know everything we know. You haven't seen everything." Ford shot back, "Why not? I thought I was supposed to see everything. You guys holding out on me?" In any case, Ford told them, "you better know more than I do because that report is one of the worst intelligence assessments I've ever read." (Tenet and McLaughlin both later said they did not recall the conversation.)

For Ford, this was a low point in the entire Iraq intelligence saga. The white-bearded Ford was a veteran intelligence professional who had worked at senior positions at the CIA, the State Department, and the Pentagon during the administrations of Ronald Reagan and the first President Bush. (Before taking the job as chief of INR, Ford had been offered a top foreign policy position in the White House by Cheney, whom Ford had worked for—and admired—when Cheney was secretary of defense.) And Ford had always gotten along well with Tenet and McLaughlin, despite the INR's dissents from key parts of the agency's prewar analysis of the Iraqi nuclear program.

Ford saw Tenet's reaction as a sign of how much the CIA director and his deputy, McLaughlin, had at stake—and of how much pressure they and the agency were under to justify their prewar findings. "It was clear they had been personally involved in the preparation of the report," Ford recalled. "As it turned out, that analysis was unprofessional and even unethical. People did funny things with the evidence; they should have been shot."

What bothered Ford the most was the circular logic in the paper. One key element of proof that the CIA had cited—it was on the first page of the white paper—was that the trailers were "strikingly similar" to the descriptions of the biolabs that had been provided by "the chemical engineer" cited by Powell in his UN speech. This was a reference to Curveball. But the CIA well knew by this point that there were serious questions about the credibility of Curveball. His reliability (and the CIA's inability to talk to him) had been the subject of angry debates within the agency for months. The CIA paper didn't acknowledge that the source on which much of its bioweapons case rested may have been a flake—or a fabricator. In fact, the same WINPAC analyst who months earlier had defended Curveball (in the face of Tyler Drumheller's warnings) had written the CIA report on the trailers. And this analyst was now using the trailers to validate WINPAC's (and the CIA's) decision to stand behind a suspect source. In Ford's view, by failing to be upfront about the questions about Curveball, the CIA had crossed a line. This was, he thought, fundamentally dishonest.

Years later, Ford was more bitter about this CIA paper than almost anything else in the Iraq weapons debate. He remained angry at its authors. "It wasn't just that it was wrong," he said. "They lied."

ON MAY 29, there was a small crisis in Dick Cheney's office. It had nothing to do with the front-page article in *The Washington Post* by Walter Pincus and

Karen DeYoung that cited Cheney's prewar assertions about Iraq's WMDs as a primary example of administration statements that now looked wrong. (In an interview for the *Post* article, Wolfowitz had denied there had been any "oversell" of the WMD threat, but he acknowledged that there "had been a tendency to emphasize the WMD issue."*) Nor was the crisis triggered by information released that day by Representative Henry Waxman, a liberal Democrat, showing that Halliburton—of which Cheney had been the chief executive officer—had received more than half a billion dollars in military contracts relating to the wars in Afghanistan and Iraq in an arrangement that did not require the firm to bid on these jobs. Instead, Cheney press aides were overwhelmed by media calls about an item in a gossip column claiming that Cheney had told subordinates, "The way to lick this recession is to get all those deadbeats out of the soup kitchens." The gossip columnist subsequently admitted she had made up this quote as a joke.

But Scooter Libby, Cheney's chief of staff, had another press-related matter on his mind this day. Pincus had been calling the White House and Cheney's office about the Kristof column.

In the three weeks since Kristof had written about the unnamed ambassador's trip to Niger, the controversy over the forged Niger documents and Bush's State of the Union comments had continued, as part of a larger debate. Bush critics were claiming that the White House had intentionally misled the American public on Iraq's WMDs. But the story of the former diplomat sent to Niger in response to an inquiry from Cheney's office hadn't registered with the media and the public.

Catherine Martin, Cheney's communications director, had taken the messages from Pincus and passed them to Libby, the vice president's chief of staff. With a veteran national security reporter sniffing around about the Niger matter, Libby figured he ought to do some intelligence gathering on his own. He called Marc Grossman, the undersecretary of state, with a request: What could Grossman tell him about this ambassador and his trip to Niger?

---

*In an earlier interview with a *Vanity Fair* writer on May 10, Wolfowitz said, "For reasons that have a lot to do with the U.S. government bureaucracy we settled on the one issue [to justify the war] that everyone could agree on which was weapons of mass destruction as the core reason, but . . . there have always been three fundamental concerns. One is weapons of mass destruction, the second is support for terrorism, the third is the criminal treatment of the Iraqi people. . . . The third one by itself . . . is a reason to help the Iraqis but it's not a reason to put American kids' lives at risk."

*Do you expect me to commit a felony by telling
you classified information?*

—Scooter Libby

13

The Leaking Begins

I N EARLY June, Bush embarked on a whirlwind overseas trip that took him from a treaty signing in Saint Petersburg to a Middle East summit in Aqaba. But the emotional high came during an exhilarating stop at Camp al-Sayliyah in Qatar. More than 1,000 troops who had taken part in the invasion of Iraq gave a thunderous welcome to the president. "You set an example of skill and daring that will stand for all time," he proclaimed. Bush said that "we've got a lot of work to do in Iraq. And we're going to stay the course until the job gets done." But he said progress was being made: "Day by day, the United States and our coalition partners are making the streets safer for the Iraqi citizens."

Nobody was more ebullient that day than Karl Rove. The White House political strategist whipped out a camera and began offering to take pictures of soldiers posing with top White House aides. "Step right up," Rove boomed. "Get your photo with Ari Fleischer—get 'em while they're hot. Get your Condi Rice."

On the way home, Air Force One, escorted by U.S. fighter planes, flew over Iraq. As the jets crossed Baghdad and dipped low, Bush huddled with Rice and Powell as they gazed out the window. The president pointed out some of the city's landmarks. Press accounts that day called it a "victory lap."

But away from the cheering troops, Bush was getting frustrated. At one point during the trip, when he and aides were reviewing a speech aboard Air Force One, Bush questioned a line that had been drafted for him. Is this true? he asked. Yes, Mr. President, he was told, it's been vetted. "Oh, yeah, just like the WMD we found," Bush snapped, according to an aide who was present. This was a snide remark, the aide said—an obvious reference to the overstated we-found-the-weapons comment Bush had made before leaving Washington. It seemed to this aide that the WMD flap was getting to the president. And when Bush was in Qatar, during a meeting with top U.S. commanders, he demanded to know who was in charge of the WMD search. He turned to Paul Bremer, his viceroy in Iraq, and asked if it was his job to find the weapons. No, said Bremer. Bush put the same question to General Tommy Franks. The general said the WMD hunt was not his responsibility. Then who? an exasperated Bush exclaimed. Someone in the meeting mentioned Stephen Cambone, referring to the undersecretary of defense for intelligence. Who's that? Bush asked.

In the weeks to come, the hunt for WMDs would get a new commander. But the search would be no more successful. The embarrassing failure to find weapons would lead to new disclosures and sharper questions about what the administration had known—or chosen to ignore—before the war. The controversy would push Joe Wilson to go public and set off open warfare between the White House and the CIA.

DAVID KAY had come to Langley to lend the CIA a hand. The former UN and International Atomic Energy Agency weapons inspector in Iraq was part of a review panel of outside experts vetting a new National Intelligence Estimate on North Korea. After Kay finished looking at the draft, John McLaughlin, the deputy director, asked to see him. He wanted to know what Kay thought of the ongoing search for weapons in Iraq. Kay, who had been in Iraq as an NBC News consultant, said he had never seen such a screwed-up operation. The MET teams had been poorly equipped. Their members hadn't been sufficiently trained in biological, chemical, or nuclear matters. They had been working off a list of suspected WMD sites that increasingly looked like a roster of dead ends. They had been relying too much on Ahmad Chalabi's INC for leads.

McLaughlin picked up the phone and called Tenet. Moments later, Kay was next door in the CIA director's office. Okay, Tenet asked him, what would you do? Not go looking under rocks, Kay said. Saddam's weapons program, he explained, must have had a tremendous infrastructure full of not only scientists and military officers but clerks, truck drivers, and janitors. Find these people, Kay said, and you'll find the weapons. And Iraq was loaded with documents. When Kay had been there, he had seen people trying to peddle former government papers. Records needed to be secured and examined. An effective search, Kay said, would have to be an intelligence-driven operation. It would require plenty of resources—meaning money. Tenet and McLaughlin listened; then the meeting was done.

A few days later, during the second weekend in June, Kay was at a spa outside Washington celebrating his wedding anniversary when Tenet tracked him down to ask if he would take over the search. Kay was being offered a unique berth: special assistant to the director of central intelligence and chief strategist for the Iraq Survey Group, the new Pentagon-created outfit now responsible for the WMD hunt. Kay would be in charge of the weapons search. He said yes, but only if the CIA would meet his demands: all the necessary resources and authority to keep the ISG focused solely on the WMD mission. "I told George, I'm taking on *your* moral hazard," Kay recalled. "*Your* agency said there were WMDs there." Tenet assured Kay he would have whatever he needed.

Tenet wanted Kay to head to Kuwait immediately and meet up with the ISG. No, said Kay. He first wanted to see exactly what the Bush administration really had known about Saddam's deadly arsenal before the war. He parked himself in a conference room at the CIA and began reviewing all the prewar intelligence on Saddam's weapons programs. "Now I'll get the good stuff," he thought to himself.

Before him were various reports. Highly classified. The best the CIA had. But as he read the documents, he shook his head. He wasn't coming across any undeniable evidence. The intelligence either was overly general or had originated with problematic sources. "On the trailers," he later said, "I cannot tell you how discouraged I was to see it was based on a single source—Curveball. No one knew his name. No American had spoken to him." He spotted the dissents of Energy Department scientists on the aluminum tubes and wondered why they had been given less weight than the evaluation of the CIA's WINPAC. The Energy Department scientists were the experts, not the desk analysts at WINPAC. Nothing was hard and strong. The more Kay read, the more disheartened he became. He thought of a favorite old tune. It was the Peggy Lee song "Is That All There Is?"

GRUFF and idiosyncratic, Walter Pincus had been covering national security issues for *The Washington Post* for decades. He had written some of the few skeptical accounts about prewar intelligence that had appeared in the paper before the war (though most had been buried inside and received little attention). In early June, with the weapons search faltering, Pincus's sources within the intelligence community were opening up. This was a sign of rising tension between the intelligence community and the White House. And Pincus and his colleague Dana Priest were taking full advantage of it.

On June 5, they reported on the paper's front page that Cheney and Libby, according to senior intelligence officials, had "made multiple trips to the CIA" over the past year to question analysts about Iraq. Two days later, Pincus and Priest had another front-page article that compared Bush's prewar public statements with a recently disclosed classified DIA report from the fall of 2002 that warned that there was "no reliable information on whether Iraq is producing or stockpiling chemical weapons."

Pincus was also still chasing the story of the unnamed ambassador in the Nicholas Kristof column of early May. It hadn't taken long for Pincus to figure out that the envoy was Wilson. Pincus contacted him, and Wilson spoke at length—on background, meaning that he would be identified only as a former ambassador. Pincus also kept pressing Catherine Martin, Cheney's chief press spokeswoman, for information. How had the trip of the former ambassador come about? What had Cheney been told about the ambassador's mission and his findings? Finally, Martin arranged for Pincus to talk with Libby.

By this point, Libby had learned some things about Wilson. After Cheney's office first heard from Pincus, Libby had received two oral reports from Undersecretary of State Marc Grossman, who told Libby that Wilson had been the unnamed ambassador who had made the trip to Niger. Then, on June 9, the CIA faxed several classified documents to Cheney's office, directing them to the personal attention of Libby and another staff member. The faxed documents referred to the former ambassador and his trip to Niger, without naming him. After receiving the documents, Libby wrote the names "Wilson" and "Joe Wilson" on the documents. And on June 10, Grossman—Libby's key contact at the State Department on this matter— had new information about the incident. It involved Joe Wilson's wife and was on his desk—in a State Department memo.

AFTER Libby had first asked Grossman for information on the Niger trip, Grossman had instructed Carl Ford, the State Department's INR chief, to prepare a memo on the Wilson issue. Ford and the INR were happy to take on this assignment. It gave them a chance to remind their bosses at State that INR had tried to wave the administration off the Niger charge. "We thought it was a travesty that anybody would have believed any of this stuff," Ford later said. He directed his staff to pull the files.

The two analysts most familiar with the Niger episode were not at INR at the moment. Doug Rohn, the Africa analyst, had left the office to become the consul general at the U.S. Consulate in Karachi, Pakistan, and Simon Dodge, the specialist on Iraqi nuclear topics, was on leave. Another INR analyst, Neil Silver, was given the job of writing the memo for Grossman. Silver collected the available records and drafted a memo that recapped the INR's initial skepticism about the Niger charge, its dissent in the NIE, and Dodge's warning that the documents were forgeries. The memo also noted that the INR had had little to do with the Wilson trip—and had even argued at the time that there was not much point to the mission. In other words, the INR had been right all along, and it was not to blame for the Wilson trip.

One of the documents Silver was using to draft the memo was Rohn's one-page account of the February 19, 2002, meeting at the CIA, where Joe Wilson had talked about the Niger deal with intelligence officers and had discussed a possible trip to Niger. Rohn's notes said that Valerie Wilson had "apparently convened" this meeting with the idea of sending her husband to Niger, and they identified her as "a CIA WMD managerial type."

Silver lifted Rohn's account of the meeting but dropped the word "apparently." In the memo for Grossman—which had been triggered by Libby's request—Silver stated as a fact that the meeting at the CIA had been "convened" by Valerie Wilson, whom he described as a "CIA WMD manager." Because he had not talked to Rohn about Rohn's notes, Silver didn't know that Rohn had entered that meeting late and wasn't really sure about

Valerie Wilson's role. (Silver had no reason to think that such details would later take on significance.) With this memo, Silver had depicted Valerie Wilson as the CIA officer responsible for the meeting that had led to the trip. Inadvertently, Rohn's uninformed impression (conveyed in a loosely worded line) was now portrayed as a hard-and-fast truth. It would soon become, in the hands of White House spinners, a political charge.

Rohn's notes and several other relevant documents were attached to the INR memo, and the memo was stamped "Secret." The key paragraphs, including the one that mentioned Valerie Wilson, were prefaced with the letters S/NF. This meant Secret/No Foreign: the information was classified and considered too sensitive to share with any foreigners. INR sent copies of the memo and the attachments to Grossman, Powell, and Richard Armitage, the deputy secretary of state. The memo did not make much of Valerie Wilson's connection to the Niger trip.

After Grossman received the INR memo, he briefed Libby again on the Wilson matter. This time, he told Cheney's chief of staff that Wilson's wife worked at the CIA and that she had been responsible for sending Wilson to Niger.

I. Lewis Libby was playing a classic Washington role: the fiercely loyal aide determined to defend his boss. And he was well suited to the task, especially if the assignment called for quiet, behind-the-scenes maneuvering.

Libby, fifty-three years old, was an important player—the hard-line chief of staff to the most influential vice president in U.S. history. But he was not especially high profile. When he attended meetings Cheney held with others, Libby often stood off to the side, deferential but paying close attention. He was known to be a well-practiced secret keeper. Friendly with a number of reporters, he would occasionally talk to them, rarely sharing anything useful or sensitive. "Do you expect me to commit a felony by telling you classified information?" Libby once huffily asked a reporter friend who tried to question him when Libby was staff director for a congressional committee investigating Chinese espionage in the 1990s. He was tight-lipped about personal matters. He would not tell friends what the "I" in his name stood for. (*USA Today* would report his first name was Irv; other publications would claim it was Irving.) He provided different explanations for his nickname, "Scooter." He rarely gave speeches or appeared on television. A *Washington Post* reporter profiling Libby once noted that he embodied a favorite saying of Cheney: "You never get into trouble for something you don't say." In one of his only TV appearances, which occurred on CNN's *Larry King Weekend* in February 2002, he defended Cheney's refusal to reveal the names of energy executives with whom the vice president's energy task force had met.

Libby, born in Connecticut and raised in Florida, was the son of an investment banker. He attended Phillips Andover prep school and then Yale, where he was taught by Wolfowitz. After graduating from Columbia Law School and working for a Philadelphia law firm, he was recruited by Wolfowitz to work at the State Deparment. Years after that, when Libby was working for Wolfowitz at the Pentagon—at the time of the first Persian Gulf War—he developed a shared interest with Cheney (then the defense secretary) in Saddam's weapons. And at the end of that war, as he later told an interviewer, both he and Wolfowitz objected to the administration's decision, urged by Colin Powell, then the chairman of the Joint Chiefs of Staff, to accept a cease-fire before the retreating Iraqi Army could be destroyed. "I was floored by the decision," Libby said. "Neither of us liked it." In that period, he also advocated building up the U.S. military to such an extent that America would be the lone superpower for decades to come.

Libby was known by friends to be a sharp, engaging conversationalist. He was married to Harriet Grant, once a lawyer on the Democratic staff of the Senate judiciary committee. He fancied himself an expert—and daring—skier. But he had the reputation of a careful, detail-oriented, cool-headed attorney. For years, Libby had represented Marc Rich, a billionaire fugitive financier who had fled to Switzerland from the United States in 1983 to avoid prosecution on evading more than $48 million in taxes and for illegally trading oil with Iran when Tehran was holding U.S. hostages. After President Bill Clinton, in the last days of his presidency, pardoned Rich, there was an uproar. Libby, who had earlier worked on the case for a Rich pardon, was called before a House committee to testify about Rich. "Did you represent a crook who stole money from the United States government?" a Democratic House member thundered at him. "No, sir," a calm Libby replied. "There are no facts that I know that support the criminality of the client based on the tax returns."

Possessing a dark sense of humor, Libby once told an aide—in the earlier days of the George W. Bush administration—that he intended to work at the White House until "I get indicted or something." But his ironic detachment vanished when it came to "the boss," as he called the vice president. "He was enamored of Cheney, he was almost an acolyte," said one friend. Libby's life revolved around Cheney. He took his vacations in Wyoming so he could be near the vice president. He even took up hunting. After September 11, he came to view Cheney as a historical figure who saw the dangers facing his country with greater clarity than anyone. In December 2001, during an interview with journalist James Mann, Libby read aloud a passage from Winston Churchill's memoir of the years leading up to World War II: "I felt as if I were walking with destiny, and that all my past life had been but a preparation for this hour and for this trial." Libby told Mann these words could be applied to Cheney in the post-9/11 period.

Libby was also a novelist who had written one book, *The Apprentice,* a tale of intrigue set in a Japanese rural inn in 1903. It took him twenty years to finish the book. At one point, Libby told Larry King, he "went out to Colorado, drank tequila and wrote. And sort of [led] the dream life." But he hadn't been happy with what he produced and threw away three hundred pages. The book, published in 1996, was sexually graphic. It included a reference to a bear copulating with young girls and a scene that featured the line, "He asked if they should fuck the deer." (As *The New Yorker* would later quip, "The answer, reader, is yes.") In one chapter, the protagonist, the innkeeper's virgin apprentice, is tortured with a hot coal for refusing to yield a secret. Libby spared few details in describing the action. Rather than reveal the truth, this young man took the pain.

PINCUS finally got Libby on the phone. Libby wouldn't say anything on the record. He wouldn't allow Pincus to refer to him as a vice presidential aide or even a White House official. He could be called only a "government official." Once granted virtually complete anonymity, Libby answered a few questions—as he tried to spin the *Post* reporter with a small piece of disinformation so Cheney wouldn't get prominent play in Pincus's story.

Libby said nothing about Valerie Wilson. He insisted that Cheney hadn't known about Wilson's trip as the Kristof column had suggested. Libby did acknowledge that the trip might have originated with a question from an aide from Cheney—but not from Cheney himself.

This was a deflection. It had been Cheney who had first asked the questions that prompted the Wilson trip. There had been nothing improper about this. But now was not the time to say that Cheney's personal interest in the purported uranim deal had spurred Joe Wilson's mission to Niger. Pincus and Priest had, days earlier, disclosed Cheney's prewar visits to the CIA. Other media reports were suggesting that intelligence analysts had been pressured by the White House before the war. Libby didn't want to see a new story revealing that a request from Cheney had led to a trip that had produced information contradicting Bush's now-controversial State of the Union claim—information that, according to the Kristof column, the White House had deliberately ignored.

Libby's fibbing worked.

Pincus's article appeared on the front page on June 12, 2003. It barely mentioned Cheney. The story reported that a "key component of President Bush's claim in his State of the Union address last January that Iraq had an active nuclear weapons program . . . was disputed by a CIA-directed mission to the central African nation in early 2002" but that the CIA had not passed on the results of this mission to the White House. Pincus quoted the unnamed ambassador (Wilson) as relating the same story he had told Kristof—how he had gone to Niger to investigate the yellowcake claims, concluded the uranium-deal story was false, and told the CIA that the documents may have been forged because the "dates were wrong and the names were wrong." Wilson later told the Senate intelligence committee that he may have "misspoken" to Pincus. He had not seen the documents and had not known what names were on them. (Wilson said to the committee that he might have become confused about his own recollections after the IAEA had reported that the names and dates on the documents were wrong and that he might have thought he had seen the names.)

Only toward the end of Pincus's story did it mention the request from an "aide" to the vice president for more information about Niger. The story caused no public uproar. The White House didn't feel compelled to respond. Reporters traveling with Bush on Air Force One didn't ask press secretary Ari Fleischer about it during a press briefing. "Nobody picked up on it," Pincus later said, not even *The New York Times*. "The *Times* never wrote a fucking word about it after the Kristof column," Pincus remarked, "and they never wrote about it after my piece."

THE story was certainly noticed inside Cheney's office. The vice president was even doing his own research on the subject.

On June 12, the day the Pincus story appeared, Cheney told Libby that Wilson's wife worked in the Counterproliferation Division at the CIA. Libby would later testify that Cheney had learned this directly from the CIA and had mentioned Joe Wilson's wife to him in a "sort of curiosity sort of fashion." (Libby's notes indicated that the vice president had received the information on Valerie Wilson from Tenet. A spokesman for Tenet later said he did not recall this.) But this was no incidental piece of information. As connoisseurs of intelligence, Cheney and Libby would undoubtedly have known that the Counterproliferation Division was part of the CIA's Directorate of Operations, the most secretive part of the agency—and home to undercover officers.*

Cheney and Libby felt under siege. Wilson, with his off-the-record comments to journalists, was running a one-man effort to challenge the White House's credibility. And Libby was convinced that high-level CIA officials, looking to duck responsibility for the apparent WMD failure, were looking to blame Bush and Cheney for having embellished the evidence about Saddam's weapons. The Pincus story had prominently quoted one unnamed senior CIA analyst as saying, "Information not consistent with the administration agenda was discarded and information that was [consistent] was not seriously scrutinized."

Two days after the Pincus article appeared, Libby met with his CIA debriefer and expressed irritation that CIA officials were making comments to reporters that were critical of the vice president's office. Libby mentioned the Niger trip, Joe Wilson, and—by name—Valerie Wilson.

WILSON was not going to let this story fade. And the administration's public response to the Niger controversy was, he later said, pushing him to do more. On June 8, National Security Adviser Condoleezza Rice appeared on *Meet the Press* and was asked by Tim Russert if Bush should retract his State of the Union sentence about Iraqi uranium shopping in Africa. She replied, "The

---

*When Libby later appeared before a grand jury and was asked, "Is it fair to say that [Cheney] had told you . . . that [Wilson's] wife worked in the functional office of the Counterproliferation of the CIA," Libby said, "Yes."

president quoted a British paper. We did not know at the time—no one knew at the time, in our circles—maybe someone knew down in the bowels of the agency, but no one in our circles knew that there were doubts and suspicions that this might be a forgery." To Wilson, it was inconceivable that nobody at high levels had been aware of his trip and his findings. Wilson called a senior administration official to complain about Rice's dismissive remarks, and, Wilson later claimed, he was told that he shouldn't expect the administration to issue any correction of the State of the Union speech. Wilson decided he might have to do so himself. He called David Shipley, the editor of the op-ed page of *The New York Times*. You can have 1,500 words to tell your story, Shipley said. But Wilson didn't start writing right away

On June 14, Wilson spoke at a forum held by the Education for Peace in Iraq Center (EPIC), a group opposed to the war, and he was unrestrained in his criticisms of the administration. He also hinted at his own personal role in the Niger imbroglio:

> I just want to assure you that that American ambassador who has been cited in reports in *The New York Times* and in *The Washington Post*, and now in *The Guardian* over in London, who actually went over to Niger on behalf of the government. . . . I can assure you that that retired American ambassador to Africa, as Nick Kristof called him in his article, is also pissed off and has every intention of ensuring that this story has legs. And I think it does have legs. It may not have legs over the next two or three months, but when you see American casualties moving from one to five or to ten per day, and you see Tony Blair's government fall because in the U.K. it is a big story, there will be some ramifications, I think, here in the United States. . . . It is absolutely bogus for us to have gone to war the way we did.

For anyone listening to Wilson's remarks, Eric Gustafson, the executive director of EPIC, later said, "it was pretty clear that he was referring to himself as the special envoy who went to Niger." Wilson was itching to come out and challenge the White House and Cheney head-on.

IN MID-JUNE, Bob Woodward was working on his next book. His *Bush at War*, an account of the Bush administration's response to September 11 and the Afghanistan War, had been a big seller. His new installment, to be called *Plan of Attack,* was focusing on the run-up to the Iraq War. Around the thirteenth of the month, he had an interview with an important and reliable confidential source in the Bush administration, during which he learned something intriguing about the Wilson mission that no other reporter knew. Woodward would later reluctantly write and talk about this conversation without identifying this official.

That source was Deputy Secretary of State Richard Armitage, according to three government officials, a lawyer familiar with the case, and an Armitage confidant.

Armitage and his boss and close friend Powell were the antihawks of the administration (even though Powell had allowed himself to become the administration's lead spokesman in making the case for war at the United Nations). A bear of a man with a cartoonish squeaky voice, Armitage was a U.S. Naval Academy graduate who had done three tours of duty in Vietnam and volunteered for combat. In the Reagan administration, he was an assistant secretary of defense—and got caught up in the Iran-*contra* investigations. Armitage (who was then, like Powell, a key aide to Defense Secretary Caspar Weinberger) told investigators he did not recall attending a meeting where Oliver North discussed providing covert assistance to the *contras*. A special counsel later concluded that Armitage had provided "false testimony" to investigators about his participation in the Reagan administration's missile sales to Iran.* In April 1989, the first President Bush nominated Armitage to be secretary of the Army, but the nomination hit trouble—in part due to his role in the Iran-*contra* affair—and Armitage hired a lawyer to help. That attorney was Scooter Libby. Armitage headed off a potentially nasty confirmation fight by withdrawing.

During the Clinton years, Armitage was an ally of the neoconservatives. In 1998, he joined Rumsfeld, Wolfowitz, and Perle in signing the Project for the New American Century letter calling on Clinton to overthrow Saddam. But in the George W. Bush administration, Armitage ended up battling his former neoconservative friends and came to view them with disdain. He routinely returned to Foggy Bottom from meetings at the White House shaking his head in amazement at the armchair warriors. "One day," said

---

*Iran-*contra* prosecutor Lawrence Walsh said he could not prove beyond a reasonable doubt that Armitage's misstatements had been "deliberate."

Powell's chief of staff, Larry Wilkerson, "we were walking into his office and Rich turned to me and said, 'Larry, these guys never heard a bullet go by their ears in anger. These guys never heard a bullet! None of them ever served. They're a bunch of jerks.'" Among his colleagues at the State Department, Armitage often referred derisively to the lack of military service or combat experience of the hawks at the White House and the Pentagon. "Those remarks were aimed at everybody," Wilkerson said, "including the president."

Armitage had a weakness: he enjoyed spreading juicy tidbits about Washington intrigue. This was no secret. In grand jury testimony during the Iran-*contra* investigation, he admitted he was "a terrible gossip" and a trader of information regarding political, policy, and bureaucratic developments. In a deposition, he told Iran-*contra* investigators, "I am pretty nosy and frankly think I've learned the lesson in a bureaucracy that the more you know, the more you can put things together." And he had recently come across one source of interesting information: the June 10 INR memo that claimed that Valerie Wilson had "convened" the meeting that had triggered Joseph Wilson's trip to Niger. (This was the memo that had been written at Libby's request.)

Toward the end of Woodward's long interview with Armitage about the road to war—in which Armitage recounted for Woodward details of the prewar tussles that had pitted Powell against Cheney and Rumsfeld— Woodward asked about Joseph Wilson. (Walter Pincus's story on the Niger mission had just been published, and Woodward had learned the unnamed envoy was Wilson.) Woodward would later recount that his source had told him that "everybody knows" Wilson was the anonymous ex-diplomat dispatched to Niger; the source also said that Wilson's wife worked at the CIA as an analyst on weapons of mass destruction and had apparently played a role in sending him to Niger. According to Woodward, his source referred to Valerie Wilson in a "casual and offhand" manner. "It was gossip," Woodward later said.

It may well have been that the first leak about Valerie Wilson was perceived by leaker (Armitage) and reporter (Woodward) as nothing more than chitchat. The initial leaker was not a White House hawk trying to discredit or harm Joe Wilson and his wife. Armitage had seemingly mentioned her either to distance his department from the Wilson mission or, simply, to share a piece of hot gossip.

Woodward wrote nothing about the Wilson affair in the *Post*. And in *Plan of Attack*, he made only one passing reference to Wilson and the yellowcake dispute. As he later explained, he didn't consider the Wilson matter important. But Armitage would soon mention Wilson's wife again to another prominent journalist, who would find it far more interesting.

THE mounting debate over the war didn't intrude on the festivities when a crowd of the capital's powerful political figures and journalists assembled on the evening of June 18 at the Army-Navy Club to honor one of its own: Robert Novak, the crusty conservative columnist for the *Chicago Sun-Times*. It was the fortieth anniversary of Novak's syndicated column, which he had originally begun writing with the late Rowland Evans. The crowd was Novak's A-list journalist pals: NBC's Tim Russert and Novak's compatriots on CNN's *Capital Gang* show, Al Hunt, Mark Shields, and Margaret Carlson. Also celebrating with Novak were a few of his high-placed sources, such as Ken Mehlman, who had just vacated his post as White House political director to manage the Bush reelection campaign. "It was a room full of old friends, a jovial back-slapping affair," recalled Carlson.

Among those having a grand time—and sitting prominently at Novak's table—was the celebrity guest of the evening, Karl Rove. In a chipper mood, Rove was wearing a large button that read, "I'm a source not a target." Rove, Carlson recalled, " thought it was really funny. He was flashing [the button] boldly and brazenly." The button's message was clear: it was better to be a source for Novak than a target. It was also an allusion to a thinly kept secret among the political cognoscenti: Rove had been feeding Novak political tidbits for more than two decades. In 1992, Rove, then an up-and-coming GOP political consultant, was fired from the reelection campaign of the first President Bush after there were complaints he had leaked damaging information to Novak about the Texas state campaign chairman, Robert Mosbacher.

Rove and Novak were "intimately close" and occasionally socialized together, according to Al Hunt. But neither spoke about it publicly. Rove was rarely mentioned in Novak's columns (although when he was, it was in a positive light). "I can't tell anything I ever talked to Karl Rove about, because I don't think I ever talked to him about any subject, even the time of day, on the record," Novak later said in a television interview. Novak and

Rove did disagree on one thing: the Iraq War. Prior to the invasion of Iraq, Novak had written columns skeptical of the coming war. He had called it an "imperial mission" and had appeared to be rooting for Powell's diplomacy. Eleven days before the invasion, Novak had said on CNN that the nuclear weapons case was weak and that the White House was pushing the WMD threat to cover its real agenda: getting rid of Saddam. "A lot of conservatives," Novak declared, were "heartsick about this prospect" of war in Iraq. But none of his remarks had caused a break with the White House.

Adam Levine, the Bush press aide, had gotten his own insight into how the Novak-Rove relationship worked months earlier when he had told Rove that he had heard John Weaver, John McCain's chief political strategist, trashing Rove at a Washington bar and accusing him of having circumvented campaign finance laws during the 2000 election. "Karl went ripshit," according to Levine. Soon afterward, Levine got a call from Novak, who repeated the story Levine had just told Rove. Novak then used Levine's confirmation of the tale as the basis for a column taking a swipe at Weaver, portraying him as a sore loser who hadn't gotten over his 2000 loss to the Bush campaign and who was spreading derogatory information about Rove to the news media. The incident illustrated how Rove used Novak to play political brushback without leaving any fingerprints.

THE run of stories about the unnamed ambassador and his trip to Niger was not over. On June 19, *The New Republic* posted online an article that yet again cited the unidentified former diplomat—and presented a muddled version of what had happened. The magazine reported, "Cheney's office had received from the British, via the Italians, documents purporting to show Iraq's purchase of uranium from Niger. Cheney had given the information to the CIA, which in turn asked a prominent diplomat, who had served as ambassador to three African countries, to investigate." If Pincus's account had understated Cheney's role, the *New Republic* piece exaggerated it. Cheney hadn't been the recipient of the documents. They had not come from the British. And Cheney hadn't passed them on to the CIA. The article contained yet another in-your-face quote from the still anonymous retired ambassador: "They knew the Niger story was a flat-out lie. . . . They were unpersuasive about aluminum tubes and added this to make their case more persuasive."

Inside Cheney's office, the story hit another raw nerve. Libby spoke on the phone with his principal deputy, Eric Edelman, who asked him if the vice president's office could release information to rebut the claim that Cheney had sent Wilson to Niger. None of the articles had claimed Cheney had ordered that an envoy go to Niamey. But the various stories were creating the impression that Cheney was a bigger player in the episode than he had been. By now, Libby knew that Valerie Wilson worked at the CIA, and he thought she had been involved in the trip. He understood this was a sensitive matter and told Edelman that he couldn't discuss it on a nonsecure phone. Then he added something revealing: if Cheney's office started slipping information to reporters about the Wilson trip, there would be complications at the CIA. Libby apparently was worried that this could create even more problems between the White House and the agency.

JUDY MILLER was on the outs—with both her paper and the U.S. military.

In recent weeks, she had gone from being one of her paper's star reporters to virtually persona non grata—as the *Times* experienced a veritable meltdown. In late April, *Times* correspondent Jayson Blair had been exposed as a plagiarist and fabricator. What might have been a midlevel controversy boiled over into the biggest scandal to rock the nation's most influential paper. And it had threatened the reign of Howell Raines, who had become widely unpopular within the newsroom for his imperious manner and other reasons unrelated to the Blair mess.

After returning to the United States in late May, Miller found her e-mail in-box flooded with eight thousand e-mails. Most were angry complaints about her prewar articles on Iraq's WMDs. On Web sites and blogs, she was being assailed for having carried the Bush White House's water. She had become *the* symbol of national media that had enabled the Bush administration to launch a war on the basis of a WMD threat that might not have existed.

Still, Miller wanted to go back to Iraq, but Roger Cohen, the foreign editor of the paper, told her, as he later said, that "there was unease, discomfort, unhappiness" over her WMD coverage. Raines and Boyd overruled Cohen, and she returned to Iraq in early June, producing little copy (though she did cowrite a piece reporting that some intelligence analysts were disputing the findings on the purported mobile bioweapons labs).

About this time, she clashed with Jim Wilkinson, the former White

House deputy communications director who was now chief of public affairs for Central Command at its headquarters in Doha, Qatar. Late one night, while he was sleeping, his cell phone went off. It was Miller, and she lit into him about the agreement that permitted military commanders to review her copy before she filed it. Now that major combat operations were over, she no longer thought it was necessary. Wilkinson viewed it differently: a deal was a deal.

As a member of the White House Iraq Group, Wilkinson, the previous September, had written the white paper for Bush's UN speech that relied in part on the flawed Miller story about the dubious INC defector Adnan al-Haideri. But now he was less appreciative of her. She was, according to Wilkinson, in a state of "hysteria." She screamed at Wilkinson that she would send her story back to New York anyway, by regular, unclassified e-mail. "What she was trying to do was use her diva status to roll me," Wilkinson later said. Wilkinson ordered her evicted from the unit. "I kicked her ass out of Iraq," he boasted.

That was it for Miller in Iraq. By mid-June, she was back in the United States. And Raines and Boyd, her supporters, were gone; both had resigned in the aftermath of the Jayson Blair scandal.* And the *Times'* Washington bureau had launched a major project to investigate what had gone wrong with the WMD intelligence. A team of reporters was assigned to the subject, and Miller joined in. But she wasn't fully with the project. Rather than figure out how faulty intelligence had been used to justify a war, she was interested in a different subject: whether the search for the WMDs had been so bungled that had there been any unconventional weapons in Iraq the military wouldn't have found them. With this notion in mind, she pursued sources who could be helpful—and soon she would be sitting across from Scooter Libby in his office.

BY NOW, some—but not all—White House aides had concluded that the administration's position on the Niger charge was untenable. In mid-June,

---

*In July, Bill Keller, a well-liked veteran at the *Times,* would be named the new executive editor. One of the top problems on his plate would be the paper's prewar coverage of the WMD issue—particularly, but not only, Miller's stories. Yet it would be nearly a year before Keller would confront this touchy matter.

the CIA produced a report that was unambiguous. "[S]ince learning that the Iraq-Niger uranium deal was based on false documents earlier this spring," agency analysts wrote in a memo to Tenet, "we no longer believe that there is sufficient other reporting to conclude that Iraq pursued uranium from abroad." It was a white flag on the yellowcake issue—and the end of the story. At the same time, David Sanger, a White House correspondent for *The New York Times* who was working on the paper's Iraq project, was pressing National Security Council officials for answers to basic, if awkward, questions: Did the White House still stand by the sixteen words in the State of the Union address about yellowcake? Did the White House have other credible evidence to support the claim beyond the Niger documents, which had now been exposed as a forgery?

The CIA memo and Sanger's queries prompted a series of internal White House discussions. Some officials, especially Robert Joseph, the hawkish NSC official in charge of proliferation issues, were resistant to any public retreat. After all, hadn't the CIA endorsed the uranium claim by including it in the NIE? "They can't walk away from the NIE, can they?" Condoleezza Rice herself asked, according to a NSC official. But Tenet had warned the NSC not to use the yellowcake charge in the Cincinnati speech. There was plenty of blame to go around. "We're all going to have to eat a little bit of this," Tenet told Rice, according to the NSC official.

There was, however, a complication. The White House had so far rested its defense on the fact that in the State of the Union address Bush had attributed the yellowcake charge to the British—and the Brits were publicly insisting that they had other reliable reporting supporting the yellowcake assertion. Skeptics inside the U.S. intelligence community were arguing that because the British wouldn't share this additional intelligence, the U.S. government couldn't evaluate its credibility. When the CIA formally asked to review the British evidence, it was rebuffed, according to Tyler Drumheller, the CIA's European Division chief. That was pretty much a tip-off, Drumheller said, that all the Brits had was the same "circular reporting" stemming from the same phony Italian documents.

While considering what—if anything—to do about those sixteen words in the State of the Union address, White House aides were closely following a political crisis in London. In late May, BBC reporter Andrew Gilligan had broadcast a sensational report claiming that a well-placed intelligence source had told him that the British white paper on Iraqi WMD released the previous September had been "sexed up" by Blair's Downing Street. The report set off an enormous controversy across the Atlantic. Blair's critics accused him of having rigged the case for war. Blair demanded a parliamentary inquiry that would put the BBC on trial for relying on an anonymous source to challenge the government's credibility. White House aides worried that walking away from the yellowcake charge would undermine—if not imperil—Blair. "There was concern," said a White House official, "that the British government might fall."

INSIDE the vice president's office, Scooter Libby and Cheney had no intention of backpedaling.

On the afternoon of June 23, Libby received a visitor in his office in the Old Executive Office Building: Judy Miller. In her notebook, Miller had scrawled her first question for Libby: "Was the intell slanted?" Libby took the occasion to gripe about the "selective leaking" of the CIA, according to Miller's notes of the conversation. He said the agency had a "hedging strategy" to protect itself in case no weapons were found: "If we find it, fine, if not, we hedged." He was angry about the media reports suggesting that senior Bush officials, including Cheney, had embraced and promoted uncertain intelligence reports about Iraq's alleged procurement of uranium in Africa. These news reports, Libby insisted, were "highly distorted." He conceded that Cheney's office had indeed asked about the supposed Niger deal (without acknowledging it had been Cheney who had asked). He told Miller that the CIA had dispatched a "clandestine guy" to Niger to check out the charge. He denied that Cheney had had anything to do with this trip and referred to Joe Wilson by name. Miller wrote in her notebook, "Veep didn't know of Joe Wilson." She also wrote, "Wife works in bureau?" That was a reference to the CIA. Miller years later said that Libby had raised the subject of Wilson's wife and had either said she was working or might be working at the CIA. (Miller apparently used the word "bureau" because she had received the impression that Wilson's wife was employed by a bureau within the CIA that handled WMD issues.)

Libby was defensive. And he was blaming the CIA, suggesting that if there had been any doubts about the WMD intelligence, the agency hadn't conveyed those uncertainties to the White House. Miller wrote in her notebook, "No briefer came in and said, 'You got it wrong, Mr. President.'"

LIBBY was no doubt hoping that Miller would be an ally in his battle with the backstabbing officials of the intelligence community—or, at least, would convey his defense of the White House in the pages of the *Times*. But no such story appeared. Libby, though, was not done pushing back. Nor was the vice president.

In late June, Cheney discussed with Bush the steady stream of negative news stories about the administration's prewar use of the Iraq intelligence, according to a lawyer close to the principals. Cheney and Bush agreed that to refute the criticism they ought to divulge portions of the classified National Intelligence Estimate on weapons of mass destruction that had hastily been prepared prior to the congressional vote on the Iraq War resolution. "The president declassified the information and authorized and directed the vice president to get it out," the lawyer said. How that would be done—who should leak the information and to which reporters—was left entirely up to Cheney, the lawyer noted.

This was an extraordinary move. Before the war, it could have been a firing offense—if not a federal crime—for a government official to disclose any of the contents of the NIE. But now, with the administration under fierce attack for having manipulated intelligence, Bush was directing the vice president to leak parts of the NIE to protect the White House. Bush aides would later say that Bush possessed the authority to engage in such an act of automatic declassification. But the information would be used selectively—not to inform the public but to buttress a political argument.

On the afternoon of June 27, 2003, Woodward showed up in Libby's office for an interview for *Plan of Attack*. He had come with an eighteen-page list of questions for Cheney—including one about Valerie Wilson. He spent some time talking to Libby, and Libby took the opportunity to counter the stories—including the Pincus piece in Woodward's own newspaper—suggesting the administration had exaggerated the uranium-shopping-in-Africa charge. Libby shared with Woodward some of the NIE. According to Woodward's notes, Libby told him that the NIE asserted that there had been an "effort by the Iraqis to get [yellowcake] from Africa. It goes back to February '02." He even used the word "vigorous" to describe those efforts, just as one sentence of the NIE had said.

But Libby wasn't exactly revealing the full truth; he was marshaling evidence to defend his client, the vice president. According to Woodward's account, Libby said nothing about the INR dissent or the qualifiers in the yellowcake section. Nor, apparently, did he tell Woodward about the CIA's recent conclusion that the Niger claim was unfounded. As for Joe Wilson and his wife, Woodward later said that he could not rule out the possibility that he had brought up the subject with Libby. But there was no reference to Valerie Wilson in his interview notes, and he had no recollection of talking with Libby about her—even though Armitage had already told him about the former ambassador's wife.

THE administration's position kept crumbling. The day before Woodward interviewed Libby, *The New York Times* broke a front-page story disclosing that State's INR had produced a June 2 classified memo disputing the CIA's finding that the trailers found in Iraq were mobile bioweapons labs. After more than three months of war, the mobile trailers were still the only find the administration had to show for its WMD hunt, and now that was officially in doubt.

And administration officials were attempting to wiggle out of their definitive prewar statements. Testifying before the House armed services committee, Wolfowitz remarked, "If there's a problem with intelligence . . . it doesn't mean that anybody misled anybody. It means that intelligence is an art not a science." At a press briefing, General Richard Myers, chairman of the Joint Chiefs of Staff, noted, "Intelligence doesn't necessarily mean something is true, it's just, it's intelligence, you know, it's your best estimate of the situation. It doesn't mean it's a fact."

IN LATE June, Robert Novak got word that a senior government official—someone he had been trying to interview for some time—had finally agreed to see him. The official was Armitage, the deputy secretary of state. For all his years in Washington, Novak didn't have a relationship with Armitage. But he knew that Armitage was the perfect source to talk to about intrigue within the Bush administration, particularly the bitter clashes between Colin Powell's State Department and the hawks in the Pentagon and the vice president's office.

In getting his interview request approved, Novak may have received be-hind-the-scenes help from another well-connected Washington player: Ken Duberstein, former chief of staff in Ronald Reagan's White House and now one of the capital's premier power brokers and lobbyists. Duberstein was a confidant of Powell. (The secretary affectionately called him "Duberdog.") Duberstein would later tell others that, while chatting with Novak about Powell, he had told the columnist, if you really want to know how Colin is doing, you should talk to Rich; he's running things day to day at the State Department. Duberstein said he would make a phone call and help smooth the way.

Novak would later not remember the conversation with Duberstein and profess to be unaware of his intervention. But he was happy, and a little sur-prised, when his interview request suddenly came through toward the end of June. It wouldn't happen right away, however. Novak's meeting with Armitage was scheduled for a couple of weeks later—right after the July 4 holiday.

AFTER naming a new global AIDS coordinator on July 2, Bush took a few questions from reporters at the White House. The first reporter he called on pointed to the increasing number of attacks on U.S. forces in Iraq and asked what Bush was doing to persuade "larger powers, like France and Germany and Russia, to join the American occupation there." Bush replied not by ex-plaining what he was doing to coax other countries to send troops to Iraq. Instead, he offered tough talk about the Iraqi insurgents, practically issuing them a dare: "There are some who feel like that if they attack us that we may decide to leave prematurely. . . . My answer is, bring 'em on."

FOUR days later, Joe Wilson outed himself within the pages of *The New York Times*. In the op-ed section of that Sunday's paper—under the headline "What I Didn't Find in Africa"—he opened his piece with a question: "Did the Bush administration manipulate intelligence about Saddam Hussein's weapons programs to justify an invasion of Iraq?" His answer: "based on my experience . . . I have little choice but to conclude that some of the intelli-gence related to Iraq's nuclear weapons program was twisted to exaggerate the Iraqi threat." And that unnamed former envoy sent to Niger? "That's me," he wrote.

Wilson described his trip, noting that the CIA had been spurred to action by an inquiry from Cheney's office. He noted that he had spent eight days in Niamey "drinking sweet mint tea and meeting with dozens of people." (Wilson's critics later pounced on the "sweet mint tea" reference and accused him of being a dilettante. That line, though, had been suggested by Wilson's editor, who was looking to add a touch of local color to the piece.) "It did not take long," Wilson wrote, "to conclude that it was highly doubtful that any such transaction had ever taken place." And he explained how the uranium industry was structured and how that made such a deal unlikely. He also acknowledged that he had never seen the forged documents but said he had been briefed before leaving about a supposed memorandum of agreement detailing the yellowcake transaction. He noted that although he hadn't filed a written report, his findings should have been documented—and should have been shared with Cheney's office. So, he asked, why had the White House continued to use the Niger charge to justify an invasion? He suggested that Congress should investigate Bush's use of the Niger charge. "[Q]uestioning the selective use of intelligence to justify the war in Iraq," Wilson wrote, "is neither idle sniping nor 'revisionist history,' as Mr. Bush has suggested."

Wilson's op-ed was the hot news of the day. And it was part of a one-man media blitz. He appeared on *Meet the Press* and went further in pointing an accusatory finger at Cheney. "The office of the vice president, I am absolutely convinced, received a very specific response to the question it asked [about the Niger deal], and that response was based upon my trip out there," Wilson said. When guest host Andrea Mitchell pressed him on this point, Wilson said he assumed Cheney had been briefed, because when he worked in the White House it was "standard operating procedure" to provide the vice president answers to questions he had posed. But Wilson was wrong. There was no evidence that Cheney had known about his trip.

The White House was aware "well ahead" of Bush's State of the Union speech, Wilson charged, that the yellowcake-from-Africa intelligence was "erroneous." Wilson also noted that the issue was greater than the question of whether Bush and Cheney had abused the prewar intelligence. The administration, he argued, had actually trivialized the WMD problem by exploiting it: "There is no greater threat that we face as a nation going forward than the threat of weapons of mass destruction in the hands of non-state actors or international terrorists. And if we've prosecuted a war for reasons other than that, using weapons of mass destruction as cover for that, then I think we've done a grave disservice to the weapons of mass destruction threat. The bar will be set much, much higher internationally, and in Congress, when . . . another administration has a true WMD problem."

In a *Washington Post* profile of Wilson by Walter Pincus and Richard Leiby, which appeared that morning, Wilson summed up what he believed was the bottom line: "It really comes down to the administration misrepresenting the facts on an issue that was a fundamental justification for going to war. It begs the question, what else are they lying about?"

Had Bush misled the country? That question had been percolating for months. Congressional Democrats had raised it; cable talk shows had mulled it over. Bush and the White House had tried to dismiss it as nothing but partisan revisionism—nothing that required a substantive response or any form of concession. Yet Wilson, though overstating his case against Cheney, had changed the equation. His attack on one sliver of the administration's brief for war had opened up much larger questions about the justification for the invasion of Iraq. "I was really mostly concerned with correcting the record on the State of the Union," Wilson later said. "I figured the WMD question would sort itself out the longer we were in Iraq." But with his *Times* op-ed—and his other media appearances—he had single-handedly intensified the assault on Bush, Cheney, and their aides.

And they would respond.

Or did his wife send him on a junket?

—Vice President Dick Cheney

14

Seven Days in July

O N SUNDAY morning, July 6, Carl Ford, the State Department's chief intelligence officer, was doing what many professional Washingtonians do on the day of rest: watching the political talk shows. And there was Joe Wilson on *Meet the Press,* talking about his op-ed piece in that day's *New York Times* and identifying himself as the former ambassador who had gone to Niger for the CIA and exposed the uranium canard. "Oh, shit," Ford recalled saying to his wife, "this probably is going to cause me to have to work today."

He was right. No sooner did the show end than his phone rang. Richard Armitage was on the line. "Were you watching TV?" he asked Ford. Powell was due to leave for Africa with Bush the next day. "We need to get him up to speed on this," Armitage said with urgency. Ford reminded Armitage that he had already sent Undersecretary of State Marc Grossman a memo on the Wilson trip and suggested he could update it. "Fine," Armitage said. But he wanted it right away. The Wilson matter was now Topic A inside the Beltway.

Ford called one of his analysts at home and told him to get to work. But it turned out that the first memo needed no updating. The new memo was just about word for word the old memo, reminding Powell that INR had had nothing to do with sending Wilson and that it had consistently argued that the Niger charge was absurd. "We basically changed the date" and the addressee, Ford said. Instead of Grossman, the recipient of the memo was now Powell. Like the first memo, this one was stamped secret and the key paragraphs were marked S/NF (Secret/No Foreign distribution). The same attachments were affixed, and the new memo repeated the same sentence about Valerie Wilson's having "convened" the February 19, 2002, CIA meeting that had led to Joe Wilson's Africa trip.

The Wilson controversy now struck Ford as more ridiculous than ever. There had never been anything to this stupid yellowcake charge, he thought. But Ford was acutely aware of the larger context. The politics were more volatile than two months earlier, when the anxiety over the missing weapons of mass destruction had started to creep into hallway conversations in the State Department. Now, Ford thought, "the whole underpinning and logic of the war was unraveling."

And the unraveling would get worse as the week proceeded. It would result in an orchestrated high-level effort to discredit Wilson and culminate in a leak that would be seized on by administration critics as prime evidence of White House desperation and deviousness—even though it was caused partly by an improbable series of accidents and misunderstandings.

MONDAY morning at the White House, officials were preparing for Bush's Africa trip. He was to leave later that day, accompanied by Powell, Rice, Fleischer, Card, and communications director Dan Bartlett—and a planeload of reporters. It was to be a five-nation tour. With the war in Iraq not abating, this trip had been designed to emphasize the compassionate side of Bush's diplomacy. The White House hoped to highlight a major new $15 billion initiative to fight AIDS on the continent and to play up a new antifamine proposal.

But the buzz within the press corps on the morning of July 7 wasn't about an anti-AIDS initiative; it was about Joe Wilson. Fleischer held a press briefing and faced a barrage of questions. "There is zero, nada, nothing new here," Fleischer said about the Wilson op-ed. "This is old news." It was the standard damage control line used by every White House: it's all been reported before. "We've said this repeatedly—that the information on yellowcake did indeed turn out to be incorrect," Fleischer remarked, maintaining that neither Cheney nor anyone else in the White House had had any reason to suspect the Niger charge prior to the State of the Union speech.

But under persistent questioning from David Sanger of *The New York Times,* Fleischer became confused on whether or not Bush's sixteen-word sentence in his State of the Union speech—which had referred to uranium shopping in *Africa,* not *Niger*—had been wrong. First, he said, "I see nothing that . . . would indicate that there was no basis to the president's broader statement." That seemed to suggest the White House was standing by the sixteen words. But moments later, Fleischer remarked, "The president's broader statement was based and predicated on the yellowcake from Niger."

"So it was wrong?" Sanger asked.

"That's what we've acknowledged," Fleischer said.

If the White House was admitting that the president had used faulty intelligence to lead the nation to war, that would be news. Sanger reminded Fleischer that White House officials previously had said that Bush's State of the Union remark had not been based entirely on the Niger charge. Let me get back to you, Fleischer said. "If you don't hear from me, just assume that there is nothing new that moves the ball today."

BUT the ball was moving. And not only because of Wilson. That day, in London, the House of Commons foreign affairs committee released a tough report questioning the Blair government's prewar intelligence on Iraq. The panel, made up mostly of Blair's Labour Party colleagues, questioned the September 2002 British white paper's "bald claim" that Iraq had tried to buy "significant quantities of uranium from Africa." The panel noted that government ministers had insisted there was "other evidence" beyond the forged Niger documents to support the assertion, but the ministers had not disclosed what that evidence was—or whether they stood behind it.* The

---

*A year later, a British parliamentary committee headed by Lord Butler described the "other intelligence" as reports of the February 1999 trip to Niger by Wissam al-Zahawie, the Iraqi ambassador to the Holy See. British intelligence had assessed that a uranium deal "could have been the subject of discussions" during the visit. This led the Butler commission to conclude that the British government's assertion about Iraq's attempts to buy uranium—and Bush's sixteen words—were "well founded." Yet the Butler commission noted that the IAEA had obtained excerpts of Zahawie's travel report, and they contained no reference to any talks about uranium. And no new intelligence had been obtained indicating the Zahawie trip had been related to uranium purchases. Moreover, the idea that Zahawie's trip could have justified Bush's assertion was a stretch: Bush had said Saddam had "recently" sought uranium from Africa. At the time of Bush's speech, the Zahawie visit was nearly four years in the past.

panel concluded that the white paper's claim about Iraq's efforts to obtain uranium in Africa at least "should have been qualified to reflect the uncertainty." Bush's definitive State of the Union remark—which attributed the yellowcake charge to British intelligence—had lost its foundation.

In Britain, this was not the biggest news about the foreign affairs committee report. The panel found that Blair and his aides generally "did not mislead" Parliament prior to the war but that Blair had misrepresented some of the intelligence on Iraq's WMDs. The committee reported that another main allegation of the British white paper—that Iraq could deploy chemical or biological weapons within forty-five minutes—"did not warrant the prominence" given to it. But the committee concluded that Alistair Campbell, Blair's communications chief, had not "sexed up" that section of the white paper, as he had been accused of doing.

With the British report questioning the yellowcake-in-Africa charge, National Security Council officials finally realized they had no defense for the sixteen words. They began crafting a concession statement.

But within the vice president's office, Libby and Cheney weren't about to step back from anything. A retreat would be a victory for Wilson—and the president's critics. And Cheney and Libby were more livid about the former diplomat than ever. Cheney, as Libby later testified to a grand jury, considered Wilson's op-ed an assault on his credibility.

Cheney had studied the piece carefully. He had a habit of clipping important articles out of the newspapers with a penknife, and he had cut out the op-ed, jotting notes on it and carefully underlining key sections. He fixed on Wilson's assertion that some of the intelligence about Iraq's nuclear program had been "twisted to exaggerate the Iraqi threat." He also underlined two of Wilson's references to the vice president's office. Above the headline, Cheney wrote in easily legible script, "Have they done this sort of thing before? Send an Amb. to answer a question?" (In the case of Wilson, the answer was yes; during an earlier trip to Niger he had, on the CIA's behalf, sought information regarding A. Q. Khan, the notorious nuclear weapons proliferator.) Cheney wondered if something fishy had occurred. He wrote, "Do we ordinarily send people out pro bono to work for us? Or did his wife send him on a junket?" A trip to one of the poorest nations in the world for no money would not normally seem a boondoggle. Yet Cheney—who had learned a month earlier that Valerie Wilson worked in the Counterproliferation Division of the CIA's clandestine service (and who had shared that specific information with Libby)—was looking for a hidden truth. He wasn't taking Wilson at his word. As he and Libby were pondering how to respond to the Wilson article, Cheney was trying to discern what *really* was behind this op-ed. He suspected it might involve Joe Wilson's wife.

Libby agreed. On the morning of July 7, Cheney's office sent talking points to Fleischer about Wilson's op-ed, noting that Cheney hadn't known anything about Wilson's trip to Niger. Hours later, Libby had lunch with Fleischer. The conversation, as Fleischer later recounted, was "kind of weird." Libby, the press secretary recalled, usually operated "in a very closed-lip fashion." But this day, Libby wanted to dish. He told Fleischer that Cheney hadn't sent Wilson to Niger. "He was sent by his wife," Libby said, according to Fleischer's subsequent testimony to a grand jury. "She works in . . . the Counterproliferation area of the CIA." Libby, Fleischer testified, also said "something along the lines of, you know, this is hush-hush, nobody knows about this. This is on the q.t." Cheney's chief of staff appeared to recognize the information he was sharing with Fleischer was significant—and classified. (Libby later would say he remembered the lunch but denied discussing Wilson's wife at it.)

That day, Armitage was pestering Ford to get the new INR memo on the Wilson trip to Powell. "Is it there yet?" he asked the State Department intelligence chief in a brusque phone call. After Bush and his entourage had left for Africa, according to Ford, the memo was faxed to Powell on the presidential jet. It was a significant moment. A secret memo reporting that Valerie Wilson had "convened" the CIA meeting that Wilson had attended was now aboard Air Force One. Any Bush administration official who read it would have had cause to wonder if there had been something odd about how the Wilson trip had come to be. Powell later recalled sharing the memo with Rice. A copy was also sent to Armitage.

Once Air Force One was in the air—and after the network news shows had wrapped up their evening broadcasts—Fleischer threw in the towel on the sixteen words. He called reporters for *The New York Times* and *The Washington Post* and engaged in a rare act: he admitted a White House mistake. "White House Backs Off Claim on Iraqi Buy," read the headline on Pincus's front-page piece in the *Post* the next morning. "Knowing all that we know now," a senior Bush administration official was quoted as saying, "the reference to Iraq's attempt to acquire uranium from Africa should not have been included in the State of the Union speech." Sanger's story in the *Times* had a senior official saying essentially the same thing about the sixteen words: "We couldn't prove it, and it might in fact be wrong."

This was a concession, albeit a limited one. Yet the Niger story was far from over.

THE next morning, Libby had another get-together with Judy Miller, this one a two-hour breakfast at the St. Regis Hotel, blocks away from the White House. Once again, Cheney had given his chief of staff the green light to disclose information from the classified National Intelligence Estimate. The idea was to strike back—at Wilson, at the critics—with the CIA's own words. Libby had also consulted David Addington, Cheney's longtime chief counsel and perhaps the White House's most notorious proponent of unbridled presidential power. Addington, according to Libby's later testimony, had reassured Libby that if Bush had authorized the disclosure of this classified information, that amounted to declassification of the material. This was the first time Libby had seen secret information declassified only on the say-so of a president. And now he was going to go further with Miller than he had with Woodward in revealing the contents of the NIE. He would be feeding sensitive information to a reporter whose stories had bolstered the WMD case for war—and who had an interest in defending the prewar claims. It was, one senior administration official later said, "Scooter's black op."

At breakfast, Miller started the conversation by asking Libby about the Wilson op-ed—a subject that, she later wrote, "agitated" Libby. Cheney's top aide insisted that the op-ed was inaccurate. And he was prepared to explain why. But first he wanted to discuss the ground rules. During their previous conversation, Libby had told Miller she could quote him in any story she might write as a "senior administration official." Now—with Wilson the subject—he insisted he be identified as a "former Hill staffer." This was technically true but disingenuous; Libby hadn't worked on Capitol Hill since the late 1990s. It was a sign that he didn't want White House fingerprints (or his own) on any article that emerged. Miller accepted these unusual conditions.*

Now cloaked with a deceptive layer of anonymity, Libby began what Miller later described as a "lengthy and sharp critique" of both Wilson and the CIA. He criticized Wilson's op-ed as part of the CIA's backpedaling on the prewar intelligence. He cited classified intelligence reports from 2002 on the Niger charge. He claimed, according to Miller's subsequent account, that an agency cable based on Wilson's trip had "barely made it out of the bowels of the CIA." He noted that the cable showed Wilson had actually returned with information indicating that in 1999 Iraq had pursued expanding commercial relations with Niger, which included (or so one Niger official thought) uranium purchases. He said George Tenet had never heard of Wilson.

When Miller tried to change the subject to Saddam's supposed chemical and biological stockpile—biochem, as she liked to say, was her specialty, not nukes—Libby kept talking about Wilson and the nuclear issue. He told her the NIE had "firmly concluded that Iraq was seeking uranium." (Libby at one point read from a piece of paper he pulled from his pocket.) He claimed that the detailed assessments in the NIE "were even stronger" than those in the slick, declassified CIA "white paper" released the previous October. But in making these assertions about the NIE, Libby was again being misleading and highly selective: the NIE hadn't "firmly concluded" that Iraq was seeking uranium. And he neglected to mention the caveats, qualifiers, and dissents within the NIE that had been left out of the white paper.

Libby once more brought up Wilson's wife's employment as a counterproliferation expert at the CIA. Miller wrote in her notebook, "Wife works

---

*Miller later wrote that she had agreed to these ground rules "because I knew that Mr. Libby had once worked on Capitol Hill." But after she was criticized for having done so, she told National Public Radio that she had planned to turn the tables on Libby. "I agreed to listen to Mr. Libby's information on the basis of his attribution as a former Hill staffer," Miller said. "It is very common in Washington to hear information on the basis of one attribution and then to go back to that source if you're going to use the information and say, 'You know, this attribution really won't fly.'" The interviewer asked, "Are you saying you do that frequently, make an agreement to hear information under one—." Miller cut her off and said, "No, I did not say I do it. I said it is often done in Washington."

at Winpac," referring to the counterproliferation unit in the CIA's directorate of intelligence. In the same notebook, Miller scribbled the name "Valerie Flame," clearly a reference to Valerie Wilson's maiden name, Valerie Plame. Later, Miller would say—somewhat improbably—that she didn't believe the "Valerie Flame" information had come from Libby, although the entry was in the same notebook as her notes from the Libby meeting. She claimed she had heard the "Valerie Flame" name from another source. She couldn't, however, recall who that source was.

After the long Miller breakfast, according to a later indictment, Libby encountered Addington in an anteroom outside Cheney's office. Libby asked a curious question: What paperwork would the CIA have if an employee's spouse took an overseas trip? He was still looking for more information on Wilson—and his wife.

BOB NOVAK, too, was looking for information that day. He was writing about Fran Fragos Townsend, the new White House counterterrorism chief. The piece he was planning was classic Novak: an insider's tale of dissension and backstabbing within the administration. Novak had spoken to aides to Attorney General John Ashcroft who were questioning the political sympathies of Townsend, a former Justice Department terrorism prosecutor who had been chief of the department's unit in charge of national security wiretaps. They were suggesting that she was a closet Democrat who might prove disloyal to Bush. Now Novak wanted to talk to Rove for this story.

But Rove was in a bind. Under normal circumstances, Rove—who zealously screened the political bona fides of administration appointees—might have been sympathetic to such a hit piece. But the president had already selected Townsend. So that morning, Rove was doing something he rarely did: he was ducking Novak's phone calls.

Novak called Adam Levine, the White House press aide who had become something of a Rove protégé, and complained that Rove wasn't calling him back. Levine promised to talk to Rove and see what he could do. In the course of the conversation, according to Levine, Novak asked him, "What do you make of the Wilson thing?" Levine replied, "I'm not working on that. You've got to talk to Scooter or Karl." That morning, Levine had run into Rove in the hallway, and Rove had seemed to have boned up on Wilson. "He's a Democrat; he's giving money to John Kerry," Levine later recalled Rove remarking.*

NOVAK had a secret source for information on Wilson and his Niger trip. On the afternoon of Tuesday, July 8, the columnist went to the State Department to interview Deputy Secretary of State Armitage, according to three government officials familiar with the meeting. This was the session that Washington power broker Ken Duberstein would say that he had helped arrange. Powell also had thought it was a good idea for his deputy to talk to the columnist. "Powell was encouraging Rich to have this get-together," a State Department official later said.

One issue Novak asked about was the Wilson trip. He wanted to know why someone who had worked in the Clinton National Security Council and who was now a vocal critic of Bush's policies in Iraq had been chosen for the Niger assignment. Novak's line of thinking paralleled Rove's. "Why in the world did they send Joe Wilson on this?" Novak recalled asking. "Why would they send him?" To answer Novak, Armitage revealed a tantalizing morsel that was in the classified INR memo: that Wilson's wife worked at the CIA on weapons of mass destruction and had suggested her husband for the mission to Niger. It was the same information Armitage had already shared with Woodward. (Novak, in a column three months later, would maintain that the remark had come from a senior administration official who was "no partisan gunslinger.")

The identity of the administration official who first divulged information about Valerie Wilson to Novak would soon become one of Washington's biggest mysteries. And months later, Armitage would be questioned by the FBI about this conversation with Novak and testify about it before a federal grand jury. After a grand jury appearance, he spoke about his testimony with his colleague Carl Ford, the INR chief. "I'm afraid I may be the guy that caused this whole thing," Armitage said, according to Ford.

---

*Wilson had contributed $1,000 to the Kerry campaign in May 2003 and had become an adviser to his campaign. But in partisan Washington, it was easy to overlook Wilson's expertise on Niger and his familiarity with the uranium trade and the fact that he was not considered a fierce Democrat or a Bush administration foe when he accepted the CIA's invitation. In 1999 Wilson had donated money to George W. Bush for his Republican presidential primary campaign.

"You're kidding," Ford replied.

"Yes," the deputy secretary of state said. "I may have been the leaker. I talked to Novak." Armitage said that he had "slipped up" and had told the columnist more than he should have, Ford recalled: "He was basically beside himself that he was the guy that fucked up. He was mad at himself. My sense from Rich is that it was just chitchat. If you know Rich, he loves to hear rumors, he loves to talk about what the latest rumors are. He was just gossiping. It wasn't malevolent." Armitage told Ford that he had confessed to the grand jury. A lawyer representing one of the most senior U.S. officials in the case said Armitage was distraught over his role as the leaker. "He was ashamed and embarrassed," the attorney said. "He felt foolish."

The series of events had been bizarre. Doug Rohn, an INR analyst skeptical of the entire yellowcake claim, had taken notes of the Wilson meeting at the CIA's Counterproliferation Division. Carl Ford, the INR head who had championed his bureau's dissents in interagency meetings, had passed a memo (based on Rohn's notes) to Powell and Armitage. And Armitage, who had broken ranks with the neoconservatives, had shared information from the memo with Novak (who actually had opposed the war in Iraq before the invasion). Though Libby and other hawkish White House officials were enraged at Wilson and scheming against him, it had been a leading member of the administration's small moderate cell who had first slipped Novak the information on Joe Wilson's wife.*

NOVAK and Rove talked on July 9. They discussed the selection of Fran Townsend to be Bush's counterterrorism chief. They also spoke about the Wilson trip. For Rove, this was no matter of gossip. The president's chief political strategist shared the same goal as Libby and Cheney: to knock Wil-

---

*On the afternoon of July 8, a friend of Joe Wilson encountered Novak on Pennsylvania Avenue, a few blocks from the White House, and struck up a conversation with the columnist. Without revealing his connection to Wilson, the friend asked what Novak thought of the ongoing Niger controversy and Wilson. The Niger dust-up was a minor matter, Novak replied, and he added that Wilson's wife was a WMD specialist at the CIA and had sent Wilson to Niger. Novak also told the friend that Wilson, as far as he was concerned, was an "asshole." After Wilson heard his friend's report of what Novak had said, he called Eason Jordan, the head of CNN's news division, and complained that Novak was irresponsibly spreading details about his wife.

son down. Still, his response to Novak was limited—at least according to the narrow accounts Rove and Novak later provided.

Novak told Rove he had learned that Valerie Wilson had been behind Joe Wilson's trip. "I've heard that," Rove replied, according to his attorney. Novak would later say he "distinctly" recalled Rove saying: "You know that, too."

And who had told Rove about Valerie Wilson? Years later, Rove would profess not to remember. But a source close to Rove suggested that the White House aide had "probably" learned it from Scooter Libby.

Rove, according to these accounts, hadn't said much to Novak. But whatever the precise words, Rove had provided his old friend confirmation of what Armitage had told the columnist. Bush's top adviser was, at the least, corroborating the disclosure of classified information, given that Valerie Wilson's employment at the CIA was an official secret. Even if this confirmation was indirect, it was enough for Novak. Thanks to Rove, the columnist now had two sources for the story—and a strong column for the following week.

ALL that week, Levine later recalled, "Scooter was going nuts." Cheney's chief of staff was incensed over the nonstop press coverage touched off by the Wilson op-ed. He talked about it repeatedly to Levine and Catherine Martin, Cheney's chief spokesperson. Libby was especially upset over the nightly commentaries of MSNBC's Chris Matthews, the garrulous host of *Hardball.* A vocal critic of the Iraq war, Matthews was on a tear over the yellowcake issue, accepting Wilson's account and hammering Cheney and Libby (by name) at every turn. Libby ordered Levine and Martin to review the transcripts of everything Matthews was saying on the subject. They did and the two press aides underlined for Libby everything they thought Matthews had gotten wrong.

Matthews had gone beyond even what Wilson had charged; he seemed to be suggesting Libby had been primarily responsible for the sixteen words. "It sounds to me," Matthews had said on his July 8 show, that "a hawk in the vice president's office, probably from Scooter Libby on down," had inserted the bogus uranium charge into the State of the Union address and that "the president went along with it without thinking." Matthews was pushing for a full-scale investigation of the yellowcake fiasco and suggesting possible witnesses from the White House, including Libby.

Libby had reasons beyond politics to be obsessed with Matthews. The talk-show host's comments were getting covered in the Arab world. They had, Libby thought, fueled anti-Semitic diatribes against the architects of the Iraq War. (Libby was of Jewish background, although not religiously observant.) This was a common complaint among the administration's neo-conservatives. When Wolfowitz had run into a *Hardball* producer at the White House correspondents' dinner two months earlier, he had said contemptuously that he would never go on *Hardball* because of what Matthews had been saying. But for Libby, it had become personal. Thanks to Matthews, he was getting international publicity—and not the kind he wanted. At some point, U.S. intelligence picked up "chatter" about possible threats against Libby, according to a close friend of Libby who discussed the matter with him. Libby said he had been forced to adopt security measures. He worried about his family. And he seemed to blame all this on Matthews and his attacks. Matthews "was his bête noire," the friend said.

Fed up, Libby directed Martin to have Levine call Matthews to complain. Levine had once been a senior producer for Matthews on *Hardball*. But the resulting phone call, according to Levine, was a disaster. Within minutes, he and Matthews were in a shouting match. Levine upbraided his old boss for having accepted Wilson's version of events. He pointed out that Matthews had been harping about the role of Libby and other neocons and that they all had Jewish names. "Some of what you're saying about this sounds anti-Semitic," Levine later recalled telling the talk-show host.

Levine didn't believe Matthews was prejudiced. But he was dutifully conveying a message from Libby. ("Scooter thinks the term 'neoconservative' is anti-Semitic," Martin once told Matthews.) Matthews was indignant and made clear that he had no intention of laying off the vice president's office. Matthews later remembered receiving a phone call from Levine, but he said he didn't recall any discussion of anti-Semitism.

Levine subsequently ran into Libby. "Have you talked to him?" Libby asked. "We need to get him to stop." When Levine reported that he had gotten nowhere with Matthews, Libby was "really upset," according to Levine. "I can't do anything more on this," the press aide told Libby. He suggested Libby call Tim Russert, who was Washington bureau chief for NBC News, and take it up with him.

Libby called Russert on July 10 to complain about Matthews. For Libby, it would be a fateful call.

According to Russert, Libby was angry. "What the hell is going on?" Libby asked him. Why, he demanded to know, was Matthews constantly mentioning only certain names when he referred to the administration officials behind the Iraq War? "It's always Libby and Wolfowitz and Perle," Libby said, according to Russert. The television host immediately assumed that Libby was accusing Matthews of focusing on people with Jewish-sounding names. Russert suggested Libby call the president of MSNBC. Russert promised to call Neal Shapiro, the president of NBC. "I immediately, obviously, called [Shapiro] and shared the complaint, which is why it was memorable in my mind," Russert said in a subsequent MSNBC interview.

Shapiro would remember the call from Russert. "Hey, I just got a phone call from Scooter Libby, and he's got real problems with Chris Matthews," Russert told him, according to Shapiro. Russert also told Shapiro that he viewed Libby's complaint as an implicit warning: if Matthews didn't tone it down, the network might find it hard to book White House guests. Shapiro spoke with Matthews's executive producer and urged him to have the talk-show host throttle back a bit. "Hey," Shapiro recalled saying, "this guy is still the vice president."

Months later, when Libby's phone call to Russert became a critical part of a criminal investigation, Libby would offer a description of this conversation completely different from Russert's and Shapiro's account.

IN AFRICA, Bush and the rest of the White House delegation were hopping from one country to the next, trying to talk about AIDS and famine relief. But throughout the week, the White House press corps wouldn't let go of the Niger scandal. At a press "availability" in South Africa on Tuesday, Bush had dodged questions from reporters trying to get him to affirm what Fleischer had already conceded—that one sentence in the State of the Union speech had been wrong. Asked whether he still believed Saddam Hussein had attempted "to buy nuclear materials in Africa," Bush responded, "One thing is for certain, he's not trying to buy anything right now."

On July 10, when John Cochran of ABC News asked Powell in Pretoria if the administration owed the world an apology for having used the yellow-cake claim, Powell dismissed the whole to-do: "This is very overwrought and overblown and overdrawn. . . . You get the information, you analyze it. Sometimes it holds up, sometimes it does not hold up." Powell also stated the trailers found in Iraq were the biovans he had spoken about during his Security Council speech, even though his own INR had challenged that conclusion weeks earlier. The purpose of those trailers, he insisted, wasn't to produce hydrogen for military weather balloons. His UN charge, he added, had "stood the test of time."

The Niger imbroglio wouldn't let up, though. The following day Pincus had a front-page piece in the *Post* quoting unnamed CIA officials as saying they had tried to dissuade British intelligence from using the yellowcake claim in its September 2002 white paper. This was more evidence of what Libby and other White House hawks suspected: that the agency was looking to escape responsibility for the yellowcake fiasco and to make it appear that administration officials eager for war had irresponsibly pushed a discredited charge. The White House had had enough.

Early that morning, while Air Force One was on its way to Uganda, Rice came to the press cabin. Shortly before, she had called Tenet in Sun Valley and woken him up in the middle of the night to tell him what was coming. (Tenet was attending a conference for corporate moguls and media bigwigs sponsored by investment banker Herbert Allen.) Having warned the CIA director, Rice, speaking on the record, fired back at the agency. "The CIA cleared the speech in its entirety," Rice told the reporters. She pointed to the still secret NIE and said it had asserted that Iraq had been "seeking yellowcake in Africa." She dismissed the INR's dissent as merely "kind of a standard INR footnote." The White House, she said, had "relied" on the NIE and the CIA. The sixteen words, she maintained, had even been reshaped so that the sentence "reflected better what the CIA thought." Then Rice made it personal: "I can tell you, if the director of central intelligence had said, 'Take this out of the speech,' it would have been gone, without question. . . . It would not have been in the speech." After holding out the sword—on which Tenet was expected to fall—she did insist that Bush retained confidence in the CIA director: "George Tenet has been a terrific DCI."

Rice's comments that morning struck reporters on the press plane as unprecedented for the Bush White House. It signaled a public rift between the White House and the CIA. For more than two and a half years, the bond between the breezy Tenet and tough-talking Bush had been as tight as any in history between a president and a CIA director. "They were like fraternity brothers," one White House official said. During a joint House-Senate investigation of the intelligence failures of 9/11, Tenet also had protected

Bush and refused to release classified documents that might have proven embarrassing to the president (who had paid scant attention to Tenet's warnings of the al-Qaeda threat). "George gave his heart and soul to the president," Buzzy Krongard, the agency's executive director and a Tenet confidant, later observed.

But the White House was under fire as it had never been before. So it dumped its misfortunes on Tenet. And Bush piled on. After Air Force One touched down in Uganda, the president headed to a meeting with the country's president, Yoweri Museveni, at the Imperial Botanical Beach Hotel. Right before the private chat began, a reporter asked Bush, "Can you explain how an erroneous piece of intelligence on the Iraq-Niger connection got into your State of the Union speech?"

"I gave a speech to the nation," Bush replied, "that was cleared by the intelligence services."

The reporter attempted a follow-up: "But, sir, how did it get into your speech if it was erroneous?"

Bush moved on to his meeting with Museveni.

That sealed it. Tenet, who had done so much to serve Bush and his Iraq agenda, would have to take the blame for the White House.

After the comments by Rice and Bush, the traveling White House reporters were ushered into a cramped holding room with phone lines. One of the reporters, *Time*'s John Dickerson, called Washington and left a voice mail message for his bureau chief, Michael Duffy, relaying the latest developments. After Duffy got it, he sent off an e-mail to a *Time* reporter working on the magazine's cover story for the week. "John reports . . . they've dimed out Tenet," it read.

AFTER the senior staff meeting at the White House that morning, Karl Rove had a brief hallway chat with Scooter Libby and passed on what must have seemed like good news during a tough week. Rove told Libby he had spoken with Novak about the Wilson affair and that the columnist had said he'd be writing a piece on the matter that would mention Valerie Wilson. Following this chat, Rove went to his office.

THIS Friday was one of Bill Harlow's most intense days as director of public affairs for the CIA. In public, the CIA's chief spokesman was known mostly for issuing no-comment responses for stories revealing the deeds or misdeeds of the agency. But Harlow, a moody, brooding part-time novelist, probably played the media better than any government press officer in town. When other government agencies, especially the FBI, had been pilloried for pre-9/11 screwups, Harlow masterfully steered criticism away from the CIA. He would dole out tips to select journalists and for big stories provide them access to senior agency officials. But the events of this week were a test of Harlow's talents.

The agency was drafting a public statement accepting responsibility for its failure to properly vet the president's State of the Union speech. Harlow would later insist Tenet had come up with the idea of the statement on his own. But there was no doubt Tenet was under extreme pressure during this period. Tyler Drumheller, the European Division chief, later recalled walking down the hallway of the seventh floor of CIA headquarters around this time and running into Krongard and another Tenet aide. The two aides said that Tenet was getting pummeled by the White House and had just gotten off the phone with Rice, who had yelled at him. "I'm not sure George isn't going to resign," Krongard said, according to Drumheller. Then Tenet wandered by. Drumheller thought he looked like hell. "I hope none of you ever aspire to be DCI [director of central intelligence]," Tenet told the group. He entered the office of James Pavitt, the chief of the operations directorate, and closed the door.

After Rice had publicly blamed Tenet, Harlow was trying to hammer out the agency's statement, going through draft after draft. He and other agency officials were engaged in a delicate balancing act. The CIA would have to accept responsibility for the foul-up, but Harlow and the others wanted to note that the CIA had never fully accepted the yellowcake story. Tenet, Krongard later said, "wanted to make clear that we weren't a total bunch of clods."

While he was working on the draft, Harlow was dealing with another knotty problem: Robert Novak. The day before, Novak had called Harlow and said he planned to write a column about Valerie Wilson's role in sending her husband to Africa. Harlow tried to wave Novak off the story. Novak would later say he had asked Harlow a narrow, specific question—whether it was true, as he had been told, that Valerie Wilson had "suggested" her husband for the trip—and that Harlow responded that she "had not authorized the mission." Harlow subsequently claimed he told Novak that Valerie

Wilson hadn't arranged for her husband's trip and had only been asked by colleagues to solicit her husband's assistance. Whatever Harlow told the columnist, the CIA spokesman wasn't sure about Valerie Wilson's precise status at the agency. Harlow knew only the basics: she worked in the Directorate of Operations, the clandestine branch of the agency. She probably was undercover, as most DO employees were. That meant there could be serious problems if Novak named her.*

On Friday, as Harlow was crashing on the agency's yellowcake statement, he checked on Valerie Wilson's position and confirmed she was indeed a "covered" (as agency people say) officer. He called Novak back. "I hope I convinced you that this is a nonstory," he later recalled telling Novak. But in case he hadn't, Harlow added, "I would ask that you not use her name." Novak asked why not. Harlow replied that she would "probably" never again be stationed overseas, but exposure of her name "would make it difficult for her to travel overseas or conduct other business for the agency."

Harlow had a dilemma. He couldn't tell Novak outright that Valerie Wilson was a covert CIA officer. To do so would be divulging classified information and violating the law. Most experienced journalists who covered the CIA usually respected his requests not to print something. But Novak wasn't going along. He subsequently claimed that he thought at the time that if naming Wilson's wife was a big deal, a senior agency official—maybe even Tenet himself—would call and ask him not to disclose her identity in his column. Nobody did. In any case, he looked up Joe Wilson's entry in *Who's Who in America* and saw his wife's name listed: Valerie Plame.

Novak proceeded to finish his column.

WHILE Bush and the Ugandan president, Museveni, were conducting their meeting, John Dickerson was chatting up Ari Fleischer, who was standing by an old yellow school bus near the filing center for the traveling press corps. Normally such informal conversations with Fleischer bore meager fruit. But this discussion was different. Fleischer, speaking on background—so he

---

*After his initial conversation with Harlow, Novak had called Wilson, who was upset that Novak had blurted out information about his wife to a stranger on the street. Novak, according to Wilson's account, apologized and asked if Wilson would confirm that his wife worked at the CIA. "I told him that I didn't answer questions about my wife," Wilson later wrote.

could be identified only as a "senior administration official"—launched into a sharp attack on Wilson. Wilson's report on his Niger trip had been sloppy and contradictory, Fleischer claimed. His trip hadn't been approved by Tenet or any other senior agency official. And Fleischer (who days earlier had been told about Wilson's wife by Libby) gave Dickerson a none-too-subtle tip: he should look into who had actually sent Wilson to Africa. Dickerson pressed Fleischer: What are you talking about? Go ask the CIA, Fleischer told him.

An hour or so later, as Bush spoke at an AIDS treatment center, Dickerson cornered Dan Bartlett, now the White House communications director. Bartlett, an unflappable young Texan, talked with Dickerson about the unseemly clash between the CIA and the White House and the potential political problems for the president. But Bartlett, too, made the point that Wilson had been sent by a relatively low-ranking agency employee, and he encouraged Dickerson to follow up. When he was done talking to Fleischer and Bartlett, Dickerson wrote down in his notebook, "Look who sent."

The Bush White House's standard operating procedure was to ignore critics and stick to its script, just push ahead. But now Dickerson sensed there was a concerted effort to bring down Wilson. There might be a story here, he thought. He called his Washington bureau and failed to reach anyone. His editors and fellow correspondents were in a meeting. It was about 10:30 A.M. in Washington.

A LITTLE after 11 A.M., Matthew Cooper placed a call to Rove. Cooper was an easygoing veteran newsmagazine correspondent; he was also a minor Washington celebrity, an amateur comic who did dead-on political impressions, occasionally performing at local comedy clubs. Cooper had just started on the White House beat for *Time* and wasn't accustomed to dealing with Rove. Earlier in the week, Cooper had called Rove's office, leaving a message that he wanted to speak about welfare reform, and had not heard back. But this morning, Cooper's phone call was more pressing. *Time* was preparing a cover story on the major event of the week: the White House's acknowledgment, triggered by the Wilson op-ed, that it had misstated a key piece of Iraq weapons intelligence.

Cooper called the White House switchboard and was transferred to Rove's office. The woman who answered the phone said she wasn't sure if

Rove was there; then she said, "Hang on," and Cooper was put through. The conversation was brief. Rove insisted he was talking on "deep background," which meant he couldn't be identified as a White House official or quoted but that the information he provided could be used. When Cooper told him, "I'm writing on Wilson," Rove interrupted, "Don't get too far out on Wilson." He proceeded to explain why. Rove then ended the conversation with a curious remark: "I've already said too much."

As soon as he hung up the phone, Cooper, at 11:07 A.M., banged out an e-mail to Michael Duffy, the bureau chief, summarizing the conversation:

> Spoke to Rove on double super secret background for about two mins before he went on vacation . . . his big warning . . . don't get too far out on Wilson . . . says that the DCIA [director of central intelligence, George Tenet] didn't authorize the trip and that Cheney didn't authorize the trip. It was, KR said, wilson's wife, who apparently works at the agency on wmd issues, who authorized the trip. not only the genesis of the trip is flawed ans [*sic*] suspect, but so is the report. he implied strongly there's still plenty to implicate iraqi interest in acquiring uranium from Niger . . . some of this is going to be dclassified [*sic*] in the coming days, KR said. don't get too far out in front, he warned then he bolted . . . will include in next file . . .
>
> please don't source to rove or even WH but have TB [*Time* reporter Tim Burger] check out with Harlow.

Cooper was being flip. "Double super secret background" wasn't an actual journalistic code; it was a reference to the scene in the film *Animal House* when John Belushi's unruly fraternity was placed on "double secret probation." That one joke aside, Cooper knew he had learned something hot during his short talk with Rove: the White House was disclosing to him that Wilson's wife was a CIA officer and had arranged the controversial trip that had caused the current storm. Right after sending the e-mail to Duffy, he sent another to Dickerson in Africa: call me on a landline.

Dickerson was in Nigeria when he got the e-mail and immediately phoned Cooper, who was excited. "The fact that he had gotten to Rove and had gotten Rove to dish—this was his second week on the job . . . it was a powerful deal," Dickerson later said. The two *Time* reporters compared notes and saw that several White House officials were pushing the same line—there was something odd about Wilson's trip and how it had come about. But Cooper had received an extra piece of information from Rove: Wilson's wife was the story. This was real news, Cooper and Dickerson figured—and it seemed to cut against Wilson. Suddenly, for Dickerson, the dots connected. "It felt like the ultimate blow against Wilson's credibility," Dickerson later said. He and Cooper agreed they would each send dispatches to their editors reporting that the White House was going after Wilson hard.

Later that afternoon, Cooper summarized what he had, or thought he had, in a file he sent for the week's cover story:

> A startling charge from a senior administration official that we need to handle with some caution. . . . The senior administration official warns that we shouldn't get too far ahead of ourselves on Wilson. The official says that Wilson was not sent by the director of the CIA or by Dick Cheney and when it comes out who sent him, it will be embarrassing. When I pressed the official, he said it was somebody at the agency involved in WMD, Wilson's wife. This guy was not an emissary, the source claimed. His report is nowhere near the truth, the official added; in fact it may be totally wrong. The Iraqis, this person said, probably were seeking Niger uranium. He said the documents will be declassified in the next few days and epople [sic] will see a different side to Wilson.

Rove, who went further with Cooper than he had with Novak, had passed Cooper a tip that disclosed classified information: the fact that Valerie Wilson worked at the CIA. And he had indicated more developments on the Niger story were on the way.

ROVE might indeed have felt he had said too much to Cooper. He was rushing to get out of the office early that day to leave for a family vacation. But just before he left, at 11:55 A.M., he typed a short e-mail to Deputy National Security Adviser Stephen Hadley that contained a different (somewhat sanitized) version of his conversation with Cooper. The e-mail, in full, read:

> Matt Cooper called to give me a heads up that he's got a welfare reform story coming.

When he finished his brief heads-up, he immediately launched into Niger/isn't this damaging/hasn't the President been hurt? I didn't take the bait but said, if I were him, I wouldn't get TIME far out in front on this.

No mention of Valerie Wilson. No mention of her employment at the CIA. No mention of Joe Wilson or his trip. In this account of the conversation, Rove hadn't said much at all.

LATE on Friday afternoon, the CIA sent its statement—written in Tenet's name—to the White House, and it was faxed to Air Force One in Africa. The statement was hedged and more equivocal than Bush officials had anticipated—and it even undercut the White House's claim that the whole Niger mess had been the CIA's fault. When senior White House officials saw it that afternoon, they did double-takes. "Well this is not what we were expecting," one NSC official recalled saying.

The statement began in a no-nonsense fashion: The CIA had approved the State of the Union speech. "I am responsible for the approval process in my agency," Tenet said. "These sixteen words should never have been included in the text written for the President." Then Tenet's statement noted, "For perspective, a little history is in order."

But in recounting that history, Tenet's statement, drafted by Harlow, emphasized the CIA's repeated warnings about the Niger charge. It mentioned that in the fall of 2002, when the British wanted to refer to the Niger claim in their white paper, the CIA had "expressed reservations about its inclusion." It stated that CIA officials had told members of Congress that they disagreed with the British on the Niger charge. It pointed out that the NIE had not relied on the uranium-in-Africa charge for its judgment that Iraq was reconstituting its nuclear program. It even noted that the NIE had included the INR's "alternate view" stating that the Niger charge was "highly dubious."

Tenet's statement did say that the inclusion of the Africa charge in the State of the Union speech had been a "mistake." But whose mistake? Many of the details also implicated the White House in this mess. Tenet's statement, which the CIA released that day, was as much a defense as a surrender.

THE next morning, July 12, Fleischer spoke to reporters at the National Hospital in Abuja, Nigeria, and pronounced the Niger matter closed. "The president has moved on," he said.

Scooter Libby hadn't.

That same morning, Libby flew on Air Force Two with the vice president to Norfolk, Virginia, to celebrate the latest addition to America's military arsenal: the USS *Ronald Reagan,* a $4.5 billion aircraft carrier. More than 20,000 sailors and their family members cheered wildly as Nancy Reagan broke a bottle of sparkling wine to christen the ship. "Today we send forth a great American ship bearing a great American name," Cheney said. "Something tells me that any potential adversary of the United States will take note when word arrives that the USS *Ronald Reagan* has been sighted offshore."

On the plane ride back, Libby was still focused on Joe Wilson. With Cheney and Cathy Martin, the vice president's spokesperson, he discussed how to handle the media requests still coming in on Niger and Joe Wilson, including one from *Time*'s Matt Cooper. Cheney, according to Libby's later testimony to a grand jury, specifically selected him, instead of Martin, to talk to the press about Wilson—and to provide "on-the-record," "background," and "deep background" statements to reporters covering the story. Cheney and Libby remained committed to a counterattack against Wilson.

Cooper, meanwhile, was urging his editor to include in the magazine's cover story the White House's assault on Wilson. When Cooper read a draft of the cover story, written by bureau chief Michael Duffy, he was disappointed there was nothing on this angle. In an e-mail to Duffy, Cooper wrote, "The piece doesn't really get at the level of infighting this week. For instance, there's nothing about the dis of Wilson which I first unearthed."

Libby and Cooper didn't talk until three that afternoon. Cooper had gone swimming at a local country club, and when Libby called, Cooper was, as he later wrote, "wet, smelling of chlorine," and sprawled on his bed. Libby initially spoke on the record and for the first time confirmed that it had indeed been Cheney who asked his CIA briefer for more information on the uranium-from-Niger issue. But Libby added that Cheney had had nothing to do with Wilson's trip and had been "unaware" of it until it became public.

Libby also spoke off the record. Cooper asked Libby if he had heard anything about Wilson's wife having been involved in sending her husband on the mission. "Yeah, I've heard that, too," Libby said, according to Cooper's account. (Libby would later give a quite different account.)

Cooper now had two sources, Rove and Libby, and he fired off another e-mail to Duffy. "Still think you oughta stick in WH v. Wilson fight," he wrote.

Later that afternoon, Libby had a more extensive phone conversation with another reporter, Judy Miller. She called him from the home she shared in Sag Harbor with her husband, Jason Epstein, a legendary publisher and the founder of the liberal *New York Review of Books*. Miller later testified that she had probably been calling others about Joe Wilson's wife by this point. And in this conversation, Libby again quickly turned to bad-mouthing Wilson. He said it was unclear whether Wilson had even spoken with the right people in Niger. In her notebook, Miller jotted, "Victoria Wilson"—once again a near-miss reference to Wilson's wife. Although Miller's memory would later be foggy on precisely who had mentioned the name, the conversation appeared to have been the third time Libby had discussed Wilson's wife with her.

That same day, Walter Pincus was working on his latest story on the Niger controversy, and he had a scoop the White House wouldn't like: that Tenet had personally intervened with the White House to keep the Niger claim out of the Cincinnati speech. (The CIA had left that incident out of Tenet's quasi–*mea culpa*.) Pincus was talking to a confidential source when this administration official "veered off the precise matter we were discussing," Pincus subsequently wrote. The official told him that the White House hadn't paid attention to Wilson's Niger mission because his wife, a WMD analyst at the CIA, had sent Wilson there on a "boondoggle." Pincus didn't really believe the claim and dismissed it. He made no reference to it in his story.

By the end of the week, Rove had discussed Wilson's wife with two reporters (Novak and Cooper). Libby had also done so with two reporters (Cooper and Miller). And Armitage had revealed Valerie Wilson's CIA connection to two reporters (Woodward and Novak). Including Pincus, five reporters had been told something by Bush administration officials about Valerie Wilson's employment at the CIA in relation to Wilson's mission to Niger.

———

ON SATURDAY, July 12, six days after Wilson's op-ed appeared, *The Washington Post* and other newspapers received the latest column from Robert Novak. It was slated to run in many newspapers on Monday. The subject was "the political firestorm" over the Wilson trip. Most of the article was a routine rendition of the Wilson mission. Novak's point was that the trip had not been all that significant because Wilson's report "was regarded by the CIA as less than definitive" and it was "doubtful Tenet ever saw it." But the sixth paragraph contained a small nugget not yet publicly known:

> Wilson never worked for the CIA, but his wife, Valerie Plame, is an Agency operative on weapons of mass destruction. Two senior administration officials told me that Wilson's wife suggested sending him to Niger to investigate the Italian report.

Novak's column made nothing more of Valerie Wilson's role.

Bush's sixteen words in the State of the Union address had sparked a Washington furor. Novak's two sentences—thirty-nine words in all—were about to cause a bigger explosion.

15

A Cover Blown

VALERIE WILSON, a suburban-style mother of three-year-old twins, was at home with her husband in the couple's well-decorated brick town house in the tony Palisades section of Washington, when she read *The Washington Post* on the morning of July 14. She stared at Robert Novak's column and could scarcely believe it. There was her name—her maiden name—and the description of her as a CIA "operative." She knew that Washington was a town fueled by leaks. But why, she wondered, would anyone have done *this*?

She had known Novak was sniffing around on the story; the columnist had called her husband for comment a few days earlier. (Wilson had said to Novak that he didn't talk about his wife.) Valerie Wilson had told her supervisors about Novak's inquiry. She had figured someone at the CIA would take care of it—talk to Novak and keep things quiet. This wasn't the first time a journalist had stumbled across the identity of an undercover CIA officer. She assumed the agency would somehow protect her.

But it hadn't. And now her cover, both professional and personal, was blown. For nearly two decades, she had maintained a secret identity. Neighbors, friends, relatives—they had no idea that Valerie Wilson, this poised and confident woman who had told everybody she was an energy analyst—was a spy.

After reading the article, Valerie Wilson zeroed in on close-to-home worries. Her career, she feared, was in jeopardy. Her previous operations—the assets and sources she had worked with—might be threatened. Brewster-Jennings & Associates, the paper-only front group that had provided cover for her and other CIA officers, could be revealed as a fake company; anyone connected to it would be compromised. Intelligence services around the globe, she assumed, were probably already running her name through their records, looking to see if she had had contact with anyone of importance to them.

Valerie Wilson started a list of what would have to be done to minimize the fallout to her operations. She would have to reconcile her deception with family, friends, and neighbors. She also worried about her safety. Who knew what some kook might do now that it had been reported she was a CIA spy? Through her anxiety, she recognized the irony at hand. The Bush administration had taken the country to war by charging Iraq was a threat based on its weapons of mass destruction. As a member of the CIA's Joint Task Force on Iraq, Valerie Wilson had tried to find the evidence that would support the president's claims. But because her husband had challenged Bush's case for war, somebody in the administration was retaliating against *her* by outing her secret CIA identity.

At the time she had no idea that the leak had been caused by both Armitage's indiscretion and Rove's desire to discredit a critic. The disclosure would effectively end Valerie Wilson's CIA career—but it also would kick off another wild week for the White House and transform the WMD controversy from a bitter political debate into a criminal inquiry that would imperil both White House aides and journalists.

VALERIE PLAME entered the CIA in 1985, recruited straight out of Pennsylvania State University and placed in the program that trained the agency's best prospects. She was twenty-two years old.

It was a go-go moment for the CIA. With Reagan in the White House and William Casey in charge, the agency, as its champions liked to say, had been unleashed. The spy service had stepped up its covert and paramilitary activities around the globe, especially in Central America, Africa, and Afghanistan. The agency's secret war against the Sandinista regime in Nicaragua was generating controversy and would soon turn into a scandal.

Plame, whose father was an Air Force lieutenant colonel who served in the National Security Agency for three years and whose mother taught elementary school, grew up in Huntington Valley, Pennsylvania, near Philadelphia, in a household with country-club Republican politics (strong on defense, conservative on fiscal policy, liberal on social matters). But she was no ideological or political partisan. She had joined the CIA not to be a covert Cold War crusader but for the simplest of reasons: she wanted to serve her country, and the work seemed interesting.

She had married her college boyfriend, Todd Sesler, and the plan was for him to sign up with the CIA, too. But after they received their security clearances, Sesler soured on becoming a spy. The marriage ended. And in September 1985, Plame found herself in a conference room in the CIA with about forty-five other new trainees. The class included trainees who would be heading toward various careers in the agency: analysts, logistics managers, technicians, operatives. Plame was in a case officer slot; she had been hired to be an undercover CIA employee who would run agents and operations overseas. She was one of the youngest in the class.

During a ten-week course, Plame and her classmates were taught the basics of the CIA: how the agency was structured, how the classification system functioned, how to create and maintain cover, how to write an intelligence report. There were classes on how the federal government functioned—on international trade, budgets, the diplomatic corps. Much of it was mundane. But present and retired case officers came in to share stories of their glory days and best operations.

During one class, a CIA official who had been stationed overseas talked about life as a case officer working under nonofficial cover (or NOC), the most perilous of agency positions. Most case officers dispatched abroad operate under what's called "official cover." They pretend to be, say, a foreign service officer and have an office in the U.S. Embassy while holding a diplomatic passport. If anything goes wrong with an operation, such an officer has the protection of diplomatic immunity. Being a NOC is different. A CIA spy with nonofficial cover will pose as, perhaps, a businessperson and have no official connection to the local U.S. Embassy. If such an officer's cover is blown, he or she is out in the cold. The embassy offers no lifeline. The officer can be arrested and imprisoned (or worse) by any government for espionage.

This former NOC told Plame's class that his cover had been as an executive for an American heavy equipment company in one of the firm's overseas offices. He had had to work during the day in his cover position; he tended to his spy tasks off the company clock. One night he came home to his apartment and noticed that things had been moved around. It looked to him as if someone had rifled through his possessions and then tried to place items back where they had been. He had a sports car registered in another name sitting in a garage a block or so away. He immediately backed out of his room, collecting only his briefcase, and went to that car. He drove four hours to the border at 180 miles per hour and then flew back to the United States. He never returned to that country.

"He told us," Brent Cavan, a classmate of Plame, said, "that you have to think about this. This is not a life for someone with a family. He had a fantastic salary with this company, but he didn't get to keep it—and he had to work two jobs. We heard lots of stuff like that. Valerie took it to heart."

Plame, according to one member of her class, was "the kid sister in the group." She came across, Cavan said, as young but "plucky," determined, ambitious, and personable. "She was physically stunning, with platinum blond hair," a fellow trainee later said. "During our first four to five minutes together, I could tell she was more of a listener than a talker. That's why she was going into the DO." The trainees didn't know each other by their full names. To her fellow trainees, she was Val P.

After the initial orientation, members of the class were assigned internships with various parts of the CIA. Then they headed to the Farm, the CIA's paramilitary training facility near Williamsburg, Virginia. Because of her young age, Plame did extra internships and headed to the Farm later.

At that facility, also known as Camp Peary, trainees were issued military-style green uniforms, boots, backpacks, and the like. They attended classes on how to do airdrops, how to navigate through tough terrain on foot at night with a compass, how to insert an operative into hostile territory from the water, how to use explosives, how to handle and fire weapons, including an AK-47.

The most intense moment at the Farm for CIA trainees came during the hostage exercise. At some point, mock terrorists would stage an ambush and take the trainees captive. The trainees would be bound, blindfolded, and thrown into a ditch. They would be taken—perhaps marched—to a makeshift prison, stripped, and forced to put on baggy clothes. They were placed in cells, some so small that the trainees could not lie down. They were forced to stand. They were not permitted to speak or sleep. Loud white noise, Arabic music, or the sound of a baby crying was played on speakers. Periodically, each trainee would be taken to an interrogation session. There would be no physical abuse, but trainees would be placed in stress positions.

The goal for each rookie was to not provide any information about him- or herself or about a fellow trainee for as long as possible. "The aim is to survive," noted Larry Johnson, another Plame classmate, "and to realize that all information is perishable and you should give it up only when you need to. You learn how to divulge it when doing so can save your life and hopefully not compromise anyone else's life."

Though all trainees knew that this was only an exercise, and that no harm could come of it, forty-eight hours of such treatment took its toll. "It still seemed real," Johnson recalled. "One woman cracked and gave me up for a Grape Nehi and a ham sandwich." Trainees came up with various ways of coping. Val P. devised her own: repeatedly dancing the hokey-pokey in her cell.

At the end of the exercise, the trainees were "rescued" by a special operations team, with guns drawn, and then the group together sang "The Star-Spangled Banner."

PLAME graduated from the Farm in the fall of 1986. The following spring she took a course in operations for trainees destined to be case officers, the elite corps of the Directorate of Operations. This covered the essence of espionage: how to recruit an agent—a foreign national who would be willing to hand over valuable information about his government, his military, his company. (In CIA lingo, agency officers are not "agents"; that word applies to foreigners persuaded by case officers to become spies.) Plame learned the basics: how to assess a potential agent, how to make contact, how to make a pitch. "Recruiting an agent is essentially selling a product," one of Plame's classmates later explained. "You're not saying this vacuum cleaner will save you work. But you're selling an idea: if you help us, you will be helping your country, your people. But every time you recruit somebody, you expose yourself. We had to be taught all this."

After her CIA education was complete, Plame was assigned to the Cyprus/Greece/Turkey desk in the European Division of the DO. She was a junior case officer, basically doing work that supported officers in the field. She studied Greek. The branch's main focus at the time was counterterrorism. The CIA's Cyprus station was a field headquarters for much of the agency's counterterror operations related to the Middle East. The branch's number one target was the 17 November leftist terrorism group working out of Greece. The agency had an intense interest in these terrorists for good reason: the 17 November group had claimed responsibility for the 1975 assassination of Richard Welch, the CIA station chief in Athens. (The group had targeted the CIA for working with the repressive military junta that ruled Greece from 1967 to 1974.) More than a decade later, the Cyprus/ Greece/Turkey desk was still looking to find Welch's killers.

In 1989, Plame was posted to the CIA station in Athens as a case officer. She served under official cover as a State Department officer, working in the U.S. Embassy there. She carried a diplomatic passport. Her task was to spot and recruit agents for the CIA. After that first tour, she obtained a master's degree at the London School of Economics and a master's in European studies at the Collège d'Europe in Bruges, Belgium.

In the early 1990s, Plame became a NOC, that most covert of covert officers. She was looking to work more on her own and to avoid what she could of the usual bureaucratic nonsense that afflicted even the government's spy services. It was uncommon for a case officer who had official cover to turn into a NOC. Plame had already established a trail as a U.S. government officer. (This meant she would not be the purest of NOCs.) She "resigned" from her cover job at the State Department and began working out of Belgium, telling those who asked that she was in the energy field. People usually didn't inquire much beyond that. Her main mission, though, remained the same as before: to gather agents for the CIA. In 1997, Plame returned to CIA headquarters.*

Back at Langley, Plame had to choose a new career path within the agency. She figured that with the end of the Cold War, the two growth in-

---

*Her reassignment might have been due to Aldrich Ames, the notorious CIA officer who had spied for the Soviets and been arrested in 1994. Ames had served on a promotion panel for DO officers, including NOCs like Plame. Agency officials who conducted a postmortem damage assessment on the Ames case feared that the Soviet mole had shared the identities of CIA officers, including NOCs, with the KGB. As a precaution, some NOCs were brought home. Within the CIA, some officers later came to believe that Plame had been among the officers whose return had been prompted by the Ames case, but it was never clear if Ames had told the Russians about her.

dustries in the intelligence field were counterterrorism and counterproliferation. She picked weapons and requested an assignment in the DO's new Counterproliferation Division, a unit Congress had pushed the CIA to create to address concerns about the spread of weapons of mass destruction.

About that time, she also moved into a Watergate apartment with Joe Wilson, who had recently served in Stuttgart, Germany, as the political adviser to the commander in chief of the U.S. armed forces in Europe. Wilson had come back to the capital to become senior director for African affairs at the National Security Council in the Clinton White House. The two had met a few months earlier at a reception at the Washington residence of the Turkish ambassador. At that party, Plame had told Wilson she was an energy executive living in Brussels. But shortly into their subsequent courtship, she disclosed her secret to him: she worked undercover for the CIA. (Later, Wilson would say that his only question at the time was, "Is your real name Valerie?") They married in April 1998, and she took his last name. Less than two years later, Valerie Wilson gave birth to twins, a boy and a girl. (Wilson had been married twice before, and his first marriage had also produced a set of boy-girl twins.) After the twins were born, Valerie Wilson was struck by postpartum depression. It lasted for months. But with the help of medication, she recovered and later became executive director of a local postpartum support group.

After a maternity leave, Valerie Wilson returned to the CIA's Counterproliferation Division in the spring of 2001. She was given a choice: she could work on North Korea or Iraq. She selected Iraq and became one of the two operations officers working for the CPD's rather modest Iraq branch. But within months, it would expand into the Joint Task Force on Iraq and assume one of the agency's most important missions: the search for intelligence on Iraq's WMDs. (She also assisted on operations related to Iran.)

Two years later, Valerie Wilson was sitting at home, staring at the newspaper and wondering whether her CIA career was over. Prior to the leak, she had started to change her status from nonofficial cover to official cover. She was in the process of leaving the JTFI to assume a personnel management position within the CIA. After sixteen years in operations, she wasn't relishing the new job. But others at the agency had advised her to put in some time as an administrator to rise through the ranks. She wanted to maintain official cover so she could return to operations. But her need for deep-cover NOC status had passed. The paperwork for this transition was in motion when Novak's column hit. Now, for the first time since she had entered the CIA, she was without any cover at all.

LATER on the morning of July 14, 2003, Joe Wilson received a call from David Corn, Washington editor of *The Nation*. In the months before the war, the two had gotten to know each other during encounters in the green-room at the Fox News Washington bureau. Corn was a Fox News contributor. And Wilson, at Corn's invitation, had written a prewar piece for *The Nation* that had assailed the "imperial ambitions" of the administration's neoconservatives. Corn had telephoned after reading the Novak column.

"You never told me your wife worked at the CIA," he said to Wilson, half jokingly.

"And I can't now," Wilson said. The tone of his voice was drop-dead serious.

Well, what can you say? Corn asked.

"I will not answer questions about my wife," Wilson replied. "This is not about me and less so about my wife. It has always been about the facts underpinning the president's statement in the State of the Union speech."

But the two discussed—in theoretical terms—the implications of the Novak column. Without acknowledging that his wife was a CIA employee of any kind, Wilson said that naming her this way could compromise all the operations she had worked on and all the networks with which she had been associated, were she a spy. "This is the stuff of Kim Philby and Aldrich Ames," Wilson said. And, he noted, if she weren't actually a CIA officer, Novak and his administration sources were inaccurately branding a woman known to friends as an energy analyst for a private firm as a CIA spy—and that wouldn't do her much good. Not giving anything away about his wife, Wilson was making a good case that this leak (true or otherwise) was bad news for Valerie Wilson—and possibly damaging to national security.

Wilson wouldn't discuss with Corn whether his wife had been involved in his trip to Niger: "I was invited out to meet with a group of people at the CIA who were interested in this subject. None I knew more than casually. They asked me about my understanding of the uranium business and my familiarity with the people in the Niger government at the time. And they asked, 'What would you do?' We gamed it out—what I would be looking for. Nothing was concluded at that time. I told them if they wanted me to go to Niger, I would clear my schedule. Then they got back to me and said, 'Yes, we want you to go.' " Wilson did note with a laugh that at the time of his Niger mission their twins were two years old and that it wouldn't have been in his wife's interest to encourage him to head off to Africa for two weeks on an unpaid gig.

But Wilson was upset and said that he regarded the leak as a warning to others: "Stories like this are not intended to intimidate me, since I've already told my story. But it's pretty clear it is intended to intimidate others who might come forward. You need only look at the stories of intelligence analysts who say they have been pressured. They may have kids in college, they may be vulnerable to these types of smears."

Corn asked if Wilson had ever heard of the Intelligence Identities Protection Act. No, Wilson said. This leak might be more serious than you think, Corn remarked. It might be a criminal offense.

NEARLY a decade earlier, Corn had published an unauthorized biography of a controversial CIA officer, Theodore Shackley, and he was familiar with this esoteric and rarely cited law, which had been passed in 1982. The act made it a crime for a government official with access to classified information to "intentionally" disclose any information that identified a "covert agent" of the U.S. government. Under this law, a government leaker could be prosecuted only if he or she had known that the outed officer was working undercover and had realized that the government was taking affirmative measures to conceal that officer's clandestine status. And the law covered only covert officers working abroad or those who had "within the last five years served outside the United States." The punishment was steep: a fine of up to $50,000 and/or up to ten years in prison. Journalists couldn't be prosecuted, unless they engaged in a "pattern" of naming intelligence officers with the intent of impairing U.S. intelligence activities.

The law had been partly a response to the December 1975 assassination of Greece station chief Dick Welch, who had been serving under State Department cover as the embassy's first secretary at the time of his murder. In the mid-1970s, Philip Agee, a CIA case officer turned vehement CIA critic, and several colleagues—often drawing on public information, such as State Department directories—published books and magazine articles listing the names of CIA officers around the world. Their stated goal was to ruin as many CIA operations as they could—and to force agency officers to return home. Welch had been on one of these lists, published in *CounterSpy* magazine in early 1975. But years before that, his name had appeared in a book called *Who's Who in the CIA,* which was written by someone named Julius Mader. The book was published in East Germany and was probably a KGB publication. Also, Welch's name and address had been published in the English-language *Athens News* the month before he was killed. In a security lapse, Welch had been living in a house known locally as the residence of the CIA station chief.

Even if Agee's actions hadn't led to Welch's murder, he and his colleagues had unquestionably exposed hundreds of CIA officers—and they kept doing so. By 1979, they had, by their own estimate, outed more than a thousand CIA employees.* Louis Wolf, a collaborator of Agee, was an editor of a publication called *Covert Action Information Bulletin,* which contained a section titled "Naming Names" dedicated to blowing the cover of CIA officers. In the summer of 1980, Wolf and his associates held a press conference in Jamaica and revealed the names of fifteen purported CIA officers working at the U.S. Embassy there, including Station Chief Richard Kinsman. Their intent was to disrupt what they claimed was CIA intervention in that nation's upcoming election. Within forty-eight hours, unknown gunmen fired shots at Kinsman's home.

The attack in Kingston further inflamed members of Congress who had been outraged for years by the CIA-outing efforts of Agee, Wolf, and others. The incident increased support for pending legislation to criminalize the exposure of undercover intelligence officers. The Reagan administration strongly supported the bill. But media advocates, including *The New York Times,* raised First Amendment concerns. Would the measure, for example, criminalize the publication of information about illegal or rogue CIA activities? ("All should hope the courts will wipe the law from the books," the *Times* editorialized as the bill moved through Congress in early 1982.) Due partly to such complaints, Congress defined the scope of the prohibited conduct narrowly. And in June 1982, the House and Senate passed the Intelligence Identities Protection Act, and Reagan signed it into law at a ceremony outside CIA headquarters.

---

*In 1979, the United States revoked Agee's passport. He eventually settled in Cuba.

As HE was talking to Wilson, Corn found a copy of the law online and remarked that it could apply to the two administration sources who had leaked the information on Valerie Wilson to Novak. (The law didn't cover Novak; by publishing just that one leak, he hadn't engaged in an Agee-like "pattern" of actions.) Has no one mentioned this to you? Corn asked. No, Wilson replied.

This might be worth an article, Corn noted. Wilson remarked that he wasn't looking to draw any additional attention to the Novak column. He seemed to be hoping that the incident might blow over.

Well, Corn said, he would mull this over. He had another piece due the next day. He would get back to Wilson.

THAT Monday morning, *Time* magazine hit newsstands with a cover story on the Niger controversy headlined, "Untruth and Consequences: How Flawed Was the Case for Going to War Against Saddam?" Citing the White House's retreat on the Niger charge, the magazine asked, "Where else did the U.S. stretch evidence to generate public support for the war?" And it noted, "the controversy over those 16 words would not have erupted with such force were they not emblematic of larger concerns about Bush's reasoning for going to war in the first place."

When Scooter Libby read the story, he once again was angry. Wilson's tale was repeated in a fashion sympathetic to the retired diplomat. The authors referred to Wilson as a "wise choice for the mission." Even worse, *Time* hadn't used all of a lengthy on-the-record quote Libby had given Cooper two days earlier, stating explicitly that the vice president had been unaware of the Wilson trip until it became public. And the *Time* story said nothing about Valerie Wilson, even though Libby had confirmed to Cooper that she had sent her husband to Niger.

After reading the *Time* article, Libby called Cooper and complained. But Cooper was not done with the Wilson story, particularly the angle he had not been able to get into the cover story: the White House campaign against Wilson. And he had another option: *Time*'s Web site. That afternoon, he sent an e-mail to Duffy and Dickerson: "Wonder if we shouldn't try to whip something up for time.com tomorrow? i've got the white house dissing wilson (as does john) and we have wilson pushing back . . . it probably won't hold the week so why not get a little juice out of it tomorrow?" Duffy replied, "Excellent idea. . . . I like it also because it shows how far these boys will go to get their way." Oddly, neither Cooper nor Duffy had noticed Novak's column.

ON TUESDAY, Corn checked in with Joe Wilson. Had anyone else, he asked the former diplomat, picked up on the leak as a possible violation of the Intelligence Identities Protection Act? Not yet, Wilson replied. In fact, Wilson said, the leak hadn't generated any media attention. He was still seething but not eager to publicize the leak. Corn mentioned he intended to write about it. "I'm not going to tell you how to do your job," Wilson said. "It's up to you."

After that, Corn called Novak and had a brief conversation with the columnist about the article. Novak said he had been tipped off by administration officials about Valerie Wilson and that he hadn't been reluctant to name her. "I figured if they gave it to me," he remarked, "they'd give it to others. . . . I'm a reporter. Somebody gives me information and it's accurate, I generally use it."

On July 16, Corn posted a piece on *The Nation*'s Web site. Called "A White House Smear," it began, "Did senior Bush officials blow the cover of a US intelligence officer working covertly in a field of vital importance to national security—and break the law—in order to strike at a Bush administration critic and intimidate others?" The article explained the possible relevance of the Intelligence Identities Protection Act, and it noted that if the leak was accurate, Valerie Wilson was "apparently" a NOC. The logic behind that assumption was straightforward. Since Joe Wilson had mentioned that Valerie was known as a private energy consultant, she would not be an official-cover CIA employee. Such CIA officers told people they were government employees working for the State Department or the Pentagon. A CIA operative who claimed to have a job outside the U.S. government was, by process of elimination, a NOC. "Will there be any inquiry?" the article asked.

This was the first article to suggest that the Plame leak might have been a federal crime. It received no attention in the media—at first. But within two days it had been read by nearly 100,000 readers on *The Nation*'s Web site, a sizable number. Other Web sites and bloggers jumped on the story and angrily asked why other Washington reporters weren't covering the leak.

AMONG the president's communications advisers, there was talk that the attack-Wilson strategy might have gotten out of hand. In a White House meeting that week, communications director Dan Bartlett, just back from Africa, talked about redirecting coverage away from Wilson and his wife—and stopping the Wilson bashing. It was unproductive and demeaning, he suggested. Bartlett, according to Adam Levine, was "against the idea of the wife as a talking point." But shifting the White House gears wouldn't be easy. Before the meeting, Levine had received another call from a cable TV reporter asking him about the information in the Novak column. Rove and Libby "are flacking this," the reporter had said to him—meaning they were encouraging reporters to write about Valerie Wilson. "Scooter and Karl are out of control," Levine told Bartlett at the meeting. "You've got to rein these guys in." Bartlett rolled his eyes and looked exasperated, but agreed. "I know, I know," he said, according to Levine.

MATT COOPER finally got to make use of the information that Rove had leaked to him and Libby had confirmed—but only after he came close to chucking it. Cooper spent two days preparing the new Wilson story with Dickerson and another *Time* correspondent, Massimo Calabresi. Then, on Wednesday afternoon, as the story was done, one of Cooper's colleagues noticed something: Novak's column. Cooper still hadn't seen it. A chagrined Cooper sent a copy of the Novak column to Duffy with a note: "I'd missed this earlier in the week. Does this obviate our doing a piece?" No, replied Duffy, because their new article had more "pushback" from Wilson.

On July 17, *Time* posted the article, which carried a triple byline—Cooper, Dickerson, and Calabresi—and a strong headline: "A War on Wilson?" The subtitle asked, "Has the Bush Administration declared war on a former ambassador who conducted a fact-finding mission to probe possible Iraqi interest in African uranium?" Its answer: "Perhaps." The article noted that the White House had been taking "public and private whacks at Wilson." It stated that "some government officials have noted to TIME in interviews (as well as to syndicated columnist Robert Novak) that Wilson's wife,

Valerie Plame, is a CIA official who monitors the proliferation of weapons of mass destruction." The phrase "government officials" was a reference to Rove and Libby. The article said these officials had "suggested" that Valerie Wilson had been "involved" in her husband's being dispatched to Niger. "That is bulls—t," the newsmagazine quoted Wilson as saying in response.

The article also referred to top administration officials who had claimed that Wilson's post-trip report had actually strengthened the case for the Niger deal because Wilson had said that in 1999 an Iraqi representative had approached Niger to revive commercial ties. Wilson, in the *Time* piece, returned the fire: "That then translates into an Iraqi effort to import a significant quantity of uranium as the president alleged? These guys really need to get serious."

The Web story included Libby's on-the-record quote about Cheney's lack of knowledge of the Wilson trip. Still, it wasn't the sort of piece Libby was looking for. It distanced Cheney from Wilson's trip. But it didn't undercut Wilson, and it didn't dwell on the Valerie Wilson angle. It suggested administration officials (meaning Rove and Libby) had been disclosing information about Valerie Wilson as part of a "war" on her husband. And it gave Wilson the last word on each of the administration's specific charges against him. "This is a smear job," Wilson was quoted as saying about the attacks on him and the allegations about his wife.

Once the story was posted, Cooper sent it to other political journalists, including Mark Halperin, who oversaw *The Note,* an ABC News tip sheet closely read by political reporters. The piece, Cooper said in an e-mail to Halperin, "might get a pop."

THAT morning's *Wall Street Journal* carried an editorial wondering why the White House had become so defensive regarding the sixteen words. The paper was in essence speaking for Libby.

"Our puzzlement," the editorialists wrote, "is even greater now that we've learned what last October's national intelligence estimate really said." The *Journal*'s editorial page had been told about parts of the NIE—but only passages that bolstered the White House's case. The editorial quoted specific sentences related to the Niger charge—but not the INR dissent—and argued that Bush had been right to include the uranium-in-Africa allegation in the State of the Union speech. The *Journal* errantly claimed that the presumably reliable British intelligence service had provided the original report on the Niger deal. (In fact, the Italians had.) And the editorial added, "The decision to disarm the Iraqi dictator wasn't based on a single intelligence report but on a mountain of evidence compiled over a dozen years."

How had the *Journal*'s conservative editorial writers gained access to these White House–friendly portions of the NIE? "This information . . . does not come from the White House," the editorial asserted, without revealing the source. But years later, a special counsel would note that Libby had passed portions of the NIE—through another government official—to the *Journal* before the editorial appeared. After trying to use Judy Miller to disseminate a distorted (dissent-free) version of the Niger story and failing, Libby had turned to *The Wall Street Journal.* This time he succeeded.

THAT day, the president's most loyal ally, Tony Blair, stopped off in Washington for a quick visit. Blair addressed a joint session of Congress and left open the possibility that no weapons of mass destruction would be located. "Let us say one thing: if we are wrong, we will have destroyed a threat that at its least is responsible for inhuman carnage and suffering," Blair said. "That is something I am confident history will forgive."

After the speech, Bush and the prime minister met at the White House and spoke to reporters. When a journalist pointed out that Blair had "opened the door to the possibility that you may be proved wrong about the threat from Iraq's weapons of mass destruction," Bush shot back, "We won't be proven wrong." He then added, "I believe that we will find the truth. And the truth is, he was developing a program for weapons of mass destruction. . . . We will bring the weapons, and of, of course—we will bring the information forward on the weapons when they find them. And that will end up—end all this speculation. . . . And that's what's going to happen." Programs and weapons: Bush was yet again merging the two.

Then Blair took off for Tokyo. While his plane was in the air, a darker Iraq weapons drama—involving intelligence, the media, and leaks—played out to a tragic conclusion in England.

Two days earlier, on July 15, the House of Commons foreign affairs committee had held a hearing to question David Kelly, a fifty-nine-year-old Oxford-educated microbiologist and former UN weapons inspector in Iraq, who had served as senior adviser to the Ministry of Defence on WMDs.

Weeks earlier, Kelly had acknowledged to his superiors that he had spoken to BBC reporter Andrew Gilligan shortly before Gilligan broadcast the story charging that the Blair administration had "sexed up" its 2002 white paper on Iraq's weapons by including the claim that Saddam could deploy chemical or biological weapons within forty-five minutes. Kelly had had qualms about this allegation, but he maintained that he hadn't told Gilligan that the dossier had been "sexed up." Blair administration officials saw Kelly as a witness who could prove the BBC report was a fabrication, and they leaked word that he had been Gilligan's source. ("It would fuck Gilligan if [Kelly] was his source," Alistair Campbell, Blair's communications chief, who had been in charge of the white paper's production, wrote in his diary.) It was unclear, though, whether Kelly had been Gilligan's main source. In any event, Kelly became the center of a media frenzy.

At the hearing, Kelly, a private man, looked nervous and uncomfortable hunched over the witness table. Some MPs loudly demanded that he explain his dealings with Gilligan, hoping to discredit the BBC reporter. MPs critical of the government suggested that Kelly was being unfairly used by Blair officials for their own political purposes. "Have you ever felt like a fall guy?" one MP asked him. "You have been set up, have you not?" Kelly spoke so quietly that the MPs could barely hear him. And when asked if he had been Gilligan's primary source, he said he didn't think so.

For years, Kelly had been a source for reporters on Iraq and weapons issues. But after being dragged into the limelight, he told friends, he felt "physically sick." He had become a battering ram for both sides in England's version of the Iraq WMD debate. Two days after the hearing, he responded to a *New York Times* reporter who had e-mailed him offering encouragement. The reporter was Judith Miller. Kelly had been a source for her on WMD issues, and at 11:18 A.M. that Thursday, he sent her an e-mail that cryptically noted that there were "many dark actors playing games." He then thanked Miller for her support and friendship.

It was the last e-mail Kelly ever sent.

That afternoon, Kelly took a long stroll down a woodland path outside the village of Southmoor, where he lived. He walked atop a small mound, swallowed tablets of coproxamol, a prescription painkiller, and then slashed his left wrist with a knife. His body was found by police the next morning.

———

THROUGHOUT that week in Washington, news continued to dribble out about those sixteen words. The story wouldn't go away. And the White House took an unusual step: it decided to publicly release certain portions of the National Intelligence Estimate on Iraq's WMDs. Scooter Libby's selective leaking of NIE excerpts to Judy Miller and *The Wall Street Journal*—leaks authorized by Bush and directed by Cheney—had not helped.

White House staffers hoped (as had Bush and Cheney) that by disclosing the NIE's chief findings—that "Baghdad has chemical and biological weapons" and "probably" would have a nuclear weapon "if left unchecked . . . during this decade"—they could demonstrate that the president had invaded Iraq on the basis of a definitive CIA judgment. But the White House, unlike Libby, also made available several of the muddled passages from the NIE (which made the overarching key judgments seem less definitive) and the various dissents, including the State Department's conclusion that the yellowcake claim was "highly dubious."

During a background briefing for reporters in the White House pressroom, Bartlett read through the NIE excerpts. He acknowledged there had been dissents on the aluminum tubes, the Niger deal, and the overall nuclear case. But he insisted it was the dominant NIE conclusions that had formed the basis of Bush's decision to go to war. When Bartlett finished his presentation, the reporters threw questions at him.

"When did the president read this NIE?" one wanted to know.

He never did, Bartlett said: "The President has been briefed on more than—countless conversations with his national—with intelligence community about the contents of the NIE. I don't think he sat down over a long weekend and read every word of it. But he's familiar, intimately familiar with the case. . . ."

"So," this reporter followed up, "this would have been read, presumably, by the national security adviser, and then she would have briefed the president on it?"

Not exactly, Bartlett said; we have "experts who work for the national security adviser who would know this information, who understand the information."

The questions kept coming. "Last week," a reporter asked, "[Rice] told us that neither she nor the president were aware of any concerns about the quality of the intelligence underlying this allegation. Given that [there] is a [dissenting] footnote [in the NIE about the Niger charge] . . . how is it possible that the national security adviser and the president would not have been aware of those reservations?"

The answer was simple, according to Bartlett: "They did not read footnotes in a ninety-page document." It was the "majority opinion" about Saddam's broader program that mattered, Bartlett said, not individual dissents about particular pieces of intelligence.

Some reporters were incredulous.

"The words 'highly dubious,' that's the State Department's intelligence arm saying 'highly dubious,'" said one. "Is the president comfortable about making assertions that the State Department thinks are highly dubious?"

Bartlett replied, "The president was comfortable at the time, based on the information that was provided in his speech. The president of the United States is not a fact checker."

The release of the NIE was supposed to tamp down the controversy, but Bartlett's concessions were damning. The White House communications director was acknowledging that Bush and Rice hadn't read the NIE and hadn't delved into details of the debate about Iraq intelligence. Even though prewar media reports had noted there was a sharp difference of opinion among analysts about the most critical piece of evidence for the nuclear case—the aluminum tubes—Bush and Rice hadn't taken any steps to get to the bottom of the dispute. Bartlett was trying to defend the White House. But he was presenting a picture of a commander in chief who had shown little—or no—interest in sorting out the disagreements among his intelligence agencies. Bush had issued definitive public statements about the gathering menace posed by Iraq's weapons programs without ever having read the fine print.*

THE Novak column had not received as much attention as some in the White House had hoped. Days after its appearance, Bush aides, including Rove, were still pointing reporters to the article and its disclosure about Valerie Wilson. On Sunday, July 20, Andrea Mitchell of NBC called Wilson

---

*A one-page summary of the NIE presented to Bush in October 2002 did include references to the dissents by the Energy Department and the State Department on the aluminum tubes. The White House never publicly indicated whether Bush had read this summary or was aware of these dissents.

and said that she was being told by sources in the White House that "the real story here is . . . Wilson and his wife." Mitchell later told *Newsweek* she said to Wilson, "I heard in the White House that people were touting the Novak column and that was the real story." She didn't say to whom she had spoken.

The next day, Rove's secretary e-mailed Levine looking for Chris Matthews's phone number. Rove had just returned from San Francisco, where he had attended the annual male-only retreat of corporate, political, and media bigwigs at Bohemian Grove and had run into Matthews. (The secretive gathering was "essentially a summer camp for rich white men" with lots of alcohol and male bonding in the woods, according to someone who attended the retreat that summer.) Rove wanted to talk to the cable television host again. Levine was nervous about Rove contacting the antiwar Matthews, who had been championing Wilson. As Levine later recounted, he sent Rove an e-mail: "Before you talk to Matthews, you need to talk to me." But it was too late. Rove had already called.

Rove's phone call with Matthews revealed much about his attitude toward the entire Wilson affair. He was not apologetic or defensive about the outing of Valerie Wilson. As Matthews later described the conversation to colleagues, Rove considered the Wilson dust-up to be a political war, and he saw Valerie Wilson as a full-fledged combatant on the other side—not an innocent bystander. Matthews was surprised by Rove's ferocity. Rove, Matthews told a colleague, was "pretty revved up on the issue" and said that the Wilsons "were trying to screw the White House so the White House was going to screw them back." After Matthews finished talking to Rove, he called Joe Wilson and, according to Wilson, said, "I just got off the phone with Karl Rove. He says, and I quote, 'Wilson's wife is fair game.' "* (A Rove spokesperson later said that Rove had called Matthews to say it was "reasonable to discuss who sent Wilson to Niger.")

---

*White House defenders were mounting their own attacks on Wilson in an effort to undermine his credibility. Clifford May, a former Republican Party spokesman and *New York Times* reporter, wrote an article for the *National Review* Web site in which he described Wilson as a "pro-Saudi leftist partisan with an ax to grind." The reference was to Wilson's affiliation with the Middle East Institute, a Washington think tank that had accepted contributions from the Saudi government and other Arab states. In a *Wall Street Journal* op-ed, Caspar Weinberger, defense secretary under Ronald Reagan, assailed Wilson for having been a "sloppy" investigator with a "less than stellar" record when he was ambassador.

ON JULY 22, *Newsday* ran a piece by Timothy Phelps and Knut Royce that drew a new round of attention to the Plame leak. The story quoted unnamed intelligence officials confirming that Valerie Wilson was an undercover CIA officer working on WMD issues and that Novak's administration sources might well have broken the law by disclosing her classified CIA employment to the journalist. The story also quoted Frank Anderson, a former CIA Near East Division chief: "When it gets to the point of an administration official acting to do career damage, and possibly actually endanger someone, that's mean, that's petty, it's irresponsible." Novak told *Newsday,* "I didn't dig it out, it was given to me. They thought it was significant, they gave me the name and I used it." That made it seem as if his sources had purposefully planted the leak with him. (Later, though, Novak would say he misspoke when he gave this account.)

Though the leak had yet to become much of a news story, at that day's White House press briefing, Scott McClellan, who had replaced Ari Fleischer as press secretary the previous week, was asked to respond to "accusations that the administration deliberately blew the cover of an undercover CIA operative, and in so doing, violated a federal law that prohibits revealing the identity of undercover CIA operatives." McClellan replied, "That is not the way this president or this White House operates."

Just that day, Democrats had started calling for an investigation of the leak. Senator Jay Rockefeller decried the leak as "vile" and a "highly dishonorable thing to do." Senator Dick Durbin accused the White House of going after anyone who questioned how the administration had made its case for war. Senator Tom Daschle urged a probe. Would the White House, the reporter asked McClellan, support an inquiry? "I think that's suggesting that there might be some truth to the matter you're bringing up," McClellan said. "I have seen nothing—I have seen nothing to suggest that there is any truth to it. . . . But let me make it very clear, that's just not the way this White House operates."

JULY 22 should have been a day of celebration at the White House. The news out of Baghdad that morning was positive: Uday and Qusay Hussein, the dictator's vicious sons, had been killed in a shoot-out with the U.S. military. Defense Department officials expressed hope that this would demonstrate to the Iraqis that the old tyrannical regime was truly gone and be a psychological blow to a resistance that had yet to wither away.

But the White House staff was in turmoil, bracing for what aides feared could be the worst day yet in the never-ending yellowcake affair. Late the previous Friday night—hours after Tenet had issued the double-edged statement accepting responsibility for the sixteen-word mistake—Mike Gerson, Bush's chief speechwriter, had discovered in his files the memo that had been sent to him and Hadley by the CIA on October 5, 2002, requesting that the White House remove the uranium claims from the Cincinnati speech. The memo not only questioned elements of the Niger case, it explicitly challenged the British government's position: "We told Congress that the Brits have exaggerated this issue." Then on Monday evening, after the White House told Tenet that it had come across the October 5 memo, the CIA had located the follow-up memo sent to Hadley and Rice on October 6, 2002. The second memo elaborated on the reasons the CIA didn't believe the uranium claims. It stated—loud and clear—that "the Africa story is overblown." Tenet forwarded a copy of this second memo to the White House on Tuesday morning.

Eleven days previously, the White House had blamed the CIA for the sixteen words. Now aides were aware of documents showing that the national security adviser, the deputy national security adviser, and the chief speechwriter had ignored clear warnings from the CIA.

The White House's position—dump-it-on-the-CIA—was no longer defendable. Hadley told his colleagues that he had simply forgotten about the memos. He offered to resign, but the president refused to accept the offer, according to two NSC officials. And White House aides decided that there would have to be another press briefing—so Hadley could come clean. It had to happen right away. Otherwise, the Bush aides figured, the CIA would leak these memos. As Bartlett and other communications staffers assembled in McClellan's office that morning to plan their press strategy, Hadley offered up a piece of *Godfather* humor. "We're here to make peace between the families," he said, according to Levine. He was referring to the White House and the CIA.

Hadley's briefing in the Roosevelt Room that day was painful for White House aides. He reported that the memos the CIA had sent him indicated that the CIA had told Congress it had "concerns" pertaining to the British intelligence on the Niger charge. (He didn't disclose that the memos said that the British had "exaggerated.") He acknowledged he should have remembered the memos and had the sentence removed from the State of the Union speech. "It is now clear to me that I failed," he said. Rice, he added, was also willing to take "personal responsibility" for the foul-up.

White House aides viewed this episode as a victory for the CIA in the postinvasion spin battle between Langley and 1600 Pennsylvania Avenue. "We should never have gotten into a knife fight with the CIA," John Gibson, the White House speechwriter, recalled saying to Gerson about this time. "Making Tenet say that statement [accepting fault for the sixteen words] was like opening up a hornet's nest. [The CIA's] job is to screw you." Gerson, according to Gibson, was thinking along similar lines. "Why can't we," he asked Gibson, "get the CIA to stop regarding the White House like a foreign government?"

INSIDE the CIA, there was anger at the White House, and the Valerie Wilson leak had intensified it. It was unclear what actual damage—if any—had been caused by the leak. Still, the idea that her identity would be exposed in the course of a political tussle rankled the rank and file. Valerie Wilson was not a widely known officer. She was one of the thousands of midlevel employees at the agency. "I asked Tenet if he knew who she was," a senior CIA official later recalled, "and he said no." But some CIA employees who had nothing to do with Valerie Wilson and her work were infuriated. "It was a matter of principle," Mike Sulick, the deputy chief of the operations directorate, said. "For somebody at the White House to be outing somebody at the agency like this—it's like giving away the name of a platoon leader in wartime. And especially coming from an administration that waves the flag and supports the troops—well, we're part of the troops."

It wasn't just troops who were upset. "George and myself and McLaughlin and [James] Pavitt [the DO chief]—everybody was pissed," said Buzzy Krongard, the agency's executive director. For all the bad blood between the White House and Langley, some senior agency officials were reluctant to believe the leak had been the product of a White House plot. But Krongard, who knew Valerie Wilson slightly, was the only senior agency official to reach out to her. He called her on the phone and said, "This is outrageous. Whatever I can do to help, let me know. The whole building is with you on this."

Wilson thanked him. But she was not so sure the rest of the agency brass was with her.

In assessing the impact of the leak, CIA officials were concerned mostly about the people Wilson had recruited over the years and the informants she had worked with, even while working on the Iraqi WMD issue. "We were more worried about her sources," said Krongard. There was also the possible exposure of Brewster-Jennings & Associates, the front company that the CIA had used to provide paper cover (as opposed to operational cover) to Wilson and other CIA operatives for tax records, insurance purposes, and other paperwork matters. (When Valerie Wilson made a contribution to Al Gore's presidential campaign in 1999, she listed her employer as "Brewster-Jennings & Associates" and her occupation as "analyst"—as Novak first revealed in early October 2003.) This firm, according to business records, had a Boston address, but there was no Brewster-Jennings office at that address.

Valerie Wilson remained worried by the disclosure. She submitted to her superiors her own assessment of the damage that could be caused by the leak. Meanwhile, she continued with her transition to the new administration job, realizing her chances of ever returning to operations were shot.

Tenet said nothing about the leak publicly. And he didn't immediately push for an investigation. "I had to remind [Pavitt] that he ought to make a referral to Justice," a senior CIA official later said. And the CIA's lawyers got on the job. On July 24, a CIA attorney left a phone message for the chief of the Justice Department's counterespionage section. It was a heads-up: The agency was reviewing the Novak column. Six days later, the CIA counsel's office sent a letter to the Justice Department's criminal division notifying it that a possible violation of criminal law had occurred. The CIA informed the division that its own Office of Security was examining the leak.

This was all standard operating procedure for leak cases. First, the CIA investigated; then, if its lawyers believed a law might have been broken, the agency requested an FBI investigation. The Justice Department even had a form—the "DOJ Media Leak Questionnaire"—that an agency had to fill out when it wanted the FBI to investigate a national security leak. There were eleven questions on the form. One asked, "What specific statements in the article are classified and was the information properly classified?" Another asked, "What effect the disclosure of the classified data might have on the national defense?" And the form requested that the agency affirm that the exposed information was truly a secret. No investigation would proceed unless the CIA indicated that Valerie Wilson's employment at the CIA had been classified information.

The Plame leak hadn't sparked much of a public controversy, but CIA lawyers were moving along methodically. The filing of a criminal leak report was not that unusual. The agency submitted about one a week, and about "99 percent of them go nowhere," as one agency official put it. But this was one Washington leak that wouldn't go away.

*I'm not sure I've spoken to anyone at that level who
seemed less inquisitive.*

—DAVID KAY, CHIEF WMD HUNTER

16

The Incurious President

IT WAS the middle of the night in Baghdad. There was a pounding on the door. David Kay got out of bed. A staff officer of the Iraq Survey Group was at the door. He had an important message for the man who had been sent to Iraq to find Saddam's weapons of mass destruction: the vice president's office had called.

Kay looked at the message. Cheney's office had a burning question for him: Had he seen a particular signals intercept? It was a highly sensitive communications intercept that had captured a snippet of conversation between two unidentified people. Cheney's aides were reading raw transcripts straight from the National Security Agency. And a Cheney staffer who had gotten hold of this piece of unanalyzed intelligence thought that it contained a reference to a WMD storage site in Iraq, even though the captured exchange didn't specifically mention weapons. What made this intercept most promising was that it had come with geographic coordinates for one of the unidentified persons. Here was a road map—finally—to Saddam's WMDs. Kay ordered his analysts to review the coordinates and went back to bed.

The next morning, his analysts checked the coordinates and discovered they referred to a site in the Bekka Valley in Lebanon—not anywhere in Iraq. This was no lead. It was nothing. But as Kay was overseeing the search for weapons in the summer months of 2003, the vice president's office urgently wanted him to come up with evidence that Saddam had maintained arsenals of weapons of mass destruction—so much so that, just as Cheney and Libby had done before the war, the vice president's aides were rummaging through top secret, unprocessed intelligence in the hope of discovering what everyone else in the U.S. government had missed. "They were reaching down and reading raw intelligence and putting their own meaning on it," said a CIA official familiar with the incident.

With the administration—and Cheney—facing increasing challenges to their prewar arguments for invasion, Kay and his Iraq Survey Group were their best hope. Nothing would trump the fuss over the sixteen words, the NIE, and the Plame leak better than a discovery of real weapons or undeniable evidence Saddam had been trying to build a nuclear bomb. But Kay, who had favored the war and who had come to Iraq believing Saddam had possessed stockpiles of chemical and biological weapons, would end up sinking, not supporting, the administration's case.

THE signals intercept was not the only intelligence tip Cheney's office urgently passed on to Kay. On another occasion, the vice president's aides sent a message to Kay and the ISG: check out this overhead photograph. It showed what looked like the opening of a tunnel on the side of a hill in Iraq. This could be where the WMDs were hidden, Cheney's office said—in caves.

When Kay and several of his analysts took a look at the photo, they burst out laughing. They knew exactly what was in the picture. It was a common practice for local farmers to use bulldozers to dig trenches into the sides of hills. Because the water table was fairly high, these trenches would fill with water and become sources of drinking water for cows. The vice president's staff hadn't discovered the elusive WMDs; it had found a bovine watering hole. "Anyone who has spent any time on the ground in Iraq immediately would recognize these as cuts that the local population made to get to ground water for their animals," Kay said later. "We reported back that we had looked at it and it was not what you thought it was. There was no point humiliating them."

Deputy Defense Secretary Paul Wolfowitz was also watching the work of the Iraq Survey Group closely, and there was a particular topic he thought deserved Kay's attention: Mohamed Atta and his alleged visit to Prague. As part of its mission, the ISG was poring over millions of documents—seven and a half miles of them. The papers, rounded up and kept in a secured facility, were being scanned into a computer database. Trying to find WMD clues in this massive amount of paper was a daunting task. (And the ISG was constantly being approached by Iraqis peddling documents on weapons—which were usually worthless or forged.) But Wolfowitz wanted Kay's WMD pursuers to look for one more thing in this monster haystack: evidence that would prove that the lead 9/11 hijacker had met with an Iraqi intelligence officer in the Czech capital five months prior to September 11. Several times Major General Keith Dayton, the military commander of the Iraq Survey Group, conveyed Wolfowitz's request to Kay. "Oh, shit," Kay said to himself, "why waste time on this?" But, he thought, it's Laurie Mylroie.

Wolfowitz's request, as Kay later put it, "bore no relationship to my mission," but he passed it along to his document exploitation crew. Don't pull anyone off the WMD beat, he told the team, but if you see anything on Atta, grab it. No records connecting Atta to Iraqi intelligence surfaced. The ISG documents examiners did find plenty of papers linking Iraqi intelligence to various terrorist groups, mostly anti-Israel and anti-Iran outfits. But nothing came up regarding operational ties to al-Qaeda.

KAY had been running the ISG's search since mid-June, working out of the Water Palace outside Baghdad. The group employed about 1,300 people, including only a couple dozen weapons experts to do the serious analysis. The game plan was not look here, look there, and hope to unearth a massive cache of deadly armaments. The mission was a human intelligence job. Kay calculated that Saddam's weapons programs had employed about 10,000 people. Get some of those Iraqis to talk, and the puzzle would be solved. He even had a slush fund of $10 million to pay informants.

Kay was starting from scratch. When he got to Baghdad, he asked for the reports of the 75th Exploitation Task Force, which had overseen the work of the two MET teams that had originally been assigned to the weapons search. But he was told there were no available records. The 75th had left nothing behind. He couldn't find out which sites had been previously inspected or which Iraqis had been interrogated. He was also dismayed that the U.S. Army had done little to secure Iraqi ammunition sites. "The military just blew this off," Kay said.

Still, Kay was optimistic, at least when he talked publicly about the weapons hunt. During an interview with NBC News' Tom Brokaw, who was in Baghdad in the middle of July, Kay proclaimed himself confident that he would uncover evidence of WMDs.* "We're finding progress reports [on WMDs]," he said to the anchor. And he added, "I've already seen enough to convince me, but that's not the standard. I've got to have enough to convince everyone of that." He said he expected to have "a substantial body of evidence" within six months.

But in his private communications to the CIA, Kay was conveying a different message. Each week, he sent e-mail updates to George Tenet and John McLaughlin. And by the end of July, Kay was telling both that his Iraq Survey Group was more likely to uncover evidence of a production surge capacity—that is, programs that could quickly manufacture a limited amount of chemical or biological weapons once there was an order to do so—but not actual stockpiles of unconventional weapons. As Kay and the ISG examined the leading elements of the prewar WMD case—the aluminum tubes, the mobile biological weapons labs, the chemical weapons depots—they were coming up empty.

The tubes were the first to go. The high-strength aluminum tubes had been central to the charge that Iraq was reconstituting its nuclear program, the one hard piece of evidence to support White House speechwriter Michael Gerson's "smoking gun in the form of a mushroom cloud" metaphor. From Cheney on *Meet the Press* to Powell before the UN Security Council, the administration's top officials had argued that the Iraqis were acquiring tubes that could be used for nuclear centrifuges. The International Atomic Energy Agency had concluded before the war that the tubes had been intended for rocket production and not centrifuges. And when Iraq Survey Group members arrived at the Nasr munitions plant, where the Iraqis manufactured their 81 mm artillery rockets, they found endless rows of the tubes. In plain sight, David Kay's weapons hunters could see the

---

*Brokaw had been at the Idaho conference with Tenet and had pressed the CIA director to let him interview Kay, who at this time wasn't talking to the media. Tenet said, sure. And CIA spokesman Bill Harlow called Kay and told him Tenet wanted him to grant Brokaw an interview.

proof for themselves. (The plant was later looted, and the ransacked tubes showed up on the streets, sold for drainpipes.)

Kay's team still had questions. Why had the Iraqis needed such high-strength tubes for rockets? ISG investigators questioned the Iraqi plant managers. They also interrogated the senior official who had overseen Saddam's military industrial commission. All the Iraqis told a consistent story: the rockets had been falling short. The problem was the propellant. But changing the propellant—the obvious solution—wasn't an option. The propellant was produced at a facility run by a friend of one of Saddam's sons. So to avoid interfering with the flow of business to a regime crony, the engineers devised a Rube Goldberg solution: lower the mass of the rockets and use tubes that had a higher strength than otherwise necessary. That was why the Iraqis had been using the Internet to procure tubes with unusually precise specifications. (The whole thing reminded Kay of some of the Pentagon's own procurement messes.) "We had this down," Kay later said. "The system was corrupt."

Before long, Kay reached a harsh but firm conclusion about one of the fundamental selling points in the White House case for war. "The tubes issue," he said, "was an absolute fraud."

Nor did the Iraq Survey Group uncover any other evidence of an active nuclear program. Team members inspected the enormous Taiwatha nuclear facility outside Baghdad and other nuclear sites. They found a decayed infrastructure, aging machine tools, and other equipment that hadn't been used for years. They interviewed Iraq's former nuclear scientists, all of whom described a nuclear program that had been dormant since after the first Persian Gulf War. They examined records trying to find any trace of signs that Iraq had been seeking uranium abroad. Once again, there was nothing. (And with no active nuclear weapons program, Iraq had had no need for hundreds of tons of yellowcake.)

The mobile biological weapons trailers weren't panning out, either. A team of Pentagon examiners and INR analysts had already disputed the CIA's finding that these trucks had been built to cook up anthrax and other biological agents. But the ISG's guiding principle was that it should do its own work and not react to previous conclusions. And it didn't take long for Kay's experts to determine that these trailers were not what the CIA—and the president—had claimed they were.

In mid-July, Hamish Killip, a veteran British weapons inspector who specialized in chemical and biological weapons, arrived in Baghdad to join Kay's team. On the way from the airport to ISG headquarters, he rode past the military camp where the trailers were being stored. He told his driver to pull over and left the car to eyeball the notorious trailers. Right away he had his doubts. The trailers were, he later said, "not a proper piece of work." They had been poorly assembled; the welding was substandard, the materials were inferior. There was no way, he thought, that they could have been used for microbiological work. "You'd have better luck putting a couple of dustbins on the back of a truck and brewing it in there," he later said.

Much of the case for the trailers had rested on the credibility of Curveball, the Iraqi defector whose account (fed through German intelligence) had been a key part of Powell's presentation to the Security Council. In May, the CIA had concluded that the trailers were biolabs because they appeared to resemble what Curveball had described before the war. If they did, it was coincidence. When Kay's investigators dug deep into Curveball's background and unearthed new information about this all-important defector, nothing in his story withstood scrutiny.

"Relatively quickly, we realized there were real problems with Curveball," Kay remembered. Kay's investigators obtained his real name from sources in British intelligence; the Germans had refused to provide it to the CIA. Then they pulled his personnel file from an Iraqi government storeroom. Curveball had claimed to be at the top of his engineering class. The ISG found that he had actually finished at the bottom. He had claimed to have been a project chief or site manager for the Chemical & Engineering Design Center, a division of the Iraqi Military Industrial Commission. Yet the records showed he had been only a low-level trainee. The file also showed Curveball had been fired from his job in 1995—two years before he claimed to have been working on building one of the biolabs, three years before he claimed to have witnessed a horrific accident involving biological weapons. After being dismissed from his job, he had ended up driving a Baghdad taxi. When the investigators interviewed his former bosses and coworkers, they all denied working on any biolabs—and dismissed Curveball's accounts as ludicrous. Some of his old friends described him as a "great liar" and "con artist." A CIA investigator working with the Iraq Survey Group said, "People kept saying what a 'rat' Curveball was." And an ISG team member later told the Los Angeles Times, "They were saying, 'This guy? You've got to be kidding.'"

Kay's investigators even tracked down Curveball's family in a middle-class Baghdad neighborhood. The Germans had consistently told the CIA that Curveball couldn't speak English and hated Americans; that was supposedly the reason the CIA couldn't talk to him. But when Kay's investigators asked Curveball's mother about this, they got a puzzled response. "No, no!" she said. "He loves Americans!" Curveball's parents took Kay's team into Curveball's old room. It was full of posters of American pop stars. "They said he always wanted to go to the United States and that he spoke English," Kay said.

Not everything was settled for the ISG. There were plenty of documents to review. Clearly, Iraq had been working on prohibited missiles. (According to Kay, former Iraqi Deputy Prime Minister Tariq Aziz told U.S. interrogators "that Saddam had said to him as long as we don't put WMDs on the end of a missile it was all right to have these missiles. Aziz said he had tried to tell Saddam that was not right.") And the ISG kept finding small laboratories in houses tucked into buildings—many of which had been ransacked, making it difficult to determine what they had been used for. Kay's specialists theorized the labs might have developed poisons to be used by Iraqi intelligence services for political assassination.

The Iraq Survey Group had no luck locating the chemical weapons arsenals Bush and others had said Saddam possessed. "We had a number of people who purported to know where CW was buried," Kay recalled. "We checked them all out, but nothing. We combed the records." And Kay found nothing to support the administration's claims that the unmanned drones—the UAVs—were being produced to carry chemical and biological payloads. Kay's investigators closely inspected the drones. "We knew the range, navigation, and payload capability," Kay said. "There was no way this was a threat to anyone."

IN WASHINGTON, Robert Joseph, the hard-line National Security Council official for proliferation issues (who had approved the sixteen words), was unconcerned about the absence of unconventional weapons in Iraq. Joseph, who had relentlessly pushed the WMD case before the war, was—on almost a daily basis—waving off the worries of his colleagues, many of whom had become quite nervous, one NSC staffer recalled. The weapons were about to turn up, Joseph assured them. "It's just a matter of time," he said on a number of occasions, recalled the NSC staffer. "We're going to find them any day now." Joseph had placed much stock in the trailers. This was the proof that the White House had been right all along, he argued. When Iraqi scientists were quoted as saying the trailers had been used to produce hydrogen for weather balloons, Joseph, with much sarcasm, dismissed the claim. "Yeah, right, give me a break," Joseph said, according to the colleague. This was, as Joseph saw it, just another Iraqi lie.

When Kay came back to Washington to brief the Senate intelligence and armed services committees in late July, he brought small comfort for Joseph and other White House true believers. On the afternoon of July 28, Tenet told Kay he should sit in on the CIA's daily morning briefing of the president the next day. But when Kay walked into the Oval Office that morning, Bush greeted him and said he was looking forward to *his* briefing. "No one told me that I was doing the briefing," Kay later recalled.

In the room with Bush were Cheney, Rumsfeld, Wolfowitz, Tenet, Rice, Card, and other aides. Kay tried to be gentle. He emphasized that the WMD hunt was still a work in progress. Answers weren't likely to be derived quickly due to various impediments: the looting, the difficulty in locating Iraqi scientists, the poor security situation. He mentioned his theory that Iraq might have had a surge production capacity for chemical weapons. But he couldn't avoid the bottom line: He had found nothing. As for the trailers, he said they were probably not bioweapons labs, as the CIA had claimed.

Kay discerned no disappointment coming from Bush. The White House had just been rocked by the controversy over the State of the Union claims and the Wilson op-ed. But the president seemed disengaged. "I'm not sure I've spoken to anyone at that level who seemed less inquisitive," Kay recalled. "He was interested but not posing any pressing questions." Bush didn't ask, Are you sure? He didn't ask about the prospects of finding actual weapons. Or whether WMDs had been hidden or spirited away. Instead, he asked, Kay, what do you need?

Patience, replied Kay. He had been on the job only five or so weeks.

I have a world of patience, Bush replied.

None of the other Bush officials grilled Kay. He was surprised by that, too. Rumsfeld, known for being rough on briefers, had mostly been quiet. "They were all deferential to Bush," Kay later said.

After leaving the meeting, Kay was perplexed and perturbed. "I cannot stress too much," he subsequently remarked, "that the president was the one in the room who was the least unhappy and the least disappointed about the lack of WMDs. I came out of the Oval Office uncertain as to how to read the president. Here was an individual who was oblivious to the problems created by the failure to find the WMDs. Or was this an individual who was completely at peace with himself on the decision to go to war, who didn't question that, and who was totally focused on the here and now and what was to come?"

Kay later met with Cheney and Libby in the vice president's office, and this session was quite different from Kay's presentation in the Oval Office. Cheney, who did most of the questioning, drilled down. He asked if Kay was relying on intelligence from the CIA or if he was finding his own facts. It was clear to Kay that Cheney was worried about the credibility of any intelligence coming out of Langley. Kay assured him that he was digging up his own information.

Cheney was very specific with Kay. He wondered if Kay had seen the intelligence—signals intercepts and satellite imagery—indicating there had been prewar movement of Iraqi trucks and aircraft across the Syrian border. He asked how Kay intended to deal with the possibility that Saddam's WMDs might have been ferried to Syria. (Kay was looking into whether any biological or chemical weapons had been produced in the years before the war. If there had been no weapons, there couldn't have been an effort to move or hide them.) Cheney even knew that Kay had been negotiating with arms dealers in Damascus, who were offering to sell the Iraq Survey Group documents on Iraq's prewar armaments deals.

"This was a vice president who was well read in the intelligence and knew the details of the WMD issue," Kay recalled. He felt no pressure from Cheney to skew his appraisal. But Kay did see a problem in Cheney's analytical view: "He kept remembering little facts that he thought proved big conclusions. The problem with intelligence is that little facts often don't prove anything, let alone something big. They're just pieces of puzzles—sometimes just pieces that don't even make a puzzle."

Two days after he briefed Bush, Kay spoke briefly with reporters in a Senate hallway and was more upbeat about the ISG's prospects than he had been with the president. "We are making solid progress," he said. The Iraq Survey Group had found "some physical evidence" related to Iraq's WMDs, he said, but he was not ready yet to talk about it. "It's very likely," he added, "that we will discover remarkable surprises in this enterprise."

WHEN Kay went back to Iraq in August, he soon found that even his "surge capacity" theory for chemical weapons didn't hold up. The ISG could find no trace of such a program. In his frank, weekly e-mail report, Kay informed Tenet and McLaughlin of his conclusions, which were becoming more solid by the week. But Tenet wasn't eager to discuss these matters with him. During his first month at the ISG, Kay had usually heard from Tenet after he sent in his weekly report. But now only McLaughlin was responding. Tenet was even skipping the weekly interagency videoconferences on the ISG's work. "Increasingly, there was no reply from George," Kay remembered. "Only John. George has a tendency not to want to hear bad news. He drew back and left John to carry the can. My suspicions were trouble for the system." And McLaughlin was not yet willing to absorb the bad news. In September, Kay met with McLaughlin and presented what his ISG had found on the tubes and the mobile weapons labs. McLaughlin, Kay recalled, wouldn't accept the findings.

"John and George had believed the WMDs were there," Kay later said. "I think they understood how weak the available evidence was. They understood the holes. McLaughlin was too good an analyst not to have seen the weaknesses. But the evidence didn't matter because the weapons would be found. They were confident the WMDs would be there. But these are the people whose antennae should've gone up." Now their antennae were withdrawn. Kay believed Tenet and McLaughlin were in denial. "I became," he noted, "the turd on the table."

THE lack of WMDs was but one worry for the Bush administration—and perhaps no longer the most pressing. As the summer of 2003 ended, it was becoming evident that the war wouldn't be over anytime soon. In early July, a testy Donald Rumsfeld had declared that there was no "guerrilla war" in Iraq. Yet chaos and conflict were spreading, as the insurgents—former Baathists, foreign jihadists, Sunni partisans, and Iraqis who just wanted Americans out of their country—adopted deadlier and more sophisticated tactics. In early August, a car bomb exploded outside the Jordanian Embassy in Baghdad, killing at least eleven people and sparking fears that guerrilla fighters were turning toward so-called soft targets. In the middle of the month, saboteurs blew up an oil pipeline in the north. On August 19, a truck bomb blew up the UN headquarters in Baghdad, killing twenty, including UN envoy Sergio Vieira de Mello. Afterward, humanitarian aid agencies began evacuating workers. Then a car bombing in Najaf killed more than a hundred people. Daily attacks were on the rise—and Iraqis' complaints about the lack of electricity, the absence of security, the slow pace of reconstruction, and rampant crime were becoming louder.

In the United States, commentators and politicians debated whether Bush had sent a sufficient number of troops to Iraq and whether it had been wise to disband the Iraqi Army. Bush aides repeatedly insisted that progress was being made. "We must remain patient," Rice said to the annual convention of Veterans of Foreign Wars. Rumsfeld downplayed the threat posed by the enemy, telling the same group, "The resistance our coalition faces today may appear more significant than otherwise might have been the case." He claimed no additional U.S. troops were needed in Iraq. Speaking to the American Legion national convention, Bush claimed that "there's steady progress toward reconstruction and civil order."

With the president's approval numbers slipping, Bush and his aides in early September—at the time of the second anniversary of 9/11—decided he should address the nation in prime time. He had spent the eight months before the invasion selling the war. Now, nearly half a year since launching it, Bush and his aides were finding they had to keep defending the policy. Speaking from the Cabinet Room, with a bust of George Washington behind him, Bush tied the war in Iraq to the post-9/11 effort to roll back "the terrorist threat . . . at the heart of its power." He depicted the Iraqi resistance as being a problem in only one area of the country. He announced he would submit a budget request for $87 billion to cover the costs of operations in Iraq and Afghanistan. He vowed not to be chased out of Iraq by "the terrorists." He said little about weapons of mass destruction.

Cheney was also unyielding.

On September 14, he appeared on *Meet the Press,* and host Tim Russert grilled him on the administration's prewar arguments. Cheney once again talked about links between Saddam's regime and bin Laden, claiming that Iraq's support for al-Qaeda was "clearly official policy." He once more cited the Czech report about Mohamed Attta in Prague as though it were still credible. He ignored the dispute over mobile bioweapons labs and insisted without equivocation that the U.S. government had found "two of them"—even though David Kay had told him that was not true.

Asked about Joe Wilson, Cheney gave no hint that he had spent June and July gathering information about the former ambassador to discredit Wilson's story. "I don't know Joe Wilson. I've never met Joe Wilson," he told Russert. "I have no idea who hired him."

Russert asked, If CIA analysts were to be proven wrong, "shouldn't we have a wholesale investigation into the intelligence failure . . ."

"What failure?" Cheney interjected.

"That Saddam had biological, chemical, and is developing a nuclear program," Russert replied.

"My guess is in the end they'll be proven right, Tim."

BUSH was now trying to build support for the war by portraying it as a struggle against terrorists: Saddam holdouts (not willing to give up power and allow a democracy to take root in Iraq) and al-Qaeda wannabes (looking to fight America wherever they could). But government experts were wrangling over whether it was that simple.

Earlier in the summer, U.S. Central Command had asked the intelligence community for a National Intelligence Estimate on the sources of violence and instability in Iraq. The request had triggered a fierce interagency battle that would continue for months. "The essential question," Wayne White, the Iraq specialist at the State Department's INR, later said, "was, who the hell is shooting at us and why?" White became involved in this project near the beginning of August, and the first draft he saw of the NIE was, in his view, "terribly one-dimensional." The anti-American fighters were dismissed as mainly former regime elements. But White believed that the insurgency was being stoked by various factors beyond the desire of former Baathists to regain power. The infrastructure was destroyed, the electricity was often off, and many Iraqis had lost jobs, had property destroyed, and had relatives killed or arrested. The country was being occupied. All of this was creating anger and resentment that was fueling the insurgents. White coined a term for the phenomenon: Pissed-Off Iraqis.

The draft NIE didn't regard the insurgency as sufficiently serious or likely to continue growing, and it contained no clear statement that the situation in Iraq would probably worsen. "Administration officials and many intelligence professionals—did not grasp," White recalled, "the depth of the political, economic, religious, ethnosectarian, and psychological well from which the insurgency was drawing much of its increasing strength." He assumed that the insurgency was not going to wind down slowly.

White took his concerns to a meeting at a CIA conference room. Analysts from various agencies—twenty or so people—sat around the table. When he voiced his reservations about the NIE draft, a vigorous debate followed. Other analysts were less worried that the insurgency would expand. White tried, as he later recounted, "to drive home the sheer magnitude of the insurgency's recruiting and support base in Iraq's Sunni Arab heartland." The national intelligence officer in charge of the estimate, according to White, was surprised by his negative take, and he didn't seem anxious to carry this message to government higher-ups. White wouldn't back down. "We got some of the changes we wanted into the draft," White recalled, "which weren't enough." At the end of the meeting, a CIA representative said she would have to see if her agency would support the downbeat revisions.

More meetings would be held regarding this NIE, and the interagency debate would continue. It was as if the government's top experts on Iraq were reflecting the views of the leaders of the administration by not coming fully to terms with the profound challenge Bush's invasion had created. But intelligence community analysts would eventually agree with White's pessimistic assessment and accept it as their official position in a formal NIE. Top administration officials, however, remained unrestrained in supplying upbeat assessments. "The level of resistance continues out there, obviously," Cheney said in mid-September, "but I think we're making major progress against it. . . . The fact is that most of Iraq today is relatively stable and quiet." Rumsfeld noted that the U.S. military was engaged in "a relatively small number of incidents per day . . . that last a relatively few minutes." U.S. forces, he claimed, were training 70,000 Iraqi troops, who would soon take over security in Iraq. "The goal," he said, "is to not spend a long time in Iraq. . . . It is moving at a very rapid pace."*

---

*In September, Rumsfeld spoke at a National Press Club luncheon, where he was asked to explain his March 30 assertion that "we know where [the WMDS] are." He replied, "Sometimes I overstate for emphasis."

IN THE weeks after the Novak column, the CIA/Plame leak received little media coverage, and the Niger controversy faded from the news. Joe Wilson, though, was still talking about it. On August 21, at a town meeting in Seattle convened by Democratic Representative Jay Inslee, Wilson said that he was hoping for an investigation of the CIA leak because "wouldn't it be fun to see Karl Rove frog-marched out of the White House in handcuffs?"

Whether Wilson knew it or not, CIA lawyers were quietly working on the case. On September 5, the agency, possibly as a reminder, faxed to the Justice Department's criminal division the letter it had sent five weeks earlier noting that a crime might have occurred. Then on September 16, the CIA provided the Justice Department with a memo outlining the results of its inquiry and requested that the FBI open a criminal investigation of the Plame leak. The CIA was asking the FBI to start an inquiry that would target the White House.

The CIA and the Justice Department managed to keep the referral under wraps for only ten days.

17

The Investigation Begins

O N THE evening of September 26, 2003, White House press aide
Adam Levine was having drinks in Georgetown with colleagues when
an urgent message popped up on his BlackBerry. MSNBC had posted a
story on its Web site reporting that the CIA had asked the Justice Department to investigate the Plame leak. The story had a grabber of a headline:
"CIA Seeks Probe of White House." The news confirmed that Valerie Wilson had been an undercover officer; otherwise the agency wouldn't have had
grounds to request an inquiry. And for the administration, the implication
was ominous: if somebody at the White House had disclosed her name, that
person could be in criminal jeopardy.

Levine shared the news with the rest of his party. One of them looked
anxious. "I got to go," said Mike Allen, a *Washington Post* White House correspondent. "I got to follow up on this." He dashed off.

The next morning, there was nothing in the *Post* or any of the other
major papers about the criminal referral. Levine was surprised, but he soon
saw that Allen was working the story hard. Throughout the day, the *Post* reporter sent him e-mails and called repeatedly. He told Levine that the *Post*
had learned that White House officials had called several reporters about
Plame. Allen didn't know who had made the calls. But he mentioned that

Rove had been involved. He wanted to talk to White House press secretary Scott McClellan, who so far hadn't returned his call.

That afternoon, about 3:00, National Security Adviser Condoleezza Rice wandered by Levine's office. She was looking to discuss her upcoming appearances on *Meet the Press* and *Fox News Sunday*—what she was likely to be asked and how she should respond. McClellan came by and joined them. As they went over what was in the news, Levine shared what he had learned from Allen—that the *Post* had evidence White House aides had called reporters about Joe Wilson's wife. If so, White House officials would be the prime targets of the Justice Department's criminal investigation. Let's "knock it down," McClellan proposed.

Levine disagreed. Allen was saying that a bunch of reporters had been called. How could McClellan, Rice, and he be certain that Tim Russert hadn't been one of them? If Rice were to deny the story on *Meet the Press* and Russert were to say he had received such a call, it would be devastating. Levine suggested that Rice rely upon a traditional dodge, saying that she could not comment on a criminal investigation. Rice said she was inclined to take this advice, but McClellan favored going on the offensive. Later in the day, McClellan told Levine that he had spoken to Rove and Rove had assured him he had had nothing to do with the CIA leak. McClellan wanted to push back hard and say that the White House's top aides had played no role in the disclosure.

That assertion wasn't true. Still, it would soon become the White House's official line. For months, the administration had been contending with the charge that it had launched an increasingly unpopular war after misrepresenting the threat from Saddam Hussein. But the dispute over Iraq intelligence had so far been a policy and political debate. The leak matter was different; the White House would now have to deal with an FBI investigation, subpoenas, and grand jury appearances, all of which could lead to indictments. Faced with a criminal investigation, the White House was about to mount a public defense based on unequivocal denials. In classic Washington fashion, the cover-up would soon become the suspected crime.

The Sunday *Post* made the leak story even hotter. Mike Allen's piece, with a double byline that included Dana Priest, repeated the news that the CIA had asked for a criminal investigation. But the article advanced the story, or seemed to:

> Yesterday, a senior administration official said that before Novak's column ran, two top White House officials called at least six Washington journalists and disclosed the identity and occupation of Wilson's wife . . . "Clearly, it was meant purely and simply for revenge," the senior official said of the alleged leak.

This made it sound as though the CIA leak in Novak's column had been the product of a vengeful and coordinated White House campaign to punish Joe Wilson for criticizing the White House. It now also looked as if Novak hadn't been the only recipient of the leak and, perhaps most surprising, that a senior official in the tight-lipped Bush White House was ratting out two of his fellow aides. Immediately Washington had a new—and serious— guessing game: Who were the two top Bush aides? (Didn't one of them have to be Rove?) Who were the six (or more) Washington reporters? Who was the *Post's* Deep Throat–like source?

When Levine read the story, it occurred to him that he had talked to Allen a number of times the previous day. Allen had mentioned that he knew about reporters getting phone calls. And Levine certainly knew that Rove and Libby had been targeting Joseph Wilson. He had confirmed some of the information Allen had told him. But he later said that he had never used the word "revenge." Still, he wondered: Was he the unnamed senior administration official who was the *Post's* secret source for this explosive allegation?

Levine also wondered about something else. The same *Post* front page had a piece by Priest disclosing that the House intelligence committee had sent a blistering letter to Tenet regarding prewar intelligence. After staffers had combed through nineteen volumes of classified material, the committee's Republican chairman, Representative Porter Goss, and its senior Democrat, Representative Jane Harman, were accusing the intelligence community of having relied on outdated, "circumstantial," and "fragmentary information" containing "too many uncertainties" in concluding that Iraq had possessed WMDs. They also stated that the CIA had a "responsibility" to correct public officials if they "mischaracterized the available intelligence." It was a clear warning: the House panel planned to hold Tenet and the CIA responsible for what was starting to look like a colossal intelligence failure—and for standing by while the White House had misrepresented the evidence.

Could it be, Levine thought, that a stung CIA was looking to divert attention from the House intelligence committee's letter by leaking the CIA referral and pointing the finger at the White House? It was only a theory. But in Washington these days—with the news out of Iraq relentlessly dismal—it didn't seem far-fetched that the CIA's press savvy spinners would do whatever they could to protect the agency and place the White House in the crosshairs.

The *Post* story on the CIA leak was consequential. With its assertion that there had been an orchestrated White House plot, the article would give administration critics (and even neutral parties) cause to call for an independent counsel to handle the leak investigation. But this pivotal article (written mostly by Allen, not Priest) was partially off the mark—due to a slight wording change in a crucial sentence.

In the paper's early edition, the words "before Novak's column ran" were not in the sentence noting that "two top White House officials called at least six Washington journalists." An editor on the *Post* national desk inserted that phrase to sharpen the copy and clarify what the editor took to be Allen's understanding of events. But the addition of those four words—"before Novak's column ran"—made a huge difference. If White House officials had called reporters about Valerie Wilson *after* the Novak column, they would have been playing a rather bruising (and arguably unethical) game of hardball: amplifying a leak of classified information and spreading information about the wife of a critic. Still, it would have been no crime to talk to a journalist about what had already been published in a newspaper column. But if Bush aides had placed the calls *before* the Novak column, they would have been divulging classified information—and perhaps violating the Intelligence Identities Protection Act.

The truth was somewhere in the middle. Armitage had been Novak's original source. But two White House officials, Rove and Libby, had spoken to at least three reporters—Novak, Judy Miller, and Matt Cooper—about Valerie Wilson before the Novak column came out. The reporters, though, had contacted them, not the other way around. After the Novak column appeared, Rove had called Matthews and angrily told the talk-show host that Valerie Wilson was "fair game." NBC News' Andrea Mitchell had reported that she had heard talk of Wilson's wife from "White House sources"—after the Novak column. The White House's anti-Wilson campaign had been less organized than depicted by the explosive *Post* story, and much (but not all) of it had occurred after the Novak column was published. Mike Allen's source had supplied him a slice of the story—with some significant details wrong.*

ON THE Sunday morning that the *Post* story appeared, the accuracy of Allen's disclosure wasn't the issue. On *Fox News Sunday,* the first questions Condoleezza Rice faced concerned Goss and Harman's tough letter to Tenet. "Did you have fresh intelligence about weapons of mass destruction in Iraq before the war began?" host Tony Snow asked. Rice replied, "Well, the president believes that he had very good intelligence going into the war and stands behind what the director of central intelligence told him going into the war." She added, "Every day David Kay says he's getting better information." Rice also noted that there was "progress being made every day" in Iraq and that life was "getting back to normal."

Then came questions about the leak investigation and White House involvement. "I'm not going to go into this," she said. On *Meet the Press,* she did the same, telling Russert, "The Justice Department will now take appropriate action, whatever that is."

ON MONDAY, the Plame leak was the news consuming Washington. Democrats were demanding a special counsel. How could John Ashcroft's Justice

---

*A day later, the paper ran another Mike Allen story referring to his source for the phone calls as an "administration aide"—not a "senior administration official" (as Allen had described him in the original story). Allen's source had been quietly downgraded. In an October 8, 2003, article on *Newsweek*'s Web site, reporters Michael Isikoff and Mark Hosenball first raised the question of the accuracy of the *Post* story. "Some government officials now believe," they reported, that "most, if not all, of these phone calls were made after the Novak column appeared." Within the *Post,* there was concern about the first article and discussions about whether any correction was warranted, according to *Post* sources. But no action was taken. The editors and reporters involved, one *Post* correspondent subsequently said, "had no real desire to let people know we fucked this up." A year later, the *Post* ran a piece by reporter Susan Schmidt noting that government investigators had been trying to confirm the allegation in Allen's story but had failed to do so. *Post* Executive Editor Len Downie declined to discuss the paper's internal deliberations relating to the story.

Department, they argued, be trusted to investigate the Bush White House, which, according to the *Post*, had mounted a covert and extensive campaign to punish an enemy? Democratic Party researchers dug up a 1999 quote from the first President Bush, a former CIA director, and e-mailed it to reporters: "I have nothing but contempt and anger for those who betray the trust by exposing the name of our [intelligence] sources. They are, in my view, the most insidious of traitors."

In the White House pressroom, reporters anxiously waited for McClellan to conduct the daily briefing. Let's hear him spin his way out of this, some were saying. McClellan appeared shortly after noon. An amiable Texan who had been with Bush for years, McClellan was relatively new on the job. At the podium, he tended to look stiff, robotically repeating his pre-scripted talking points. This briefing would be his biggest challenge.

"Has the president tried to find out who outed the CIA agent?" asked Helen Thomas. "And has he fired anyone in the White House yet?"

"First of all, that is not the way this White House operates," McClellan replied. "The president expects everyone in his administration to adhere to the highest standards of conduct. No one would be authorized to do such a thing."

CBS News' Bill Plante asked if Bush and the White House were going to take a "proactive role" to determine if a White House official had leaked information regarding Valerie Wilson. McClellan answered, "Do you have any specific information to bring to my attention suggesting White House involvement?" McClellan was saying that the White House had no information of its own and no intention of gathering any. But if reporters wanted to tell the White House who their sources were, the White House would look into the matter. This was a none-too-subtle hint to the press corps: Do you really want to go down this road?

And the questions started coming about Rove. Was he in any way involved in the leak to Novak?

"I've made it very clear, from the beginning, that it is totally ridiculous," McClellan said. "I've known Karl for a long time, and I didn't even need to go ask Karl, because I know the kind of person that he is, and he is someone that is committed to the highest standards of conduct." But McClellan added, "I have spoken with Karl about this matter. . . . I've made it very clear that he was not involved, that there's no truth to the suggestion that he was."

What about the vice president? Could McClellan say categorically that Cheney hadn't been involved?

"I've made it clear that there's been nothing, absolutely nothing brought to our attention to suggest any White House involvement, and that includes the vice president's office," he remarked.

McClellan also issued a rather definitive statement. Bush, he said, had "made it very clear to people in his administration that he expects them to adhere to the highest standards of conduct. If anyone in this administration was involved in it, they would no longer be in this administration."

THAT evening, the Justice Department informed Alberto Gonzales, the White House counsel, that a criminal investigation was under way, and it asked the White House to instruct its staff to preserve any records related to the case, including records of contacts with Novak.

When the White House senior staff assembled in the Roosevelt Room for a meeting the next morning, a somber Gonzales relayed the news. All members of the staff were instructed to go review all their files and turn over to the counsel's office any material relevant to the investigation.* All members of the staff were to cooperate fully with the inquiry. "It was a very dramatic moment," a senior staff member said. Gonzales looked gravely serious. Members of the Bush White House tended to pride themselves on their probity, believing they were quite different from the occupants of the ethically challenged Clinton White House. A criminal investigation—that was what happened to them, not us, the staffer thought. Judging from Gonzales's tone, this staffer believed that anyone who didn't cooperate would be fired.

Rove was at the meeting, seated as usual across from Card and Gonzales at the grand conference table, and Libby, as always, was in a chair slightly behind. Neither said a word. The senior staffer had heard the gossip that the two of them might somehow have participated in the CIA leak. No way those rumors could be true, the staffer thought.

---

*Some administration critics later jumped on the fact that Gonzales waited almost twelve hours to instruct White House aides to preserve their notes and e-mails. "Every good prosecutor knows that any delay could give a culprit time to destroy the evidence," griped Senator Charles Schumer. But given that the leak had occurred more than two months earlier, any White House staffer determined to destroy relevant evidence had already had ample time to do so.

That day, Bush reinforced the point that McClellan had made. Talking briefly to reporters after meeting with business executives in Chicago, Bush said, "If there is a leak out of my administration, I want to know who it is. And if the person has violated law, the person will be taken care of."

When a reporter said, "Yesterday, we were told that Karl Rove had no role in it," Bush interrupted and said, "Yes."

"I don't know of anybody in my administration who leaked classified information," Bush continued. "If somebody did leak classified information, I'd like to know it, and we'll take the appropriate action. . . . And if people have got solid information, please come forward with it. . . . And we can clarify this thing very quickly if people who have got solid evidence would come forward and speak out. And I would hope they would. And then we'll get to the bottom of this and move on. . . . I want to know who the leakers are."

With Bush and McClellan saying they had no idea who the leakers were, Rove and Libby made no public statements about the case. Nor did Cheney.

MEANWHILE, a full-force shoutfest was under way among pundits, politicos, and cable show talking heads. The leak case now had all the ingredients of a Washington scandal: an alleged crime, high-level suspects in the White House, and a Justice Department investigation. To White House allies, it was a phony controversy ginned up by Democrats trying to smear the president for a war they had never really supported in the first place. Ed Gillespie, the head of the Republican Party, dismissed Wilson as a "partisan." Bill Kristol claimed that the leak case was really a tale of "the enemies of the hawks in the administration us[ing] this . . . unfortunate revealing of Mrs. Wilson's name as a weapon—quite skillfully—against people in the White House." The editorial page of *The Wall Street Journal* called Wilson "an open opponent of the U.S. war on terror" and argued that the public "had a right to know" about Valerie Wilson and her CIA job.

The president's critics were hailing Wilson as a heroic whistle-blower and decrying the CIA leak as a grievous blow to national security. "Someone high in the administration committed a felony," thundered *New York Times* columnist Paul Krugman. "End of story." Speaking on PBS's *NewsHour,* Larry Johnson, a CIA classmate of Valerie Wilson and a Republican, proclaimed, "This is not about partisan politics. This is about a betrayal."

Robert Novak felt the need to defend himself. On October 1, he published a column to explain what had happened and to "protect my own integrity and credibility." Novak wrote that he had not received a "planned leak." His first source—a senior administration official—had told him about the CIA employment of Joe Wilson's wife as an "offhand revelation," he claimed. The CIA had not warned him that publishing her name—which, he noted, was listed in *Who's Who in America*—would endanger her or anyone else. He did regret describing her as an "operative," calling it a term he had "lavished on hack politicians." But he then cited an "unofficial source" at the CIA who had assured him (wrongly) that Valerie Wilson "has been an analyst, not in covert operations." Novak also wrote, "It was well known around Washington that Wilson's wife worked for the CIA." But he offered no real proof of this.

After reading Novak's column early that morning, Richard Armitage became alarmed. From home, he called his boss, Colin Powell. "I'm sure he's talking about me," Armitage said. The deputy secretary was in distress. "He was very unhappy and upset with himself," said another State Department official who spoke to him that day. But Powell wondered if Armitage was overreacting. Perhaps, he thought, Novak might be referring to someone else. At Powell's suggestion, Armitage tracked down Ken Duberstein, who was in New York on business, and asked him to call Novak and find out if he indeed was the columnist's primary source. Powell also called Duberstein and made the same request. When Duberstein called Novak, the columnist brushed him off. "Why would he think that he's the person?" Novak replied, declining to confirm his source to Duberstein.*

But neither Powell nor Armitage really needed Novak's confirmation to realize what had happened. By mid-morning, Powell had called William Taft IV, the department's top lawyer. Taft then phoned Armitage and debriefed him. Powell, Taft, and Armitage knew they had a tremendous problem.

Taft, an old Washington hand, had been deputy secretary of defense during the Reagan administration and had lived through the Iran-*contra*

---

*This flurry of phone calls would later draw intense scrutiny from FBI agents and prosecutors who were at first suspicious that the four men might have been coordinating their stories. But Powell and Duberstein maintained they had only been trying to ascertain the facts.

scandal with both Powell and Armitage. He later maintained that there had never been any question as to what action they should now take. There would be no cover-up. "We decided we were going to tell [the investigators] what we thought had happened because that's what the president had directed," said Taft. He notified the Justice Department's criminal division that Armitage had information for them about the CIA leak case. An interview was scheduled for the next day.

But there was another, more sensitive phone call to make—to the White House.

Taft felt obligated to inform Alberto Gonzales, the White House counsel. But Taft, Powell, and Armitage feared that the White House would leak that Armitage had been Novak's source to deflect attention from itself and to embarrass State Department leaders who had never been enthusiastic about the president's Iraq policy. Public disclosure could be harmful not only for Armitage but for Powell (who had encouraged his deputy's meeting with Novak).

So when Taft called Gonzales, he was oblique. He told the White House counsel that the State Department possessed information relevant to the investigation—without mentioning Armitage—and that he had already contacted the Justice Department. Taft asked the White House lawyer if he wanted to know the details. Gonzales said no. It was exactly the answer Taft wanted; Armitage's central role in the leak case would stay secret.

ON OCTOBER 1, McClellan took another pounding in the briefing room: Why didn't Bush do anything back in July, when the leak first occurred? Would he order his staffers to take polygraph examinations? Does the White House condone the Republican attacks on Wilson's credibility? McClellan had no direct answers, but he added, "The president is focused on getting to the bottom of this." Congressional Democrats—led by Senator Chuck Schumer—kept pushing for a special counsel. (News accounts noted how Rove, a possible target, had once done campaign work for Attorney General John Ashcroft.) Senator Arlen Specter, a Republican, said, "Recusal is something Ashcroft ought to consider."

THE next day, two FBI agents and a Justice Department prosecutor interviewed Armitage in his office at Foggy Bottom. Taft sat in on the session.

Armitage acknowledged that he had talked to Novak. But there were key details he said he could not recall. How had he first learned about Valerie Wilson? He wasn't sure. What about the INR memo drafted in response to Libby's request? Did Armitage realize that the information in this memo about Valerie Wilson had been designated secret? He hadn't noticed that. Armitage was cooperating—but, some investigators thought, not explaining everything.

There is a standard question FBI agents always ask at the end of interviews in criminal investigations: Is there anything else you think we should know? Armitage didn't volunteer a pertinent fact: that he had previously passed the same information to Bob Woodward. (He later told colleagues he had forgotten this.)

Armitage was due to be in Central Asia that day, as part of a previously scheduled trip that would take him to Tajikistan, Uzbekistan, and Kazakhstan before he headed to Afghanistan and Pakistan. But due to the leak investigation, he canceled the first part of the trip and removed the stops in Central Asia from his itinerary. State Department spokesman Richard Boucher told reporters that Armitage's departure had been "delayed due to a very brief illness."

THE news on October 2 was unsettling for the White House on another front: David Kay was in town to provide closed-door briefings to the House and Senate intelligence committees on his interim findings.

"We have not yet found stocks of weapons," Kay said in a statement released by the CIA. His summary was devastating: his Iraq Survey Group had not "been able to corroborate the existence of a mobile BW production effort."* He reported that Iraq's chemical weapons stockpiles had apparently been destroyed after the first Persian Gulf War and that he'd found no evidence of any ongoing major nuclear program. He did note that the ISG had

---

*Toward the end of October, Kay's investigators concluded that Curveball was nothing but a fabricator and that his reporting was all false. But WINPAC officers at CIA headquarters, as well as McLaughlin and Tenet, continued to support Curveball. Kay was now certain that the trailers were not WMD labs. He initially considered unconvincing the theory that they were facilities for producing hydrogen for military weather balloons. "Then we found out," he said, "that in the 1980s the Iraqis got a mobile production unit [for making hydrogen] from a European country. Rather than go back and buy another, they made some."

come across "dozens of WMD-related program activities," including clandestine labs run by Iraqi intelligence (apparently for the production not of biological weapons but of poisons for use in assassination operations). Saddam, Kay said, had not given up his "aspirations and intentions" to acquire weapons of mass destruction in the future. But on every key prewar claim—a revived nuclear program, WMD-carrying unmanned drones, stockpiles of chemical and biological weapons—Kay had uncovered nothing.

"I'm not pleased," huffed Senator Pat Roberts, the Republican chairman of the Senate committee, after Kay testified. And Senator Jay Rockefeller, the senior Democrat on the committee, referring to the Bush administration, asked, "Did they mislead us, or did they simply get it wrong? Whatever the answer is, it's not a good answer."

Kay's interim report had created much discomfort at the CIA. During the two weeks he had spent preparing it, working out of an office at CIA headquarters, he had shared drafts with McLaughlin and Tenet. Neither was happy. Tenet challenged Kay on the absence of chemical stockpiles. McLaughlin, Kay recalled, resisted his conclusions that the aluminum tubes hadn't been for a nuclear program and the trailers weren't mobile biolabs. The CIA deputy director was getting complaints from the analysts at WINPAC, who were insisting Kay had it wrong. McLaughlin urged Kay not to say anything too definitive about the empty-handed weapons hunt. Kay disagreed. "I went there to find WMDs," he later said, "and if I went up on the Hill and didn't say that I hadn't found any, all dialogue would be over." He placed that fact high up in his testimony. "I knew the agency was going to be unhappy and disturbed by these conclusions," Kay said. "But if anyone was disturbed, I was disturbed. I had thought there were WMDs. I was not just discomforting the CIA. I was discomforting myself."*

After Kay was done with this round of hearings, Tenet and McLaughlin told him that they had received calls from White House officials asking why

---

*Kay's report prompted I-told-you-sos from former UN inspectors. Rolf Ekeus, a Swedish diplomat who had overseen UN inspections in Iraq in the 1990s, said the Kay report had come as no surprise to him. UN experts, he noted, had much earlier concluded that "Iraq was just working on preserving their capability to eventually reestablish their weapons." He added, "I think the Americans were misled" about the WMD threat. Hans Blix, who had overseen the prewar UN inspections, said, "It's a long way from finding some minor things, as [Kay] did, to concluding Iraq was an imminent danger. . . . In many cases, Kay's report says [the programs he discovered] may be suitable for this or suitable for that. Well, a butcher's knife is also suitable for murder."

Kay had started out by saying weapons had yet to be found. Couldn't that, they asked, have been buried?

The day after the Kay report came out, a CBS News/*New York Times* poll reported that 53 percent of Americans believed the Iraq War was a mistake. Only a slight majority of 51 percent approved of Bush's performance in office. The presidential election was thirteen months away.

THE leak scandal was consuming much of the Washington media, but the editors and writers at *Time* had a distinct challenge. They realized the White House hadn't been truthful. McClellan had said Rove wasn't involved. Yet Cooper, Dickerson, Michael Duffy, the bureau chief, and others at the newsmagazine knew Rove had tipped off Cooper that "Wilson's wife" worked at the CIA. They were aware that Libby had confirmed it. (Novak, of course, also knew that the White House denials about Rove were untrue.)

The newsmagazine pulled together a cover story about the leak case. It delicately danced around the issue of its own role. The story quoted McClellan as denying the Rove allegation: "There is simply no truth to that suggestion." But the story offered no rebuttal from its own correspondents or editors. Rove and Libby hadn't spoken on the record; the magazine felt it had to respect their confidences. Duffy, who authored the cover story based on reporting from Cooper, Dickerson, and eight other correspondents, later said that there had been no discussion within the magazine about whether it should have challenged McClellan's denials based on what he and the magazine's reporters knew. Nor did they talk about whether Cooper and others should have called Rove and pressured him to correct McClellan's denials. "I don't think it occurred to me," Duffy said. "This is one of those rare situations where I didn't tell the reader everything we knew because we thought there was a higher journalistic principle involved." But Duffy's story did hint at the dilemma the magazine's reporters faced: "any reporter who might have learned Plame's name in a leak is duty bound to shut up about it, even to federal investigators, if the situation comes to that." The story foreshadowed the fight ahead: "The ultimate irony is that the Administration may now be depending on journalists' rectitude. In the prelude to and particularly in the aftermath of the war, Bush's aides at times questioned the patriotism of the press; that some of those officials may now be depending on the silence of the media in the face of a national-security investigation made some Bush allies uncomfortable." That is, Rove and Libby were relying upon Matt Cooper and his colleagues and editors at *Time*.

About this time, Libby, apparently worried that McClellan hadn't sufficiently protected him and the vice president's office as much as he had Rove, sent the White House press secretary talking points. They were practically a script: "I've talked to Libby. I said it was ridiculous about Karl. And it is ridiculous about Libby." McClellan adopted Libby's spin. The day after the *Time* story appeared, he told the White House press corps that he had spoken to Rove, Libby, and NSC aide Elliott Abrams and that each had categorically denied they had leaked information on Valerie Wilson. That day, Bush remarked to reporters, "I have no idea whether we'll find out who the leaker is—partially because, in all due respect to your profession, you do a very good job of protecting the leakers."

How much could the White House count on the reporters to keep silent? Protecting confidential sources is a fundamental tenet for professional journalists. There is often no other way for a reporter to pry loose essential information (particularly concerning national security matters) than by assuring an informed source that his or her identity won't be disclosed. But the practice can also be overused. Sources granted anonymity are free to push their own agendas and vendettas—to use reporters as much as reporters use them.

The legal rights journalists had to protect their sources, especially during a federal criminal investigation, were shaky. And the Justice Department, prodded by the White House, was becoming increasingly aggressive in mounting leak investigations. In the past, department officials had been reluctant to subpoena journalists, but the rules were changing. Prosecutors and FBI agents assigned to recent leak cases had grumbled: Why shouldn't we subpoena reporters and force them to testify? What makes the reporter-source relationship sacred?

Veteran FBI agent Jack Eckenrode was looking to change the playing field. A dogged investigator who reminded some of the Tommy Lee Jones character in *The Fugitive,* Eckenrode was accustomed to chasing after sensitive targets. In the late 1990s, he had spearheaded an investigation probing Clinton White House fund-raising that had led to the convictions of some of the president's dubious fund-raisers. In the summer of 2002, the FBI brass assigned Eckenrode to another dicey case: the leak of a National Security Agency intercept that had exposed an egregious intelligence community mistake related to 9/11.

On September 10, 2001, the electronic eavesdropping machines of the NSA captured a conversation between two al-Qaeda operatives that contained two chilling phrases: "Tomorrow is zero hour" and "The match begins tomorrow." The conversation wasn't translated by NSA until two days later—after the attacks. In a private hearing on June 19, 2002, Michael Hayden, then the NSA director, had briefed the Senate and House intelligence committees on this snafu. Hours after his testimony, CNN's David Ensor broadcast a report disclosing the contents of the intercept; other news outlets produced their own reports. The leak embarrassed—and infuriated—the White House.

Cheney called Senator Bob Graham, who was chairing the intelligence committee, and threatened him: if the intelligence committees didn't put a stop to such leaks, the White House would cut off cooperation with the committee's inquiry into pre-9/11 failures (a probe the White House had never been enthusiastic about). Graham asked the FBI to investigate, and Eckenrode was put in charge.

The FBI and federal prosecutors soon had a primary suspect: Senator Richard Shelby of Alabama, the ranking Republican on the intelligence committee. But to make a case, Eckenrode and other investigators concluded, they would have to question reporters who had talked to the senator—and haul them before a federal grand jury if they refused to testify.

When Eckenrode asked his superiors for permission to subpoena the reporters, he met with stiff resistance. At a tense meeting at Justice Department headquarters, Michael Chertoff, then the assistant attorney general in charge of the criminal division, told Eckenrode that the FBI agent and his colleagues didn't understand the broader "policy implications" of taking this step, according to law enforcement sources familiar with the investigation. Chertoff was sticking to established Justice Department guidelines: federal prosecutors were authorized only to subpoena members of the news media as a last resort. But members of Eckenrode's FBI team wondered if Chertoff's boss, Ashcroft, a former Republican senator, was derailing a probe that might incriminate one of his old GOP colleagues. Eckenrode wrote a long, impassioned letter to senior Justice officials, arguing it made no sense to conduct leak investigations if the department was unwilling to use all the tools available. His point—shared by federal prosecutors assigned to the case—was,

If you want us to conduct these sorts of inquiries, let us do our job. If not, don't waste our time.

Eckenrode and the prosecutors never got the green light to go after reporters in the NSA case, and that investigation (like many leak probes) fizzled out. But in the fall of 2003, Eckenrode's boss told him he had another big case to add to his workload: the CIA leak. A week or so later, FBI Director Robert Mueller popped his head into Eckenrode's office to offer encouragement. "Take it wherever it goes," Mueller told him.

Eckenrode had every intention of doing just that.

ONE of Eckenrode's first steps was to contact the man responsible for the disclosure of the leak: Robert Novak. He asked to interview the columnist. By now, Novak had hired James Hamilton, a well-known Washington criminal defense attorney, and Hamilton had advised Novak that there'd be no legal basis for refusing to cooperate with the investigation if he were subpoenaed by the grand jury. Saying no to a grand jury could subject the columnist to imprisonment and steep legal costs—that he would have to pay largely out of his own pocket.

On October 5, 2003, Novak appeared on *Meet the Press* and declared, "I will not give up the source." He added, "If I were to give up that name, I would leave journalism." But he didn't say that he was about to meet with the FBI. Two days later, Eckenrode and two colleagues showed up at the offices of the Swidler Berlin law firm, where Hamilton worked, to question Novak there.

Years later Novak wrote that he did not reveal his sources to the FBI at this meeting. But Eckenrode (thanks to Taft's phone call to the Justice Department) already had a pretty good idea of the identity of Novak's chief source: Richard Armitage. He didn't need Novak to give up the name. At this early stage of the probe, he wasn't ready to press the issue. Novak later recounted that he did "disclose how Valerie Wilson's role was reported to me"—without mentioning any names.

After the FBI interview, neither Novak nor Hamilton said anything publicly about the meeting. And for the next three years, neither would disclose that Novak was cooperating with the leak investigation—leaving journalists, lawyers, and others following the case to wonder what Novak was up to.

THREE days later, Eckenrode questioned Novak's other source, Karl Rove, who had hired a criminal defense lawyer named Robert Luskin. (A former Justice Department prosecutor and Democrat, Luskin was a law partner of Rove's friend and Bush campaign lawyer Ben Ginsberg.) In his interview with the FBI, Rove acknowledged that he had told Novak he had "heard" Wilson's wife worked at the CIA, a source familiar with his account later told reporters.

The FBI had obtained Rove's phone records showing that he had talked to Novak days after news of the leak investigation broke. This had given the investigators reason to wonder whether the columnist and his old source were colluding. Rove acknowledged the two had spoken but said that nothing untoward had happened.

It was barely two weeks into the investigation, and the FBI essentially knew the identity of the senior administration officials in Novak's column. But discovering their names and making a criminal case were two different things. The FBI would have to show that the leakers had divulged classified information they had received through official channels. But Rove said to Eckenrode that he couldn't remember where and from whom he had first heard about Wilson's wife. And the subject of Rove's phone conversation with Matt Cooper of *Time* didn't come up.

Four days after that, on October 14, Eckenrode interviewed Scooter Libby. Unlike Rove, Libby didn't say he couldn't remember how he had first heard about Valerie Wilson. He offered the FBI a specific recollection. The vice president's chief of staff said it had been Tim Russert of NBC News—in that July 10, 2003, phone call—who had told him Wilson's wife worked for the CIA. Libby didn't mention to Eckenrode all that had come before that conversation: his gathering of information on the Wilsons, the INR memo commissioned for him that referred to Valerie Wilson, his discussion with Cheney about Valerie Wilson (in which the vice president had said she worked in the Counterproliferation Division of the CIA's operations directorate). Libby told Eckenrode that Russert had said "all the reporters knew" about Valerie Wilson and that he (Libby) had expressed surprise at this news. Libby also confirmed that he had spoken to Matt Cooper two days later on July 12. But he claimed he had merely told Cooper that reporters were telling the administration Wilson's wife worked at the CIA, and that he didn't know if that was true.

This was Libby's defense. He hadn't disclosed any classified information and hadn't violated the Intelligence Identities Protection Act because he hadn't really known anything about Valerie Wilson's employment at the CIA. He had only picked up some unofficial scuttlebutt from Russert and then had passed it on to Cooper without vouching for the information. Under the Intelligence Identities Protection Act, it was a crime to disclose an undercover CIA officer's identity only if the leaking government official had "authorized access" to classified information about the officer and realized that the officer was a covert employee. If Libby had merely conveyed an unconfirmed tip he had received from a reporter—as opposed to disclosing information he had officially obtained—he wouldn't be covered by the act. And if he had not known for sure that Valerie Wilson was an undercover employee, he would not have broken the law. Moreover, with this account, Libby was keeping Cheney out of the picture. In Libby's telling, Cheney was not a party to any plot to assail a critic.

But at this point Libby's defense already had one big potential flaw. He had identified two specific reporters with whom he had spoken—Russert and Cooper. Yet both men remembered their conversations with Libby differently. If they talked, he would be in trouble.

WITH the hunt for weapons in Iraq a dud, administration officials were playing up other rationales for the war. In late October, Undersecretary of Defense Douglas Feith sent the Senate intelligence committee a classified report entitled "Summary of Body of Intelligence on Iraq–al Qaeda Contacts." The memo, recapping the work of the intelligence cell Feith had set up before the war, cited fifty examples of purported contacts between Saddam's regime and bin Laden's murderous outfit (many of which had already been discounted or dismissed by intelligence analysts). It rehashed the Atta-in-Prague allegation and al-Libi's claims about poisons training. Within two weeks, the Feith report was leaked to the neoconservative *Weekly Standard,* and Stephen Hayes, a correspondent for the magazine, published a cover story entitled "Case Closed: The U.S. Government's Secret Memo Detailing Cooperation Between Saddam Hussein and Osama bin Laden." The piece, which received much media attention, quoted the Feith memo extensively and concluded forcefully, "There can no longer be any serious argument about whether Saddam Hussein's Iraq worked with Osama bin Laden and al Qaeda to plot against Americans." The hawks couldn't claim there were weapons when none had yet been found, but they could at least argue that a clear-eyed reading of assorted intelligence fragments revealed that bin Laden and Saddam had been thick as thieves—and, weapons aside, that would be enough to justify the war.

Yet later on the same day *The Weekly Standard* posted its story, the Pentagon, in a highly unusual move, immediately distanced itself from Feith's secret memo and released a statement noting the undersecretary's report was based on "raw reports or products" and was "not an analysis of the substantive issue of the relationship between Iraq and al Qaeda." In other words, the Defense Department didn't stand by it. The Pentagon statement also denounced the leak of the classified memo as "deplorable" and possibly illegal.

Not long afterward, the CIA sent Feith a list of corrections that needed to be made to his memo—and disputed the reliability of several of the alarming reports he had cited. The memo, for instance, had recycled from Feith's earlier slide show the suspect story about bin Laden's meeting with Iraq's intelligence chief in Sudan in 1996, and his memo had attributed the information to a "well placed source." Not so, the CIA said—noting the information had come from a thirdhand source through a foreign intelligence service. The CIA disputed the Feith memo's claim that Abu Musab al-Zarqawi, the notorious terrorist leading a segment of the insurgency in Iraq, had been harbored by Iraqi intelligence before the war. Prior to the invasion, the White House had cited Zarqawi's alleged presence in Iraq as evidence of an Iraq link to al-Qaeda. Now the CIA believed it wasn't certain that Zarqawi's travels through Iraq had been known to Saddam's government, as Zarqawi may have been traveling under an alias.*

The case for the Saddam–bin Laden connection was as flimsy as it had always been. Feith and *The Weekly Standard* were doing what they could to keep it afloat—as the main reason for war was slipping away. And they found at least one major champion: Dick Cheney. In an interview with the *Rocky Mountain News*—one day after Powell said he had seen no

---

*Months later, Tenet would testify in Congress that the CIA "did not agree with the way the data was characterized" in the Feith memo.

"smoking-gun, concrete evidence" on the al-Qaeda–Iraq connection—the vice president pointed to the *Weekly Standard* article based on the Feith memo as the "best source of information" on the supposed relationship. Just as he had done with *The New York Times*' story on the aluminum tubes more than a year earlier, Cheney (who usually deplored leaks) was touting a leak of classified information to buttress the administration's case for war— a leak that yet again rested on dubious intelligence.*

IN LATE October, Deputy Secretary of Defense Paul Wolfowitz flew to Baghdad to take a look for himself. The Saturday he arrived, a convoy of civilian contractors came under mortar attack from insurgents, and a U.S. Army Black Hawk helicopter was shot down, killing one of its crew members. That evening, at a reception at the al-Rashid Hotel, Wolfowitz was greeted by his old ally Chalabi. "They know you're here," Chalabi told him, according to a source present for the conversation. "I wouldn't stay at the al-Rashid tonight."

The warning struck some in Wolfowitz's party as creepy. Did Chalabi know something? But it was too late for Wolfowitz to change his lodgings. That night six to ten explosive projectiles struck the hotel, hitting the floors below where Wolfowitz and his party were staying. The attack shattered scores of windows, blew off doors, and filled hallways with smoke—but Wolfowitz, though shaken, was uninjured. The next day, a suicide bomber drove a car into the Red Cross headquarters, killing twelve people; two dozen others were killed in attacks elsewhere that day.

Speaking to reporters on October 27 after meeting with Bremer in Washington, Bush declared progress was being made in Iraq and that the rising number of attacks was a reaction to this progress—a sign that the insurgents were desperate. He added, "The overall thrust is in the right direction." At a press conference the next day, he said that in the coming year—an election year, he noted—Americans would have to be "patient" regarding Iraq.†

---

*Cheney would go even further than the Feith memo. In an interview with NPR, he would claim that "there's overwhelming evidence" of an Iraq–al-Qaeda connection and note that Abdul Rahman Yasin, one of the attackers in the 1993 World Trade Center bombing, had been "put on the payroll and provided a house, safe harbor and sanctuary" in Iraq. This was one of Laurie Mylroie's arguments. He would also say the trailers found in Iraq were definitely mobile bioweapons labs.

†Two weeks earlier, Rumsfeld had written a memo in which he described the wars in Iraq and

Then, on November 2, a grisly horror occurred: a U.S. Chinook helicopter was shot down over Fallujah. Sixteen U.S. soldiers were killed and another twenty wounded, making it the bloodiest day for Americans since major combat operations had ended in April. The insurgents' use of a missile signaled that the United States was facing a more sophisticated and dangerous enemy.

Iraq was now not only the number one policy worry for the White House but the biggest potential political problem for the up-and-running Bush reelection campaign. And within the Bush campaign, it was an issue of great sensitivity.

The day of the Fallujah crash, an Associated Press reporter, Scott Lindlaw, called the campaign for comment. Lindlaw mentioned to press secretary Terry Holt that he had previously talked to another campaign official, who had casually said to him—on background—that the campaign hoped there wouldn't be more days like this one in Iraq. It was an innocuous remark. Nevertheless, Lindlaw's prospective story sent the campaign office into a panic. There had been a stern directive issued to all the staffers: Don't talk about Iraq at all. Someone had disobeyed that command. The Bush campaign ordered its own leak investigation.

All of the campaign's phone records were reviewed. These records showed that one staffer, Brad Dayspring, a media coordinator for the northeastern states, had been in phone contact with Lindlaw in recent days. Holt called Dayspring into his office and had the phone records on his desk. He could see there had been two calls—one to and one from Lindlaw's number. Dayspring acknowledged that he had spoken to the AP reporter—but about a Pennsylvania steel issue, not Iraq. It didn't matter. "This isn't going to work," Holt brusquely told him. He was being fired.

Dayspring was stunned. He had worked for George W. Bush for four years. He appealed his dismissal to campaign higher-ups but was told it was pointless. Ken Mehlman, who had just moved from Rove's office to become the Bush-Cheney campaign manager, had signed off on his dismissal. Holt later said that Dayspring had violated a "basic ground rule" forbidding campaign staffers from talking to the press.

The incident never became publicly known. But word of Dayspring's

---

Afghanistan as "a long, hard slog" and observed, "Today, we lack metrics to know if we are winning or losing the global war on terror."

firing spread among Bush aides. Some were amazed and even alarmed that the campaign had instant access to staff members' phone calls. The episode reinforced the edict that Rove and Mehlman wanted enforced: Nobody should even mention Iraq. Inside campaign headquarters, the war in Iraq—the signature initiative of George Bush's presidency—was a forbidden subject.

IN EARLY November, a new National Intelligence Estimate arrived on the state of the Iraq insurgency. This was the document INR analyst Wayne White had tried to strengthen, starting in August, to reflect his "Pissed-Off Iraqis" analysis. The NIE, according to White, ended up being a "very strong warning" to the White House and the Pentagon about "the seriousness of the insurgency." But it left open a fundamental question: What should be done about it? There were no easy answers, said White: "One thing was clear right from the beginning. We did not have enough troops in Iraq." This was not stated in the NIE; such documents weren't supposed to prescribe policy. But that was the document's message. Yet the White House and the Pentagon continued to issue statements that the troop level was fine.

The reports from the field were dire as well. In early November, the CIA station chief in Baghdad sent Washington his latest review of the conditions in Iraq. This report—called an "aardwolf"—depicted a deteriorating situation. According to John Maguire of the CIA's Iraq Operations Group, the aardwolf described recent trends as profoundly troubling. One ominous development was that small units of insurgents had begun confronting coalition forces in tactical maneuvers—meaning the insurgents were beginning to act like a cohesive military force. The aardwolf reported that the Iraqi people—angry (or pissed off, as White would say) about the lack of electricity and the slow pace of reconstruction—were becoming worried and fearful. It stated that the U.S.-led coalition forces were losing control of some areas of the country. The report maintained that an increasing number of Iraqis were concluding the United States could be defeated in Iraq and were starting to support the resistance. Bush's effort to rebuild the country and birth a democracy, the aardwolf warned, was in danger of collapse.

The Baghdad station's report landed in the White House with a bang and sparked anger—at the CIA. When a NSC staffer read the document, he was blown away. "It was a very dark day," this official later said. The report, he recalled, said that "all the trends were in the wrong direction, and it could get far worse." According to this NSC staffer, the predominant reaction to the report at the White House was that the CIA was "fucking us again."

Days later, Bush asserted, "We've made a lot of progress on the ground."

FBI AGENT Jack Eckenrode was committed to taking the leak probe as far as he could. Late in the year, he came up with a plan to have White House aides sign statements waiving any confidentiality agreements they had with journalists. It was an idea drawn from his recent experience in the FBI inspection division, which investigated alleged misconduct by his fellow FBI agents. In those cases, Eckenrode routinely asked the agents under suspicion to sign statements waiving their rights to counsel. After all, if they worked for the FBI (and wanted to keep working for the FBI), they should have nothing to hide. And they were expected to cooperate fully with bureau investigators. Since the president had instructed White House aides to cooperate fully in the CIA leak case, shouldn't they sign similar waivers undoing whatever agreements they had with reporters? With such waivers in hand, Eckenrode would have some leverage with the journalists whose testimony he would need. He could say to the reporters, your source says he or she has no problem with your talking. So talk.

The waivers, signed by White House staffers under prodding by Eckenrode, would be dismissed by most reporters as inherently coercive. A reporter couldn't rely on such a document to determine if his or her source really wanted the reporter to talk to the FBI. But there was little doubt that the waivers, the wording of which Eckenrode worked out with Justice Department lawyers, made members of the White House staff squirm. Libby's lawyer later said his client had had no choice but to sign the waiver; otherwise, he'd probably be fired. The waivers were a signal. Most leak cases weren't vigorously investigated. This one would be.

WITH Eckenrode chasing Rove (and others), his inquiry, which was being monitored by the criminal division of the Justice Department, created a problem for Attorney General John Ashcroft, who was receiving Eckenrode's progress reports. Rove had formerly worked for Ashcroft as a campaign consultant in the 1980s and 1990s. Ashcroft's political committees had paid Rove nearly $750,000. Democrats were howling that Ashcroft couldn't be trusted to oversee an investigation of the White House and the man who had helped him become a governor and a senator. They argued that Ashcroft ought to step aside and hand the case to a special counsel.

In late October, during the confirmation hearings of James Comey, who had been nominated to be deputy attorney general, Senator Chuck Schumer held up a chart that looked like octopuses wrestling with one another. It was entitled "A Tangled Web . . . ?" and it showed the various connections between Ashcroft, his chief of staff, the White House, Rove, Gonzales, and others. (The chart noted that Bush and acting Deputy Attorney General Robert McCallum had gone to Yale together and had been members of "the ultra-secretive brotherhood of the Skull and Bones society.") Schumer, who had helped Comey become U.S. attorney in New York two years previously, wanted a special counsel for the leak case, and he wanted to hear Comey say he was amenable to that.

Comey wouldn't discuss the particulars of the leak case. But he assured Schumer he believed in erring "on the side of caution" on ethics issues. "I don't care about politics," he said. "I don't care about expediency. I don't care about friendship. I care about doing the right thing."

Comey was confirmed by the Senate on December 9. Schumer called to congratulate him and added, I'm giving you a month to get settled— meaning that Schumer would not hassle him about the leak case for several weeks. But Schumer made it clear: he expected Comey to do the right thing.

DAYS earlier, Joe and Valerie Wilson had been in the news again. *Vanity Fair* magazine had sent out advance copies of a long article on the Wilson affair, and the piece included a two-page photo of the Wilsons sitting in his Jaguar convertible with the White House in the background. In the shot, Valerie Wilson was wearing large sunglasses, and a scarf was wrapped around her head—intended as a disguise. But Joe Wilson's critics pounced. Two months earlier, Wilson had said on *Meet the Press* that his wife "would rather chop off her right arm than say anything to the press, and she will not allow herself to be photographed." His critics accused the Wilsons of being publicity hogs, and they pointed to the photo as evidence Valerie Wilson was not too concerned about her cover and personal security.

With bloggers and journalists following every twist in the Wilson affair, any new development was fodder for instant analysis and argument. Referring to the *Vanity Fair* photo, popular conservative blogger Glenn Reynolds wrote: "Sorry—if you're really an undercover spy, and really worried about national security, you don't do this sort of thing. Unless, perhaps, you're a self-promoter first, and a spy second. Or your husband is." Tim Noah, the "Chatterbox" columnist for *Slate,* noted that the photo had followed the Wilsons' joint appearance at several high-profile Washington events and wrote, "Plame's extended striptease, enthusiastically barked by her husband, now has Chatterbox wondering how much of Wilson's story to believe. (It also has Chatterbox wondering when the couple will start renting themselves out for birthday parties.)"

Valerie Wilson apologized to her superiors for having allowed herself to be photographed. But Joe Wilson later argued that the photo had in no way affected his wife's already blown cover: "With proper precautions taken, I saw no reason to deprive ourselves of the pleasure of being photographed together as the happily married couple that we are."

ON DECEMBER 13, there was—finally—good news out of Iraq. Saddam Hussein was found by a team of U.S. Special Forces hiding in a hole six feet underground nine miles from his hometown of Tikrit. The once brutal sixty-six-year-old tyrant looked bewildered and pathetic. He had a pistol with him but never fired it. He also had $750,000 in $100 bills. In Baghdad, as the news spread, Iraqis took to the streets to celebrate, dancing, honking their horns, and shooting guns into the air. In Washington, officials were exultant. The president gave a short televised speech. "This afternoon, I have a message for the Iraqi people," he said. "This event brings further assurance that the torture chambers and the secret police are gone forever."

Commentators speculated that the capture of Saddam would break the back of the insurgency. Perhaps the president's vision of a free, democratic, and peaceful Iraq would prevail after all. Perhaps the dictator would even cooperate and tell coalition forces where his missing weapons of mass destruction were.*

---

*Three days later, ABC News' Diane Sawyer asked Bush if December 13 was "the best day" of his presidency. No, he said, the best day had been Inauguration Day. She also asked him to

COMEY didn't need a month to figure out what to do about the leak case. The attorney general's top aides were political operatives whose first allegiance was to Ashcroft. They realized that any further involvement on Ashcroft's part would hurt their boss, who hadn't abandoned the idea of running for office again. Comey discussed the matter with Ashcroft, and on December 30, the deputy attorney general called a surprise press conference at the Justice Department. Comey announced that in "an abundance of caution," he and Ashcroft had decided the attorney general and his entire personal staff should remove themselves from the case.

Comey then revealed a bigger surprise: he was going to hand over the leak case to his close friend and colleague Patrick Fitzgerald, the U.S. attorney in Chicago. Fitzgerald would be appointed special counsel. Comey praised Fitzgerald, noting that he had a "sterling reputation" and was "absolutely apolitical." Comey and Fitzgerald had years earlier worked cases together at the U.S. attorney's office in New York. He was, Comey remarked, "Eliot Ness with a Harvard law degree and a sense of humor."

The deputy attorney general told the reporters he was delegating all authority for the investigation to Fitzgerald. This special counsel wouldn't have to report to him or anyone else at Justice. Comey was granting Fitzgerald extraordinary powers that no other federal prosecutor in the country had. Even independent counsels of the past, such as Kenneth Starr, had at least been accountable to a three-judge panel that oversaw their work. Fitzgerald would be answerable to no one.

Eckenrode didn't know Fitzgerald. But he met him at the Justice Department that day and gave him a crash briefing on the case. He handed his new boss a thick binder filled with forty dense FBI reports, known as 302s, that summarized the interviews Eckenrode and his team had conducted to date. Eckenrode then drove him to Reagan National Airport, and the two had a beer while waiting for Fitzgerald's plane. They talked about their New Year's

---

respond to polls showing that 50 percent of the public believed his administration had exaggerated the evidence on Iraq's WMD and connections to al-Qaeda. Bush maintained that he had "operated on . . . good sound intelligence." When Sawyer noted that Bush officials had said prior to the war that Iraq had actual weapons of mass destruction, not merely programs or the intent to acquire WMDs, Bush responded, "So what's the difference?"

Eve plans. Eckenrode would be spending it with his family. Fitzgerald, a longtime bachelor, mentioned he had a date with a woman he'd been seeing.

On New Year's Day, Fitzgerald called Eckenrode at home. He wanted to talk about those 302s. Fitzgerald had read them all. Having mastered the most obscure details, he started questioning Eckenrode about the interviews. He tossed out ideas—brilliant ones, Eckenrode thought—for moving the case forward.

Pat, Eckenrode interrupted, how was your New Year's Eve? How did your date go? Oh that, Fitzgerald said. He explained that he had worked late at the office. Eckenrode had the impression that the date never came off—and that Fitzgerald had spent New Year's Eve reading 302s. (A Fitzgerald spokesman later denied that the prosecutor had "stood up" his date.)

The conversation prompted Eckenrode to think: Wow, this is one serious prosecutor.

Don't go down this road, Pat.

—FLOYD ABRAMS, FIRST AMENDMENT LAWYER

18

The Prosecutor Versus the Press

WHEN DEPUTY Attorney General Comey compared Pat Fitzgerald to Eliot Ness of *The Untouchables* fame, he wasn't joking. The forty-three-year-old prosecutor had gotten his job as U.S. attorney because a Republican senator had been looking for a no-nonsense, nonpolitical crime fighter. As Illinois's only Republican senator in 2001, Peter Fitzgerald (no relation) had the opportunity to recommend to the White House a candidate for the important and much coveted U.S. attorney post in Chicago. Peter Fitzgerald had never heard of Patrick Fitzgerald. But the senator wanted an outsider. He wanted somebody who—like Ness, the incorruptible revenue agent dispatched to clean up the Al Capone mob—would be beholden to nobody in Chicago and willing to take on the state's perennially corrupt political establishment.

The senator called around, looking for the best assistant U.S. attorney in the country. Both FBI Director Louis Freeh and Mary Jo White, the Clinton-appointed U.S. attorney in New York, gave him the same answer: Patrick Fitzgerald. The senator interviewed the prosecutor, and his search was over. "You could just see, without question, he was an incredible straight shooter, a real straight arrow," the senator recalled.

Not everyone wanted the prosecutor from New York. House Speaker

Dennis Hastert was an old ally of the state's former Republican governor George Ryan (who was already under investigation by the U.S. attorney's office that Fitzgerald had been chosen to head). Hastert didn't want an outsider for the state's most sensitive prosecutorial post; he had his own candidate from inside Illinois. He complained to the White House. But Senator Fitzgerald by custom had the prerogative, and the Chicago media were in his corner on this issue. Patrick Fitzgerald got the nod. Months later, though, when Senator Fitzgerald was meeting with Karl Rove about another U.S. attorney selection in the state, the White House political adviser started yelling at him about the Patrick Fitzgerald pick. You got great headlines for yourself, Rove told him, but you ticked off the base.

PATRICK FITZGERALD, as Senator Fitzgerald saw him, was "straight from central casting." He grew up in Brooklyn, the son of two Irish immigrants. His father was a doorman at a ritzy apartment building on Manhattan's Upper East Side. He went to Amherst and studied math and economics. He was, his friends recalled, a brilliant problem solver with a phenomenal memory. Six feet two and over 200 pounds, he was an avid rugby player. After graduating Harvard Law, Fitzgerald entered private practice, got bored, and joined the U.S. attorney's office in New York. He soon developed a reputation as an aggressive, methodical investigator with plenty of patience and not much taste for compromise.

He put behind bars big-time heroin dealers, Mafia capos (including John Gambino), and a group of Islamic terrorists, including the radical blind cleric Omar Abdel-Rahman, for conspiring to blow up the World Trade Center and other New York City landmarks. His colleagues marveled at his ability to master the small details of a case and weave them into a larger narrative that made sense to a jury. They also ribbed him for his eccentric bachelor ways; once he accidentally left a lasagna in the oven for three months.

Following his conviction of the blind sheik in 1995, Fitzgerald focused on the little-noticed activities of an obscure Saudi financier named Osama bin Laden. Fitzgerald spent years tracking bin Laden, flying overseas with FBI agents to gather evidence and question witnesses. By the spring of 1998, Fitzgerald had filed the first sealed indictment against bin Laden—

for conspiracy to attack U.S. military facilities. And Fitzgerald became known as the Justice Department's premier expert on al-Qaeda. In the spring of 2001, he convicted the bin Laden operatives who had bombed two U.S. embassies in Africa. As a safety precaution, he did not receive personal mail at his home.

When he arrived in Chicago, Fitzgerald declared he was neither a Democrat nor a Republican. He declared himself an independent—and then proved it. He launched a wide-ranging probe into hiring practices at City Hall, a frontal attack on the Democratic organization of Chicago Mayor Richard Daley. And days before Comey handed him the CIA leak case, Fitzgerald filed a ninety-one-page indictment against the GOP ex-governor George Ryan on corruption charges.

He had one of the biggest and most significant caseloads in the nation and worked legendarily long hours, occasionally spending the night on a pullout sofa in his office. "Do I have zeal? Yes, I don't pretend I don't," Fitzgerald once told an interviewer. "As a prosecutor, you have two roles: Show judgment as to what to go after and how to go after it. But also, once you do that, to be zealous. And if you're not zealous, you shouldn't have the job."

His track record wasn't perfect; critics pointed to an excess of zeal, particularly in one case: Fitzgerald's pursuit of two large Chicago-area Islamic charities, the Global Relief Foundation and Benevolence International Foundation. Not long after he took over the Chicago U.S. attorney's office in mid-2001, Fitzgerald launched a criminal investigation of both groups, suspecting they had been funneling money to al-Qaeda. In late December 2001, FBI agents raided the offices of both charities, and the groups' assets were frozen. The charities were forced to shut down. But Fitzgerald wasn't able to bring terrorism-related charges against either. The 9/11 Commission later concluded that the U.S. government's treatment of the two charities "raises substantial civil liberties concerns"—an implicit slap at Fitzgerald.

But Fitzgerald came to believe that his Global Relief case had fizzled because it had been compromised—by the media. The day before the raid on Global Relief, *New York Times* reporter Philip Shenon had called the charity and asked about an impending law enforcement action. Fitzgerald and the FBI were convinced charity officials, in response to Shenon's call, had removed incriminating documents from the premises. So Fitzgerald launched a new investigation to find the source who had tipped off the *Times*. On August 7, 2002, he sent the *Times* a letter, asking to question Shenon about his sources and to inspect the reporter's phone records. "We believe," Fitzgerald wrote, "that freedom of the press neither protects the potentially criminal conduct of the government source in sharing this information with Mr. Shenon nor countenances Mr. Shenon's decision to relay that information privately to the subject of the search."

The *Times* turned Fitzgerald down. In the paper's response, *Times* lawyer George Freeman argued that the First Amendment "protects us from having to divulge confidential source information to the Government." But officials and editors at the paper worried that Fitzgerald wouldn't accept this far-from-certain legal point, and they were right.

Fitzgerald kept digging, and, thanks to secret national security wiretaps on the charity and testimony from charity officials, he eventually pieced together the story: Shenon had been tipped off to the Global Relief raid not by a government source but by a *Times* colleague, Judy Miller. Fitzgerald also had transcripts of a phone call made by Miller to the officials of another Islamic charity under government surveillance, the Holy Land Foundation, shortly before the FBI raided its offices. Someone in the U.S. government, Fitzgerald assumed, was leaking sensitive law enforcement information to Miller.

In the summer of 2003, Fitzgerald stopped by the office of Mark Corallo, the chief of public affairs at the Justice Department. Fitzgerald wanted to subpoena the phone records of Shenon and Miller. (Under department guidelines, subpoenas for news media records first had to be approved by Corallo, who turned down most of them.) Fitzgerald explained the case to Corallo. The public affairs chief feared that subpoenaing the *Times* would create a firestorm. "We were already being accused by the ACLU and our critics of creating a secret police force through the PATRIOT Act, and now we were going to be seen as trampling on the First Amendment," he later said. Ashcroft would get pummeled. And the evidence to justify the subpoena would have to be kept secret. Corallo was appalled that the *Times* might have tipped off a terror target. He asked Fitzgerald to do more work and figure out if there was a way "that part of the story could be told."

Fitzgerald agreed. Months later, he was still actively pursuing the case, determined to find Miller's source, when he sat down with Jack Eckenrode and began plotting out the CIA leak investigation.

THE president's speechwriters had a challenge. It was mid-January 2004, and they were drafting the annual State of the Union speech. The troubles in Iraq weren't letting up, but the Baathist regime had been destroyed, Saddam had been captured, and an interim government was forming. There was enough material to work with for a section in which the president could proclaim progress.

But what to say about Iraq's nonexistent weapons of mass destruction? Saddam's WMDs had been the president's public rationale for war. The speechwriters bandied different ideas about. One writer suggested using the past tense; have the president say Saddam *had* WMDs. After all, he had—in the 1980s. But this time, the NSC wasn't going to allow them any liberties. They were told to stick exactly to the language David Kay had used when he had presented his interim report three months earlier. So in his State of the Union addresss on January 20, 2004, Bush said of Iraq's weapons, "We're seeking all the facts. Already, the Kay Report identified dozens of weapons of mass destruction–related program activities."*

A week later, Kay offered a far more honest and memorable line.

He was back in the United States, having just resigned from the Iraq Survey Group. (In November, General John Abizaid, who had replaced Tommy Franks as head of Central Command, tried to change the mission of Kay's Iraq Survey Group to include counterinsurgency work. Kay resisted, and when he lost the fight he quit the ISG post.) Testifying before the Senate armed services committee on January 28, with only four lines of hand-scrawled talking points, Kay told the panel, "We were almost all wrong—and I certainly include myself here." The WMDs weren't hidden; they hadn't been produced in the first place. Despite Kay's sweeping statement, not everybody had misjudged Saddam's capabilities. Some intelligence analysts and UN inspectors, particularly those who questioned the nuclear claims, had gotten important parts of the story right. In any event, Kay said an independent commission was needed to investigate the Iraq intelligence failure. But his testimony made it seem as though the WMD debate was all but over.†

---

*Sitting with Laura Bush in the U.S. Capitol that night was Ahmad Chalabi, whose INC had provided faulty WMD intelligence from fabricators.

†As Kay was leaving the ISG job, he later recalled, Tenet said to him that no matter what Kay had found (or not), Tenet would always believe there had been chemical weapons in Iraq.

Kay's blunt words produced anguish among some members of Congress. Democratic Senator Bill Nelson, a former astronaut from Florida, was especially upset by one aspect of Kay's testimony: that he had found no evidence supporting the administration's prewar claim that Iraq had unmanned drones that could attack the United States with chemical or biological weapons. In an angry speech on the Senate floor that day, Nelson noted that he had attended classified briefings in which "I was looked at straight in the face and told that UAVs could be launched from ships off the Atlantic coast to attack eastern seaboard cities of the United States." He was "given that information as if it were fact," Nelson said, and it had influenced his decision to vote for the war. Now he was learning it was not true *and* that Air Force intelligence had disagreed with that assessment. (The Air Force dissent had been in the National Intelligence Estimate, which few senators had read.) "We need some answers," Nelson demanded.

The next day Kay met with Bush at the White House. Cheney, Rice, and Card were there, too. This time—unlike at Kay's previous meeting with Bush in July—the president asked a lot of questions: How did we get it wrong? What had Saddam been up to? Kay went through the whole Curveball disaster. Cheney, who was present, had no questions for him. (Days earlier, Cheney had insisted the trailers found in Iraq were definitely bioweapons labs.) Discussing Kay's findings, Bush showed no anger. He didn't ask Kay, could you be wrong? "The president accepted it," Kay recalled. "There was no sign of disappointment from Bush. He was at peace with his decision to go to war. I don't think he ever lost ten minutes of sleep over the failure to find WMDs."*

THE CIA director, though, was feeling defensive. On February 5, 2004, Tenet gave a speech at Georgetown University on "something important to

---

*With Democrats, especially the party's presidential candidates, calling for an independent investigation of the WMD intelligence failure, Bush declared on January 30, "I, too, want to know the facts." But he initially declined to endorse an outside commission. His aides told reporters they were worried an inquiry might produce information harmful to Bush's reelection effort. A week later, as political pressure mounted, Bush appointed an "independent" commission to study the WMD intelligence, with the White House picking all its members. The commission would not have to issue a report until March 31, 2005—months after the election.

our nation and central to our future: how the United States intelligence community evaluated Iraq's weapons of mass destruction programs." He had two main points to make: U.S. intelligence had not gotten it all wrong *and* the CIA had not distorted its findings to enable a White House hell-bent on war.

Tenet started off by declaring that intelligence is not a black-and-white business: "In the intelligence business, you are almost never completely wrong or completely right. That applies in full to the question of Saddam's weapons of mass destruction." He conceded only a few mistakes. The agency, he said, "may have overestimated" the progress Iraq had made toward developing a nuclear weapon. (He noted the NIE had contained dissents related to Iraq's nuclear weapons program—but he failed to mention WINPAC's aggressive promotion of the aluminum tubes and Niger allegations.) The CIA, he reported, was "finding discrepancies" in some of the claims made by its human sources about the mobile bioweapons labs but had been unable to "resolve the differences." This was a watered-down reference to the Curve-ball mess.* As for chemical weapons, he claimed more time was needed to search for them.

Tenet now made points he hadn't emphasized before the war. The NIE had said Iraq possessed weapons of mass destruction, but, he noted, the analysts who had written it "never said there was an 'imminent' threat." And the analysts had "painted an objective assessment . . . of a brutal dictator who was continuing his efforts to deceive and build programs that might constantly surprise us and threaten our interests." It was "an estimate," he said—not a firm and hard conclusion.

Tenet also referred—for the first time in public—to "sensitive reports" that had come from a source who "had direct access to Saddam and his inner circle." That source, he said, had insisted Saddam was "aggressively and covertly" developing a nuclear weapon, "stockpiling chemical weapons," but only "dabbling" with biological weapons with limited success.

This source, whom Tenet didn't identify, was Naji Sabri, the Iraqi for-

---

*The day before the speech, CIA officers briefed Tenet that most analysts now believed Curveball had been a fabricator. But Tenet and other CIA managers were reluctant to declare Curveball a total loss. In March, CIA officers would finally interview Curveball and find he couldn't explain the various discrepancies in his reporting. In May, the CIA would recall all of Curveball's reporting.

eign minister who had passed word to CIA Paris station chief Bill Murray that Saddam had nothing like the weapons capability that the Bush administration was claiming. But Tenet in his speech inflated what Sabri had said, according to Tyler Drumheller, the European Division chief of the CIA's Directorate of Operations.

Drumheller had handled Murray's reporting on Sabri, and he had drafted several paragraphs on the Sabri operation for Tenet's speech. But Tenet and his speechwriters had changed Drumheller's proposed language, Drumheller later said. Drumheller had written, in his view, a more precise account of what Sabri had actually told the CIA: that Saddam had talked about pursuing a nuclear weapons research program but was far from developing a weapon and that he had given up on maintaining chemical weapons, dispersing what was left of his arsenal to provincial political leaders. Drumheller didn't think Tenet was lying. The director was "parsing the language" to "maintain some level of respectability," Drumheller said. "He was spinning."

Tenet was implicitly saying, We did our job; if you don't like the results, talk to the White House. Tenet and McLaughlin may have even believed this. About the time of the speech, a senior CIA official subsequently recalled, "McLaughlin said to me, 'For the want of a few adverbs and adjectives we would have been fine.' He said to me, 'It's not an intelligence failure.' I said to him, 'What is it, a success?' He didn't have much of a response."

AFTER devouring Eckenrode's collection of 302s on New Year's Eve, Patrick Fitzgerald moved quickly on the CIA leak case. In mid-January, he requested records from the White House, including documents and e-mails relating to any conversations aides had had with reporters about Joseph Wilson.

On January 14, Fitzgerald arrived at the law offices of Swidler Berlin to interview Robert Novak. Thanks to Eckenrode's efforts, the prosecutor had in hand three waivers. One was signed by Armitage, one by Rove, and one by Bill Harlow, the CIA spokesman. This was everyone Novak had spoken to for his column. This created, as Novak later wrote, a "dilemma." Like other journalists, he considered these waivers to be meaningless. But his lawyer, James Hamilton, had told Novak that he would have little chance of prevailing in court if he didn't answer Fitzgerald's question.

This was the crunch time for Novak. In October, Eckenrode had not pushed Novak to disclose his sources. Now Fitzgerald wanted the columnist to name names. And Novak did. As Novak subsequently wrote years later, "I answered questions using the names of Rove, Harlow and my primary source"—meaning Armitage. Six weeks later Novak would testify before Fitzgerald's grand jury.

Fitzgerald not only needed to know the identity of the leakers; he had to determine if there had been a violation of the Intelligence Identities Protection Act, a poorly drafted law that established several hard-to-prove criteria. There were other legal issues, too. Another law, the Espionage Act, could be read to cover the leak of classified information—though prosecutors had never used the law in a case like this. Conspiracy charges could be a possibility—and that might cover both the leakers and their colleagues or superiors.

Fitzgerald also expanded the scope of his investigation. He got Comey to write him a new letter (which wasn't made public at the time) that clarified he had the authority to investigate not just any underlying crimes connected to the leak but perjury, obstruction of justice, the destruction of evidence, and related crimes.

Then Fitzgerald started calling top White House officials before the grand jury.

Rove appeared twice in February. He acknowledged his brief conversation with Novak but denied he had spoken to anybody at *Time*. Then Libby appeared before the grand jury twice, on March 5 and March 24. Libby may have felt locked in by the statements he had previously given to the FBI—at a time when he probably hadn't envisioned a prosecutor like Fitzgerald taking over the case. He offered a convoluted explanation of his actions (and state of knowledge) in the weeks prior to the Novak column that outed Valerie Wilson.

Before the grand jury Libby conceded that Cheney had first told him in mid-June 2003 that Wilson's wife worked at the Counterproliferation Division of the CIA's operations directorate. Libby had no choice but to acknowledge this. It was in his notes. Libby was a meticulous note taker; Fitzgerald had copies of his notes detailing his conversations with Cheney on the subject. But Libby claimed he had forgotten all about this crucial fact—Valerie Wilson's employment at the CIA—and wouldn't learn it anew until he called up Tim Russert on July 10, 2003, and Russert told him about Wilson's wife.

Referring to that conversation, Libby said, "It seemed to me as if I was learning it for the first time." Libby wasn't saying that the call with Russert had reminded him of a fact that had slipped his mind; he was maintaining that he had completely forgotten what he had learned weeks earlier from his boss—and that Russert's reference to Valerie Wilson hadn't even refreshed his memory. It was an odd defense: I knew, I forgot, I learned it again, and I forgot I had known it already.

Testifying to the grand jury, Libby maintained that Russert had said to him, "Did you know that Ambassador Wilson's wife . . . works at the CIA? . . . All the reporters know it." And Libby described his reaction to Russert:

> I remember being taken aback by it . . . and I said, no I don't know that. And I said, no, I don't know that intentionally because I didn't want him [Russert] to take anything I was saying as in any way confirming what he said, because at that point in time I did not recall that I had ever known, and I thought this is something that he was telling me that I was first learning.

As for his conversations with Matt Cooper and Judy Miller, Libby testified that he had told both that he had heard from "other reporters" that Wilson's wife worked at the CIA and that she had had a hand in sending him to Africa. But he testified that he had told these reporters that this wasn't information he knew on his own. "I didn't know he had a wife," Libby told the grand jury. "That was one of the things I said to Mr. Cooper. I don't know if he's married."

In questioning Libby before the grand jury, Fitzgerald and his team focused on the vice president. They asked Libby again and again about his conversations with Cheney. Libby acknowledged that Cheney had been "upset" about the Wilson op-ed and that the vice president had discussed it with him "on multiple occasions each day." Libby said that Cheney "wanted to get all the facts out about what he had or hadn't done" regarding Wilson's trip to Niger. Cheney, Libby added, "was very keen on that, and said it repeatedly. Let's get everything out." Libby testified that Cheney asked, is this normal for them to just send somebody out like this un-compensated, as it says. He was interested in how did [this] person come to be selected for this mission. And at some point . . . [his] wife worked at the Agency, you know, that was part of the question.

Libby was careful on a critical point, however. Cheney had written questions about Valerie Wilson on his copy of Joe Wilson's July 6 op-ed article, including the one asking if Wilson's wife had sent him on a "junket." But Libby, in his second grand jury appearance, claimed he had not talked with Cheney about the role Wilson's wife might have played in the trip until more than a week later—after the Novak column was published on July 14 (and when it would no longer have been a crime to pass along the information to anybody outside the government).

Judging from their questions, the prosecutors found this hard to believe. In Libby's telling, during the week following Wilson's op-ed, he and Cheney had spoken multiple times "each day" about all the vice president's various concerns related to the Wilson trip—except the one issue that had become the subject of a criminal investigation. During his second grand jury appearance, Libby was asked:

As you sit here today, are you telling us that his [Cheney's] concerns about Ambassador Wilson, his concern that he's working pro bono, his concerns that he's an ambassador being sent to answer a single question, his concern that his wife may have sent him on a junket, would not have occurred between July 6th and July 12th when you were focusing on responding to the Wilson column but instead would have occurred much later?

Libby replied:

The only part about the wife, sir, I think might not have occurred in that week.

Was Libby concocting a story to protect himself? Or was it to protect his boss? After all, if Libby had leaked classified information at the urging of the vice president, Cheney could be vulnerable to a conspiracy charge.

None of this was public at the time. Even the fact that Libby and Rove had appeared before the grand jury had gone unnoticed by the press. But by the time Libby was done testifying at the end of March, two things about the case were clear to the investigators. One was that the actions of the vice president were central to the leak investigation. The other was that there would be no way to test the truthfulness of Libby's implausible account other than to talk to Tim Russert, Judy Miller, Matt Cooper, and any other reporters with whom he might have spoken. And if the journalists wouldn't agree to talk, Fitzgerald would have to subpoena them.

THE spring of 2004 was an ugly time in Iraq. On March 31, 2004, four U.S. contractors for Blackwater Security were ambushed and killed in the city of Fallujah. Their bodies were burned, ripped from their vehicles, and dragged through the streets by an angry mob shouting "Death to America." Five days later, U.S. Marines cordoned off the city of 300,000 and began a block-by-block search for the insurgent leaders responsible for the atrocities. At the same time, the radical Shiite cleric Muqtada al-Sadr exhorted his followers to "terrorize" and expel the American occupiers; his black-clad private militia, known as the Mahdi Army, overran Iraqi police and seized control of government buildings in Najaf and several other Iraqi cities. Amid fears of a breakdown in law and order, Bush sounded a defiant note: "America will never be run out of Iraq by a bunch of thugs and killers."*

But the chief political worry for the White House was the impact the war would have on the election. Senator John Kerry, who weeks earlier had clinched the Democratic nomination, was attacking Bush hard on Iraq. Kerry, who had voted for the Iraq War resolution, called Bush's Iraq policy "inept" and "one of the greatest failures of diplomacy and failures of judgment that I have seen in all the time that I've been in public life." He accused Bush of not acknowledging that the problems in Iraq were severe and "complicated," and he called for Bush to do more to involve other nations and to hand over the rebuilding of Iraq to an international entity. Kerry suggested more troops were needed in Iraq. (The neoconservative *Weekly Standard* applauded Kerry for that.) But Kerry aides told reporters that the

---

*Days earlier, at the annual black-tie Radio and Television Correspondents' Association dinner, Bush had joked about the missing WMDs. As part of a humorous slide show, he flashed pictures of himself looking out the window of the Oval Office and looking under the furniture, and he said, "Those weapons of mass destruction have got to be somewhere."

senator had no plans to deliver a policy speech about Iraq anytime soon. They said they expected the war to be the bloody backdrop of the presidential campaign. Bush aides expected the same.

The news out of Iraq didn't improve. In April, 134 American soldiers were killed in Iraq; it had been one of the bloodiest months yet. And there were the pictures from Abu Ghraib prison that showed Iraqi detainees being sexually humiliated, taunted, and mistreated by American military guards. The grotesque images, rebroadcast throughout the Arab world by the Al-jazeera satellite network, created a new crisis of legitimacy for the American mission in Iraq. The president's approval rating was declining. Some polls showed Kerry leading Bush.

Within the CIA, there was a growing sense of gloom. The CIA's John Maguire, who had plotted the overthrow of Saddam for years, was beside himself. He had helped write a February 2004 aardwolf from the agency's Baghdad station, warning once again that the insurgency was gaining strength and becoming self-sustaining. But the White House hadn't wanted to hear it. The only feedback Maguire got from headquarters on the aardwolf was that Rice was "furious" at this description of the insurgency.

But Maguire was trying to do something about the problem. He and other CIA officers gathered hundreds of former officers of the disbanded Iraqi Army in the al-Rashid Hotel that spring, having been assured that Army Lieutenant General Ricardo Sanchez, the American military commander in Iraq, would come and talk to the group about how they could be rehired for the new Iraqi Army. Yet neither Sanchez nor any of his deputies showed up; Maguire's unemployed officers went home angry and resentful. Maguire was enraged. The episode was indicative of the entire U.S. approach to the occupation, which had begun, as Maguire saw it, with the senseless de-Baathification policy. "A historic opportunity was being squandered," Maguire later remarked. The country was being lost "through arrogance and ignorance." The arrogance was "the idea that we can impose something on a two-thousand-year-old society." The ignorance was bone-headed, ideologically driven policies such as de-Baathification and the dissolution of the army, which had fueled the anti-American insurgency. Yet neither the White House nor its emissaries in Baghdad were listening.

At times, the situation inside the Green Zone had an almost surreal quality. Maguire and the CIA station chief would attend Bremer's morning senior staff meetings. They would try to talk about the deteriorating security problems—and would get no response. "You'd sit in the meetings and you could hear the mortars going off, the windows were rattling," Maguire recalled. But nobody would say a word about what was going on. It was as though nothing was happening. Bremer, Maguire said, "would just sit there, staring at his boots. He was a weird man."

In May, Maguire's friend, former General Mohammed Abdullah al-Shahwani, who had been the chief of the CIA-trained Scorpions, was named as the interim director of the new Iraqi intelligence service. While he was in the Washington area for a short visit, Shahwani was invited to the White House. When he showed up, he was ushered into the Oval Office to meet with Bush. Cheney, Rice, Tenet, and Card were there, too. The president invited Shahwani to sit down right next to him. Tell me, Bush said, what's going on in Iraq.

"Sir, I'm going to tell you something," the Iraqi intelligence chief said. "You need to know the truth. Baghdad is almost surrounded by insurgents. The situation is not improving." Shahwani pointed out to the president that the road from the Baghdad airport to the Green Zone in the center of the city was no longer secure. "If you can't secure the airport highway, you can't secure all of Iraq," Shahwani remarked.

There was an awkward silence in the room. Shahwani noticed the leaders of the American government exchanging glances. It was as though they had never heard this—or that nobody was supposed to speak so bluntly with the president. Bush was surprised by the downbeat assessment, Shahwani thought. Cheney said nothing. Shahwani did most of the talking, and no one asked him for any advice. It seemed strange. After a few minutes, the president got up, had his picture taken with Shahwani, and exchanged a few pleasantries. Then he gave the Iraqi a souvenir tie clip bearing Bush's signature. Rice took the Iraqi intelligence chief aside. "I want to see you before you leave," she said. Shahwani went off with Rice. She asked, What can we do? What do you need? Let me know. Shahwani said he would and soon left for Baghdad. But he never again heard from the White House. He left the meeting believing Bush hadn't gotten the picture.*

---

*More than a year later, *The Washington Post,* citing classified documents, disclosed that members of Shahwani's CIA-created Scorpions had been involved in the brutal November 24,

In May, the CIA station in Baghdad sent another aardwolf to headquarters. It reiterated the bad news of the station's previous reporting—but, according to Maguire, it conveyed (or tried to convey) a greater sense of urgency. The insurgency, the cable noted, was expanding.

The White House had a daunting problem. While boasting of progress to bolster the president's reelection campaign, it couldn't publicly recognize Iraq was a mess and policy shifts were necessary. In Baghdad, Bremer was working furiously to transfer sovereignty to a new interim government at the end of June—which the White House was pointing to as the next big step forward. But as many experts and commentators outside the administration were saying, securing the country and defeating the insurgency would probably require more American troops. In a candid memo to Rice, Larry Diamond, a senior adviser to the Coalition Provisional Authority in Baghdad, wrote, "In my weeks in Iraq, I did not meet a single military officer who felt, privately, that we had enough troops. Many felt we needed (and need) tens of thousands more soldiers and . . . at least another division or two." Without more U.S. troops, he warned, "I believe we are in serious and mounting danger of failing in Iraq."

Diamond, a Stanford political science professor, had been friendly with Rice when she had been the university's provost. She had personally asked him to go to Iraq. But his tough memo elicited no response. That wasn't surprising. For the White House, sending more Americans to Iraq would be an admission of error and miscalculation. And acknowledging mistakes wasn't part of the president's campaign.

2003, death of an Iraqi general named Abed Hamed Mowhoush, who had turned himself in. While being questioned by American military interrogators at a detention facility, Mowhoush was stuffed into a sleeping bag. He died of suffocation. But two days earlier, four Scorpions and a CIA case officer had interrogated Mowhoush. According to U.S. military records reviewed by the *Post,* the Scorpions had beat him with fists, a club, and a rubber hose until he was nearly senseless. An Army memo said this beating "complicated" the "circumstances surrounding the death." John Maguire, the CIA officer who had helped develop the Scorpions, later maintained the four Scorpions had only questioned Mowhoush and that "there was nothing to substantiate" the allegation that the Scorpions had beaten him. A U.S. Army interrogator was later convicted of negligent homicide. No CIA officer or Scorpion was charged with any crime.

In late May, Iraqi police, supported by American soldiers, raided the Baghdad home and offices of Ahmad Chalabi, who had become a member of the Iraqi interim governing council created by the U.S. government. U.S. troops seized computers, records, and rifles from two offices of Chalabi's Iraqi National Congress. An Iraqi judge said the raids were part of an investigation of assorted crimes: torturing people, stealing cars, seizing government facilities. One of the arrest warrants was for Aras Habib, the INC's intelligence director. Habib had run the group's controversial "intelligence collection program," which had supplied fabricating defectors and bogus information to dozens of media outlets before the war. He also had been suspected by the CIA of being an Iranian agent for years—ever since Bob Baer and Maguire had dealt with him in the mid-1990s.

Chalabi complained that the raid was retaliation for his criticism of the American management of the occupation. "I call to liberate the Iraqi people and get back our complete sovereignty," he said, "and I am raising these issues in a way that the Americans don't like." But media reports, obviously based on leaks from U.S. officials, disclosed that Chalabi, who openly maintained ties with Iranian officials, was under investigation by the FBI for having handed top secret American information to Iran. He had allegedly told the Iranian intelligence chief stationed in Baghdad that the United States had cracked the code of the Iranian spy service. Condoleezza Rice promised there would be a full criminal inquiry. (The Pentagon's $340,000 monthly payments to the INC had recently been cut off.)

Chalabi denied the charge, and his American advocates, including Richard Perle and Jim Woolsey, claimed all these anti-Chalabi actions were politically motivated. Perle insisted that the CIA and DIA were mounting a "smear campaign" against his friend.

As for Habib, he vanished around the time of the raid on the INC headquarters. His suspicious disappearance raised an intriguing and significant question: Had the fellow responsible for slipping bogus INC "intelligence" on Iraq's supposed WMDs to U.S. officials and journalists—information concocted to start a war—done so at the behest of Iranian intelligence? Had the U.S. government and the American public been the target of an Iranian intelligence operation designed to nudge the United States to war? These were questions U.S. intelligence agencies never seriously investigated.

FOR a year, *The New York Times* had been under pressure from readers, bloggers, and press critics who were demanding the paper explain its prewar reporting on Iraq's nonexistent weapons of mass destruction, especially the work of Judy Miller. Executive Editor Bill Keller, burdened by other problems at the paper, had resisted calls to look backward. But shortly before the paper's ombudsman—a new post created in the wake of the Jayson Blair scandal—was to address the issue, the paper published an unusual (and unsigned) editor's note about its coverage. The note stated that there had been "an enormous amount of journalism that we are proud of" but in "a number of instances" the coverage "was not as rigorous as it should have been." The paper had relied too much, the editors said, on "information from a circle of Iraqi informants, defectors and exiles bent on 'regime change'"—most prominently Ahmad Chalabi, who had been a "favorite of hard liners within the Bush administration" and a "paid broker" of information from Iraqi exiles. The "problematic" articles included the front-page September 8, 2002, story on the aluminum tubes—the Michael Gordon/Judy Miller piece cited by Cheney on *Meet the Press* as he kicked off the administration's campaign to portray Iraq as a threat. The editors also questioned Miller's postwar April 21, 2003, report on the baseball-capped Iraqi scientist, noting the paper had never established the "veracity of this source" or his claims. It wasn't even clear, the editors noted, that he was a scientist.

The paper also distanced itself from Miller's front-page piece on Adnan Ihsan Saeed al-Haideri, the INC-coached defector who had claimed there was an extensive network of secret WMD facilities in Iraq (and who had been judged a fabricator by the CIA). This was the article that had been used as source material for the White House white paper released to support the president's UN speech in September 2002. "In this case it looks as if we, along with the administration, were taken in," the editor's note said. Miller had been the author or coauthor of four of the six problem-ridden articles cited by the editors, though the note mentioned no names.

Sometime after the editor's note appeared, Keller received a nighttime phone call in his kitchen from an agitated Judy Miller. The *Times* reporter told him that she was standing in the living room of al-Haideri's home in northern Virginia. She said he was about to be deported and that she needed to do a story right away exposing this terrible injustice. Keller was furious. Months earlier, he had told Miller to stop reporting on Iraq and weapons of mass destruction. It was as though she hadn't gotten the message or was just ignoring him. And here she was, still protecting and promoting a defector who had led the *Times* (and its readers) astray. It was as if she were still fighting the last war.

Keller had no interest in another al-Haideri story.

PATRICK FITZGERALD was proceeding methodically with the CIA case, and he had finally reached a line he was more than willing to cross. In May, he went after Tim Russert and Matt Cooper, both of whom Libby had mentioned during his convoluted grand jury testimony. Russert was essentially Libby's alibi. And Cooper was—in Libby's account—another witness who could back up Libby's claim that he had merely passed along gossip, not official classified information about Valerie Wilson that he had learned from Cheney, the CIA, and the State Department.

Fitzgerald contacted *Time* and asked the magazine and Cooper to cooperate with his investigation. He approached *Newsday* and asked to interview reporters Timothy Phelps and Knut Royce, who had written a piece confirming that Valerie Wilson worked at the CIA. Fitzgerald also asked *The Washington Post* if he could interview two of its reporters: Walter Pincus and Glenn Kessler. Pincus had cowritten a piece the previous October noting that an unnamed *Post* reporter had been told by an administration official that Wilson's wife was a CIA employee who had sent her husband on a boondoggle. Pincus had been referring to himself, but Fitzgerald didn't know that. He had obtained White House phone records showing that Libby had spoken to Kessler. So Fitzgerald wanted to know what Kessler and Libby had discussed. (As it turned out, it was not the Joe Wilson matter.)

Unlike Robert Novak, who had secretly cooperated, *Time* and *Newsday* turned Fitzgerald down flat. Fitzgerald responded right away. On May 21, he subpoenaed Russert and Cooper. *Time* and NBC said they would fight Fitzgerald. "Time Inc.'s policy is to protect confidential sources," declared Robin Bierstedt, deputy general counsel for the magazine. NBC News said the subpoenas would have a "chilling effect" on its ability to report the news. The subpoenas were not front-page news, but they caused alarm throughout the media. As some media commentators saw it, Fitzgerald had declared war on a bedrock principle of modern-day journalism: protecting anonymous sources. *Time* and NBC filed motions in U.S. District Court in

Washington to quash Fitzgerald's subpoenas, claiming a First Amendment privilege. But *Post* lawyers and editors started pondering if there was a way to sidestep a showdown with the prosecutor.*

Floyd Abrams, the renowned First Amendment lawyer who was representing both Cooper and the *Times,* called Fitzgerald and asked to meet with him. Fitzgerald agreed, and Abrams flew out to Chicago in June. "Don't go down this road, Pat," Abrams urged him. Did the prosecutor realize what he was doing? "I tried to persuade him to avoid the coming confrontation," Abrams later said. "I argued he really shouldn't do it [subpoena reporters] unless it was absolutely essential to the case." Fitzgerald was respectful—and absolutely unmovable. "He told me he had thought this through and he would not have started unless he was prepared to go to the end of the road legally."

Abrams pleaded with Fitzgerald to look at the broader implications. "I told him this was a bad thing as a policy matter for the country. It was a bad thing for the Bill of Rights." But Fitzgerald replied that he had "looked into the law" and was confident he would prevail. "When I walked out, I knew there was no way to resolve this," Abrams later said. "I thought it was hopeless."

Having kicked off a battle with the media, Fitzgerald also called on the White House. In separate sessions in June, he interviewed Cheney and Bush. Each had a private attorney present. Neither was put under oath. Fitzgerald spent seventy minutes with Bush. The White House called it an "interview," not "questioning."

ON JUNE 3, CIA Director George Tenet submitted a letter of resignation to Bush. He told the president he was resigning for personal reasons. Bush appeared before reporters on the South Lawn of the White House and announced Tenet's departure. He said that Tenet had done a "superb job."

---

*Editors and lawyers at the *Post* worked out a deal with Fitzgerald related to Kessler. After receiving a limited waiver from Libby, Kessler, in an interview with Fitzgerald, noted that his conversation with Libby hadn't covered the Wilson matter. The *Post* was looking to duck a full brawl with Fitzgerald. "We wanted to establish a base of cooperation with Fitzgerald to protect Walter [Pincus] from having to reveal his source," a *Post* source later said. "And we didn't want to challenge this in court and end up with an unfavorable appeals court or Supreme Court ruling. We worried that there were Supreme Court justices just waiting to take away the secret-source privilege."

Tenet was not with him. After speaking for two minutes, Bush left without taking questions.

As Tenet departed, the original case for the war seemed to be falling apart on another front. On June 16, the independent 9/11 Commission found "no collaborative relationship" between Iraq and al-Qaeda. After an exhaustive examination of intelligence community documents on the subject, the panel's staff said it discovered instances from the early 1990s in which bin Laden had "explored possible cooperation with Iraq"—but no evidence that these contacts had led to any sustained relationship or any cooperation on attacks against the United States.* Two weeks later, *Newsweek* reported that Ibn al-Shaykh al-Libi, the al-Qaeda commander who had been the main source for the president's and Powell's claims that Iraq had trained al-Qaeda in the use of "poisons and deadly gases," had recanted his story.

Then, on July 9, 2004, the Senate intelligence committee released a devastating 511-page report that chronicled the missteps, miscalculations, and shoddy judgments of the U.S. intelligence community prior to the war. The report concluded that the CIA and other agencies had succumbed to unfounded "groupthink" assumptions in determining that there had been weapons of mass destruction in Iraq. The intelligence agencies, the committee said, had reached conclusions that were either "overstated" or "not supported by the underlying intelligence." The report offered the first public glimpse into the Curveball debacle and new details about other Iraq intelligence fiascos, including the bizarre Niger saga. It also pointed out that the CIA had had no spies inside Iraq after 1998 and had been unable to get any firsthand information on its own about what was going on inside the country. The report, approved unanimously by the GOP-controlled panel, offered no criticism of Bush, Cheney, and other administration officials for having stretched the intelligence community's flawed assessments. Senator Pat Roberts, the chairman of the Senate intelligence committee, had decided that

---

*The day after the 9/11 Commission report came out, Bush insisted, "There was a relationship between Iraq and al-Qaeda." He noted that "Iraqi intelligence officers met with bin Laden, the head of al-Qaeda, in the Sudan"—even though the thirdhand report of this meeting (which supposedly occurred after bin Laden had left Sudan) had been discounted by U.S. intelligence. That same day, Cheney, in an interview, again asserted that the Atta-in-Prague report might be credible—even though the CIA, FBI, and the 9/11 Commission had found there was nothing to support it.

his committee's examination of how the White House had used the faulty intelligence about Iraq would be put off—until after the election.* The committee also delayed its investigation of two other controversial matters: the work of Doug Feith's intelligence cell at the Pentagon and the influence of Ahmad Chalabi's Iraqi National Congress on prewar intelligence. The committee's report rejected the charge that the White House had pressured intelligence analysts, but Democrats on the committee noted they disagreed with that conclusion.†

The same day while speaking at Kutztown University in Pennsylvania, Bush thanked the intelligence committee for the report. He conceded there had been "some failures" and remarked, "Listen, we thought there was going to be stockpiles of weapons. I thought so; the Congress thought so; the UN thought so. I'll tell you what we do know. Saddam Hussein had the capacity to make weapons. . . . He had the intent." But UN inspectors hadn't said there were weapons stockpiles before the war. In fact, during their pre-invasion inspections, they had found no evidence of stockpiles. And Bush didn't note that many of the members of Congress who had thought there were WMD stockpiles had been led to that view by briefings given by his administration. "They haven't found the stockpiles," Bush repeated, "but we do know he could make them."

THE CIA leak case had changed its public complexion. It now seemed to be more about the confrontation between Patrick Fitzgerald and the news media than the leak itself. Fitzgerald, Eckenrode, and their investigators were still searching for evidence and trying to determine if there were criminal charges to be brought against Libby, Rove, and others. But they did so

---

*After the 2004 election, Roberts tried to ditch this part of the investigation. But after being criticized for that, he decided this part of his committee's investigation would look at what both Republicans and Democrats had said about Iraq's WMDs going back over ten years. Still, the inquiry would be placed on a slow track and take years to complete.

†The Senate intelligence committee report raised questions about Joe Wilson's version of events relating to the origins of his Niger trip. It noted that a colleague of Valerie Wilson in the Counterproliferation Division had said that she had "offered up" her husband's name. Joseph Wilson later maintained that after the Senate report came out this CPD officer told Valerie Wilson that he had been misquoted and that he had written a memo stating that. But the officer's supervisor would not permit him to send it to the committee, according to Joseph Wilson.

quietly and produced few, if any, leaks about their actions—which was un-characteristic for a scandal-driven criminal probe in Washington. Fitzgerald, appropriately enough, was a leak-proof special counsel.

So the news of the case—when there *was* news of the case—centered on the public tussle between Fitzgerald and the media. And it seemed as though the hard-nosed prosecutor had the upper hand. In a landmark 1972 case *Branzburg v. Hayes,* the Supreme Court had ruled 5 to 4 that a journalist's pledge to protect a confidential source must yield to a grand jury subpoena. The court declared that a grand jury investigating a crime must have access to "every man's evidence," and that included evidence from reporters. Floyd Abrams had been wrestling with the implications of *Branzburg* for three decades. He had argued for years there was some wiggle room in a concur-ring opinion by Justice Lewis Powell that suggested there should be a bal-ancing test between the needs of the prosecutor and a free press. Abrams tended to be an absolutist on such matters and thought Fitzgerald had to be resisted. This was, he believed, the time to take a stand.

Other media lawyers looked at the particular facts of the leak case and had doubts about turning it into a crusade for media rights. They argued caution. After all, this was not about protecting a courageous whistle-blower who seemingly had exposed government corruption or malfeasance. It was about protecting high-level government officials who had been trying to tarnish a critic without leaving fingerprints. Was this case worth fighting over? Should journalists risk jail for this? A loss here—especially if it came in the form of a bad Supreme Court decision—could be a blow for journalism. Maybe this was a fight to avoid.

NBC News, after first opposing Fitzgerald's subpoena, relented. When U.S. District Court Judge Thomas Hogan rejected the network's challenge to the subpoena for Tim Russert's testimony, the network's lawyers decided to negotiate a deal with the prosecutor. On August 7, 2004, Russert quietly gave a deposition to Fitzgerald about the conversation he had had with Libby a little more than a year earlier. Under the terms hammered out with Fitzgerald by NBC, the prosecutor could only question the talk show host in a narrow fashion. But Russert did answer queries about the critical parts of that July 10, 2003, phone call.

Libby had told FBI agents and Fitzgerald's grand jury that Russert had told him it was common knowledge among reporters that Wilson's wife worked at the CIA. That had never happened, Russert told Fitzgerald. He said he had no recollection of knowing anything about Wilson's wife when he had spoken to Libby that day "so it was impossible for me to have [told Libby] that." Russert maintained he hadn't learned about Wilson's wife until he read about her the following week in Robert Novak's column. When he did see Novak's column, Russert testified, his reaction was, "Wow. When I read that, it was the first time I knew who Joe Wilson's wife was and that she was a CIA operative. . . . It was news to me." As Russert remembered it, Libby's phone call on July 10 had been only about Chris Matthews. He would later tell colleagues that "not one word" Libby had attributed to him was true.

Fitzgerald now had direct testimony contradicting what the vice president's chief of staff had told the grand jury. And his witness was about as credible as they come: a respected and widely known newsman.

Fitzgerald pushed ahead. Two days after Russert's testimony, he served Pincus with a subpoena. On the same day, Judge Hogan unsealed a ruling he had made three weeks earlier in which he had found *Time*'s Cooper in contempt for refusing to testify to Fitzgerald's grand jury. "We're going to appeal it as far as it goes," said *Time* Managing Editor Jim Kelly. But if the appeal failed, Cooper would face jail and *Time* could be fined $1,000 a day.

The leak case was front-page news once again—but as a battle between the prosecutor and the media. This had become the most significant clash of this sort in decades. "I think we're going to have a head-on confrontation here," remarked Lucy Dalglish, executive director of the Reporters Committee for Freedom of the Press. "I think Matt Cooper is going to jail."

Fitzgerald was not done targeting journalists. On August 12, he subpoenaed Judy Miller. He was now attacking the *Times*—and Miller—from two directions. While moving against Miller on the CIA leak case, Fitzgerald, who was still U.S. attorney in Chicago, was also pressing ahead on the Islamic charities case. He had recently notified the *Times* that he had been authorized by the Justice Department to subpoena the phone records of Miller and Shenon. (As Fitzgerald subpoenaed journalists in the CIA leak case, one name was conspicuously absent from the list of recipients: Robert Novak. Some reporters following the case assumed—correctly—the conservative columnist was cooperating.)

The First Amendment face-off that Abrams had feared back in June had arrived—on two fronts. Fitzgerald's double assault pushed him, Bill Keller, and Arthur Sulzberger, the *Times*' publisher, to resist at all costs. As Sulzberger saw it, nothing less than the future of American journalism was at stake. And Miller was at the center of this crusade.

FOR Cooper, there did seem to be an easy way out. Fitzgerald was interested primarily in what Cooper had to say about Libby. With Libby's phone records in hand, Fitzgerald assumed that Libby had been the administration source who had told *Time* about Joe Wilson's wife. But Libby had said little to Cooper about Wilson's wife. When Cooper had asked Libby about Valerie Wilson during a July 12, 2003, phone call, Cheney's chief of staff had said only, "Yeah, I've heard that too." The conversation seemed relatively innocuous and certainly not worth going to jail over.

The night before he was to be sentenced to jail, Cooper called Libby. "I've been called before the grand jury," Cooper said, "and I think they're going to ask me about a conversation we had about a year ago. Most of it was on the record, but part of it wasn't, and I wanted to see if I could get your permission to talk about the part that wasn't on the record." Cooper had reason to hope; Libby had granted personal waivers to Russert and the *Post*'s Kessler. Libby told him that "to be safe" Cooper's lawyer should talk to Libby's lawyer. If it was okay with them, it was okay with him, Libby said. With this call, Cooper and *Time* were making their first accommodations with the prosecutor, just as *The Washington Post* and NBC News had already done.

Abrams, representing Cooper, talked to Libby's lawyer and then reached an arrangement with Fitzgerald. On August 23, 2004, Cooper arrived in the Washington office of Abrams's law firm for his deposition. It was a big moment for Fitzgerald. He was convinced Libby had been Cooper's main source for the *Time* Web article that had mentioned Wilson's wife—so convinced that the prosecutor had agreed to limit his questioning to Cooper's conversations with Libby. There would be no questions about anybody else or any other subject. If Cooper testified that Libby had provided him the information on Wilson's wife, Fitzgerald would have two witnesses who contradicted Libby's testimony. With that, he could indict the vice president's chief of staff for perjury and possibly for the leak itself.

But when Cooper answered his questions, Fitzgerald didn't hear what he had expected. From what Cooper was saying, it was clear the *Time* reporter had learned about Wilson's wife before he had spoken to Libby. Fitzgerald had Cooper recount his brief conversation with Libby over and over to make sure he wasn't missing anything. Fitzgerald took a break so he could go huddle with his cocounsel. Then he came back and asked the same questions again. "He was obviously surprised at how little Matt had to say," Abrams recalled.

Cooper's account did conflict with Libby's testimony. According to the *Time* reporter, Libby had not said to him that reporters had told the White House Wilson's wife worked for the CIA and that he (Libby) didn't even know that Wilson had a wife. So with Cooper, Fitzgerald did have one more journalist who could testify that Libby wasn't telling the truth.

Yet Fitzgerald had a new and frustrating mystery. Cooper obviously had another source: an administration official who had first told him about Valerie Wilson. Fitzgerald and Eckenrode had interviewed every Bush administration official who they thought could possibly have been *Time*'s source. Nobody other than Libby had acknowledged talking to Cooper about Wilson's wife. Somebody must have lied. Fitzgerald was determined to find out who it was.

WMD—I got it totally wrong. . . . If your sources are wrong,
you are wrong.

—JUDITH MILLER, *NEW YORK TIMES* REPORTER

19

The Final Showdown

IT WAS the second night of the Republican National Convention—
August 21, 2004—and Karl Rove was sitting in the CNN booth at Madison Square Garden. He was granting a rare television interview. Asked by reporter John King about the Democrats' depiction of him as the president's political wizard, Rove responded with a laugh. "Dr. Evil," he cracked, might be the better description.

He then tore into John Kerry, the Democratic presidential candidate, assailing him as a "far left" candidate not "in sync" with America's values. Rove distanced the Bush campaign—somewhat—from controversial TV ads being aired by a group called Swift Boat Veterans for Truth that accused Kerry of having exaggerated his Vietnam combat record. But he quickly added that he understood why some veterans were mounting this attack. Rove cited Kerry's stint as a leader of the Vietnam War protest movement and claimed that Kerry had routinely portrayed his fellow servicemen as "war criminals." Rove was deftly managing to disavow the ads while reinforcing their message.

King next turned to a subject Rove didn't want to talk about: the CIA leak investigation. Administration officials had been questioned in the probe, King noted. "Can you tell us," he asked, "that you had nothing to do with—"

Rove cut him off: "I didn't know her name. I didn't leak her name. This is at the Justice Department. I'm confident that the U.S. attorney, the prosecutor who's involved in looking at this, is going to do a very thorough job of doing a very substantial and conclusive investigation."

That's all Rove would say, that he didn't leak her *name*. But it seemed to King that the Bush campaign was concerned. Bush aides could control the campaign's message—on Iraq, on terrorism, on the flaws of John Kerry. But they couldn't control Fitzgerald. There was "some worry in the Bush campaign," King said that night, that this "could be the October surprise"— political shorthand for a last-minute development that can influence an election. "If there are indictments or any progress in that investigation," King noted, "that could be one of those events that tends to redirect the campaign."

Rove had to be hoping that the truth would stay hidden.

Two nights later, on September 2, as wildly cheering delegates chanted "Four more years," President Bush strode to the stage to accept his party's nomination for a second term. It was a chance to define his presidency— and present the war on his terms.

John Kerry, in his acceptance speech at the Democratic National Convention at the end of July, had accused Bush of having misused the WMD intelligence and of having failed to prepare adequately for the postinvasion challenges in Iraq. "I will be a commander in chief who will never mislead us into war," he had said. With Iraq still insecure and unstable, Kerry's attack appeared to work. He emerged from the convention in a strong position: slightly ahead of the wartime incumbent in the polls. But the days that followed were rough for Kerry. An orange terror alert had shifted media attention to the war on terrorism—the president's strong suit. Kerry also failed to respond quickly to the Swift Boat attacks on his war record. Although most of the charges were quickly debunked by mainstream news organizations, the political assault on Kerry's credibility took its toll.

Now, as Bush stood before the thousands of Republican delegates, he sought to turn the tables on Kerry in an acceptance speech that again cast Iraq in the context of the broader war on terror. September 11, he declared, "requires our country to think differently" and confront threats "before it is too late." As the crowd chanted "USA! USA!" Bush reminded his audience that John Kerry and his running mate, John Edwards, had supported the October 2002 war resolution: "Members of both political parties, including my opponent and his running mate, saw the threat and voted to authorize the use of force." The United Nations had passed a unanimous resolution calling on Saddam to disarm, but, Bush claimed, the dictator had refused. "And I faced the kind of decision that comes only to the Oval Office, a decision no president would ask for but must be prepared to make," Bush said.

"Do I forget the lessons of September eleventh and take the word of a madman?"

"No!" roared the delegates.

"Or do I take action to defend our country? Faced with that choice, I will defend America every time!"

FIVE days later, on Tuesday, September 7, Army specialist Yoe M. Aneiros Gonzalez of Newark, New Jersey, was killed in Iraq on his twentieth birthday. He left behind an eighteen-year-old widow. Aneiros, who had hoped to become a doctor, had been riding in a patrol vehicle in the Baghdad neighborhood of Sadr City when he was hit by a rocket-propelled grenade. His death and those of two others killed in fierce fighting in Sadr City that day brought the American death toll in Iraq to over 1,000. News reports noted that nearly two thirds of those deaths, 647, had occurred since May 1, 2003, when President Bush had flown onto the USS *Abraham Lincoln* and declared the end of major combat operations while standing beneath a banner that proclaimed "Mission Accomplished."

At the Pentagon, Defense Secretary Donald Rumsfeld acknowledged this milestone, telling reporters that fighting terrorism "has its cost." He sought to keep the number in perspective. "Hundreds were killed in Russia last week," he said, referring to a ghastly shoot-out with Chechen terrorists at a school in Beslan. He also reminded reporters that the country was this week commemorating the third anniversary of September 11, when "3,000 citizens of dozens of countries" were killed.

Bush issued a brief statement from the White House. "We mourn every loss of life," he said. "We will honor their memories by completing the mission."

After learning that Scooter Libby had not been Matt Cooper's original source about Joe Wilson's wife, in September Patrick Fitzgerald issued the *Time* reporter a new subpoena. He was demanding that Cooper testify again and hand over the rest of his notes and e-mails on the subject. Fitzgerald was, as Cooper later put it, asking "for everything in my notebook."

At the same time, *The New York Times,* led by Sulzberger, was vowing to fight all the way to the Supreme Court to keep Judy Miller from having to testify. The firm stance adopted by Sulzberger and the *Times* greatly influenced *Time* magazine executives. Norman Pearlstine, editor in chief of all Time Inc. publications, and Sulzberger had lunch. The *Times* publisher talked about the importance of mounting a united and total resistance to Fitzgerald. Once *The New York Times* became involved, one *Time* executive later said, "We were going to wave the flag of the First Amendment for as long as we could." The *Times* was leading *Time* into battle.*

But it was a losing battle, probably doomed from the outset. Other First Amendment lawyers looked at the case and saw no way around the Supreme Court's *Branzburg* decision, which stated reporters had no privilege protecting them from testifying in grand jury investigations. Moreover, unlike *Branzburg,* which had partly involved a reporter's sources for a story on hashish production in Kentucky, the CIA leak investigation concerned a potential national security breach, a probe in which the stakes could be much higher. The news organizations were on weak ground. "From the start, our chances were significantly less than even," Floyd Abrams, the First Amendment expert representing the *Times* and *Time,* acknowledged after the case was over.

The decisions the two news organizations made at this point would later be second-guessed, and for good reason. The *Times'* editors had never sat down with Miller, reviewed her notes, and determined exactly what had happened between her and Libby. They had no idea of the extent to which Libby had tried to use her to justify the administration's prewar positions and how much he had disclosed to her about the Wilson matter. "There was a lack of due diligence," one veteran *Times* correspondent later said. "They decided to fight a battle without having the basic information about what

---

The Washington Post had not signed up for this fight. Walter Pincus worked out a deal that allowed him to testify to the grand jury without disclosing the identity of his source, who testified to the grand jury separately.

had happened." And there was disquiet within the newsroom about Miller. After the sustained pummeling she had taken over her Iraq WMD reporting, she seemed to many of her colleagues to be a little too eager to be the star in a major First Amendment clash.

At *Time,* Cooper appeared less excited about the prospect of becoming a press rights martyr, especially if it meant going to jail. But there was a way for him to avoid prison. In August, Cooper had asked Libby for a personal waiver so he could talk to the prosecutor about their off-the-record conversation. Libby, having little real choice (given the president's admonition that everybody cooperate with the investigation), had granted it, and Cooper had testified. Cooper could have done the same thing with Rove—and put the White House strategist in the same box. The magazine's editors and lawyers discussed this option, yet they chose not to pursue it—a decision that had the effect of protecting Rove and the president.

There were compelling legal reasons for *Time* and Cooper to hold back. Any effort by Cooper to reach out to Rove would undercut the argument that Abrams was planning to make in court about the need to protect confidential sources. But according to persons familiar with the magazine's own internal deliberations, there was another factor: *Time* Managing Editor Jim Kelly and other editors feared that any approach by Cooper could put the magazine in the position of influencing events. And *Time* didn't want to be in such a spot, especially during an election campaign. "There was a lot of concern about getting involved in the middle of the election," Richard Sauber, Cooper's lawyer, later said. Another source who participated in the magazine's discussions about the Rove matter, added, "There was an enormous reluctance to do that before the election. The idea of the magazine's White House correspondent asking Rove what he wanted of him was deeply troubling."

Just as had been the case with its October 2003 cover story on the CIA leak, the magazine was sitting on vital information that would have undermined the White House's credibility. *Time*'s editors, as they saw it, were acting in defense of an important journalistic principle: protecting sources. But the net result was a journalistic paradox: one of the country's most important news organizations—whose core mission is telling the truth—was concealing an important truth about the subject of a major criminal investigation involving the White House. Its silence was enabling Rove and the White House to maintain a false public position: that the most influential aide to the president had not leaked information about the identity of a CIA officer.

ON OCTOBER 6, Charles Duelfer, David Kay's successor as head of the WMD-hunting Iraq Survey Group, presented his comprehensive report to Congress. It appeared to be the final verdict on the WMD question, and it further shredded Bush's primary rationale for the war.

Shortly before Kay had left the post in early 2004, he had readied another report that essentially conveyed what he had told Congress: there had been no weapons of mass destruction. But once Duelfer took over, he sidelined Kay's report. This afforded war supporters and senior CIA officials—still smarting from Kay's "we-were-all-wrong" pronouncement—the opportunity to say, let's see what Duelfer can find. As Rod Barton, an Australian weapons inspector with the ISG, later recalled, Tenet had visited the ISG in February 2004, as Duelfer was taking over, and conveyed this message: "There are weapons out there; we just have to find them." Duelfer represented a last chance for administration officials still hoping to find evidence to support the dire and dramatic prewar assertions they had made to justify the war.*

But Duelfer let them down. His report was more definitive—and more damning—than Kay's findings. Saddam's WMD capability, it said, "was essentially destroyed in 1991." The report noted that Saddam had wanted to "re-create" his weapons programs—but only after sanctions were gone and the Iraqi economy had stabilized. The report explained that Saddam's main motivation for desiring unconventional weapons had been to deter Iran, which was presumed to have such weapons of its own. Duelfer's report noted that at the time of the invasion Saddam had no "plan for the revival of WMD."

In recent weeks, Bush had repeatedly insisted that Iraq had been a "gathering threat." But the Duelfer report showed there had been nothing gathering about it. So why hadn't Saddam cooperated completely with the UN

---

*Barton and another weapons inspector resigned from the Iraq Survey Group when Duelfer killed Kay's final report, which, among other things, reported that it was now certain that the trailers were not bioweapons labs but facilities that made hydrogen for military weather balloons.

inspectors to prove he had no WMD programs? Duelfer personally concluded that Saddam had been engaged in an impossible double game: trying to persuade the West that he had no WMDs while maintaining enough ambiguity that his historical foe, Iran, couldn't be certain that was true.

The day following the release of the Duelfer report, Bush spoke to reporters about it for three minutes. "Iraq," he conceded, "did not have the weapons that our intelligence believed were there." Yet he added, "Based on all the information we have today, I believe we were right to take action. . . . He retained the knowledge, the materials, the means, and the intent to produce weapons of mass destruction." That is, Saddam had had everything but the weapons and the actual programs to make them. Bush took no questions.

THE next day, October 8, Bush and Kerry held their second debate, this one at Washington University in St. Louis. During the first encounter, a week earlier, Kerry had tried several times to score points by attacking Bush and his decision to invade Iraq, calling the war a "colossal error of judgment." Bush had assailed Kerry for having first voted to authorize the use of force and then criticizing the war, suggesting Kerry was a flip-flopper.

At the second debate, Bush was asked by a woman named Linda Grabel if he could "please give three instances in which you came to realize you had made a wrong decision." Bush looked as if he were caught off guard. He acknowledged he might have made some "tactical decisions" that future historians could question. But on the big decisions, such as invading Afghanistan and Iraq, he had no regrets. "That's really what you're—when they ask about the mistakes, that's what they're talking about," Bush said. "They're trying to say, 'Did you make a mistake going into Iraq?' And the answer is 'Absolutely not.' It was the right decision."

Bush then cited the Duelfer report as proof, asserting that it "confirmed that decision today, because what Saddam Hussein was doing was trying to get rid of sanctions so he could reconstitute a weapons program." But Bush was overstating Duelfer's conclusions. The report said that Iraq had had no programs and had maintained only vague ambitions to pursue WMDs in the future. Bush finished his answer by noting, "I'm fully prepared to accept any mistakes that history judges to my administration, because the president makes the decisions, the president has to take the responsibility."

Five days later, there was one last presidential debate, hosted by Arizona

State University in Tempe. The focus was domestic affairs; the war in Iraq wasn't discussed much. Kerry said Bush had "rushed us into a war" and "we are not as safe as we ought to be." Bush declared he had a "comprehensive strategy" to "chase down the al-Qaeda" and that he had "held to account a terrorist regime in Saddam Hussein."

The next morning, Rand Beers, a terrorism expert who had resigned from Bush's National Security Council staff and now was a top adviser to Kerry, flew back to Washington from Phoenix. Sitting next to him on the plane was David Corn, who had been covering the debate for *The Nation*. Beers told him that he was satisfied with Kerry's performance in the debates, but he was frustrated that Kerry's criticism of both Bush's decision to go to war and the administration's poor planning for the postinvasion period was getting lost in the campaign wash. The attacks on Kerry's war record, the claim that Kerry had flip-flopped on the war, the charge that Kerry's plan for Iraq (which called for increasing international participation in rebuilding and securing Iraq) was not really a plan—all of that was distracting from the Kerry campaign's efforts to highlight Bush's pre- and postwar blunders.

But, Corn asked, wasn't Kerry in an impossible position? He couldn't promise a solution to the mess Bush had created. His position on Iraq had been full of nuances that didn't fit on bumper stickers. And consider this, Corn said: Kerry first came to public attention as a Vietnam vet who testified in Congress against the war and said, "How do you ask a man to be the last man to die for a mistake?" If he were elected president, wouldn't Kerry—since he wasn't in favor of a withdrawal—be doing exactly that: asking U.S. troops in Iraq to die for a mistake? And if the international community failed to respond to his call and Kerry was left to fend in Iraq alone, what would—and could—he do? Perhaps, Corn remarked to Beers, you ought to be careful what you wish for.

Beers recognized the dilemmas at hand. His voice became quiet. He described some of his talks with Kerry about Iraq—and what they might do were Kerry to win: "Sometimes, when it's late at night, at the end of a long day, we look at each other, and we say, 'What the fuck are we going to do?'"

ON OCTOBER 13, 2004, Judge Hogan held Matt Cooper in contempt a second time and threatened to send him to jail for up to eighteen months if he didn't testify to Fitzgerald about all of his sources for the leak story.

Hogan had also held Judy Miller in contempt the week before. After the hearing, Cooper said, "No reporter should have to go to jail for doing his job." But he was now closer to a painful choice: reveal a source or be locked up in prison. Hogan's decision regarding Cooper was reported the next day in *The New York Times* and *The Washington Post*.

The day after that, Rove made his third appearance at the federal court-house and changed his story.

During his two February 2004 appearances before the grand jury, Rove had denied having talked to Cooper. But now Rove conceded he had spoken to the *Time* reporter after all. He testified that he still didn't remember the conversation, his lawyer said later. But Rove could no longer dispute that it had occurred, for on this day he handed over what he claimed was a recently discovered copy of the July 11, 2003, e-mail he had sent to Deputy National Security Adviser Stephen Hadley. This was the short e-mail in which Rove had told Hadley that "Matt Cooper called" about a welfare reform story and then switched the subject to "Niger/isn't this damaging/hasn't the President been hurt?" By giving this e-mail to Fitzgerald, Rove was acknowledging to the prosecutor that he hadn't told the full story the first two times he was questioned before the grand jury.

Rove was now in Fitzgerald's crosshairs, and the prosecutor had a whole new set of questions: Why hadn't Rove disclosed the conversation with Cooper earlier? Why hadn't Rove, Hadley, or the White House turned over the e-mail previously? This was the sort of document covered by subpoenas from the Justice Department and Fitzgerald; it should have been produced months ago.

Sorting this out would preoccupy Fitzgerald. He had to determine if Rove had originally lied to the grand jury to conceal his conversation with Cooper. An obvious issue for Fitzgerald and his investigators was whether Rove was now acknowledging the Cooper phone call because Cooper had just been held in contempt and might be compelled to testify about his conversation with Rove. Rove's testimony made it even more imperative for Fitzgerald to get Cooper's account—and his notes.

There was another piece to this puzzle. A hard copy of the Hadley-Rove e-mail turned over to Fitzgerald (which was independently obtained by the authors) showed that it had been printed out of Rove's White House computer on November 25, 2003. One of Rove's assistants, B. J. Goergen, had searched the computer that day at the request of Rove's attorney, Robert

Luskin. So why had it taken Rove nearly eleven months to turn it over to Fitzgerald? For a year and a half, Rove would remain in legal jeopardy, as Fitzgerald would attempt to unravel this mystery.

But on October 15, 2004, none of this was publicly known. Reporters covering the case had no inkling that Rove's earlier testimony was now contradicted by a piece of evidence that he had not disclosed for almost a year. The news stories that day merely reported that Rove had been spotted going into the grand jury. They quoted Luskin saying that his client was not a target of the investigation and "has been cooperating fully from the beginning."

With only three weeks to go to the election, the public was unaware that Rove was suspected by Fitzgerald of having lied to the grand jury to hide his role in the CIA leak.

On November 2, 2004, Bush was reelected, capturing 51 percent of the popular vote to Kerry's 48 percent. The Republicans strengthened their hold over both houses of Congress. There had been no blowups in the CIA leak case. And Bush's selling of the war hadn't come back to haunt him. A *Newsweek* poll taken the week before the election found that 43 percent of Americans—a large bloc but not a majority—thought that Bush and his administration had purposefully misled the public about the prewar intelligence and the case for invading Iraq. According to a Harris poll, 46 percent believed that "what we were told by the government before the war about weapons of mass destruction and links to al Qaeda" was "misleading." By election day, almost half of America had concluded that Bush had falsified his argument for war—but a slight percentage more believed he had acted in good faith.

Two days later, a buoyant Bush held a White House press conference and declared, "I earned capital in the campaign, political capital, and now I intend to spend it. It is my style."

Less than two weeks after Bush's reelection, Colin Powell resigned. Bush quickly picked Condoleezza Rice to be his next secretary of state.

On December 14, 2004, Bush staged an extraordinary ceremony at the White House to present the Presidential Medal of Freedom, the country's highest civilian honor, to three architects of the Iraq enterprise: Tenet, Franks, and Bremer. Bush kidded and teased the CIA director for having the "demeanor of a longshoreman" and for chewing on unlit cigars. He credited Tenet as being "one of the first to recognize and address the threat to America from radical terrorist networks." He praised the CIA's role in the war in Afghanistan and its efforts to dismantle the leadership of al-Qaeda. He made no mention of the prewar intelligence on Iraq. A few days before the ceremony, it had been reported that Tenet had signed a $4 million contract to write a "candid" account of his tenure as CIA director. There was immediate speculation that Tenet would use the book to blame the White House for the Iraq WMD debacle. Not long after the ceremony, Tenet decided to postpone the book. He explained that he needed more time to do the research and "to gain the necessary perspective." He didn't yet know what he wanted to say.

FITZGERALD's investigation moved relentlessly forward, as he zeroed in on the reporters he wanted as witnesses. On December 8, a three-judge federal appeals court panel heard oral arguments regarding *The New York Times'* and *Time* magazine's appeals of the contempt orders issued against Judy Miller and Matt Cooper. The large hurdle facing the news organizations became apparent when Judge David Sentelle, a cantankerous conservative, interrupted Floyd Abrams and demanded to know how this case differed from *Branzburg,* the 1972 Supreme Court ruling that reporters have no privilege to refuse to testify in criminal investigations. When Abrams didn't offer a satisfactory answer, Sentelle grew testy. "If there's an answer to my question, I'd love to hear it," the judge snapped. "I take it you don't have one since you haven't advanced it yet, given three, four, or five opportunities."

When Cooper interviewed Bush in the White House that month, the president cracked, "Cooper! I thought you'd be in jail by now." Cooper replied, "What can I say, Mr. President. The wheels of justice grind slowly."

FOR the Bush White House, the WMD controversy was done. In January 2005, the Iraq Survey Group shut down for good. At a press briefing, reporters pressed McClellan to respond to this finale. "If the information about WMDs is wrong, as we all agree now, is there no consequence?" one asked.

Bush's "focus," McClellan replied, "is on helping to support those in the region who want to move forward." Days later, *Washington Post* reporters interviewed Bush aboard Air Force One. "In Iraq," they said, "there's been a steady stream of surprises. We weren't welcomed as liberators, as Vice President Cheney had talked about. We haven't found the weapons of mass destruction as predicted. The postwar process hasn't gone as well as some had hoped. Why hasn't anyone been held accountable, either through firings or demotions, for what some people see as mistakes or misjudgments?" Bush brushed aside the suggestion that anyone had to be held responsible: "Well, we had an accountability moment, and that's called the 2004 election." On January 20, during his second inaugural address, Bush proclaimed that America's security depended upon advancing "liberty in other lands." He did not utter the word "Iraq."

Ten days later, millions of Iraqis participated in the first post-Saddam election. The violence in recent weeks had been discouraging. The governor of Baghdad had been assassinated. A helicopter crash and insurgent attacks had resulted in thirty-seven dead American troops in one day. But the election was a stirring moment—an optimistic one—with Iraqis leaving polling places and brandishing a purple finger that showed they had voted. The images of smiling Iraqi women in black *abayas* emerging from polling booths was heartening. When Bush delivered his 2005 State of the Union speech three days later, some members of Congress held up fingers that had been dyed purple.

ON FEBRUARY 15, 2005, Fitzgerald won a key victory. The appeals court panel ruled three to nothing that Miller and Cooper had to testify or face jail. "There is no First Amendment privilege protecting the evidence sought," the majority opinion stated. In a concurring opinion, Judge David Tatel, a Clinton appointee, cited the fact that forty-nine states and the District of Columbia offered some protection to reporter-source confidentiality (though no federal law did so). Tatel stated that he believed in a "balancing test" to determine whether a reporter should be forced to disclose his or her sources. There were cases when leaks of even classified information produced important public benefits that justified protecting confidential sources, he wrote. (He cited as one example the prize-winning series cowritten by Miller that had alerted *New York Times* readers to the threat from al-Qaeda months before the September 11 attacks.) But in ten redacted pages, Tatel discussed the secret grand jury evidence that Fitzgerald had presented to the court to demonstrate his need for the two reporters' testimony. Although the public—and the lawyers for the news organizations—couldn't read these pages, Tatel concluded that this secret evidence showed that in this case the balance was in the prosecutor's favor. The leak of Valerie Wilson's identity had "marginal news value," he wrote, and compelling the reporters to identify their sources was "essential" to "remedying a serious breach of the public trust."*

The *Times* and *Time* announced they would appeal the decision to the Supreme Court.

The prospect of imprisonment transformed Miller into a First Amendment crusader. The *Times* reporter, whose reporting on Iraq had caused so much controversy, struck a defiant note. "I have to be willing to go to prison," Miller told CNN. "I think the principles at stake in this case are so important to the functioning of a free press and to the confidentiality of sources that I just have to be willing to do that." Lucy Dalglish, executive director of the Reporters Committee for Freedom of the Press, observed, "This has rehabilitated her image a bit."†

Though the *Times*—Miller, Sulzberger, and Keller—displayed a united front in public as advocates for media rights, cracks were forming. Miller didn't trust Keller after the May 2004 editor's note questioning her WMD-related reporting. She worried he wouldn't want to identify the paper fully with a reporter accused of having helped the Bush White House. And a few weeks earlier, she had retained her own lawyer, Robert Bennett, one of Washington's premier criminal defense attorneys, whose clients had included Bill Clinton in the Paula Jones case and Caspar Weinberger during the Iran-*contra* affair. (Matt Mallow, a corporate lawyer and friend, had pushed

---

*In the redacted pages, some of which would be released a year later, Tatel noted that Fitzgerald had already obtained evidence contradicting Libby's grand jury testimony. He wrote, "The special counsel appears already to have at least circumstantial grounds for a perjury charge." Tatel maintained that perjury "is itself a crime with national security implications."

†Most news organizations were generally supportive of *Time* and *The New York Times,* but some professional journalists were troubled. In a May 13, 2005, column, David Ignatius of *The Washington Post* noted that Fitzgerald appeared to be probing into perjury by one or more high-level government officials. If that were indeed the case, Ignatius wrote, it raised questions as to whether reporters were still obligated to protect the officials under investigation. "Does a reporter's confidentiality agreement extend to protecting a cover up?" he asked.

Miller to retain her own counsel, arguing that Floyd Abrams and the *Times'* in-house lawyers were being paid by Sulzberger, not her.) "I don't want to represent a principle," Bennett told her when he was hired. "I want to represent Judy Miller." During their first meeting, he had explained to her that not only could she be cited for civil contempt for refusing to cooperate with Fitzgerald, she could face a criminal contempt charge and a prison sentence of five years. She had walked out of the meeting terrified, wondering if the *Times* and she shared all the same interests.

For his part, Cooper seemed no more eager to play the crusader. After the appeals court panel ruled against him and Miller, he said, "You'd have to be catatonic not to be unsettled by the prospect of a jail sentence. Great career move? I had a pretty good career already."*

BUSH'S commission on WMD intelligence concluded its investigation at the end of March and released a 692-page report. Its overall finding was no news flash: "the Intelligence Community was dead wrong in almost all of its pre-war judgments about Iraq's weapons of mass destruction. This was a major intelligence failure." The commission warned that the "harm done to American credibility by our all too public intelligence failings in Iraq will take years to undo." It reported that intelligence analysts who had handled WMD issues had told the commission they hadn't been directly pressured to "skew or alter any of their analytical judgments." But, the panel added, "it is hard to deny that intelligence analysts worked in an environment that did not encourage skepticism about the conventional wisdom."

As had the Senate intelligence committee, Bush's commission, cochaired by Judge Laurence Silberman, a Republican, and former Senator Chuck Robb, a Democrat, ignored a key issue: whether Bush and his aides had

---

* On February 24, 2005, *The New York Times* won a victory over Fitzgerald on another front: a federal judge in New York blocked the prosecutor's attempt to obtain the phone records of Miller and Philip Shenon in the Islamic charities case. The judge ruled that the reporters had a qualified privilege to protect their confidential sources and that Fitzgerald hadn't "reasonably exhausted" alternative means of finding out who had leaked word of the December 14, 2001, FBI raid on Global Relief. Abrams hailed the decision as a "substantial vindication of the right of journalists to protect their sources." But Fitzgerald appealed. In August 2006, a federal appeals court overturned the ruling and said Fitzgerald could inspect Miller's and Shenon's phone records.

overstated and misrepresented the intelligence they had received from the intelligence agencies. The commission noted in a footnote:

> There is a separate issue of how policymakers used the intelligence they were given and how they reflected it in their presentations to Congress and the public. That issue is not within our charter and we therefore did not consider it nor do we express a view on it.

The war was two years old, and no official body in Washington had yet examined how Bush and his aides had used the intelligence. The commission hadn't even interviewed Bush or Cheney during its fourteen-month investigation.

IN IRAQ, it was another bloody spring. In May, about 600 Iraqi civilians and 250 Iraqi police officers and soldiers were killed in car bombings, suicide bombings, and attacks. Responding to this rise in violence, the new Iraqi government launched a major counterinsurgency campaign in Baghdad, employing 40,000 Iraqi troops. As this effort was under way, the police chief of Basra admitted he had lost control of three quarters of his officers and that sectarian militias had infiltrated his force and their loyalists were using these posts to assassinate opponents. The intense pitch of insurgent and sectarian attacks continued into June.

Vice President Cheney, though, saw grounds for optimism. "The level of activity that we see today from a military standpoint, I think, will clearly decline," he said on *Larry King Live*. "I think they're in the last throes, if you will, of the insurgency."

THE final showdown in the CIA leak case began on June 27, 2005, when the Supreme Court, without any comment, declined to consider the appeal filed by *The New York Times* and *Time* to Judge Hogan's contempt order. Responding to the Supreme Court action, Sulzberger noted that Miller was honor-bound not to disclose her source.

At a hearing two days later, Judge Hogan gave Miller and Cooper one week to comply—or face the consequences. Hogan also told lawyers for

Time Inc. that he was prepared to impose large fines on the company if *Time* didn't turn over Cooper's notes and e-mails. When one of *Time*'s lawyers, Theodore Boutrous, said the magazine was "grappling with" what to do, Fitzgerald shot back, "I don't understand what *Time* can deliberate about. They don't have a right to break the law. We shouldn't allow people to think court orders are sort of optional."

Fitzgerald had a point. *Time* was owned by a publicly traded corporation (Time Warner). If it defied a court order—and that would cost the corporation lots of money—the corporate parent could face repercussions from federal regulators and its own shareholders. The decision about what to do was left with Norm Pearlstine, Time Inc.'s editor in chief.

The next day, after much agonizing, Pearlstine decided to turn over Cooper's notes to Fitzgerald. "I found myself really coming to the conclusion that once the Supreme Court has spoken in a case involving national security and a grand jury, we are not above the law," he said to explain his decision. Sulzberger told the Associated Press that he was "deeply disappointed" by Pearlstine's decision.*

Among the materials *Time* gave to Fitzgerald was Matt Cooper's e-mail showing that Karl Rove had been his source about Valerie Wilson's employment at the CIA.

THAT week, *Newsweek* reporter Michael Isikoff was working the CIA leak story. He had been told by several sources that Rove was the unidentified Bush administration official Cooper was protecting—and that the subpoenaed *Time* e-mails would show that conclusively. Late on the afternoon of June 29, Isikoff e-mailed Rove. He told him he planned to report this and asked for his comment.

A few hours later, Robert Luskin, Rove's attorney, called Isikoff on his

---

*Shortly after Pearlstine handed Cooper's notes and e-mails to Fitzgerald, he went to Washington to meet the Washington bureau staff. He reiterated his reasoning for cooperating with Fitzgerald. The editors and writers did not hide their anger. Michael Weisskopf, a reporter who had lost a hand while covering the war in Iraq, said that he had always considered Pearlstine a "journalistic giant"—but he could not fathom his decision. This was a moment to stand up, Weisskopf told him. Other reporters noted that sources were telling them that they could no longer cooperate with *Time*. "Cooper sat there looking distressed," one participant recalled. "Norm was startled by the level of anger. It was clear to everyone our reputation had suffered."

cell phone. He professed that Rove had nothing to worry about. His client, Luskin once again said, had fully cooperated with Fitzgerald and was not a target in the investigation. "Karl has never knowingly disclosed classified information," he remarked. "Karl did not tell any reporter that Valerie Plame worked for the CIA."

But Isikoff pressed Luskin. He told the lawyer he had sources assuring him that Rove was identified in Cooper's e-mails. How did Luskin account for that? Had Rove spoken to Cooper that week or not? Luskin dodged this question a bit; then he acknowledged—first on background, later on the record—that Rove indeed had a brief call with Cooper. But the lawyer claimed that all Rove had said to Cooper was that *Time* shouldn't get too far out on the Wilson story and that Tenet was going to be putting out a statement on the Niger matter that afternoon. That was it, merely a helpful heads-up, according to Luskin.

This was a partial breakthrough in the story: Rove had talked to Cooper. But it was short of what Isikoff had been told by other sources—that Rove had provided Cooper the key information about Wilson's wife. The story that Isikoff ended up writing was toned down. When it came to Rove, his editors wanted to be careful. The piece reported only that Rove had been "one of the sources" for Cooper's article. It quoted Luskin as denying that Rove had disclosed anything to Cooper about Valerie Wilson. But the story did quote another lawyer for a White House official saying there was "concern" among Bush aides about Fitzgerald's focus on Rove.

The story prompted reporters to start pushing Luskin, and Rove's lawyer responded by spinning away. To a *Washington Post* reporter, he said, "Who outed this woman? . . . It wasn't Karl." To the *Los Angeles Times,* he called the *Newsweek* account "70 percent wrong" and added, "I state categorically that my client did not disclose Valerie Plame's identity to Matt Cooper or anyone else." He told *The Wall Street Journal* that Rove had not asked any reporter to treat him as a confidential source regarding Valerie Wilson and "if Matt Cooper is going to jail to protect a source, it's not Karl he's protecting."

Luskin's comment to *The Wall Street Journal* appeared on July 6, 2005, the day Cooper and Miller were scheduled to be sentenced to jail. (*Time* had handed over Cooper's e-mails, but Fitzgerald still needed Cooper's testimony about them—and Cooper was still standing on principle.) That morning, Richard Sauber, Cooper's lawyer, read the *Journal* article with great interest.

He was on his way back from a family vacation in Alaska, switching planes in Chicago, so he could be in the courtroom in Washington at 2 P.M. for the hearing before Hogan. As he fixated on Luskin's quote, he thought he saw an opening—but he knew he had to move fast.

Cooper so far had showed no sign of wavering, but he was torn. "Nobody knew what Matt would do," one of his editors later said. Cooper and his wife, Mandy Grunwald, a Democratic political consultant who was the daughter of a venerated *Time* editor, had a six-year-old son. He wanted to do the right thing as a journalist, Sauber later said, but he understandably had no interest in becoming an inmate. Just in case, Sauber had recently arranged for a prison consultant to brief Cooper on how to prepare for jail: how he should handle himself with other prisoners, how and when to make eye contact, how to avoid becoming a target.

From the airport in Chicago, Sauber called his client. Cooper hadn't accepted the general waiver that Rove and other White House officials had been compelled to sign. But, Sauber told Cooper, if Luskin was willing to say to Sauber what he had told the *Journal,* that could be considered a "personal" waiver. Sauber quickly called Luskin, and Luskin said he would have to check with his client.

A frenzied series of phone calls ensued. Luskin called Rove, Fitzgerald, and then Sauber. And shortly after 12:30 P.M., Sauber faxed to Luskin a proposed statement that Rove "affirms his waiver of any claim of confidentiality he may have concerning any conversation he may have had with Matthew Cooper of Time Magazine during the month of July 2003."

In authorizing his lawyer to accept the statement, Rove wasn't acting out of compassion for Cooper's plight. Anytime in the past year, he could have called Cooper—or had Luskin call Sauber—and spared the reporter his agony. But once Sauber made the request, Rove had little choice. Asking Cooper to stay silent could be construed as obstruction of justice by Fitzgerald.

Ninety minutes later, Cooper and Miller were in Courtroom 8 in the federal courthouse. Standing before Judge Hogan, Miller read a statement. "If journalists cannot be trusted to guarantee confidentiality," she said, "then journalists cannot function and there cannot be a free press." She called her refusal to testify "an act of civil disobedience." Hogan was unmoved. "I have a person in front of me who is defying the law." He ordered her sent to jail. She was taken into custody by three court officers. Shackles were placed on her hands and feet, and she was driven to the Alexandria Detention Center in Virginia. As she passed the U.S. Capitol and other government buildings—where she had roamed as a reporter—she thought, "My God, how did it come to this?"

After Miller had been escorted out, Cooper stood up to deliver a statement. He had woken up that morning, he said, prepared to go to jail. He had already said good-bye to his son when he had received an unexpected phone call. "A short time ago, in somewhat dramatic fashion," Cooper told the court, "I received an express, personal release from my source. It's with a bit of surprise and no small amount of relief that I will comply with this subpoena."

COOPER wouldn't publicly identify his mystery source. The assumption of most of the reporters at the courthouse that day was that it must have been Rove. But Luskin once again muddied the picture. He told reporters that it wasn't Rove who had called Cooper and freed him to testify. Isikoff was taken aback. Had he and *Newsweek* been wrong to point the finger at Rove?

But Rove's attorney—unknown to the reporters—was again being disingenuous. It was technically true that Rove hadn't called Cooper. Rather, Rove's attorney (Luskin) had called Cooper's attorney (Sauber). The bottom line, though, was the same: Rove had been Cooper's source, and it was Rove who, through Luskin, had given Cooper his personal waiver. Yet Rove's lawyer was doing everything he could to keep this from becoming public.

The day following the court hearing, Isikoff called one of the sources, who reassured him that a *Time* e-mail turned over to Fitzgerald showed Rove was the culprit. You see how they spin their way out of everything, Isikoff said. There's only one way to prove it was Rove, he told his source, I need the Cooper e-mail.

Isikoff and his source met the next day in a dark corner of an out-of-the-way restaurant at an early hour, before the lunch crowd arrived. The source slipped Isikoff a copy of the e-mail. It was more damning than Isikoff had expected.

It was the e-mail Cooper had sent to his editors: "Subject: Rove/P&C," for personal and confidential. The e-mail stated that Cooper had spoken to Rove "on double super secret background" and that Rove had told him that

"Wilson's wife, who apparently works at the agency on wmd issues," had "authorized the trip."

In one short paragraph, the e-mail blew apart Rove and Luskin's deceptions and the White House's denials of the past two years. This was hard evidence that Rove had leaked and that he and the White House had covered up his role in the scandal. When Isikoff returned to the *Newsweek* offices, he shared the e-mail with the magazine's senior editors. "Wow," said Tom Watson, *Newsweek*'s national editor, "I don't know that I've ever seen a smoking gun before."

Still, the editors wanted to know who had provided it. Isikoff explained that the source was insistent: the reporter wasn't to disclose the source's identity to anyone, not even his editors. There was some back-and-forth over this at the magazine. But Isikoff's editors were eventually satisfied the e-mail was real. Once Isikoff had it in hand, he was able to get other sources to confirm its authenticity. When he called Luskin for comment and started reading the e-mail to him, the lawyer asked him to slow down so he could start typing. It was clear Luskin had no idea what it said or how much his client was implicated by Cooper's own words. Still, the lawyer was unruffled. This is consistent with what Karl has been saying all along, he said without missing a beat.

THAT Sunday, the *Newsweek* story hit the Web and caused a stir. It was undeniable proof that Rove had passed classified information about Valerie Wilson to a reporter. True, Rove hadn't sought out Cooper to slip him the secret, in classic Washington leak fashion. He had blurted it out in a brief telephone conversation in response to the reporter's question. But at stake was the credibility of everything the White House had been saying since the controversy began.

On Monday, July 11, when Scott McClellan, the White House press secretary, took to the podium, the press corps ripped into him. It was as if the reporters were venting pent-up frustrations that had been gathering for years. AP's Terry Hunt initiated the barrage: "Does the president stand by his pledge to fire anyone involved in the leak?"* McClellan responded that

---

*In June 2004, Bush had reaffirmed his pledge to dismiss anyone who had committed this leak.

"while that investigation is ongoing, the White House is not going to comment on it." An angry David Gregory of NBC News grilled the press secretary. "This is ridiculous!" Gregory exclaimed, adding, "Do you stand by your remarks from that podium or not?" And so it went. McClellan turned every question away with the same line. When did Bush learn that Rove had leaked the information? Would the president take any action now that it was clear Rove had been one of the leakers? Did Bush still have confidence in Rove? "I'm simply not going to comment on an ongoing investigation," McClellan said.

Luskin had his own spin for reporters. He told them that when Rove had talked to Cooper about Wilson's wife, he hadn't identified her *by name.* He had only referred to "Wilson's wife." Yet days later, Rove was also tied to the original leak: the Novak column. On July 15, *The New York Times,* citing a source "who had been officially briefed on the matter," reported that Rove had been Novak's second source on the CIA leak story.

Rove was now fingered as a source for the two reporters who had written articles disclosing Valerie Wilson's CIA connection. Democrats jumped on the disclosures. Aides to Senator Harry Reid, the Democratic leader in the Senate, spent a day preparing a sixteen-page background memo on the leak, asking "When did President Bush learn any details of this incident?" Representative Henry Waxman circulated a memo maintaining that Rove had violated the agreement on handling classified information signed by senior government officials. He noted that under existing rules, Rove, whether or not he had committed a crime, could lose his security clearance or face dismissal for this violation.

On July 17, 2005, *Time* published an article by Matt Cooper describing his appearance before Fitzgerald's grand jury five days earlier. Cooper had previously not publicly identified his primary source. But with his e-mail about Rove now public, there was no reason to hold back. In this piece, he reported he had told the grand jurors about his conversation with Rove. Cooper also revealed for the first time that he had previously told the grand jury that Scooter Libby (who had granted Cooper a personal waiver) had been another source for him regarding Wilson's wife and the Niger trip. Now two top White House officials were publicly identified as leakers. The next day, Bush was asked if he would stick to the White House position that anyone involved in the leak would be fired. He said, "If someone committed a crime, they will no longer work in my administration." With Rove and Libby exposed, the president was raising the bar.

JUDY MILLER was still in jail two months later when she received a letter from Scooter Libby.

She wasn't in a country club facility. The Alexandria jail was also home to Zacarias Moussaoui, the convicted terrorist. She was living in an 80-square-foot-cell, sleeping on a mat on a concrete slab, and brushing her hair with a toothbrush. She wore a dark green uniform. Her lawyer repeatedly told reporters that she was being treated like any other prisoner. There was one exception: she had been receiving a parade of high-profile visitors. The notables included Sulzberger, Keller, Tom Brokaw, *Wall Street Journal* Managing Editor Paul Steiger, former senator Robert Dole, UN ambassador John Bolton, former White House terrorism czar Richard Clarke, weapons inspector Charles Duelfer, and Senators Chris Dodd and Arlen Specter. "She looked radiant and seemed aglow with purpose," said one friend who visited her in prison early on in her ordeal. Miller, this visitor recalled, was "full of urgent talk about the need to pass a shield law [to protect reporters] on the Hill." Miller reported that she was angling for a job in the laundry and had already made connections with the right people. "She was counting the number of letters she got each day—they were in the many dozens—but she was concerned because they were dropping off," this friend said. Miller was also upset that there wasn't more press coverage of her case. Each day, she would check the outdated copies of *The New York Times* she could get in prison and was disappointed there weren't news articles about her situation.

While maintaining a brave face to her jailhouse visitors, Miller was worried. Judge Hogan's contempt citation would keep her locked up until Fitzgerald's grand jury expired at the end of October. But Bennett, her lawyer, had called Fitzgerald in August and was convinced that the prosecutor intended to convene a new grand jury and keep Miller in jail for another eighteen months if she didn't talk. There was also the lingering possibility of what Bennett had warned her about nearly a year earlier—that Fitzgerald could seek criminal charges against her that could lead to additional prison time. Miller wanted a way out.

She and Bennett had been discussing approaching Libby and asking him for a specific personal waiver, like the waiver Rove had granted Cooper. Sulzberger was cool to the idea. As Miller later told others, Sulzberger, her old friend, favored an absolutist position: we don't cooperate with law enforcement, we don't testify in court. Abrams, too, was wary of her taking a step that could be portrayed as a retreat. Miller was annoyed. Sulzberger was asking her to stay in jail to prove a point. Why not, she asked, reach out to Libby and see what happens? Why stay in jail to protect a source who was willing to release her from her promise? She wasn't prepared to remain behind bars for another eighteen months to five years if she didn't have to.

Sulzberger, Miller later told colleagues, tried to talk her out of approaching Libby. But Bennett went ahead. He contacted Libby's attorney. Fitzgerald stepped up the pressure on his own. On September 12, he wrote a pointed letter to Libby's lawyer, Joseph Tate, reminding him that his client had signed a written waiver releasing reporters from any pledge of confidentiality. If Libby was unwilling to affirm that directly to Miller, Fitzgerald noted, one reason might be that "Mr. Libby had decided that encouraging Ms. Miller to testify to the grand jury was not in his best interest."

It was a clever move on Fitzgerald's part. Libby was boxed in. Either he granted Miller the personal waiver she wanted, or he would be all but acknowledging to the prosecutor that he had something to hide. And so, three days later, Libby wrote Miller the get-out-of-jail card she was seeking—but a rather odd one with some intriguing literary flourishes.

"Dear Judy," Libby began the note. "Your reporting, and you, are missed. Like many Americans, I admire your principled stand. But, like many of your friends and readers, I would welcome you back among the rest of us, doing what you do best—reporting." Libby said that he would give her a "waiver of confidentiality." He noted that "every other reporter's testimony makes clear that they did not discuss Ms. Plame's name or identity with me." Then the onetime novelist wrote:

You went to jail in the summer. It is fall now. You will have stories to cover—Iraqi elections and suicide bombers, biological threats and the Iranian nuclear program. Out West, where you vacation, the aspens will be already turning. They turn in clusters, because their roots connect them. Come back to work—and life.

Aspens connected by roots? Was he suggesting that he and Miller were somehow tied together below the surface? Was Libby attempting to shape what Miller would say to the grand jury?

A coded message or not, the letter was what Miller wanted. But she still insisted on hearing directly from Libby. On September 19, the lawyers—Bennett and Tate—arranged a conference call with Libby and Miller from her jailhouse phone. It was an awkward conversation. "I'm sorry you're in jail, Judy," Libby said. "I am, too," she replied. "The food is not very good." Libby then told Miller he wanted to "encourage" her to testify to "help both of us . . . get this matter behind us," according to an account later provided by Tate. Libby said that he "hadn't fully understood" that she had gone to jail just because of him and that he had thought there might be others she was protecting, according to Miller's account. She asked him, " 'Do you really want me to testify? Are you sure you really want me to testify?" Libby replied, according to her, "Absolutely. Believe it. I mean it."

The phone call provided Miller with the "personal waiver" she thought was necessary to vindicate her position. She agreed to testify. On September 29—after serving eighty-five days—she was released. Sulzberger proclaimed victory. "Judy has been unwavering in her commitment to protect the confidentiality of her source," he said. Sulzberger and Keller greeted her warmly and whisked her away to the Ritz-Carlton hotel for a massage, a manicure, a martini, and a steak dinner.

The next day, September 30, Miller testified before the grand jury for three hours. But her account was muddled. She described her July 8 breakfast meeting with Libby at the St. Regis Hotel, when—after insisting on being described as a "former Hill staffer"—Libby had attacked Joe Wilson and told her (wrongly) that Wilson's wife worked at WINPAC, the CIA center that specialized in analyzing weapons of mass destruction. But Miller had "no clear memory of the context" of the conversation about Wilson's wife, she later wrote. Nor could she explain the "Valerie Flame" entry in the same notebook. She thought she might have gotten that from another source—but she had no idea who that might be. She also couldn't explain why she had written "Victoria Wilson" in a notebook containing notes from her July 12 phone interview with Libby.

Miller returned to *The New York Times* building on October 3, 2005. But she didn't receive the heroine's welcome she might once have anticipated. She was by now a problematic figure. She had ended up accepting an arrangement similar to those reached by the other reporters pursued by Fitzgerald.* (Lucy Dalglish of the Reporters Committee for Freedom of the Press noted that the outcome of the Miller case could embolden other prosecutors to imprison reporters, for it had worked in this instance.) Her prewar reporting was seen as an embarrassment by most of her colleagues. And her First Amendment fight had been tainted by the recent revelation that it had been Cheney's chief of staff—an arch proponent of the discredited intelligence she had championed—whom she had gone to jail to protect. Miller was worried about the reaction she would get from her colleagues.

After she entered the newsroom, she gave a brief speech about how her case had been a victory for press freedom and the First Amendment. But the response was "quite frosty," one reporter recalled. The applause was tepid. A team of *New York Times* correspondents had been assigned by Keller to write an exhaustive reconstruction of the entire case. One was veteran investigative reporter Don Van Natta, Jr. "A lot of people in the newsroom came up to me afterward and said they hoped I could explain to them what the great victory for the First Amendment was," Van Natta later recalled.

A short time later, Miller discovered in her desk a notebook of her June 23, 2003, meeting with Libby at the Old Executive Office Building—an interview she said she had completely forgotten to tell Fitzgerald about. The discovery prompted a frantic call to her lawyer and a trip back to Washington for more testimony before Fitzgerald. The notebook contained entries from the discussion she had had with Libby about Joe Wilson that day, including the words "wife works at bureau?" She told Fitzgerald she didn't know why the entry said "bureau." She thought it meant a "bureau" at the CIA. This was the third reference in her notebooks to Valerie Wilson that she said she couldn't explain.

After all the drama of a historic First Amendment battle, the results

---

*Right after Miller left jail, her legal team and Libby's entered into a public squabble. Libby's lawyer, Joseph Tate, claimed that the accommodation that had been reached could have been struck a year earlier because Libby had signed a waiver and Tate had told Abrams that Miller should accept it. But Abrams said that Tate had told him that this waiver was not voluntary because Libby would have been fired had he not signed it. Still, the tussle raised a question: Could Miller have resolved this issue without going to jail, and could she have testified to Fitzgerald a year earlier (and before the presidental election)? When later asked whether there had been an earlier mix-up between Abrams and Libby's lawyer, Miller said, "If you ever get into a situation like I did, make sure you know the difference between a criminal defense lawyer and a First Amendment lawyer."

were meager. For the prosecutor who had relentlessly pursued her, Miller turned out to be anything but the ideal witness. Her memory was clouded, and her notes were confusing—and this jumble was mostly beneficial for Scooter Libby. Still, her testimony confirmed the bare minimum: that Libby, contrary to what he had told the grand jury, had talked to Judy Miller about Joe Wilson's wife and her employment at the CIA.

ON OCTOBER 16, the *Times* published its lengthy reconstruction—authored by Van Natta and three other reporters—along with a sidebar by Miller recounting her testimony before the grand jury. The article was the equivalent of picking at an open scab. The "Miller case" was no tale of a heroic battle for reporters' rights. It was a mess of conflicting interests, unresolved disputes, and journalistic missteps. The article noted that when Managing Editor Jill Abramson was asked what she regretted about the paper's handling of the episodes, she remarked, "The entire thing." And Miller, in this piece, offered a simplistic, self-excusing explanation for her flawed prewar reporting: "WMD—I got it totally wrong. . . . If your sources are wrong, you are wrong. I did the best job that I could."*

Several days later, on October 21, Keller sent a memo to the staff saying he wished that "we had dealt with the controversy over our coverage of WMD as soon as I became executive editor." But, he explained, the paper at that time had still been reeling from the Jayson Blair fiasco. "By waiting a year to own up to our mistakes," he continued, "we allowed the anger inside and outside the paper to fester. Worse, we fear, we fostered an impression that *The Times* put a higher premium on protecting its reporters than on coming clean with its readers." Keller noted that Miller "seems to have misled" an editor "about the extent of her involvement" in the leak case. He added, "if I had known the details of Judy's entanglement with Libby, I'd have been more careful in how the paper articulated its defense, and perhaps more willing than I had been to support efforts aimed at exploring compromises."

---

*In a first-person account accompanying the *Times* piece, Miller noted that Fitzgerald had asked her how she had interpreted Libby's strange reference to aspens in his letter to her. Rather than supply a straight answer, she wrote that she had recounted the last time she had seen Libby: at a rodeo in Jackson Hole, where he had been wearing jeans and a cowboy hat.

The next day, *Times* columnist Maureen Dowd published a piece, headlined "Woman of Mass Destruction," excoriating Miller for her "leading role in the dangerous echo chamber" that had led to war.

A glorious campaign for reporters' rights had ended up as a bitter family fight—poisoned by Miller's prewar reporting.

ON THE morning of October 28, 2005, Bush delivered a speech on the war on terrorism to a group of 2,500 military members and local business and political leaders in Norfolk, Virginia. No tickets for the event had been made available to the general public. The number of American troops killed in Iraq had recently topped 2,000. Public opinion polls showed support for the war weakening. And in the wake of the administration's ineffective response to Hurricane Katrina, the withdrawal of the underwhelming Harriet Miers as a Supreme Court nominee, and the collapse of Bush's campaign to privatize a portion of Social Security, the president's approval rating had fallen below 40 percent—then a record low for his presidency. (Within days, a CNN/*USA Today*/Gallup poll would find that 53 percent believed that the Bush administration had deliberately misled the public about Iraq's weapons of mass destruction—an increase from a year earlier—and a *Washington Post* poll would report that 58 percent doubted Bush's honesty, the first time a majority of Americans questioned his integrity.) As Bush took the stage, he half joked, "It's good to be out of Washington."

His forty-minute-long speech was a full-throttle defense of his Iraq policy. The mission in Iraq, he said, was to defeat anti-American terrorists in league with (the still-at-large) Osama bin Laden. "We must recognize Iraq as the central front in our war against terror," he said. Even though experts in and out of the government were suggesting that the Islamic jihadists in Iraq affiliated with al-Qaeda made up only a small slice of the insurgency, Bush equated the entire insurgency with bin Laden's murderous band. He referred to Iraq as "the heart" of power for al-Qaeda and its allies, and he suggested that if the United States were to disengage in Iraq, bin Laden would be "in control of Iraq." (He was ignoring the Sunni, Shiite, and Kurdish forces.) He noted that "progress isn't easy, but it is steady." And Bush declared, "We will never back down, never give in, and never accept anything less than complete victory."

He received a long standing ovation.

THREE and a half hours later, Patrick Fitzgerald came to the podium in a conference room at the Justice Department. Scores of reporters and dozens of cameras were present. Next to him was FBI Special Agent Jack Eckenrode. That morning, the grand jury in the CIA leak case had issued a five-count indictment against Scooter Libby, charging him with one count of obstruction of justice, two counts of perjury, and two counts of making false statements. The indictment accused Libby of having lied during his interviews with FBI agents and his two grand jury appearances about his role in the leak and his conversations with Tim Russert, Matt Cooper, and Judy Miller.

The indictment revealed some of what Fitzgerald had uncovered: that Libby had obtained information from the CIA about Valerie Wilson; that Cheney had told him that Joe Wilson's wife worked at the CIA's Counterproliferation Division; that Libby had disclosed the CIA connection of Wilson's wife to Miller and confirmed it to Cooper; that Russert had contradicted Libby's claim that he (Libby) had learned about Wilson's wife from the *Meet the Press* host. The indictment asserted that Libby had talked to "Official A"—a "senior official in the White House," who soon would be identified as Karl Rove—who had acknowledged speaking about Wilson's wife with Bob Novak before the leak story ran.

The indictment indicated that Libby had discussed Wilson's wife with no fewer than eight U.S. government officials, including Cheney; David Addington, Cheney's chief counsel; and White House press secretary Ari Fleischer; as well as Rove—and all this before he had spoken to Matt Cooper on July 12, 2003 (when, Libby claimed, he had told the *Time* reporter he didn't even know that Joe Wilson had a wife). Given the number of witnesses, Fitzgerald's indictment presented a strong case that Libby had lied. And it undercut the administration's claim that the White House hadn't been involved in the leak. It suggested that Libby and Rove had been at the center of it. Conspicuously absent from the indictment was any allegation that Libby, or anyone else, had violated the Intelligence Identities Protection Act, the law banning the disclosure of the identity of covert CIA officers. The strict standard of the law—that the violator had to be aware of the covert status of the officer—was difficult to prove. Nor were there any charges against Rove, Matt Cooper's original source about

Valerie Wilson, or against Richard Armitage, who had gotten the whole thing rolling by talking to Novak.

The prosecutor began with an opening statement noting that Valerie Wilson's status as a CIA officer was "classified" and "not widely known outside the intelligence community." Realizing that some of his critics had claimed no law had been broken in the outing of Valerie Wilson, he said, "It was known that a CIA officer's identity was blown, it was known that there was a leak. We needed to figure out how that happened, who did it, why, whether a crime was committed, whether we could prove it, whether we should prove it." And in such an investigation, he said, it was crucial that witnesses tell the grand jury the truth. "Given that national security was at stake," Fitzgerald said, "it was especially important that we find out accurate facts." Libby, he said, had impeded this investigation by telling a false cover story. That was why he had been indicted.

Then Fitzgerald took questions. Was the investigation finished? "The substantial bulk of the work in this investigation is concluded," he said. Was this another case of a leak investigation that did not end with a leak prosecution? Fitzgerald argued that the charges he had filed against Libby were as serious as leaking. Had the vice president encouraged Libby to leak or lie? "We don't talk about people that are not charged with a crime in the indictment," Fitzgerald replied. Is Karl Rove off the hook? Same answer. Fitzgerald wouldn't answer questions about what damage had been caused by the outing of Valerie Wilson or whether Novak had cooperated with the investigation. Would he be issuing a final report explaining what he had uncovered? "I do not have the authority to write a report."

One reporter asked Fitzgerald if the Libby indictment was a "vindication" of the "argument that the administration took the country to war on false premises." Fitzgerald gave a firm reply: "This indictment is not about the war. . . . This is simply an indictment that says, in a national security investigation about the compromise of a CIA officer's identity that may have taken place in the context of a very heated debate over the war, whether some person—a person, Mr. Libby—lied or not. The indictment will not seek to prove that the war was justified or unjustified. . . . I think anyone who's concerned about the war and has feelings for or against shouldn't look to this criminal process for any answers or resolution of that."

———

Patrick Fitzgerald was right. The indictment was not about the war. It was not even about the leak. But it was about a lie. And that lie had come about because the most senior officials of the White House, including Bush and Cheney, had been determined to counter the claim that they had misled the nation into a war that had not gone well. They refused to concede that they had misrepresented the intelligence and had hyped the threat to win public and congressional approval for the invasion of Iraq. And in all the time since Bush had told the American public that there was "no doubt" that Saddam Hussein posed a pressing WMD danger to the United States, there had been no official scrutiny of the administration's use of the prewar intelligence. The selling of the war had escaped investigation.

That day, Scooter Libby resigned his post in Cheney's office. The vice president released a statement calling him "one of the most capable and talented individuals I have ever known."* The White House sent a memo to staffers reminding them not to talk about the ongoing leak investigation.

Bush watched the first fifteen to twenty minutes of Fitzgerald's press conference in his private dining room. Shortly after the prosecutor finished, the president spoke for two minutes on Libby's resignation. He noted that "we're all saddened by today's news"; but, he added, "I got a job to do."

---

*To replace Libby as his national security adviser, Cheney picked John Hannah, whom Ahmad Chalabi's Iraqi National Congress had previously identified as its contact person in Cheney's office. As his new chief of staff, Cheney tapped David Addington, who had been Cheney's legal counsel and who had been accused by human rights advocates of drafting policies that led to the abusive treatment of prisoners in Afghanistan and Iraq.

The administration sold it the way it sold it. That's history.

—DOUGLAS FEITH, UNDERSECRETARY OF DEFENSE

Afterword: No Regrets

LATE ON the afternoon of June 12, 2006, Karl Rove was sitting in a plane at Baltimore/Washington International Airport, heading toward Manchester, New Hampshire, when he received an e-mail on his Black-Berry from his lawyer: FITZGERALD CALLED. CASE OVER. After investigating Rove for nearly two and a half years and calling him before the grand jury five times, Patrick Fitzgerald had determined that he didn't have enough evidence to indict the White House aide for perjury, obstruction, or any other crime in connection with the leak of Valerie Wilson's CIA identity. Rove was a free man. When he arrived in New Hampshire, he was re-lieved—and pumped.

Rove had come to the Granite State to be the star attraction at a fund-raising dinner for the local Republican Party. His talk that night was vintage Rove, only more so—a nasty, polarizing speech that blasted Democratic critics of the war. Rove assailed not just Senator John Kerry (whom he and Bush had vanquished a year and a half earlier) but also Representative John Murtha, a longtime Democratic hawk who had initially supported the war but was now calling for withdrawing U.S. troops. "They are ready to give the green light to go to war," Rove said of Kerry and Murtha, "but when it gets tough, and when it gets difficult, they fall back on that party's old pat-tern of cutting and running. They may be with you at the first shots, but they are not going to be with you for the last, tough battles." If Murtha's advice was followed, Rove declared, Iraq would become "a launching pad for the terrorists to strike the United States and the West." He added, "We were absolutely right to remove [Saddam] from power and we have no excuses to make for it."

Unencumbered by worries of indictment, Rove was dipping into a familiar playbook. Ever since September 11, he had sought to divide the electorate on the national security issue and exploit the public's fears for the president's benefit. With polls showing support for the Iraq War steadily sinking, Rove was seeking to redefine the debate for the fall congressional elections—once again casting the Democrats as untrustworthy custodians of the public safety. But in going after Murtha and depicting him as a pusillanimous "cut-and-run" man, Rove was being especially audacious. As a young man, Rove had escaped the Vietnam draft with a student deferment (even though he was for a period only a part-time student at the University of Utah). Now he was impugning the moral courage and commitment of Murtha, who had served thirty-seven years in the Marines and had been decorated for valor in combat. Rove wasn't just countering a policy critique of the war; he was seeking to delegitimize another Iraq War critic. This was the sort of conduct that had gotten Rove, Libby, and the White House into trouble in the first place.* The speech was a clear sign that Bush's number one aide was unrepentant—about the war, about the leak, about how he and the White House played politics, about everything. He had good reason to be. As the Associated Press's Pete Yost noted in a story the next day, "The decision not to charge Karl Rove shows there often are no consequences for misleading the public."

THE previous October, shortly before Fitzgerald indicted Libby, the prosecutor had been close to indicting Rove for perjury stemming from his initial

---

*After the New Hampshire speech, Murtha went on *Meet the Press* and criticized Rove for "sitting in his air-conditioned office with his big, fat backside, saying, 'Stay the course!' " Once again advancing a Rove attack, Robert Novak, four days later, wrote a column swiping at Murtha. He dug up an issue from Murtha's distant past: the fact that twenty-six years earlier, Murtha had been investigated by the FBI in the Abscam congressional bribery probe. (Murtha hadn't been charged with any crimes.) Novak belittled Murtha's efforts to force a troop withdrawal from Iraq. "Murtha now wears his heroic combat record like a suit of armor," Novak wrote.

testimony, in which he had denied talking to Matt Cooper about Valerie Wilson. Fitzgerald visited the Washington law offices of Luskin. He told Luskin he was considering bringing charges, Luskin later said. But the ever-facile lawyer presented an explanation that saved Rove.

The key issue for Fitzgerald and his investigators was why Rove had changed his testimony. He had first told the grand jury in February 2004 that he hadn't had any conversation with Cooper about Valerie Wilson. Then, eight months later, he had handed over an e-mail showing that he had talked to Cooper about the Wilson affair (though he still claimed not to recall this phone call). Trying to explain this away, Luskin told Fitzgerald about his occasional chats over drinks at a Washington restaurant called Cafe Deluxe with Viveca Novak, a seasoned reporter at *Time*. (She is no relation to Bob Novak.)

During one of these conversations, Luskin had said to her, "Rove doesn't have a Cooper problem"—meaning Rove hadn't been Cooper's source. "That's not what I hear," Novak shot back. It was a casual if careless remark, for Novak figured Luskin was spinning her and that he had to know his client had talked to Cooper. Luskin, though, was surprised by Novak's comment. He ordered Rove's aides to check Rove's computer for any e-mails containing a reference to Cooper or *Time*. It was only then that the e-mail Rove had sent to Hadley after talking to Cooper—which noted that Rove had spoken to Cooper about the Wilson matter—had turned up, Luskin subsequently said. It had been missed in an earlier White House search. And, according to Luskin, it was this e-mail that had prompted Rove to acknowledge the conversation he had forgotten about.

This was the e-mail that had been printed out by a Rove aide on November 25, 2003. Luskin claimed that his critical conversation with Viveca Novak had occurred in October 2003. That made sense: an October conversation had led to a November search. But if Luskin and Rove had the Hadley e-mail in hand in November 2003, why did Rove wait nearly a year to turn this important evidence over to Fitzgerald? (The subpoena Fitzgerald had sent to the White House certainly covered this e-mail.) And if the e-mail had been found and given to Luskin in late November 2003, why did Rove, at his first grand jury appearance three months later, not disclose at that point that he had spoken to Cooper?

According to another lawyer representing a White House witness in the leak case, Luskin's explanation was this: Rove's office had given Luskin a folder full of e-mails that included the one Rove had sent to Hadley. But Luskin hadn't noticed the important Hadley e-mail until October 2004, just before Rove was about to go back to the grand jury for the third time (and right after Matt Cooper had been held in contempt for the second time). Preparing for Rove's return to the grand jury—and aware of Fitzgerald's renewed interest in Cooper—Luskin looked closely through the file he had gotten from Rove's office. Luskin later admitted he might have screwed up, the attorney said. His mistake: missing the Hadley e-mail before Rove's first grand jury appearance in February 2004. In other words, a careful Washington defense lawyer who had been assiduous enough to ask for a search of his client's computer had overlooked a crucial piece of evidence—and did not realize he had had it in his possession for almost a year. Was this plausible? A question for Fitzgerald was whether Luskin had really screwed up or was covering for his client.

There was another problem with Rove's defense. When Fitzgerald brought Viveca Novak before his new grand jury in the fall of 2005, he discovered there was a conflict between her account and Luskin's. She recalled that her key conversation with Luskin had occurred in March or May 2004, months after the Hadley e-mail had been printed out of Rove's computer.* Though she couldn't remember which month it had been—were you wearing an overcoat? Fitzgerald had asked her—Novak was certain it had happened after her October 2003 meeting with Luskin and no earlier than a January 2004 get-together at Cafe Deluxe. Novak's testimony suggested that her conversation with Luskin about Cooper hadn't precipitated Luskin's request for a search of Rove's computer—for it had occurred after the search. This undermined Luskin's complicated argument for Rove's innocence.

Trying to sort all this out, Fitzgerald called Rove back for a fifth grand jury appearance in April 2006. Once again, the issue was whether Rove had really forgotten about his conversation with Cooper or not—whether he had been truthful during his first two grand jury appearances.

Whatever his suspicions about Rove's account, Fitzgerald was a profes-

---

*After Luskin had disclosed his off-the-record conversation with Viveca Novak to Fitzgerald, Novak arranged to talk informally to the prosecutor—without consulting her editors. "Unrealistically," she later wrote, "I hoped this would turn out to be an insignificant twist in the investigation." She later testified officially, with the knowledge of her editors. The episode led to her departure from *Time*.

sional who would not indict a suspect unless he believed he could establish guilt beyond a reasonable doubt. And perjury is notoriously difficult to prove, especially when a witness claims he or she had forgotten a conversation. Rove hadn't told the grand jury about his conversation with Cooper at first—purposefully or not. But he then came forward with the incriminating Hadley e-mail and conceded he must have talked to Cooper. Fitzgerald didn't have a parade of witnesses contradicting the White House aide's account—as he did with Libby. Though Luskin's explanation was murky—and inconsistent with Viveca Novak's account—it could create a reasonable doubt in the minds of a jury. After hearing from Rove this fifth time, Fitzgerald concluded he didn't have a case to make.

As for the leak itself, Fitzgerald never seriously considered bringing a case against Rove under the law that much of the media had focused on: the Intelligence Identities Protection Act. To win a conviction, Fitzgerald would have had to establish that Rove had been aware that Valerie Wilson was a "covert" CIA employee, and demonstrating state of knowledge is often a difficult task for a prosecutor. Fitzgerald and his team did seriously consider using a vaguely worded provision of the Espionage Act, a World War I–era statute that makes it a crime to communicate any information relating to the "national defense" to any person not authorized to receive it. (The law also has a provision that allows government officials to be charged for "gross negligence" for failing to protect national defense information with which they have been entrusted.) But that law had rarely been used, and some legal experts worried that doing so in this case could create a dangerous precedent. It would effectively turn the archaic statute into a de facto Official Secrets Act—the law in Great Britain that makes it a crime to disclose any classified information. That would be a major and disturbing development, both for the news media and for the public. It would have a chilling effect on investigative reporting relating to national security and government excesses and abuses. In the end, Fitzgerald chose not to take that road.

Still, the basic facts were not in dispute. In his zeal to defend the Iraq War and tear down a critic of the president, Rove had confirmed a leak of classified information to Bob Novak and then had offered the same information about Valerie Wilson's employment at the CIA to Matt Cooper. He had done so with relish. Valerie Wilson was "fair game," Rove had privately remarked to Chris Matthews. Then he and the White House had falsely denied his (and Libby's) involvement in the leak, maintaining a cover-up for two years. And after the disclosure of the smoking-gun Cooper e-mail in July 2005, the White House had steadfastly refused to comment—or honor its pledge to dismiss anyone involved in the leak. But after years of investigating, Fitzgerald decided that Rove had done nothing for which he could be indicted. The leak was "smarmy politics," one senior law enforcement official familiar with the case said. It was sloppy and reckless. But it wasn't criminal.

The day after the media reported that Rove was in the clear, Bush said, "I've made the comments I'm going to make about this incident, and I'm going to put this part of the situation behind us and move forward." But, in fact, Bush had never addressed the situation. Since the disclosure of the Cooper e-mail—which proved that Rove had leaked Valerie Wilson's CIA identity—nearly a year earlier, the president had declined to say anything about Rove's conduct. Nor had he said anything about the White House's previous false claim that Rove (and Libby) had had nothing to do with the leak. Bush had also declined to reveal what he had known—if anything—about the matter. The president and his press secretary had repeatedly claimed they couldn't comment on the investigation (or anything related to it) while the inquiry was under way. Now that the Rove investigation was completed, Bush would say nothing more. "I obviously, along with others in the White House, took a sigh of relief when he [Fitzgerald] made the decision he made," the president said at a June 14, 2006, press conference, when asked if he approved of Rove's actions in the leak episode. As for his onetime pledge to fire anyone who had been involved in the leak, Bush also made it clear that that was now off the table, at least as far as his closest adviser was concerned. "I trust Karl Rove, and he's an integral part of my team," he said.

The stonewall strategy had worked.

THE original leaker in the case also got off, but only after Fitzgerald had intensely investigated his conduct—twice.

Richard Armitage had contacted investigators early on and confessed that he had talked to Novak about Wilson's wife. He felt terrible about it, he told friends. It had been, he told them, a stupid mistake. Still, the investigators had questions about whether Armitage had been completely candid. Was it truly pure happenstance that Novak's meeting with Armitage—facilitated by Washington power broker Ken Duberstein and encouraged by Colin Powell—had occurred just as the Wilson affair was blowing up in the second week of July 2003? Had Armitage not realized the information he was sharing with Novak had come from a classified memo—the same memo Armitage had asked Carl Ford to fax to Colin Powell after Joe Wilson's appearance on *Meet the Press*? Had Armitage merely slipped a piece of gossip to the columnist in a casual manner while chatting about other topics, as Novak had claimed? Or had he purposefully disclosed what he believed was Valerie Wilson's role in her husband's controversial trip to distance the State Department from this mess and, in a way, blame the CIA?

Armitage's truthfulness had been an issue during the Iran-*contra* investigation, a fact surely known to Fitzgerald. But when Fitzgerald was seeking to wrap up the investigation in October 2005, he didn't have proof that Armitage had testified falsely in this case. As with Rove and Libby, Fitzgerald never contemplated bringing a case against Armitage under the Intelligence Identities Protection Act. He also decided not to seek charges against him under the Espionage Act, even though, as the original leaker to Novak, the former deputy secretary of state was the closest candidate for prosecution under the law. Fitzgerald figured he was done with Armitage. But that was not the case.

After Fitzgerald unveiled his indictment of Libby, Armitage again contacted the prosecutor, according to two knowledgeable sources familiar with the events. There was something, he said, that he hadn't told the prosecutor about: his earlier conversation with Bob Woodward of *The Washington Post*.

Armitage's belated confession was awkward for both himself and others. It placed Armitage in a difficult spot. He was admitting he had not told Fitzgerald the whole story. And this meant that Fitzgerald had misstated a fact of the case. At the press conference announcing the Libby indictment, Fitzgerald had stated that the vice president's chief of staff "was the first official known to have told a reporter" about Valerie Wilson when he had talked to Judy Miller on June 23, 2003. But Armitage had already spoken to Woodward about her more than a week earlier. Armitage's last-minute admission to Fitzgerald thus ensnared yet another journalist in the case. Fitzgerald had to bring Armitage back before the grand jury. But he also needed to hear from the famed Watergate reporter about what he knew and when he knew it.

After Woodward obtained a waiver from Armitage, the *Post* lawyers worked out an arrangement with Fitzgerald, and Woodward provided a sworn deposition to Fitzgerald on November 14, 2005, that focused narrowly on his Armitage conversation. ("I was astounded that we were able to do this," Woodward subsequently said, "because other people got in this confrontation with [Fitzgerald]. He was quite respectful of the First Amendment.") Then late the next day, Woodward and the *Post* revealed that Woodward had cooperated with Fitzgerald—without identifying Armitage. Woodward released a statement acknowledging he had been told about Joe Wilson's wife by a confidential source while conducting interviews for his book *Plan of Attack* in mid-June 2003. He had not told his editors about this conversation until October 2005, fearing that if any reference to this conversation appeared in the *Post* he could be subpoenaed. Woodward did say he had mentioned to a fellow *Post* reporter, Walter Pincus, that Wilson's wife worked at the CIA. But Pincus told the *Post* that he didn't recall that: "Are you kidding? I certainly would have remembered that."*

Woodward's late cameo role in the scandal prompted criticism of the *Post* reporter. He had long been disdainful of Fitzgerald's investigation. In an appearance on Larry King's cable show the night before the Libby indictment was issued, Woodward had discounted the leak as innocent "gossip" and "chatter" and dismissed the notion of charging any officials, even with perjury. Months earlier, on National Public Radio, he had called the leak case "laughable because the consequences are not that great." But Woodward had known that one of his sources had told him the same information at issue in the investigation—and he had good reason to believe the source was a prime subject of Fitzgerald's probe. "I had long suspected my source was Novak's source," Woodward said in a 2006 interview. But, he said, he hadn't learned it for sure until days before Fitzgerald's press conference.

As a reporter, Woodward certainly had well-founded concerns about Fitzgerald's investigation and the prosecutor's pursuit of journalists. But he had opined on the case publicly without disclosing he had a keen personal

---

*Judy Miller was at a conference on blogging in New York City the morning the news broke about Woodward's involvement in the leak case. As she read the *Post* article and Woodward's statement on the newspaper's Web site for the first time, she could hardly contain herself: "This is weird. . . . Do you realize the ramifications of this? This guy knew before I did." She then dashed off to call her lawyer.

interest in the matter. Woodward apologized to the *Post*'s editors about the matter. Len Downie, the paper's executive editor, said that Woodward had "made a mistake" but that this error ought to be balanced against the journalist's long record of "outstanding reporting."

For Fitzgerald, the important question was, what had prompted Armitage to come forward? According to Woodward, he himself had been the trigger.

Appearing again on *Larry King Live,* this time a week after his deposition with Fitzgerald, Woodward explained what had happened. When he had watched the Fitzgerald press conference, Woodward said, he had been surprised to hear the prosecutor say that Libby was the first administration official to have passed information on Valerie Wilson to a reporter. "I went, 'Whoa,'" Woodward said. He realized that Armitage had told him about Valerie Wilson ten days before Libby had told Judy Miller. Woodward then went into what he termed an "incredibly aggressive reporting mode." He immediately called his source—meaning Armitage (whom Woodward was not naming publicly)—and asked, "Do you realize when we talked about this and exactly what was said?" His source replied, "I have to go to the prosecutor. I have to tell the truth." And he did, and he released Woodward to testify about it. But Armitage wouldn't allow Woodward to identify him publicly.

Here was yet another matter for Fitzgerald to investigate. Had Armitage merely forgotten that he had also given information about Valerie Wilson to Woodward until he was reminded by Woodward following the Fitzgerald press conference? In his interview with Larry King, Woodward said, "I made efforts to get the source, this year, earlier, and last year, to give me some information about this so I could put something in the newspaper or a book. So, I could get information out, and totally failed." Woodward's remark was incriminating for Armitage. It strongly suggested that if Armitage had forgotten about his conversation with Woodward, the *Post* reporter had reminded him about it at least twice. Each time Woodward brought up the subject, the reporter later said, his source had quickly cut him off after one sentence. Woodward had asked questions along the lines of, "What about the Fitzgerald investigation? I heard you testified before the grand jury." But the response from his source, he said, was abrupt: "It was, Boom. End of conversation. Not going there." If Woodward's account was accurate, Armitage hadn't come clean on this leak until after the Libby indictment *and* after Woodward had pressed him yet again. Had he been hiding his conversation with Woodward from the prosecutor?

Once the Woodward disclosure occurred, Armitage was "very depressed," according to one friend. Another friend said, "A lot of us were worried about Rich." But Fitzgerald chose once again not to charge him—and the prosecutor, following standard grand jury rules, never disclosed anything about Armitage's role in the leak.

Armitage, who was now running an international consulting firm, rebounded. In June 2006, the day after Fitzgerald ended his investigation of Rove, Armitage appeared on PBS's *Charlie Rose Show* and refused to answer the talk-show host's gentle questions as to whether he had been Woodward's source. Asked about his role in the leak case, he said, "Oh, I'm not worried about my situation." Days later, he told *The Australian* newspaper that the level of violence in Iraq was worsening dramatically, that the attacks were fueled mostly by sectarian conflict, and that he believed the Iraqis would soon ask the United States to leave Iraq.

SCOOTER LIBBY was the only one of the leakers to remain in jeopardy. Determined to protect Dick Cheney, Libby had told a convoluted story under oath: I knew; I forgot; I learned it again from journalists, not from the vice president. After he was indicted in October 2005, Libby, facing a prison term of up to thirty years and fines of $1.2 million, mounted an aggressive defense. He hired a battery of top-tier defense lawyers, whose fees were covered by the newly formed Libby Legal Defense Trust. The fund's advisory board was studded with prominent Republicans and neoconservatives, including ex–CIA Director Jim Woolsey, former Senator Fred Thompson, Cheney adviser Mary Matalin, and publisher Steve Forbes. The outfit, which was not a tax-deductible charity, was chaired by Melvin Sembler, the Florida supermarket magnate and GOP fund-raiser who had been the Bush-appointed U.S. ambassador to Italy at the time the Niger documents surfaced. By the spring of 2006, the trust had raised about $2.5 million.

Libby's legal team, led by a flamboyant courtroom fighter named Ted Wells and a pit-bull litigator named William Jeffress, Jr., churned out motions seeking access to mountains of highly classified documents, reporters' notebooks, and the grand jury testimony of various witnesses. The essence of Libby's defense was that he had been far too busy with matters of war and peace to remember accurately what he had said about such a trivial matter as the employment of Joe Wilson's wife. (Libby's problem wasn't only that he claimed to have forgotten what had happened; he had given the FBI and the grand jury specific recollections contradicted by others.) The early pretrial squabbling did reveal that Cheney had taken a rather direct interest in Wilson's op-ed piece and trip, and it indicated that the Libby trial could include a dramatic moment: Dick Cheney testifying. The trial was scheduled for early 2007.

If convicted, Libby could appeal. Beyond that, the ultimate escape for Libby could be a pardon from President George W. Bush.

THE leak case, notwithstanding the Libby trial, seemed finished. But the same week that Rove got off, the issue that had triggered the leak—the reasons for the Iraq War—was back in the news. While the White House and its prowar allies were talking up Bush's recent surprise trip to Baghdad and the attack that had killed terrorist leader Abu Musab al-Zarqawi, the House of Representatives was having a full-force floor debate on the Iraq War. It was the first time the House had thoroughly debated the war since the vote in October 2002 that had handed Bush the authority to invade Iraq. Looking toward the coming congressional elections, GOP leaders had introduced a resolution that declared that Saddam had "constituted a threat against global peace and security," that the U.S. military had "scored impressive victories in Iraq," that the Iraq War was "part of the Global War on Terror," and that no date should be set for withdrawing U.S. troops from Iraq. It was all part of Rove's strategy of taking a potential liability—the war in Iraq—and turning it into an asset. For the White House, the sales campaign was never over.

For two days, as violent attacks continued unabated in Iraq, the House debated this symbolic resolution, and Republicans and Democrats tangled over whether Saddam had posed such a danger. Representative Lloyd Doggett, a Texas Democrat, said, "This war was launched without an imminent threat to our families. . . . Radical 'know it all' ideologues here in Washington bent facts, distorted intelligence, and perpetrated lies designed to mislead the American people into believing that a third-rate thug had a hand in the 9/11 tragedy and was soon to unleash a mushroom cloud." Representative Murtha argued that U.S. troops were caught within a deteriorating sectarian conflict and the number of attacks was on the rise. "Every day it gets worse," Murtha said. Republicans defended the decision to invade Iraq and, as Rove had done, characterized any discussion of withdrawing troops (or setting a timetable for withdrawing troops) as gutless cutting and running. "It is time to stand up and vote," declared Representative Charles Norwood, Jr., a Georgia Republican. "Is it al-Qaeda, or is it America?"

The House voted 256 to 153 for the GOP's complete-the-mission resolution, with merely three Republicans opposing the party. According to a *Wall Street Journal*/NBC News poll, only 41 percent of Americans now said Bush had been right to launch the Iraq War.

Four days after the vote, the American death toll in Iraq reached 2,500.

WHAT had gone wrong? Bush, Cheney, Rumsfeld, Wolfowitz, Rice, and other administration officials had set themselves up by using the most drastic and forceful rhetoric in persuading the nation that the war was necessary. They had approached the invasion of Iraq as though it were a political campaign. They pushed aside doubt, they exaggerated, they shared information with the public selectively. Rather than argue that it was prudent to assume the worst about Saddam, they asserted that they *knew* the worst to be true.

The intelligence community was both a help and a hindrance to the hawks. It did produce a National Intelligence Estimate that supported the White House's general line: Saddam had WMDs. But it also produced dissents and caveats on critical components of the WMD argument, even as the intelligence community was often at war with itself. The analysts in the CIA's WINPAC pushed the aluminum tubes, stuck with the Niger charge, and defended Curveball, while other experts, analysts, and officers challenged them. Why had WINPAC consistently overestimated the threat on the basis of thin evidence? "Iraq and the WMD came hard on the heels of 9/11—after we're accused of not having enough information and of not connecting dots," said Stanley Moskowitz, the chief of CIA congressional affairs, shortly before his death in 2006. "It put the agency in the psychology of 'Oh shit, we can't be too timid.' And if you have a predisposition, you have a tendency to raid the data to support that. Also, if you understate the threat, it will be at the peril of American cities. People were scared. You can't divorce that from the environment in which people looked at Iraqi intelligence."

So WINPAC won one tussle after another, as George Tenet and John

McLaughlin failed to referee these all-important disputes. They also failed to correct (publicly or privately) Bush, Cheney, and others who overstated the flimsy intelligence. Too many within the intelligence community, as the postmortem reports noted, lost the ability to assess the available intelligence free of assumptions and free of the obvious context: Bush was heading to war with Saddam with or without compelling intelligence. And even though the CIA refused to accept the neoconservatives' obsessive belief (based more on presumption than evidence) that Saddam and bin Laden were partners in terrorism, Tenet, in the days before the vote on the Iraq War resolution, protected the White House on this front by dismissing the significance of his own agency's skeptical view on this contentious issue. "Tenet led us into a bad place" said a senior CIA official who worked closely with him. He had been concerned more with supporting the president than with informing him. Years later, John McLaughlin still had no clear explanation of how the CIA had failed on the prewar intelligence: "We're not going to understand all the dimensions of this for some years. We need to get more distance from it."

Watching from inside the CIA, Paul Pillar, the national intelligence officer for the Middle East who was tormented by his own role in drafting the misleading CIA white paper on Iraq's WMDs, came to believe that the main motivation of Bush administration officials was, as he later put it, "to stir up the politics and economics of the Middle East and use regime change in Iraq as a stimulus for regime change and other kinds of changes elsewhere in the region." The overriding impetus was not a WMD threat but a desire to remake the Middle East. Yet WMD and terrorism had been the dual pitch. "If you want to sell anything," Pillar explained, "the best way to do it would be to link to what had become after 9/11 the main concern of the American people." And at that time it was al-Qaeda and September 11. Bush and his aides, Pillar argued, had engaged in the selective use of intelligence to create the "impression of an alliance" between Saddam and bin Laden. There was, he said, a steady flow of "rhetorical coupling" in which Bush administration officials repeatedly mentioned Iraq and 9/11 in the same breath. "The overall judgment of the analysts," Pillar said, was that "what you had [regarding Baghdad and al-Qaeda] was more in the nature of two organizations that were trying to keep track of each other." There was no operational alliance, nor was it likely one would emerge.

Speaking about this at the Council on Foreign Relations nearly three years after the invasion of Iraq, Pillar was asked by a journalist why Bush hadn't made the *real* case for war and sought support for reshaping the geopolitics of the region. "It's a lot harder," Pillar replied, "to make a case based on that . . . than it is to make a case built on fear, based on fears of weapons of mass destruction and mushroom clouds and dictators putting WMD in the hands of terrorists. . . . That is a debate I wish we had. . . . The American people have a right to know the real reason we make major initiatives like going to war."

"Then he lied," a questioner asserted.

"Your word, not mine," Pillar quietly said.

Whatever Bush and his aides actually believed about Saddam, his weapons, and his alleged ties to al-Qaeda, they didn't review the existing intelligence assiduously to validate those beliefs. And they were hardly careful in how they represented that intelligence to the public, often embellishing the data. When intelligence collided with their beliefs, they blew it off. Not surprisingly, Doug Feith later suggested that after September 11 the case for war in Iraq was self-evident and that the administration shouldn't have gotten bogged down in the details of WMDs. "My basic view," he said in 2006, "is, the rationale for the war didn't hinge on the details of this intelligence even though the details of the intelligence at times became elements of the public presentation. . . . The administration sold it the way it sold it. That's history."

Downplaying the postinvasion challenges was another essential part of the sales pitch. Worse, though, was that the Bush White House appeared to believe its own rhetoric: that there would be no need for a large and costly occupation force after the war, that Iraqi oil revenues would finance reconstruction, that Iraqis would be ever grateful to the Americans. Bush and his top aides neglected to plan seriously for the problems—almost all of which had been predicted—that followed the invasion. But had the White House acknowledged prior to the war that hundreds of thousands of troops would have to stay in Iraq after the invasion, that Iraq might well be racked with sectarian violence, and that the cost of the war would surpass hundreds of billions of dollars, the public might have been less supportive of the invasion. The desire to sell a war of choice trumped prudent planning and public candor about the difficulties ahead.

Not long before Rove was let off the hook, Zarqawi was killed, and Congress debated the war, Bush held a joint press availability with Prime Minister Tony Blair in the White House. Both men hailed what they claimed was progress in Iraq. In his opening comments, Bush noted that there had been "missteps" and "mistakes." As this short Q&A session was about to end, a reporter asked both leaders what "missteps and mistakes in Iraq" they regretted most.

When Bush was asked two years earlier at a press conference to name a specific mistake he had committed, he had frozen: "You know, I just—I'm sure something will pop into my head here in the midst of this press conference, with all the pressure of trying to come up with an answer, but it hasn't yet." In a speech in December 2005, he had said his administration had "fixed what has not worked" in Iraq—a slight admission of mistakes. And in April 2006 Bush had acknowledged there were some "tactics . . . that we could have done differently," without detailing them. This time Bush responded quickly with an example of a misstep: "Saying 'bring it on,' kind of tough talk, you know, that sent the wrong signal to people. I learned some lessons about expressing myself maybe in a little more sophisticated manner—you know, 'wanted dead or alive,' that kind of talk. I think in certain parts of the world it was misinterpreted, and so I learned from that."

Bush said nothing about his own decision making. Nothing about any policy choices. Nothing about how he had depicted the supposed WMD threat. Nothing about the planning for the postinvasion period. Blair then noted, "We could have done the de-Baathification in a more differentiated way." But Bush had no reflection to offer on that strategic error or the disbanding of the Iraqi Army—or on the issue of troop levels. The only mistake that he had made was rhetorical.

When Bush had campaigned for governor in the early 1990s, he had flown about on a plane called *Accountability One*. When he ran for president in 2000, Bush claimed accountability as one of his campaign themes, and his aides dubbed his campaign jet *Responsibility One*. But there has been no accountability for those who were wrong about Iraq—about the threat or about what would come after the invasion. Bush fired no one. Nobody resigned in disgrace. There were no consequences.

Dick Cheney continued on as the most influential vice president ever, never publicly conceding that he had repeatedly overstated the intelligence on Iraq's WMDs and the purported Saddam–al-Qaeda connection. In a June 2006 interview, Cheney stood by his claim of a year earlier that the Iraqi insurgency was in its "last throes." He also said, "I don't think anybody anticipated the level of violence that we've encountered," wiping from history the Army War College report of January 2003 warning that "ethnic, tribal and religious schisms could produce civil war" after Saddam fell.

Donald Rumsfeld stayed at the Pentagon, even after he came under attack from former generals who assailed him for his arrogant ways and for overseeing the biggest screwups of the war. Rumsfeld was still in charge of a war against an insurgency that he hadn't prepared for and that he had at first refused to recognize as a threat. Paul Wolfowitz, who miscalculated key elements of the war, was awarded the Medal of Freedom by Bush and then handed a plum job: president of the World Bank. (After delivering a speech on trade issues in December 2005, Wolfowitz was asked, "How do you account for the intelligence failures regarding weapons of mass destruction in Iraq?" He replied, "Well, I don't have to. . . . We relied on the intelligence community.") Condoleezza Rice, who failed to broker the critical intelligence disputes before the war began and didn't even read the NIE, was promoted to secretary of state after Colin Powell left. Powell, the reluctant warrior who had allowed himself to be the pitchman for the administration's shoddy case for war, went on to join a venture capital firm in Silicon Valley and became a board member of Revolution Health Group. Doug Feith, who believed that he and his analysts were perceptive enough to see the hidden al-Qaeda–Saddam conspiracy missed by the rest of the intelligence community, resigned from the Pentagon, became a fellow at the Hoover Institute and a cochair of a task force on fighting terrorism at Harvard University's John F. Kennedy School of Government, and started writing a memoir about his participation in the war on terrorism. He was named a visiting professor and "distinguished practitioner in national security policy" at Georgetown University.

George Tenet, after canceling one lucrative book contract, landed another, and he joined the board of Guidance Software and became an adviser to the Analysis Corporation, which tracks potential terrorist threats. John McLaughlin received a fellowship at the Johns Hopkins School of Advanced International Studies and became an on-air analyst for CNN. Tommy

Franks resigned from the military, wrote a book, hit the speakers' circuit, and joined the corporate boards of Bank of America and Outback Steakhouse. Paul Bremer wrote a book, too, and served as chairman of the advisory board of a company that said it "secures the homeland with integrated products and services." Stephen Hadley replaced Rice as national security adviser. Scott McClellan resigned as White House press secretary in May 2006. Bush press aide Adam Levine left the White House to work as a vice president for corporate communications for Goldman Sachs and then later as a managing director of Public Strategies, an Austin-based lobbying and communications firm whose vice chairman, Mark McKinnon, had been the president's chief media adviser. Karl Rove remained in the White House. Only Scooter Libby had to leave. He joined the conservative Hudson Institute as a senior fellow focusing on terrorism. *The Washington Post* reported that his salary would be close to the $160,000 he had received yearly at the White House.

Ahmad Chalabi never explained how all those INC-connected defectors had gotten it wrong—and expressed no public regrets about the fabricated intelligence they had passed to the U.S. government and the media. In February 2004, *The Daily Telegraph* of London reported that in an interview Chalabi "shrugged off charges that he had deliberately misled U.S. intelligence" and said, "We are heroes in error." Speaking at the American Enterprise Institute in the fall of 2005, Chalabi, then a deputy prime minister of Iraq, denied having made that comment. "The fact that I deliberately misled the U.S. government, this is an urban myth," he added. Asked where the WMDs were, he said, "It is not useful for me to comment on it. . . . We are not engaged in this debate in Iraq." Shortly before his visit to the AEI, *The Wall Street Journal* reported that the FBI's investigation of Chalabi's alleged leaking of U.S. secrets to Iran had been halfhearted. Though fifteen months had passed since the inquiry was launched, Chalabi had yet to be questioned. "The investigation just went away," CIA officer John Maguire later noted. Despite the serious charge that Chalabi had passed top secret U.S. intelligence information to Tehran, on this swing through Washington he had no problem arranging meetings with Rice and Treasury Secretary John Snow.

But Chalabi didn't fare as well as he had hoped to in the new Iraq. In the December 2005 election, his party (a renamed version of the Iraqi National Congress) garnered less than 1 percent of the vote and failed to win any seats in the new Iraqi Parliament. At that point, he lost his post as a deputy prime minister, and months later he had to give up his position as interim oil minister. Longtime Chalabi watchers, though, cautioned that no one should ever count him out.

In the summer of 2006, Laurie Mylroie, the academic who had claimed Saddam was the real power behind al-Qaeda, was an active participant on an INC e-mailing list. She was still an AEI adjunct fellow. She expressed no concerns her theories had not proven right. As she had once told *Newsweek*, "I take satisfaction that we went to war in Iraq and got rid of Saddam Hussein. The rest is details."

Judy Miller left *The New York Times* in November 2005. After the huge legal battle with Fitzgerald, she and her editors were drained and distrustful of each other. And her departure wasn't without conflict. Miller had been under consideration to receive a $1 million prize endowed by a Romanian-born Israeli businessman and philanthropist named Dan David. But the *Times* editors refused to endorse her nomination for the award, concluding that a $1 million gift from an Israeli foundation to a *Times* correspondent who had covered the Middle East raised ethical concerns. The paper's decision ended Miller's chances to win the money. After leaving *The New York Times*, the journalist considered starting a blog but instead continued writing as a freelancer. In May 2006, she wrote a two-part piece for *The Wall Street Journal* on the CIA's success in persuading the Libyan government of Moammar Qaddafi to give up its weapons of mass destruction program. The article supported the Bush administration's contention that the war in Iraq had persuaded Qaddafi to forego his WMD programs. Jacqueline Shire, a senior analyst at the Institute for Science and International Security (which had challenged the articles Miller had cowritten on the aluminum tubes), criticized Miller for overstating the case and making it seem that Libya had been closer to developing a nuclear bomb than it had been. After the whole WMD controversy, Miller still spoke favorably of Chalabi, describing him as one of the "smartest people" she had ever met.

Naji Sabri, the Iraqi foreign minister who had passed the word to the CIA that Saddam had no active WMD programs, in 2006 was teaching journalism as an assistant professor at Qatar University.

In the summer of 2006, Robert Novak broke his silence about the CIA leak case. In a July 12 column, he revealed for the first time that he had named his sources in an interview with Fitzgerald and had testified before the grand jury in early 2004. He said that when he had appeared before the grand jury he had read a statement saying he was discomforted by having to disclose confidential conversations with his sources. He defended his decision to testify, noting, "It should be remembered that the special prosecutor knew their identities and did not learn them from me." Novak still wasn't naming Armitage. He insisted that Valerie Wilson's "role in initiating Wilson's mission" had been "a previously undisclosed part of an important news story."

Valerie Wilson left the CIA at the end of 2005. In July 2006, she and her husband filed a civil lawsuit in federal court against Cheney, Rove, Libby, and unnamed White House officials. The Wilsons argued in the legal complaint that these officials had violated their constitutional rights by conspiring to "discredit, punish, and seek revenge against them." Valerie Wilson was also writing a memoir, tentatively titled *Fair Game*—the term Rove had used with Chris Matthews to describe what he considered her.

On a Saturday morning in late spring 2006, John Maguire sat in a booth at a diner in suburban Virginia. He was just back from Iraq. He was no longer a covert warrior for the CIA. He was a business consultant—oil, Internet services, airplane sales. And he had been trying to drum up deals in Iraq. Not in Baghdad but in the north, the Kurdish area, from where he had once run secret anti-Saddam operations. Baghdad was too dangerous.

Maguire, who had helped craft the secret plan for sabotage and assassination in Iraq, was dispirited about the way things were going in the country he had tried to set on the right path. "It's so fucked up," he said. "We have everything working against itself. It's chaos there." Iraqis couldn't get to work. Government ministries were not functioning. U.S. security consultants and bodyguards, retained by various U.S. military and civilian agencies, were too high profile. Some had recently shot at a crowd to make Iraqis back up. Scores of Iraqi civilians were being killed each day in sectarian violence. The fabric of society had been ripped apart. "There are young guys living like they're in a Mad Max movie, robbing members of their own tribes," Maguire bemoaned. "How do you come back from complete chaos and lawlessness?"

A chance to get Iraq right, he noted, had been lost—by big blunders. "The White House says we made tactical mistakes," he remarked. But it was more than that: "We made huge strategic errors." De-Baathification, dissolving the army, refusing to recognize the immediacy of the insurgency, not preparing postinvasion plans for running a government and maintaining the critical infrastucture—the Bush administration had botched all of this. "People led us into the abyss," Maguire said. And, he added, Bush was "totally responsible. He's the guy. His team has failed him."

The original error, he noted, was how the war had been sold: weapons of mass destruction. For more than a decade, Maguire had been working on and off to get rid of Saddam—because, he thought, Saddam was a monstrous dictator who had brutalized his own people and been a destabilizing force in the region. If regime change in Iraq could be achieved, he believed, the dynamic in the entire Middle East could shift. For Maguire, that was enough of a reason for war. This view hadn't been far from that of the neoconservative hawks. But he parted with some in the administration when it came to using WMDs to justify an invasion of Iraq. Before the war, he had feared that this argument would be counterproductive. "It seemed very risky to base a war on an issue that you would have to prove the minute you entered the country," he explained. "We believed there would be a ton of WMDs. But we thought, 'I hope we find a shitload when we come in. If we don't find a warehouse of weapons, it will be ugly as hell.'"

And, in Maguire's view, it had also been just as big a mistake for the administration to claim that Saddam's regime was supporting al-Qaeda. "We never had anything that said that," he noted. Sure, Maguire said, the Iraqi intelligence service had tracked al-Qaeda—just the way any intelligence service would. And yes, there had been occasional meetings. That's what intelligence agencies do. But "the way this was cast [by the White House] created a picture that was different than reality."

Before the war, as they plotted to overthrow Saddam, Maguire and his partner Luis would have long soul-searching discussions about the enterprise they were about to undertake. They occasionally wondered if the whole project was a bridge too far. "This was a huge task of enormous magnitude," Maguire said. He admired Bush for having embraced such a grand endeavor. But after the invasion, he was frustrated that there was "nobody sitting in the driver's seat" who understood just how big the job was and how much time and effort it would take to make a post-Saddam Iraq work.

He angrily recalled attending two meetings at the Pentagon around the end of 2002 or the start of 2003, at which forty to fifty people from various government agencies assembled to discuss postinvasion matters. He and others asked a series of questions: How could Baghdad be secured? How would the United States respond to an insurgency, if one emerged? How would the American occupiers make sure the power grid and water system worked? "The Pentagon people"—Feith, his assistant Bill Luti, and others— "said, 'We've got it covered,'" Maguire remembered. The CIA people weren't invited to subsequent sessions. "This was the part that interested them the least," Maguire said. "And it was the most important part, the hardest part. There was no question we'd get to Baghdad in no time. We better have a plan for when we get there. But we had nothing but four PowerPoint pages. It was arrogant. We used to joke about the Ph.D. club— Wolfowitz, Feith. They knew best." Iraq, he noted, was now indeed a central front in the war on terrorism—"and we set the conditions for how that happened. This is a self-inflicted mess."

Still, Maguire had no regrets about having helped to start the war. Invading Iraq had been right, he believed. And he hadn't given up. He believed Iraq would eventually "evolve into something manageable." But he was at a loss to say how this would happen. He expected the situation to get worse—much worse—before it improved. "Baghdad will be on fire," he remarked.

And he wondered who could rescue Iraq from the chaos. A few days earlier, Maguire said, he and his wife had been watching the news. A report had come on about a war council Bush had held that day with his top advisers at Camp David. At one point, Bush and his most senior aides— all wearing casual clothes—had left the wood-paneled meeting room and walked outside so Bush could take a few questions from the press pool. As the president stood beneath the tall trees of the presidential retreat and declared that it was "important that we succeed in Iraq," he was flanked by Dick Cheney, Donald Rumsfeld, and Condoleezza Rice. Looking at this scene, Maguire's wife turned toward her husband. "Do you see," she asked, "any faces besides the same old faces that got us into this mess?"

Maguire was stumped. He didn't have an answer.

LIST OF ABBREVIATIONS

AEI . . . . American Enterprise Institute
BND . . . . German Federal Intelligence Service
BW . . . . biological weapons
CBRN . . . . chemical, biological, radiological, or nuclear (materials)
CPD . . . . Counterproliferation Division of the Directorate of
Operations (CIA)
CW . . . . chemical weapons
DGSE . . . . French General Directorate for External Security
DIA . . . . Defense Intelligence Agency
DO . . . . Directorate of Operations (CIA)
IAEA . . . . International Atomic Energy Agency
INC . . . . Iraqi National Congress
INR . . . . State Department's Bureau of Intelligence and Research
IOG . . . . Iraq Operations Group (CIA)
ISG . . . . Iraq Survey Group
JTFI . . . . Joint Task Force on Iraq (CIA)
MET . . . . Mobile Exploitation Team, 75th Exploitation Task Force
MOIS . . . . Iranian Ministry of Intelligence and Security
NESA . . . . Near East and South Asian division (CIA)
NIE . . . . National Intelligence Estimate
NOC . . . . nonofficial cover
NSC . . . . National Security Council
ORHA . . . . Office of Reconstruction and Humanitarian Assistance
PDB . . . . President's Daily Brief
ROCKSTARS . . . . code name for Iraqi spies used by the CIA
SISMI . . . . Italian Military Intelligence and Security Service
S/NF . . . . Secret/No Foreign distribution
UAV . . . . unmanned aerial vehicle
WHIG . . . . White House Information Group
WINPAC . . . . Center for Weapons Intelligence, Nonproliferation, and
Arms Control (CIA)
XTF . . . . 75th Exploitation Task Force

NOTES

MUCH OF this book concerns the perils of anonymous sources. In the months before the invasion of Iraq, reporters, relying on unnamed sources, published and
broadcast stories that inflated the threat posed by Iraq. After the invasion, senior
Bush officials, hiding behind the cloak of anonymity granted by reporters who need
access to high-level officials, leaked classified information to discredit a White House
critic.

Yet anonymous sources are essential to any effort to pierce the spin and cover
stories put forward by governments and other institutions. There is, unfortunately,
no way a journalist can thoroughly describe the internal workings and decisions of
the White House, the Pentagon, the State Department, the intelligence community—
or those of a federal criminal investigation—without relying on anonymous sources.
Prior to the Iraq War, anonymous officials in the intelligence agencies did tell some
reporters that the intelligence on Iraq's WMD programs and Baghdad's alleged links
to al-Qaeda was not as strong as the Bush administration claimed. Those sources
were correct. But the stories based on their leaks did not receive sufficient attention—not nearly as much as the articles, citing unidentified sources, that reported
the dictator of Iraq was a WMD danger and in league with al-Qaeda.

In this book, we have tried to use anonymous sources judiciously. We always
asked sources to go on the record. When we cite unidentified sources, we try to describe them with as much detail as they would permit.

The Bush administration has made it harder for journalists to find and use
anonymous sources. It has vigorously chased after leakers and threatened to prosecute some for unauthorized disclosures that shed light on potential abuses, such as
domestic wiretapping and secret CIA prisons. The administration's actions have sent
a chill through the ranks of the federal government. It is an unfortunate irony of the
CIA leak case that Patrick Fitzgerald's probe, which targeted wrongdoing by senior
administration figures, may have contributed to that chill by inhibiting midlevel
whistle-blowers.

Several potential sources declined to speak to us, citing the administration's
crackdown. Often they demurred with a familiar-sounding explanation: "I'd like to,
but *these days* . . ." If senior White House officials can get away with leaking classified
information to undermine a policy foe but lower-ranking officials are scared into

silence and cannot share with reporters important truths the government will not admit, the public is not served.

For this book, we conducted more than two hundred interviews with scores of participants in the chronicled events. Most of the quotes in the book are drawn from these interviews. The sources for quotes that did not come from our interviews—and were not public statements—are noted below. Public statements by George W. Bush, Dick Cheney, Donald Rumsfeld, Paul Wolfowitz, Colin Powell, Condoleezza Rice, Scott McClellan, and other administration officials can generally be found on the Web sites of the White House, the Pentagon, and the State Department.

INTRODUCTION

The account of George W. Bush on the White House lawn and his response to Helen Thomas's questions is based on interviews with Adam Levine. The authors obtained a copy of the "prebrief" memo for Bush's interview with Frank Sesno; this copy includes Bush's handwritten notes. (Ari Fleischer did not respond to interview requests.) For Dick Cheney's trips to CIA headquarters, interviews with John Maguire, Michael Sulick, and confidential interviews with other CIA sources. For Cheney and the Niger charge, see Senate Select Committee on Intelligence, *Report on the U.S. Intelligence Community's Prewar Intelligence Assessments on Iraq* (Washington, D.C.: U.S. Senate, 2004), pp. 38–39 (hereinafter *SSCI Report*). The reference to I. Lewis "Scooter" Libby receiving copies of NSC memos and his office reviewing raw NSA intercepts is based on confidential interviews with White House officials. For Libby's information requests to the CIA, "Government's Response to Court Orders of February 23 and 27, 2006," *United States of America v. I. Lewis Libby,* United States District Court for the District of Columbia, CR. NO 05-394 (RBW), March 2, 2006, pp. 15–16.

The description of the Anabasis project is based on interviews with Maguire, Tyler Drumheller, and Bob Graham, chairman of the Senate intelligence committee at the time, as well as confidential interviews with a White House official. See also Bob Woodward, *Plan of Attack* (New York: Simon & Schuster, 2004), pp. 68–74. Woodward describes portions of this project—without disclosing its name—elsewhere in the book. For Barry Goldwater's "I am pissed off" letter, *Congressional Record,* November 5, 1991, p. S15923. For Cofer Black's speech, interviews with Drumheller and a confidential counterterrorism official who heard Black's remarks. The description of Valerie Wilson's work at the CIA, her stint at the CPD's Joint Task Force on Iraq, and the operations of the JTFI is based on confidential interviews with CIA sources. For Bush's comments to Sesno, an unedited transcript of the interview obtained by the authors.

CHAPTER 1: A WARNING AT THE WHITE HOUSE

The account of the Cabinet Room meeting is based on interviews with Tom Daschle, Dick Gephardt, Dick Armey, and Trent Lott. Terry Holt described his telephone call from Dan Bartlett and his conversation with Armey after the White House meeting in an interview with the authors. See also *Plan of Attack*, pp. 169–172. (Woodward's account does not include Armey's previously unreported warning to Bush.) The letter Bush handed out can be found at http://archives.cnn.com/2002/ALLPOLITICS/09/04/bush.letter/index.html. The John Yoo Justice Department memo can be found on the Justice Department's Web site at www.usdoj.gov/olc/warpowers925. htm. A copy of the Karl Rove PowerPoint presentation was obtained by the authors. Thomas Wilson's March 2002 testimony can be found at www.fas.org/irp/congress/2002_hr/031902wilson.pdf. Wilson's comment—"I didn't really think they had a nuclear program"—is from an interview with the authors.

The Downing Street memos are available here: www.afterdowningstreet.org/?q=node/840. Zinni's speech can be found at www.npr.org/programs/morning/zinni. html. For Lott's comments on Bush and his phone call with Cheney, see Trent Lott, *Herding Cats: A Life in Politics* (New York: Regan Books, 2005), pp. 235–236. For Cheney's briefing on Capitol Hill, confidential interviews with participants. For the account of the Senate intelligence committee hearing, interviews with Graham and Carl Levin, and see Bob Graham with Jeff Nussbaum, *Intelligence Matters* (New York: Random House, 2004), pp. 179–180.

CHAPTER 2: THE NEW PRODUCT

The account of the White House's use of the "smoking gun" phrase is based on a confidential interview with a White House official. The account of *The New York Times'* aluminum tubes story is based on confidential interviews with *Times* reporters and editors. The story of Joe Turner and the aluminum tubes is drawn from interviews with David Albright, Houston Wood, Robert Kelley, and Greg Thielmann and confidential interviews with CIA officials and an intelligence analyst at the Lawrence Livermore National Laboratory. See also *SSCI Report*, pp. 84–93; Barton Gellman and Walter Pincus, "Depiction of Threat Outgrew Supporting Evidence," *The Washington Post*, August 10, 2003; Dafna Linzer and Barton Gellman, "CIA Skewed Iraq Report, Senate Says," *The Washington Post*, July 11, 2004; and David Barstow, William Broad, and Jeff Gerth, "How White House Embraced Suspect Iraq Arms Intelligence," *The New York Times*, October 3, 2004. (Turner did not respond to an interview request.) For the Durbin letter to George Tenet, *SSCI Report*, p. 12.

CHAPTER 3: A SPEECH AND A SPY AT THE UNITED NATIONS

The account of the TelePrompTer incident is based on confidential interviews with NSC staffers and *Plan of Attack,* pp. 183–184. The story of Bill Murray and Naji Sabri is drawn from interviews with Drumheller, Maguire, and a confidential source. For Maguire's response to Bush's UN speech and his inspection of the INC, Maguire interviews. The White House white paper, "A Decade of Deception and Defiance," can be found at www.whitehouse.gov/news/releases/2002/09/20020912. html. For Chalabi's participation in the 1995 coup, Kenneth Pollack, *The Threatening Storm: The United States and Iraq: the Crisis, the Strategy, and the Prospects After Saddam* (New York: Random House, 2002), pp. 71–73. Robert Baer's quote about the Chalabi coup appeared in Seymour Hersh, *Chain of Command: The Road from 9/11 to Abu Ghraib* (New York: HarperCollins, 2004), p. 164. For Maguire's meeting with Chalabi, interviews with Maguire and another CIA officer. For the CIA's suspicions about Aras Habib, interviews with Maguire and Baer. Zaab Sethna's remarks come from an e-mail exchange with the authors. For the INC's "information collection program," see Mark Hosenball and Michael Hirsh, "Chalabi: A Questionable Use of U.S. Funding," *Newsweek,* April 5, 2004, and Jonathan Landay, Warren Strobel, and John Walcott, "U.S. Still Paying Group That Provided False Iraqi Intelligence," Knight Ridder, February 22, 2004.

For David Wurmser's reference to Chalabi as a "mentor," see David Wurmser, *Tyranny's Ally* (Washington, D.C.: American Enterprise Institute, 1999), p. xxi. For Habib's role as head of the INC's "information collection program," see Knut Royce, "Named in Arrest Warrant," *Newsday,* May 21, 2004, and Douglas McCollam, "The List," *Columbia Journalism Review,* July–August 2004.

For R. James Woolsey's role in the Khodada incident, interview with Woolsey. Francis Brooke's "go get me a terrorist" quote can be found in Bryan Burrough, Evgenia Peretz, David Rose, and David Wise, "The Path to War," *Vanity Fair,* May 2004. For information on the "INC-linked" defector who talked to *Vanity Fair* about Salman Pak, *SSCI Report,* p. 332. The al-Haideri episode is based on an e-mail exchange with Sethna and two accounts: Jonathan Landay and Tish Wells, "Iraqi Exile Group Fed False Information to News Media," Knight Ridder, March 16, 2004, and James Bamford, "The Man Who Sold the War," *Rolling Stone,* November 17, 2005.

The account of Howell Raines and Judy Miller at the *Times* is based on interviews with Stephen Engelberg, Craig Pyes, Richard Burt, and numerous *Times* reporters and editors. A copy of the Pyes e-mail was obtained by the authors. Engelberg described Miller's near story on the al-Qaeda intercept. See also the Miller interview at www.navyseals.com/community/articles/article.cfm?id=9591. The account of the second Miller-Gordon piece on aluminum tubes is drawn from interviews with Albright and *Times* sources.

CHAPTER 4: ONE STRANGE THEORY

The account of Woolsey's trip to London is based on interviews with Woolsey, Drumheller, and other senior government officials. Also see Jonathan Landay and Warren Strobel, "Former CIA Director Used Pentagon Ties to Introduce Iraqi Defector," *Knight Ridder*, July 16, 2004. The transcript of the AEI press briefing on September 14, 2001, is available at www.aei.org/events/filter.all,eventID.366/transcript.asp. Mylroie's role as a back-channel diplomat is based on interviews with Amatzia Baram and Daniel Pipes and an e-mail exchange with Judith Miller.

For Mylroie's own account of her theories about Saddam Hussein, see Laurie Mylroie, *Study of Revenge: Saddam Hussein's Unfinished War Against America* (Washington D.C.: AEI Press, 2000). For the CIA's and FBI's assessment of her ideas and for details related to their investigations, confidential interviews with officials in each agency. For Ramzi Yousef's background, see Steve Coll, *Ghost Wars: The Secret History of the CIA, Afghanistan, and bin Laden, from the Soviet Invasion to September 10, 2001* (New York: Penguin, 2004), pp. 247–251. An excerpt from Mylroie's e-mail to Pipes was shared with the authors. The reference to Mylroie's and Wolfowitz's ties to the Telluride network is based on interviews with Francis Fukuyama and a representative of the Telluride Association in Ithaca, New York. See also James Mann, *Rise of the Vulcans: The History of Bush's War Cabinet* (New York: Viking, 2004), pp. 23–24. (Wolfowitz's office did not respond to interview requests for this book.) For Mylroie's relationship with Chalabi and the INC, interviews with Baram and an INC official. For Mylroie's appointment to a Pentagon advisory board, an interview and e-mail exchange with Pipes.

Richard Clarke's account of the April 2001 deputies meeting comes from Richard Clarke, *Against All Enemies* (New York: Free Press, 2004), pp. 231–232. The *Clean Break* study can be found at www.iasps.org/strat1.htm. The Project for a New American Century letter to Clinton can be found at www.newamericancentury.org/iraq clintonletter.htm. The group's founding statement can be found at www.newamerican century.org/statementofprinciples.htm. For Paul O'Neill's account of Bush's desire to topple Saddam, Ron Suskind, *The Price of Loyalty* (New York: Simon & Schuster, 2004), p. 86. Clarke's encounter with Bush in the Situation Room is based on Clarke's book (pp. 32–33) and an interview with a confidential source. For Wolfowitz's post-9/11 memos, see National Commission on Terrorist Attacks upon the United States, *The 9/11 Commission Report* (New York: W. W. Norton, 2004), pp. 335–336 (hereinafter *9/11 Commission Report*). For Wolfowitz's March 17, 2002, lunch with British Ambassador Christopher Meyer, see Meyer's March 18, 2002, memo (which is part of the Downing Street memos). The July 23, 2002, memo is also part of that collection.

CHAPTER 5: THE NIGER CAPER

The account of the drafting of Bush's September 12, 2002, speech is based on interviews with John Gibson and the *SSCI Report,* p. 49. (Michael Gerson did not respond
to requests for an interview.) The story of Rocco Martino and the Niger documents
is drawn from interviews with FBI officials, Alain Chouet, and Drumheller, a three-
part series in *La Repubblica* in October 2005 by Carlo Bonini and Giuseppe D'Avanzo,
and an interview Martino granted *Il Giornale* that appeared on November 5, 2005.
All quotes from Martino come from the Italian articles. See also Bob Drogin and
Tom Hamburger, "Niger Uranium Rumors Wouldn't Die," *Los Angeles Times,* February 17, 2006; Jay Solomon and Gabriel Kahn, "The Italian Job," *The Wall Street
Journal,* February 22, 2006; and Michael Smith, " 'Forgers' of Key Iraq War Contract
Named," *The Sunday Times,* April 9, 2006. For Antonio Nucera's comment on help-
ing La Signora, "L'ex 007 del SISMI, 'Io, Martino e la fonte segreta,' " by Gian Marco
Chiocci and Mario Sechi, *Il Giornale,* November 6, 2005.

For information on Wissam al-Zahawie's visit to Niger, see Report of a Committee of Privy Counsellors, *Review of Intelligence on Weapons of Mass Destruction,*
July 14, 2004, p. 124 (this report is better known as *The Butler Report*). The Zahawie
quotes come from e-mails he sent the authors. The account of the U.S. intelligence
community's handling of the Niger intelligence comes from *SSCI Report,* pp. 36–51.
For the CPD employee's quote regarding the request from the vice president's office,
a confidential interview.

The account of Joseph and Valerie Wilson's involvement in the Niger trip is
based on the *SSCI Report,* confidential interviews with CIA officials and others, interviews with Joseph Wilson and Doug Rohn, and Rohn's memo, which was released
by the State Department under the Freedom of Information Act. Wilson's own account is in Joseph Wilson, *The Politics of Truth: Inside the Lies That Led to War and
Betrayed My Wife's CIA Identity* (New York: Carroll & Graf, 2004), pp. 39–43. His
trip to Niger and his subsequent debriefing are covered in the *SSCI Report* and *The
Politics of Truth.* The INR memo, "Niger: Sale of Uranium to Iraq Is Unlikely," was
obtained by Judicial Watch under the Freedom of Information Act. The summation
sent to Armitage was released under a FOIA request by the authors. The quotes from
Chouet come from e-mail exchanges with the authors. For Murray's "Eiffel Tower"
cable, a confidential interview. The British white paper on Iraq's WMDs can be
found at www.the-hutton-inquiry.org.uk/content/dos/dos_1_0055to0107.pdf.

CHAPTER 6: THE SECRET DIGGERS

The account of the Feith slide show is based on copies of the slides obtained by the
authors from the office of Carl Levin and *SSCI Report,* pp. 309–312. For the FBI report on Atta's family, a confidential interview. The CIA and FBI investigations of the

Atta-in-Prague charge are drawn from Michael Isikoff, "The Phantom Link to Iraq," *Newsweek,* May 6, 2002, and *9/11 Commission Report,* pp. 228–229, 522; and from confidential interviews with CIA and FBI investigators. The reference to Ahmad Hikmat Shakir can be found in the *9/11 Commission Report* on page 519. The 9/11 Commission's finding regarding the alleged bin Laden meeting at a farm in Sudan is explained in its report, p. 468.

For Donald Rumsfeld's meeting with influential Washingtonians, a confidential interview with a participant. For Hans Blix remark, Lawrence Freedman, "War in Iraq: Selling the Threat," *Survival,* Summer 2004. For an account of what happened—or didn't happen—with al-Midhar and al-Hazmi, two of the 9/11 hijackers, see *9/11 Commission Report,* pp. 266–272. The report is also the source for Wolfowitz's charge that the CIA lacked imagination in dealing with terrorism, pp. 335–336. The accounts of Feith at White House meetings are based on confidential interviews with White House and State Department officials. For Feith's dealings with other government officials, confidential interviews. The account of Feith's intelligence unit is based on interviews with F. Michael Maloof, Thomas Wilson, and a confidential INC source, and the *SSCI Report,* pp. 307–312, 362–364. The *SSCI Report* covers the "Iraq and al-Qaida" study on pp. 305–306, and it refers to the CIA ombudsman and possible politicization of intelligence on pp. 359–361. Feith's comments on the competing theories of intelligence are from an interview with the authors.

CHAPTER 7: A TALE OF TWO SOURCES
The account of the assassination plot against George H. W. Bush and the subsequent fate of the plotters is based on interviews with Edward ("Skip") Gnehm and a confidential government source. For Armey's reaction to Bush's comment, interview with Armey. See also Paul Quinn-Judge, "CIA Report Casts Doubt on Kuwait Assertion of Plot on Bush," *The Boston Globe,* May 27, 1993, and Seymour Hersh, "A Case Not Closed," *The New Yorker,* November 11, 1993. For Bush's breakfast with congressional leaders, confidential interview. The account of the September 24, 2002, hearing is based on interviews with Joseph Biden and Chuck Hagel and confidential interviews with other participants.

The story of Ibn al-Shaykh al-Libi is based on confidential interviews with senior FBI and CIA officials. The State Department's 2001 human rights report can be found at www.state.gov/g/drl/rls/hrrpt/2001/. The February 2002 DIA memo on al-Libi was released by Levin in October 2005. It can be found at levin.senate.gov/newsroom/release.cfm?id=248339. See also Michael Hirsh, John Barry, and Daniel Klaidman, "A Tortured Debate," *Newsweek,* June 21, 2004; Michael Isikoff, "Forget the Poisons and Deadly Gases," *Newsweek,* July 5, 2004; and Michael Isikoff and Mark Hosenball, "Al-Libi's Tall Tales," Newsweek.com, November 10, 2005.

For Armey's briefing with Cheney, interviews with Armey. The policy briefings for House Democrats were described by Henry Waxman in an interview. He shared his notes from these sessions with the authors. The story of the Biden-Lugar-Hagel resolution and Dick Gephardt's role is based on interviews with Biden, Hagel, Lott, and Gephardt, and confidential interviews with congressional staffers. For Bush's order to Lott, see *Herding Cats,* p. 240.

The tale of Curveball is based on interviews with Drumheller and a confidential CIA source and on the accounts in the *SSCI Report,* pp. 152–154, and Commission on the Intelligence Capabilities of the United States Regarding Weapons of Mass Destruction, *Report to the President of the United States* (2005), pp. 83–85 (hereinafter *Robb-Silberman Report*). See also Bob Drogin and John Goetz, "How U.S. Fell Under the Spell of 'Curveball'," *Los Angeles Times,* November 20, 2005.

CHAPTER 8: BENT WITH THE WIND

Peter Zimmerman's reaction to the NIE is based on interviews with him. Portions of the NIE were declassified by the White House in July 2003. They can be found at www.fas.org/irp/congress/2003_cr/h072103.html. For the quote from the unnamed Energy Department official—"DOE did not want to come out before the war"—see *Robb-Silberman Report,* p. 75. For the intelligence analyst's quote on the prewar perspective of intelligence analysts, *SSCI Report,* p. 505. For Pillar's observations regarding pressure on analysts, Paul Pillar, "Intelligence, Policy, and the War in Iraq," *Foreign Affairs,* March–April 2006. Simon Dodge's actions regarding the NIE and the Niger charge and Robert Walpole's decision to include it are referenced in the *SSCI Report,* pp. 51–54. For the WMD Commission report quote, *Robb-Silberman Report,* p. 14.

Graham's reaction to the NIE and his and Levin's request for a declassified white paper are based on interviews with Graham and Levin and *Intelligence Matters,* pp. 180–181. For Pillar's role in drafting the CIA white paper, interviews with Pillar. The CIA white paper can be found at www.cia.gov/cia/reports/iraq_wmd/Iraq_Oct_2002.htm.

Graham's response to the CIA white paper comes from interviews with Graham; *Intelligence Matters,* p. 185; and Bob Graham, "What I Knew Before the Invasion," *The Washington Post,* November 20, 2005. For Levin's reaction to the CIA letter, an interview with Levin. The CIA letter on Saddam, terrorists, and WMDs can be found at www.fas.org/irp/cia/product/iraq-wmd.html. It cites the October 2, 2002, exchange between Levin and John McLaughlin. For Tenet calling a *New York Times* reporter, Levin interview and a confidential interview with a *Times* reporter.

The account of the drafting of Bush's Cincinnati speech is based on interviews with Gibson and another White House speechwriter and on *SSCI Report,* pp. 55–57. For McLaughlin's October 2 testimony, *SSCI Report,* p. 54. Walpole's presence at that hearing comes from an interview with a confidential CIA official. For Levine in the Situation Room, interviews with Levine.

The account of Elisabetta Burba's meeting with Martino and her subsequent dealings with editors and the U.S. Embassy is based on interviews with her and Ian Kelly. For CIA station chief Jeff Castelli's handling of the Niger documents, Drumheller interviews. (Castelli's name was published in *La Repubblica*'s Niger series in October 2005.) For Brent Scowcroft's letter to the White House regarding Joseph Wilson, an interview with Scowcroft. See also *The Politics of Truth*, pp. 296–97.

CHAPTER 9: A SECRET IN THE NEVADA DESERT

The account of the Scorpions at the Nevada training camp is based on interviews with Maguire, one of the Scorpions, Drumheller, an NSC official, Graham, and a White House official. For Mohammed Abdullah al-Shahwani's background, interviews with Maguire and one of the Scorpions. See also Marie Colvin, "Revealed: CIA's Bungled Iraqi Coup," *The Sunday Times* (London), April 2, 2000.

For the Sufi mystic at the Marrakesh restaurant, interviews with Maguire. See also *Plan of Attack*, pp. 144, 210–212. For Biden's phone call with Colin Powell, interview with Biden. For Tommy Franks's deployment order, Michael Gordon and Bernard Trainor, *Cobra II: The Inside Story of the Invasion and Occupation of Iraq* (New York: Pantheon Books, 2006), p. 95. For Cheney's meeting with Victor Davis Hanson, an unpublished interview with Hanson conducted by one of the authors. The account of Luis and Maguire's conflict with other CIA officers regarding the Jordanian car operation and other Anabasis matters is based on interviews with Maguire. See also James Risen, *State of War: The Secret History of the CIA and the Bush Administration* (New York: Free Press, 2006), pp. 79–83.

For Simon Dodge's review of the Niger documents, *SSCI Report*, p. 58, and interview with Dodge. For Wayne White's reaction to the documents, an interview with White. For the December 17, 2002, WINPAC paper, John Bolton's connection to the State Department fact sheet, Dodge's continuing efforts related to the Niger documents, the Energy Department analyst's quote, and the WINPAC analyst's quote about the Niger papers, *SSCI Report*, pp. 60–62.

The account of the dispute within the CIA over Curveball is drawn from *Robb-Silberman Report*, pp. 95–101, and a confidential interview with a CIA source. The issue of the January 2003 spin tests of the aluminum tubes is covered by *Robb-Silberman Report*, p. 70. The IAEA meeting with Joe Turner and the quote from one participant is drawn from "How White House Embraced Suspect Iraq Arms Intelligence," *The New York Times*, October 3, 2004. For Shahwani and the Scorpions in Jordan, interviews with Maguire and one of the Scorpions. For the work of the CIA's Joint Task Force on Iraq, interviews with confidential CIA source.

CHAPTER 10: THE FINAL PITCH

The account of the drafting of the State of the Union address is based on interviews with Gibson and Matthew Scully and confidential interviews with other White House officials and a CIA official. *SSCI Report* covers the interactions between Alan Foley and Robert Joseph at pp. 64–66. See also White House press briefing by senior administration official, July 18, 2003. (This official was not identified publicly; it was Dan Bartlett, White House communications director.) For Joseph Wilson's reaction to the State of the Union speech, *The Politics of Truth,* pp. 312–314.

For the preparation of Powell's presentation at the United Nations, interviews with Lawrence Wilkerson and confidential interviews with a State Department official and a White House official. Also *SSCI Report,* pp. 66–67, 366–367; "Testimony of Lawrence Wilkerson," Senate Democratic Policy Committee hearing, June 26, 2006; *Plan of Attack,* pp. 288–292; and Burrough, Peretz, Rose, and Wise, "The Path to War," *Vanity Fair,* May 2004. Powell's reaction to de Villepin's January 20 statement is based on a confidential interview with a State Department official. For the INR's memos critiquing the draft of the Powell speech, *SSCI Report,* pp. 423–430.

The account of the January 31, 2003, Bush-Blair meeting is based on a secret memo written by a Blair aide. Portions of this memo have been published; see Philippe Sands, *Lawless World* (London: Penguin, 2005), pp. 273–274, and Don Van Natta, Jr., "Bush Was Set on Path to War, Memo by British Adviser Says," *The New York Times,* March 27, 2006. The authors have reviewed a copy of this memo.

For Woolsey, Mohammad al-Harith, and the Pentagon intelligence officer, interviews with Woolsey; Jonathan Landay and Warren Strobel, "Former CIA Director Used Pentagon Ties to Introduce Iraqi Defector," Knight Ridder, July 16, 2004; and *SSCI Report,* p. 247.

The account of the Curveball dispute and its relation to the Powell speech is based on *Robb-Silberman Report,* pp. 102–105; *SSCI Report,* pp. 243–251; and interviews with Drumheller. For Phil Mudd's call to Tenet and Tenet's attempt to reach Wilkerson, interviews with Wilkerson. For Biden's phone call with Powell, interview with Biden. For Wilkerson's comments regarding Powell's use of the al-Libi charge, "Testimony of Lawrence Wilkerson," Senate Democratic Policy Committee hearing, June 26, 2006. For Powell's comments on his UN speech, interview with the authors.

CHAPTER 11: BEST-LAID PLANS

The account of Wayne White's preparation of the "No Dominoes" study is based on interviews with White and Greg Miller, "Democracy Domino Theory 'Not Credible,'" *Los Angeles Times,* March 14, 2003. The Stiglitz and Bilmes war costs study can be found at www.2.gsb.columbia.edu/faculty/jstiglitz/download/2006_Cost_of_War_in_Iraq_NBER.pdf. For General Tommy Franks's use of the "lord mayor" phrase, interviews with White House official. See also *Cobra II*, p. 160. The account of Phase IV planning within the Third U.S. Army is based on interviews with Colonel Kevin Benson. For the preparation of the Army War College's Strategic Studies Institute study, interviews with one of the report's coauthors and another War College source. The study can be found at www.strategicstudiesinstitute.army.mil/pdffiles/PUB708.pdf.

Pillar described the post-Saddam report he prepared for the CIA in an interview and e-mail exchange. See also the transcript of a talk he gave at the Council on Foreign Relations in Washington, D.C., on March 7, 2006, which can be found at www.cfr.org/publication/10097/intelligence_policy_and_the_war_in_iraq_rush_transcript_federal_news_service_inc.html. For the description of the Future of Iraq project, interview with a State Department official; David Phillips, *Losing Iraq: Inside the Postwar Reconstruction Fiasco* (Westview Press, 2005), p. 128; Eric Schmitt and Joel Brinkley, "State Dept. Study Foresaw Trouble Now Plaguing Iraq," *The New York Times,* October 19, 2003; and James Fallows, "Blind into Baghdad," *The Atlantic Monthly,* January–February 2004. Murray's continuing pursuit of Naji Sabri is based on confidential interviews with CIA officials.

The account of Jacques Baute and the Niger documents is based on an interview with him and an e-mail exchange with Zahawie. For the DIA memo sent to Rumsfeld on the yellowcake charge, the WINPAC reports, and the CIA Sense of the Community Memorandum, see *SSCI Report,* pp. 69–71. For the Iraqi defector who provided fabricated intelligence about chemical weapons and for the CIA's rejection of the UAV charge, see *Robb-Silberman Report,* pp. 128–129, 132–140. The account of Miller at the book party is based on an interview with a confidential source. For Gibson's conversation with Sean McCormack, interview with Gibson. For Levine's conversation with Tim Russert, interviews with Levine.

CHAPTER 12: THE MISSING WEAPONS

The story of the ROCKSTARS and the bombing raid targeting Saddam is based on interviews with Maguire and *Cobra II*, pp. 176–177, and *Plan of Attack*, pp. 383–399. The role of the Scorpions and the Anabasis sabotage program is drawn from interviews with Maguire and one of the Scorpions. For the celebratory dinner held by Cheney, *Plan of Attack*, pp. 409–412. A University of Chicago summation of what was looted from the Iraqi National Museum can be found at http://oi.uchicago.edu/OI/IRAQ/iraq.html. See also Andrew Lawler, "Mayhem in Mesopotamia," *Science,* August 1, 2003. Benson's briefing of General William G. Webster is based on interviews with Benson. The account of the atmosphere in the White House regarding the unfound WMDs is based on interviews with Levine and four other White House officials. For Gerson's remark on WMDs and Bush's legacy, a confidential interview with a White House source. Carl Ford's review of the incoming intelligence on Iraq's WMDs is based on interviews with him.

Victoria Clarke's approval of Miller's embed assignment is based on an interview with Clarke and an e-mail written by Eugene Pomeroy that was shared with the authors. For Miller in the desert, a confidential interview. Steven Erlanger's reaction to the Miller story about the scientist in a baseball cap and the subsequent *Times* meeting is based on interviews with Erlanger and other *Times* employees. The Pomeroy e-mail quoting Colonel Richard McPhee was obtained by the authors. For Gellman's effort to follow up Miller's story, interviews with Gellman. For Miller's role in the transfer of Saddam's son-in-law and her attempt to block the order recalling MET Alpha, Howard Kurtz, "Embedded Reporter's Role in Army Unit's Actions Questioned by Military," *The Washington Post*, June 25, 2003. The account of Miller's interactions with MET Alpha is also based on interviews with Pomeroy. A full copy of Miller's note protesting the order recalling MET Alpha was obtained by the authors. Miller's e-mail to John Burns about Chalabi was first disclosed in the Kurtz article mentioned above. A copy of Miller's May 5, 2003, e-mail to Raines and Gerald Boyd was obtained by the authors.

The account of Joseph Wilson's appearance at the gathering of Democratic senators is based on interviews with Wilson and another participant at the meeting. For Wilson's account of his pretrip meeting at the CIA, see *The Politics of Truth*, p. 14. For Paul Bremer's orders on de-Baathification and dissolving the Iraqi Army, see L. Paul Bremer III, *My Year in Iraq: The Struggle to Build a Future of Hope* (New York: Simon & Schuster, 2006), pp. 39–42. This account is also based on interviews with a senior NSC official and Maguire. See also *Losing Iraq*, pp. 143–153.

The account of the dispute over the CIA paper on the purported bioweapons trailers is based on interviews with Ford, Albright, a senior DIA analyst, and a former weapons inspector specializing in biological weapons. For Walter Pincus's pursuit of the Niger trip story, interviews with Pincus.

CHAPTER 13: THE LEAKING BEGINS

Karl Rove's horsing around at Camp al-Sayliyah is based on Mike Allen, "President: 'Truth' on Arms Will Be Found," *The Washington Post*, June 6, 2003. The account of Bush's "just like the WMD we found" remark comes from a confidential interview with a White House oficial. For Bush's conversation in Qatar about who was in charge of the WMD hunt, Massimo Calabresi and Timothy Burger, "Who Lost the WMD?," *Time*, July 7, 2003. The account of David Kay taking over the WMD hunt is based on interviews with Kay. For Pincus's continuing pursuit of the Niger trip story, interviews with Pincus. For Libby's receiving oral reports from Marc Grossman on the Wilson trip, the CIA faxing classified documents to Libby, and Libby writing

"Wilson" on the documents, see "Indictment of I. Lewis Libby," U.S. District Court for the District of Columbia, October 31, 2003, pp. 4–5 (hereinafter "Libby Indictment"). The indictment can be found at www.usdoj.gov/usao/iln/osc/documents/libby_indictment_28102005.pdf.

The account of the drafting of the INR memo is based on interviews with Ford and the memo itself (the cover letter of the memo notes that Neil Silver drafted it). For Grossman's subsequent briefing of Libby, see "Libby Indictment," p. 4.

Libby's remark to a friend—"Do you expect me to commit a felony . . . ?"—is based on a confidential interview with that friend. The referenced *Post* profile of Libby is Mark Leibovich, "In the Spotlight and on the Spot," *The Washington Post,* October 23, 2005. For Libby's remarks about the first Bush administration's decision to accept a cease-fire in Iraq, *Rise of the Vulcans,* p. 191. For Libby's quip that he intended to stay in his job until "I get indicted," see Leibovich, "In the Spotlight and on the Spot." For Libby's interview with Mann, *Rise of the Vulcans,* p. 294. For *The New Yorker's* article on Libby's novel, Lauren Collins, "Scooter's Sex Shocker," *The New Yorker,* November 7, 2005. For Joseph Wilson's statement that he had misspoken to Pincus and his explanation, *SSCI Report,* p. 45.

The account of Cheney telling Libby that Wilson's wife worked at the CIA and Tenet's role in this incident is based on "Libby Indictment," p. 5, and David Johnston, Richard W. Stevenson, and Douglas Jehl, "Cheney Told Aide of CIA Officer, Lawyers Report," *The New York Times,* October 25, 2005. (In the course of his investigation, special counsel Patrick Fitzgerald obtained copies of Libby's notes that mentioned this conversation with Cheney about Valerie Wilson.) Libby's "curiosity sort of fashion" remark is found in Judge David Tatel's concurring decision in "In Re: Grand Jury Subpoena, Judith Miller," February 15, 2005, p. 31 (hereinafter "Tatel Decision"). For Libby's June 14 meeting with a CIA briefer, "Libby Indictment," p. 5. For Wilson's reaction to Condoleezza Rice's appearance on *Meet the Press* and his subsequent actions, *Politics of Truth,* p. 332. The account of the fortieth anniversary party for Robert Novak is based on interviews with attendees, including Al Hunt and Margaret Carlson, and John Barron, "D.C. Bigwigs Toast Novak's 40th Year," *Chicago Sun-Times,* June 20, 2003. For Rove leaking information to Novak in 1992, Elisabeth Bumiller, "Rove and Novak, a 20-Year Friendship Born in Texas," *The New York Times,* August 6, 2005. Libby's discussion with Eric Edelman is described in "Libby Indictment," p. 6.

The account of Armitage's interview with Woodward is based on confidential interviews with colleagues of Armitage and a government official familiar with the conversation. Woodward later issued a statement about this conversation, without identifying Armitage as his source; see Bob Woodward, "Testifying in the CIA Leak Case," *The Washington Post,* November 16, 2005. See also Jim VandeHei and Carol

Leonnig, "Woodward Was Told of Plame More Than Two Years Ago," *The Washington Post,* November 16, 2005. See also Marie Brenner, "Lies and Consequences; Sixteen Words That Changed the World," *Vanity Fair,* April 2006.

For the Iran-*contra* special counsel's findings regarding Armitage, Lawrence Walsh, "Final Report of the Independent Counsel for Iran/Contra Matters," United States Court of Appeals for the District of Columbia Circuit, 1993, pp. 379–380, 431–438 (hereinafter "Iran/Contra Final Report"). For Armitage's complaining to Wilkerson about the lack of military service by administration officials, interviews with Wilkerson. The reference to Armitage's grand jury admission that he was a "terrible gossip" can be found in "Iran/Contra Final Report," p. 431; see note 211. The "pretty nosy" quote can be found in "Report of the Congressional Committees Investigating the Iran-Contra Affair," vol. 2 (Depositions), Appendix B, 1988, p. 147. For Woodward's characterization of Armitage's remarks as "casual" and "gossip," see Brenner, "Lies and Consequences; Sixteen Words That Changed the World."

For Roger Cohen's quote regarding "unease" over Miller's WMD coverage, Don Van Natta, Jr., Adam Liptak, and Clifford Levy, "The Miller Case: A Notebook, a Cause, a Jail Cell and a Deal," *The New York Times,* October 16, 2005. The account of Miller's clash with Jim Wilkinson is based on interviews with Wilkinson and Defense Department e-mails obtained by the authors. The account of Miller's involvement in the paper's postinvasion WMD project is based on interviews with a *Times* reporter who worked on the project.

For the mid-June CIA memo on the alleged Iraq–Niger deal, *SSCI Report,* p. 71. The account of the internal White House discussions about the Niger charge is based on confidential interviews with White House officials. For Miller's meeting with Scooter Libby on June 23, "Libby Indictment," p. 6, and Judith Miller, "My Four Hours Testifying in the Federal Grand Jury Room," *The New York Times,* October 16, 2005. For Cheney and Bush's discussion about selectively releasing portions of the NIE, interviews with a confidential source. Woodward described his June 27 meeting with Libby in "Testifying in the CIA Leak Case," *The Washington Post,* November 16, 2005. Libby's use of the word "vigorous" was reported in Barton Gellman and Dafna Linzer, "A 'Concerted Effort' to Discredit Bush Critic," *The Washington Post,* April 9, 2006. For the Novak-Duberstein conversation, interviews with confidential sources. Novak said he did not recall the conversation.

CHAPTER 14: SEVEN DAYS IN JULY

The account of Ford's involvement in preparing the updated INR memo is based on interviews with him. The memo itself was declassified and released by the State Department under the Freedom of Information Act. The report of the House of Commons foreign affairs committee can be found at www.publications.parliament.uk/pa/cm200203/cmselect/cmfaff/813/81303.htm. The Butler Report can be found at www.butlerreview.org.uk. The account of the deliberations within the White House regarding what to say about the sixteen words is based on confidential interviews with White House sources. Portions of Libby's grand jury testimony were attached to a legal filing submitted by Special Counsel Patrick Fitzgerald; see "Reply to the Response of I. Lewis Libby to Government's Response to Court's Inquiry Regarding News Articles the Government Intends to Offer at Trial," *United States of America v. I. Lewis Libby,* United States District Court for the District of Columbia, CR. NO 05-394 (RBW), May 24, 2006, Exhibits A–C (hereinafter "Libby Grand Jury Testimony Excerpts"). The copy of the Wilson op-ed annotated by Dick Cheney was filed by Fitzgerald with the U.S. District Court in Washington, D.C.; see "Government's Response to Court's Inquiry Regarding News Articles the Government Intends to Offer as Evidence at Trial," *United States of America v. I. Lewis Libby,* United States District Court for the District of Columbia, CR. NO 05-394 (RBW), May 12, 2006, Exhibit A. (As of mid-2006, most of Fitzgerald's filings could be found at www.usdoj.gov/usao/iln/osc/index.html.)

For Cheney's office sending talking points to Ari Fleischer and for Libby's lunch with Fleischer, see transcript of the May 5, 2006, hearing in the Libby case, p. 13; "Libby Indictment," p. 7; and "Tatel Decision," p. 32. For Libby's July 8 breakfast meeting with Miller, see "Libby Indictment," p. 7, and Miller, "My Four Hours Testifying in the Federal Grand Jury Room." For Libby consulting with David Addington regarding the disclosure of classified information, see "Libby Grand Jury Testimony Excerpts." For Cheney authorizing Libby to talk to Miller about the NIE, see "Government's Response to Defendant's Third Motion to Compel Discovery," *United States of America v. I. Lewis Libby,* United States District Court for the District of Columbia, CR. NO 05-394 (RBW), April 5, 2006, pp. 19–23 (hereinafter "Government's Response to Defendant's Third Motion"). For Libby's meeting with Addington in an anteroom, "Libby Indictment," p. 7.

The account of Novak trying to talk to Rove about Fran Townsend is based on interviews with Levine. Novak's meeting with Armitage is based on confidential interviews with three government officials. Powell's involvement in this meeting is based on an interview with two government officials with direct knowledge of the meeting. Novak described this meeting in an interview with Fox News, July 12, 2006. For Armitage's confession to Ford, interviews with Ford. For Novak's encounter with a friend of Joseph Wilson, *The Politics of Truth,* p. 343.

Novak's July 9 conversation with Rove is based on interviews with Rove's attorney and Novak's interview with Fox News. (In an interview with authors, Novak said the phone call might have happened July 8.) Novak also described this conversation—without naming Rove—in a column published October 1, 2003. Novak identified Rove as his second source in a column published on July 12, 2006.

For Libby's anger with Chris Matthews and Levine's phone call with Matthews, interviews with Levine. For Libby's phone call to Russert, interviews with Russert. See also "Libby Indictment," p. 7. For Russert's call to Neal Shapiro, an interview with Shapiro. A description of Rice's phone call to Tenet can be found in Ron Suskind, *The One-Percent Doctrine: Deep Inside America's Pursuit of Its Enemy Since 9/11* (New York: Simon & Schuster, 2006), pp. 243–244. The authors obtained a copy of Michael Duffy's e-mail noting, "they've dimed out Tenet."

For Rove's brief hallway chat with Libby, "Libby Indictment," p. 8. The account of Bill Harlow's efforts to draft a statement for Tenet is based on a confidential interview with a CIA official. For the interactions between Harlow and Novak, see "Tatel Decision," p. 38; Novak's October 1, 2003, column; and Walter Pincus and Jim VandeHei, "Prosecutor in CIA Leak Case Casting a Wide Net," *The Washington Post*, July 27, 2005. Wilson's description of his phone conversation with Novak can be found in *Politics of Truth*, pp. 343–344. Harlow's "I hope I convinced you" remark comes from an interview with Harlow. John Dickerson described his interactions with White House officials in two articles he wrote for *Slate*; see John Dickerson, "Where's My Subpoena?" *Slate*, February 7, 2006. Dickerson was also interviewed by the authors.

For Cooper's phone conversation with Rove, Matthew Cooper, "What I Told the Grand Jury," *Time*, July 25, 2005. Cooper's e-mail to Duffy about his conversation with Rove was obtained by one of the authors and first disclosed by *Newsweek* in July 2005. A portion of Cooper's file for the cover story was obtained by the authors. A copy of Rove's e-mail to Hadley was obtained from a confidential source.

For the conversation between Libby and Cheney on the vice presidential plane, "Libby Indictment," p. 8; Barton Gellman, "A Leak, Then a Deluge," *The Washington Post*, October 30, 2006; and "Libby Grand Jury Testimony Excerpts." Cooper's e-mails to Duffy about the "dis of Wilson" and the "WH v. Wilson fight" were obtained by the authors. For Cooper's phone call with Libby, Matthew Cooper, "What Scooter Libby and I Talked About," *Time*, November 7, 2005. See also "Libby Indictment," p. 8. Miller described her July 12 conversation with Libby in "My Four Hours Testifying in the Federal Grand Jury Room." See also "Libby Indictment," p. 8. Pincus described his conversation with an unidentified administration official in Walter Pincus, "Anonymous Sources: Their Use in a Time of Prosecutorial Interest," *Nieman Reports*, Summer 2005.

CHAPTER 15: A COVER BLOWN

The account of Valerie Wilson's reaction to the Novak column is based on confidential interviews. See also *The Politics of Truth*, pp. 345–346. The account of Valerie Plame's early life and CIA training is based on interviews with sources close to her and several CIA classmates, including Larry Johnson, Brent Cavan, and James Marcinkowski. See also, Vicky Ward, "Double Exposure," *Vanity Fair*, January 2004; Richard Leiby and Dana Priest, "Spy Next Door," *The Washington Post*, October 8, 2003; and Douglas Jehl and David Stout, "Cover Story Kept Work for CIA a Secret," *The New York Times*, October 2, 2003. The account of her early CIA assignments is based on interviews with Fred Rustmann, a former CIA official who supervised Valerie Plame, and confidential CIA sources. Joe Wilson's quote—"Is your real name Valerie?"—can be found in *The Politics of Truth*, p. 243. For her decision to join the Iraq branch of the CPD, a confidential interview with a CIA source. For her shift to a personnel management position, a confidential interview with a CIA source.

For an account of Philip Agee's CIA-naming campaign and the passage of the Intelligence Identities Protection Act, see Philip Agee, *On the Run* (Secaucus, NJ: Lyle Stuart, 1987). See also Congressional Research Service, "Intelligence Identities Protection Act," October 2003, and Committee on the Judiciary, U.S. Senate, *Intelligence Identities Protection Act of 1982*, 1982.

The account of Libby complaining to Cooper is based on "What Scooter and I Talked About," *Time*, November 7, 2005. Copies of Cooper's e-mail to Duffy and Dickerson and Duffy's reply were obtained by the authors. Bartlett's response to the Wilson bashing is based on interviews with Levine. (Bartlett did not respond to requests for comment regarding this and other scenes in the book.) A copy of Cooper's e-mail to Duffy about the Novak column was obtained by the authors. A copy of Cooper's e-mail to political journalists about his Wilson story on the *Time* Web site was obtained by the authors.

Libby's transmission of NIE excerpts to *The Wall Street Journal* is referenced in "Government's Response to Court's Inquiry Regarding News Articles the Government Intends to Offer as Evidence at Trial," *United States of America v. I. Lewis Libby*, CR. NO 05-394, May 12, 2006, p. 8.

For the "It would fuck Gilligan" quote, see Liane Katz and Matthew Tempest, "Kelly Naming Would 'Fuck Gilligan'—Campbell," *The Guardian*, September 22, 2003. For David Kelly's e-mail to Miller, see Warren Hoge with Judith Miller, "British Arms Expert at Center of Dispute on Iraq Data Is Found Dead, His Wife Says," *The New York Times*, July 19, 2003.

For Andrea Mitchell's remark to Joseph Wilson regarding the "real story," see *The Politics of Truth*, p. 5. The account of Rove seeking to speak to Matthews is based on interviews with Levine. For Rove's phone call with Matthews, interviews with confidential sources. For "fair game" comment, Evan Thomas and Michael Isikoff, "Secrets and Leaks," *Newsweek,* October 13, 2003.

Excerpts of the memos the CIA sent the White House on October 5 and 6, 2002, can be found in *SSCI Report,* pp. 56–57. Stephen Hadley's offer to resign, his "make peace" quote, and the account of the White House deliberations on these memos are based on interviews with confidential White House sources. For the CIA's response to the leak, confidential interviews and a January 30, 2004, letter sent by Stanley Moskowitz, director of congressional affairs for the CIA, to Representative John Conyers. The letter is found in *The Politics of Truth,* p. 359. A copy of the DOJ Media Leak Questionnaire was obtained by the authors.

Chapter 16: The Incurious President

The account of David Kay being asked by Cheney's office to investigate the NSA intercept is based on interviews with a confidential government source. The watering-hole episode and Wolfowitz's requests regarding Mohamed Atta are based on interviews with Kay. For Kay's activities in Iraq and his interactions with Tenet and McLaughlin, interviews with Kay. The account of Hamish Killip's inspection of the purported biological weapons labs is based on interviews with him. For Killip's "dust-bins" quote, see Drogin and Goetz, "How U.S. Fell Under the Spell of 'Curveball'," *Los Angeles Times,* November 20, 2005. This *Los Angles Times* article details many other aspects of the Curveball saga. The *Robb-Silberman Report* also covers the work of Kay and the Iraq Survey Group related to Curveball. For the references to Curveball as a "liar," "con artist," and "rat," see *Robb-Silberman Report,* p. 223. The quote from Curveball's mother can be found in the *Los Angeles Times* story.

For Robert Joseph's attitude toward the unsuccessful WMD hunt, an interview with a confidential White House source. The account of Kay's meetings with Bush and Cheney is based on interviews with Kay. For the drafting of the NIE on the Iraqi insurgency, interviews with Wayne White.

Chapter 17: The Investigation Begins

The opening anecdote about Levine and Mike Allen is based on interviews with Levine, who also described the White House deliberations involving Rice and Scott McClellan on the leak matter and his subsequent involvement in the leak story. The account of *The Washington Post*'s handling of the Mike Allen story and the reaction inside the paper to the article is based on confidential interviews with *Post* employees. For the White House staff meeting regarding the leak investigation, an interview with a confidential White House source who attended the meeting.

The account of Armitage acknowledging his role as the leaker—and the subsequent phone calls—is based on interviews with confidential sources. For the quote from William Taft IV, interview with the authors. For the FBI's interview with Armitage, interviews with confidential sources.

A copy of Kay's interim report can be found at www.cia.gov/cia/public_affairs/speeches/2003/david_kay_10022003.html. For Kay's investigator's conclusions about Curveball—and WINPAC's reluctance to accept them—see *Robb-Silberman Report*, pp. 107, 123. For Kay's acceptance of this finding and Tenet's and McLaughlin's reaction to his findings, interviews with Kay. For Rolf Ekeus's quote regarding the Kay report, Bob Drogin and Greg Miller, "Inspectors Find Aims, Not Arms," *Los Angeles Times*, October 3, 2003. For Hans Blix's response to the Kay report, Bob Drogin, "Botched Iraqi Arms Deal Is Detailed," *Los Angeles Times*, October 4, 2003.

A reference to Libby passing talking points to Fleischer can be found in "Government's Response to Defendant's Third Motion," p. 28. The account of Jack Eckenrode's investigation of the NSA leak is based on interviews with Graham and confidential congressional and law enforcement sources. For Robert Mueller telling Eckenrode to take the leak case "wherever it goes," an interview with a confidential law enforcement official. For Eckenrode's interview with Novak, Robert Novak, "My Leak Case Testimony," syndicated column, July 12, 2006, and interviews with confidential law enforcement official. For Eckenrode's interviews with Rove and Libby, interviews with confidential sources.

Details about the Feith memo—"Summary of Body of Intelligence on Reporting Iraq–al Qaeda Contacts"—and the CIA's response to it can be found in Senator Carl Levin, "Report of an Inquiry into the Alternative Analysis of the Issue of an Iraq–al Qaeda Relationship," October 2004. The report can be found at http://levin.senate.gov/newsroom/supporting/2004/102104inquiryreport.pdf. See also Stephen Hayes, "Case Closed," *The Weekly Standard*, November 24, 2003.

The account of the dismissal of Bush campaign worker Brad Dayspring is based on interviews with confidential sources. For the White House's reaction to the November aardwolf from the CIA station in Baghdad, interviews with Maguire and a confidential White House source.

For Eckenrode's use of the waivers, interviews with confidential sources. The account of Valerie Wilson's apology for posing for *Vanity Fair* is based on interviews with confidential CIA sources. For Joseph Wilson's defense of the photograph, *The Politics of Truth*, pp. 409–410. The account of Fitzgerald reading leak case files on New Year's Eve is based on interviews with a confidential source.

CHAPTER 18: THE PROSECUTOR VERSUS THE PRESS
The account of Senator Peter Fitzgerald's selection of Patrick Fitzgerald for the U.S. attorney position is based on interviews with Senator Fitzgerald. For details on Patrick Fitzgerald's background—and his "I have zeal" quote—see Peter Slevin, "The

Prosecutor Never Rests; Whether Probing a Leak or Trying Terrorists, Patrick Fitzgerald Is Relentless," *The Washington Post,* February 2, 2005. For the 9/11 Commission's conclusion on Fitzgerald's raids on the two Islamic charities, see *9/11 Commission Report,* p. 472. Fitzgerald's August 7, 2002, letter to *The New York Times* and the paper's response can be found in "Exhibits to Affirmation of Patrick Fitzgerald," *New York Times v. Gonzales,* United States District Court for Southern District of New York, Civ. 7677, November 19, 2004. For Fitzgerald's continuing investigation of the Islamic charities leak and his request to issue subpoenas, interviews with Mark Corallo. For Bush's 2004 State of the Union speech, confidential interviews with White House speechwriters. Kay described his January meeting with Bush in an interview with the authors. Tenet's speech can be found at www.cia.gov/cia/public_affairs/speeches/tenet_georgetown. Drumheller described his participation in the drafting of the speech in interviews with the authors.

For Fitzgerald's interview with Novak, Robert Novak, "My Leak Case Testimony," syndicated column, July 12, 2006, and interviews with a confidential law enforcement source. For Libby's testimony before the grand jury, "Libby Grand Jury Testimony Excerpts." For Maguire's actions in Iraq in the first months of 2004, interviews with Maguire. The account of Shahwani's visit to the Oval Office is based on interviews with confidential sources. For the involvement of Scorpions in the Abed Hamed Mowhoush incident, see Josh White, "Documents Tell of Brutal Improvisation by GIs; Interrogated General's Sleeping-Bag Death, CIA's Use of Secret Iraqi Squad Are Among Details," *The Washington Post,* August 3, 2005. Larry Diamond describes the memo he sent Rice in *Squandered Victory: The American Occupation and the Bungled Effort to Bring Democracy to Iraq* (New York: Times Books, 2005), pp. 61–62. Articles that reported Aras Habib's arrest warrant include Michael Isikoff and Mark Hosenball, "Rethinking the Chalabi Connection," Newsweek.com, May 19, 2004 (updated May 20, 2004), and Scott Wilson, "U.S. Aids Raid on Home of Chalabi; Iraqi Criminal Probe Seeks Associates of Ex-Ally of Pentagon," *The Washington Post,* May 21, 2004.

For Miller's phone call to Bill Keller about Adnan Ihsan Saeed al-Haideri, interviews with confidential *New York Times* sources. The account of *The Washington Post*'s cooperation with Fitzgerald is based on interviews with confidential *Post* sources. For Floyd Abrams's meeting with Fitzgerald, interviews with Abrams. For the Senate intelligence committee report's reference to Valerie Wilson having "offered up" her husband's name, *SSCI Report,* p. 39. For Joseph Wilson's assertion that the CPD officer claimed he was misquoted in the report, *The Politics of Truth* (New York: Carrol & Graf Publishers, paperback edition, 2005), p. lvi.

Russert's grand jury testimony can be found in "Tatel Decision," pp. 31–32. For Russert's "not one word" quote, an interview with Russert. Cooper described his phone conversation with Libby in "What Scooter Libby and I Talked About," *Time,* November 7, 2005. The account of the Cooper deposition is based on interviews with a law enforcement official and lawyers involved in the case, including Abrams.

CHAPTER 19: THE FINAL SHOWDOWN

Cooper's "everything in my notebook" quote comes from Susan Schmidt, "Reporter Held in Contempt of Court Again in Leaks Probe," *The Washington Post,* October 14, 2005. For Abrams's assessment that "our chances were significantly less than even," Floyd Abrams, *Speaking Freely: Trials of the First Amendment* (New York: Penguin, 2006), p. 292. The accounts of the internal discussions at *The New York Times* and *Time* about the leak case are based on confidential interviews with employees at each publication.

Charles Duelfer's final report on WMDs in Iraq can be found at www.cia.gov/ cia/reports/iraq_wmd_2004/. Rod Barton wrote about Tenet's visit in his March 29, 2004, resignation letter. It can be found at www.abc.net.au/4corners/content/2005/ 20050214_rodbarton/resignation.htm. For Duelfer's personal conclusion on Saddam Hussein's WMD, a confidential interview with a source who helped draft the Duelfer report.

The account of Rove's October 2004 grand jury appearance (during which he turned over the Hadley e-mail) is based on a confidential interview with a source close to Rove. For Cooper's exchange with Bush, Cooper, "What I Told the Grand Jury," *Time,* July 25, 2005. The reference to Miller's concerns about her relationship to the *Times'* legal team and her hiring of Robert Bennett is based on confidential interviews and interviews with Robert Bennett. See also Brenner, "Lies and Consequences; Sixteen Words That Changed the World," *Vanity Fair,* April 2006. For Cooper's "great career move," see Howard Kurtz, "Contempt & Praise for Reporter: Facing Jail, Judith Miller Gains Support for Stance," *The Washington Post,* February 16, 2005. The *Robb-Silberman Report* footnote on its lack of conclusions on how policy makers used prewar intelligence can be found on p. 247. For Norman Pearlstine's meeting with the *Time* Washington bureau, confidential interviews with *Time* employees present at the meeting.

Richard Sauber described his role in the last-minute negotiations between the Cooper and Rove camps in an interview with the authors. A copy of the proposed statement Sauber sent Rove's lawyer was obtained by the authors. For Miller's efforts to find a way out of jail and her subsequent interactions with Libby, interviews with Bennett, Abrams, Joseph Tate, and confidential sources. See also "The Miller Case: A Notebook, a Cause, a Jail Cell and a Deal," *The New York Times,* October 16, 2005. A copy of Libby's letter to Miller can be found at www.nytimes.com/packages/pdf/ national/nat_MILLER_051001.pdf.

For Miller's testimony to the grand jury, "My Four Hours Testifying in the Federal Grand Jury Room," *The New York Times,* October 16, 2005. The account of the public squabble between Miller's and Libby's lawyers is drawn from letters written by Abrams (representing Miller) and Tate (representing Libby). Miller's remark about knowing the "difference between a defense lawyer and a First Amendment lawyer" was made to one of the authors at a blogging conference in November 2006.

For Miller's return to the *Times,* interviews with Don Van Natta, Jr., and confidential *Times* sources. Keller's October 21, 2005, memo can be found at http://poynter.org/forum/view_post.asp?id=10541.

AFTERWORD: NO REGRETS

The account of Karl Rove learning of Fitzgerald's decision not to prosecute him is based on interviews with a confidential source and Anna Schneider-Mayerson, "Rove Case Lawyer Blackberries Karl: Fitzgerald Called," *The New York Observer,* June 19, 2006. For Pete Yost's observation on the end of the Rove investigation, Pete Yost, "Analysis; Telling the FBI the Truth Saved Rove; Misleading Public Helped White House," Associated Press, June 13, 2006.

The account of Robert Luskin's interactions with Viveca Novak and how Luskin used these meetings to defend Rove is based on interviews with Luskin, Viveca Novak, and a lawyer representing a White House official in the leak case. See also Viveca Novak, "What Viveca Novak Told Fitzgerald," Time.com, December 11, 2005. The account of Fitzgerald deciding not to charge Rove with a crime is based on confidential interviews. For Fitzgerald not seeking charges against Armitage and Armitage contacting the prosecutor after the Libby indictment, interviews with confidential sources. For Woodward's role in this episode, "Testifying in the CIA Leak Case," *The Washington Post,* November 16, 2005, and "Woodward Was Told of Plame More than Two Years Ago," *The Washington Post,* November 16, 2005. For Woodward's "I was astounded" quote, transcript of *Larry King Live,* CNN, November 21, 2005. Miller shared her reaction to the news of Woodward's involvement in the leak case with one of the authors at a conference on blogging on November 16, 2005. Woodward's quotes regarding his suspicions about his source being Novak's source and his source's refusal to discuss this are from interviews with the authors.

Moskowitz's "not connecting the dots" quote comes from an interview he granted the authors shortly before his death in 2006. For Pillar's quotes, see the transcript of his Council on Foreign Relations presentation in Washington, D.C., on March 7, 2006. Feith's quote—"The administration sold it the way it sold it"—is from an interview with the authors.

ACKNOWLEDGMENTS

ALL BOOKS are collaborations.

We are fortunate to share the same agent, Gail Ross, who was a full partner—perhaps a majority partner—in this project. She conceived the idea, put the authors together, and gave the book its name. *Hubris* would not exist had it not been for her. Her enthusiasm was matched by that of Steve Ross, the publisher at Crown, who fully backed this project from start to finish—and never once expressed concern (at least not to us) about the tight deadline set for the book. Rick Horgan, our editor at Crown, was a steady and calm force. His comments improved the manuscript and encouraged us to keep moving.

We owe our gratitude to the entire team at Crown for working hard to bring this book to life: Cindy Berman, Amy Boorstein, Tina Constable, Jill Flaxman, Linda Kaplan, Min Lee, Matthew Martin, Julian Pavia, Philip Patrick, Laura Quinn, Annsley Rosner, Barbara Sturman, and David Tran. Chris Jackson, once an editor at Crown, also deserves credit for getting us started. Howard Yoon, an associate of Gail Ross, provided valuable input.

Cora Currier contributed essential research services. She was a diligent and good-natured colleague who dug out detail after detail, often unearthing facts we didn't know existed. Sam Schramski took on last-minute research projects, fact-checked the final chapters, and helped bring the project over the finish line. We thank him for the long hours he put in when we needed assistance most. Clarisse Profilet aptly and cheerfully handled the initial research tasks for this book. We could not have written this book without their help. They will always have our thanks—and recommendations for any job applications.

MICHAEL ISIKOFF thanks his editors and colleagues at *Newsweek,* first and foremost, onetime Washington Bureau Chief and now Assistant Managing Editor Daniel Klaidman, who provided wise counsel and support at every stage and gave him the freedom to pursue this project, indulging the author far more than other bosses might have. He also expresses his appreciation to the rest of the *Newsweek* brass: President Richard Smith, Editor Mark Whitaker, Managing Editor Jon Meacham, National Editor Tom Watson, and Periscope Editor Nancy Cooper. He has especially benefited from the insights of his longtime sidekick and "Terror Watch" colleague

Mark Hosenball, who knows more about the subject of this book—most notably the machinations of the Chalabites—than any other journalist in the Western world, as Meg Ryan can readily attest. During Isikoff's reporting on the war on terror and Iraq intelligence screwups over the past five years, the *Newsweek* research staff, especially Ruth Tenenbaum, Judy Ganeles, and Sam Register, tenaciously hunted down hard-to-find information and checked facts on a moment's notice in the face of countless deadlines. Jamie Reno, as always, was helpful in San Diego. The reporting and writing of Isikoff's *Newsweek* colleagues—particularly John Barry, Howard Fineman, Michael Hirsh, Wes Kosova, Evan Thomas, and Richard Wolffe—informed his understanding of this subject. The logistical support of Gail Tacconelli and Steve Tuttle was indispensable. Isikoff would also like to salute the ultimate boss, Donald Graham. All journalists should be fortunate enough to work for a supreme leader whose first instinct is to stand by the troops when they come under fire.

As always, Isikoff would like to thank his ever-supportive family: Trudy Isikoff, who kindled his interest in politics many years ago; Nancy Isikoff and the entire Falby clan: Bruce Falby, Jacob Falby, Daniel Falby, and Anna Falby. A special word above all goes to Willa Isikoff, never far from the author's thoughts. A superb wordsmith on her own, Willa will someday write far better books than this one.

For her wisdom, wit, unflagging support, and endless patience, Isikoff thanks—and offers his love to—Mary Ann Akers. This book would never have been finished without her. But that is only the beginning of the author's debts.

DAVID CORN thanks his colleagues at *The Nation* magazine, especially Editor and Publisher Katrina vanden Heuvel, who allowed him to take time away from his magazine duties to work on this book—and who enthusiastically encouraged him over the past years to pursue the lines of inquiry that led to *Hubris*. Victor Navasky, now publisher emeritus, will always have Corn's gratitude for naming him Washington editor and granting him free rein. President Teresa Stack was rather understanding about the leave that made this book possible. Ari Berman, a reporter in the magazine's Washington bureau, offered companionship and moral support. Contributing Editor Marc Cooper was always available with sage counsel, especially at the most difficult moments. His friendship is deeply treasured by the author.

Corn thanks others at *The Nation* who have enabled him to do the work he thoroughly enjoys: Amiri Barksdale, Roane Carey, Joan Connell, Scott Klein, Judith Long, Peggy Randall, Betsy Reed, Peter Rothberg, Karen Rothmyer, Mary Taylor Schilling, Peggy Suttle, Lisa Vandepaer, and Mike Webb.

Corn also is grateful for the support provided by an assortment of friends, relatives, and colleagues during this project—and during a time when he was not always able to reciprocate: Ruth Corn, Ken Corn, Gordon Roth, Diane Corn, Steven Corn, Barry Corn, Amy Corn, Coby Laanstra-Ypma, Jan van der Baan, Fokke Laanstra, Nynke Laanstra, Stephanie Slewka, Horton Beebe-Center, Tim Weiner, Kate Doyle, Micah Sifry, Jack Shafer, Julian Borger, Bertis Downs, Henry von Eichel, Andrew Cockburn, Leslie Cockburn, Kirk Lamoreaux, Julie Burton, Roger Hickey, Conrad Martin, Steven Prince, Alex Walker, Reid Cramer, Sonya Cohen, Sally Kern, Stephen Kern, Jenny Apostol, Marco DiPaul, Ted Mankin, Joe Pichirallo, and Mitch Kaplan. Peter Kornbluh deserves a special mention for constantly supplying sound advice and never-ending encouragement.

Most of all, Corn thanks Maaike and Amarins, his daughters, and Welmoed Laanstra, his wife, for the daily joy and nourishment they provide him. Welmoed, be it duly noted, was another full partner in this project. She maintained the Laanstra-Corn household, as one member disappeared all too often, and managed to remain a visionary in her own field. This book could not have happened without her patience and exceptional (and inspiring) fortitude. For this and so much more, Corn loves and admires her. And Maaike, seven years old, and Amarins, five years old, understood (mostly) why their father occasionally had to turn down their invitations to read together or play—and began writing their own books.

We also thank our sources, especially those who trusted us with their confidences. Any mistakes in this book, of course, belong only to the authors—not our sources. And we can blame each other.

INDEX